Wo...
Cri... Media

Women in True Crime Media

The Spectacle of Female Victims and Perpetrators

JEN ERDMAN

McFarland & Company, Inc., Publishers
Jefferson, North Carolina

LIBRARY OF CONGRESS CATALOGUING-IN-PUBLICATION DATA

Names: Erdman, Jen, 1982– author.
Title: Women in true crime media : the spectacle of female victims and perpetrators / Jen Erdman.
Description: Jefferson, North Carolina : McFarland & Company, Inc., Publishers, 2022 | Includes bibliographical references and index.
Identifiers: LCCN 2022022465 | ISBN 9781476681252 (paperback : acid free paper) ∞ ISBN 9781476646183 (ebook)
Subjects: LCSH: Female offenders in mass media. | Victims of crimes in mass media. | Women—Crimes against—United States. | Female offenders—United States. | True crime stories—United States—History and criticism. | True crime television programs—United States—History and criticism. | BISAC: SOCIAL SCIENCE / Women's Studies | TRUE CRIME / General
Classification: LCC P94.5.W652 U647 2022 | DDC 302.23082—dc23/eng/20220615
LC record available at https://lccn.loc.gov/2022022465

BRITISH LIBRARY CATALOGUING DATA ARE AVAILABLE

ISBN (print) 978-1-4766-8125-2
ISBN (ebook) 978-1-4766-4618-3

Front cover image: © 2022 AlexVH/Shutterstock

Printed in the United States of America

McFarland & Company, Inc., Publishers
Box 611, Jefferson, North Carolina 28640
www.mcfarlandpub.com

Contents

Preface

My first memory of true crime is reading a book containing a story about the disappearance, and subsequent reappearance, of Agatha Christie in 1926. As I read that in the backseat of my mother's green Geo Metro on the way to a doctor's appointment, I wondered if I was the only one who found these kinds of stories utterly fascinating.

Since that afternoon in that Geo Metro, I've devoured as much true crime as possible.

For many years, that meant made-for-TV movies or dramatized paperback books. *Unsolved Mysteries* and *Forensic Files* had to satisfy our cravings, but before streaming, it was a very limited supply. The 21st century burst onto the scene with 24-hour cable channels, streaming platforms with our old and new favorites, and thousands upon thousands of podcasts.

This project began as a conference paper on one such podcast, *My Favorite Murder*, and the misconception that true crime only became "popular" in the 21st century. Karen and Georgia of *My Favorite Murder*, along with Ash and Aliana of *Morbid*, and countless others, are reframing true crime so that the female victims who have been forgotten for decades are put at the forefront of the story where they belong.

In an effort to continue the work they have begun, I have chosen specific women whose stories have been manipulated by popular culture. Some are victims, and some are perpetrators—yet all of them have had their histories manipulated until public memory no longer recognizes the truth. By examining the various pop culture iterations that have contributed to a false memory, we can begin to understand the role that it plays in how women are discussed and remembered in the true crime genre.

One glaring drawback of this project is the lack of diversity. The women chosen for each chapter were chosen because of the wealth of pop culture iterations available for analysis. News media and Hollywood are, and have been, overwhelmingly focused on White female victims. Even in 2021, there were far more documentaries, news reports, and podcasts about White victims than victims of color. Until there is a holistic shift in the way victims of color are represented in popular culture, a follow-up study cannot be done.

Introduction

As America experiences the '20s once again, comparisons are inevitable. The 1920s and the 2020s have a shocking number of similarities, among them multiple "trials of the century" and a populace captivated by true crime. More than a quarter of the top 100 podcasts ranked by Apple Podcasts are categorized as true crime. There are no fewer than three television channels solely dedicated to telling true crime stories. One of these channels, Oxygen, had been a faltering channel dedicated to "high drama" programming. When the network made the decision to dedicate a block of programming to true crime in 2015, its "viewership increased by 42%."[1] The network rebranded as entirely dedicated to true crime by 2017. Most mainstream networks have dramas that frequently include the phrase "ripped from the headlines." Media have always turned toward true crime as a bottomless font of money. "If it bleeds, it leads" has long been the reigning attitude of news media companies around the world. It is not long after a crime splashes across the headlines before it appears in *Law & Order*, a made-for-TV movie, or an Investigation Discovery special.

Over the last century, there have been three waves of media coverage of true crime. Each wave has its own strengths and weaknesses, with the genre growing as the century progresses. Print was the only avenue for true crime as the 20th century began, but as with each of these eras, the quality differed greatly. Once film and later television entered onto the stage, true crime stories began to appear on the big and small screen. In the 21st century, these same true crime stories are now appearing on the latest technology platform, podcasts.

History of True Crime

With this latest wave of true crime that began in 2015–2016, a great deal of attention has been paid to examining why there is such a rabid audience for murder and the macabre. The reality of the situation is that humans have always been interested and even obsessed with true crime. Within a century of the invention of the printing press, by about 1550, the first crime pamphlets—usually either sensationalism or a morality warning—were published in England. Those who could consume these (a) were literate and (b) were able to afford to buy these pamphlets—namely the upper and middle classes. By the 19th century, the penny press was created, which introduced widespread crime journalism. From 1889 until the 1950s, William Roughead, a Scottish lawyer and amateur criminologist, wrote and published essays on the murder trials he attended in Great Britain. Roughead published his first collection in 1913 and continued publishing until his death in 1952. American Edmund Pearson began publishing his true crime stories in 1924 in magazines like *The New Yorker* and *Vanity Fair*.

Magazines served as a bridge between the penny press of the 19th century and the true crime of the modern era. A "golden age" of circulation, 1930s–1960s, proved that true crime magazines were the dominant form of crime narration.[2] *True Detective Mysteries*, one of the first and most popular publications, was strongest during the 1920s and 1930s. As that era saw a spike in organized crime and gang wars, there was a focus on glorifying law enforcement, which tends to lead to either a manipulation of the women involved or a deletion of them altogether.

True Crime in the Modern Era

The beginning of the modern era of true crime is usually attributed to Truman Capote's novel *In Cold Blood*. Heavily based on the true story of the Cutter family, who were killed in their Holcomb, Kansas, home in 1959, *In Cold Blood* was published in 1965. The book immediately sold out in Kansas and sold millions of copies in the United States. Translated into more than 30 languages, it proved people all over the world were eager for true crime. Capote made it clear that the true crime genre had massive opportunity for profitability.

With the dawn of the 1970s, more true crime books hit the bookstores to meet the increasing demand. After the Manson Family murders in 1969, the prosecutor in the case, Vincent Bugliosi, wrote his account of the crimes and trial, *Helter Skelter*. A fascinating insider account of the Manson family, *Helter Skelter* sold at least seven million copies by Bugliosi's death in 2015. According to several articles, this makes *Helter Skelter* the best-selling true crime book of all time, but given the breadth of the genre, one has to be a little skeptical of that fact. In 1979 Norman Mailer released *The Executioner's Song*, a novel about the events leading up to the execution of Gary Gilmore in 1977. Mailer won a Pulitzer Prize, the first for the true crime genre.

The first female author to enter the modern true crime genre became arguably the most famous true crime author of all time, Ann Rule. With the 1980 publication of *The Stranger Beside Me*, Rule began a prolific career in true crime writing. She is usually the first or only author in the genre that most people know, with good reason. Over her career, which spanned 1980–2014, Rule published 35 books. However, her first book is a shining example of the close relationship that women have always had with true crime and often the criminals themselves. *The Stranger Beside Me* discusses the life and crimes of Ted Bundy, who confessed to the killing of at least 30 women. True to the title, Rule knew Bundy—they worked beside each other at a suicide hotline in the early 1970s. Rule began as yet another voice that always ends up on the news saying, "But he seemed so nice and normal."

True Crime on the Screen

"Ripped from the headlines" did not originate with Dick Wolf and *Law & Order*. Before moving pictures, nickelodeons were using true crime stories to draw crowds. Once the technology advanced, killers and their victims appeared on the silver screen, making the "consumption and enjoyment of true crime narratives … a multisensory experience."[3] The beginning of true crime films also ushered in true crime as a group activity. Viewing films, particularly in the years before home viewing became common, was done exclusively in a group, sometimes with those in one's friend group. With this evolution, those interested in true crime began to be able to be more open with that fascination.

Putting true crime stories on the big screen presents filmmakers with a host of challenges, chief among them their duty to truth, history, and to the victims. As will be discussed below, the majority of attention has been paid to the offenders, not to the victims. Exploits of offenders are often dramatized even further for the excitement of an audience, but little to no thought is given to the victims. For some productions, victims were erased entirely, reduced to a body on a screen. It is entirely worse when one examines how female victims are portrayed. Again, they may be reduced to a corpse on the screen, but often are dressed in skimpy clothes or even nude, whether that was the truth from the case file or not. The advent of true crime in films increases the sexualization of female victims; vicious crime creates a voyeurism where the audience may see even more of the actor's body.

Beginning in the 1980s, with the advent of cable channels and sensationalized movies of the week, movies based on recent crimes were made at an alarming rate. The film that is often cited as the catalyst for this is

The Burning Bed, which aired on NBC on October 8, 1984. *The Burning Bed* serves as the bridge between the old true crime medium, print—as the movie was based on the 1980 book by the same name by Faith McNulty—and on-screen media. While not the first movie based on real-life events, it has become shorthand for the first made-for-TV movie "ripped from the headlines." Over the ninety-five-minute film, Farrah Fawcett's Francine Hughes sets her sleeping husband on fire after thirteen years of domestic abuse. Named the seventh greatest American made-for-TV movie of all time, *The Burning Bed* was called "a landmark in terms of content, depicting domestic violence as an unambiguous horror and a human rights violation."[4]

True Crime in the 21st Century

The idea of podcasting was first proposed in 2000, but *The Backstage Pass*, which launched in October 2003, is often considered the first podcast. Within a few years, thousands of podcasts had popped up, mirroring the radio dramas and episodic soap operas of the early and mid–20th century. As with most technology-heavy arenas, early podcasting skewed heavily male. Pioneer podcasts included *This American Life*, hosted by Ira Glass, and *The Ricky Gervais Show*, hosted by the British comedian a few years after starring in the UK version of *The Office*.

A journalist who worked for *This American Life*, Sarah Koenig, is credited with igniting the latest wave of true crime fanaticism with her podcast, *Serial*. In the first season, focused on the 1999 murder of Hae Min Lee, Koenig proved that there were millions of fans rabid for true crime. Ranked number one on the iTunes podcast charts even before it aired, *Serial* inspired countless others to start their own shows whether they follow Koenig's more professional journalistic approach or a more relaxed, between friends, conversational style.

Podcasts like *My Favorite Murder*, *Wine & Crime*, *White Wine True Crime!*, and dozens more have an audience that skews about 70 percent female.[5] This is not surprising, as women—"forever at a higher risk … to be raped, killed, or abused by a male partner and to be harassed merely by walking down the street"—have a vested interest in hearing and learning from true crime stories.[6] Anecdotal evidence from the podcasts—emails and tweets from listeners—shows that women often cite the podcasts as helping them avoid danger, stick together as women, and "fuck politeness," as *My Favorite Murder* often says.

A study published in *Social Psychological and Personality Science* in 2010 gives statistical evidence to prove that women more than men are drawn to true crime. Women "preferred true crime books over other books based on violent topics."[7] Also in this study, it was found that women expected to enjoy books on true crime more than men did while men expected to enjoy books on war or other types of violence more than women did.[8] This study also gave some insight into why this is the case. When choosing books on true crime, women are more statistically likely to choose a book that covers the killer's motives over books that do not. This helps to confirm what has long been thought to be a reason for women's interest in true crime—to help them avoid becoming a victim of crime themselves. This is not an unfounded fear. "While men are four times more likely to be homicide victims, women comprise 70% of victims killed by an intimate partner—twice the rate of men."[9]

At the forefront of this latest wave of true crime is the podcast *My Favorite Murder*, also known as *MFM* by fans. Created in 2016 by Karen Kilgariff and Georgia Hardstark, the podcast had nearly 250 episodes as of fall 2020. As Georgia explained in the first episode, the phrase "favorite murder" is not actually favorite "like I love this murder. It's the one I really want to talk to you about, because it's so insane."[10] For every episode, each woman covers a crime that has caught their interest but in a hilarious, Wikipedia version of the story. Fans get all the salient details with a healthy dose of comedy, friendship, and real talk. In the three and a half years since the first episode, Karen and Georgia[11] have completed several world tours; the fans have created at least 400 Facebook groups with names like Disnerderinos; Rollerinos; Thou Shall Not Murder; Die Bart Die (*The Simpsons*); Slayerinos (*Buffy*); My Favorite Avada Kedavra; Runnerions; Body Positive Murderinos; Etsy Murderinos; and dozens more connected to cities and states around the world. More than 800 listings have been posted on Etsy for *MFM* themed merchandise.

But *MFM* has had a massive impact on women that goes beyond social media groups and merchandise. Many of the traditional true crime stories/publications/films/documentaries focus almost exclusively on the perpetrator; Karen and Georgia (along with most of this new wave of true crime content creators) give the spotlight to the victims of the crimes—almost exclusively women. Molly Fitzpatrick, in an article for *Rolling Stone*, said, "[W]hat's most radical about *My Favorite Murder* is how it recasts the victims in these stories—who are often women—as real people, so much more than the chalk-outline plot devices on a common TV procedural."[12] Also at the forefront of this agenda to remember the victims is *Real Crime Profile*, hosted by a former FBI profiler, Jim Clemente, and former New Scotland Yard behavioral analyst Laura Richards. Over the course of over two hundred episodes, the hosts have championed the victims, male and female, who have been lost in the shadow of the perpetrators.

Other podcasts are beginning to follow suit. In the wake of the Black

Lives Matter and the #MeToo movements, podcasts are at the forefront of the changing narrative in true crime. Those with female hosts, like *My Favorite Murder*, *Morbid*, *Wine & Crime*, and others, especially want to offer a revised history where women are finally treated fairly. In some cases, that means actually being included for the first time. In others, it means the decades-long manipulation of the woman is being righted.

Scope of Study

The ten decades of the 1920s through 2010s have been specifically chosen as they better epitomize the 20th century than the years 1900–2000. The 1900s and 1910s had far more in common with the preceding century, while the First World War changed essentially everything forever. Nineteen twenty was also chosen as the beginning for this study, as that decade began the modern era of true crime. With infamous crimes like the Leopold and Loeb case, Sacco and Vanzetti, the "Monkey Trial" of Dayton (TN), and countless others, the crime beat was a sure beat for journalists of the day. The wealth of sources makes the cases from the 1920s and after prime targets for authors, producers, and podcast hosts.

It would be nearly impossible to cover the sheer number of cases involving women throughout the last hundred years in one book without causing a paper shortage. Instead, specific case studies have been chosen, each involving a woman who has been covered by a variety of media. In most of the cases, the women, like most of the women connected to crimes, are the victims. However, there are a few women who serve as examples of other ways crime affects women—as the loved ones of the perpetrators and as the perpetrators themselves.

Chief among the reasons why these specific case studies were chosen was the amount of popular culture surrounding each woman. To be able to study how popular culture has treated women, there needs to be a combination of books, film, television, and podcasts on the subject. A few of the women are very well known and have been covered at length, such as Sharon Tate; however, this project examines all women from a different perspective. While the details of each case are included, each chapter examines how the women have been revictimized by pop culture, sometimes decades after their deaths.

One obvious limitation to this study is the lack of Black and Indigenous women, women of color and those in the LGBTQ+ community among those chosen as cases. This is entirely the fault of the pop culture industry. It is well known within true crime communities that victims in those communities mentioned above are far less represented by the news media, and shows or films about their deaths are nearly non-existent. While there are several reports and studies that show the dramatic difference in the "violence experienced by white women and women of color," there has been "little written acknowledging the difference in news reporting."[13] One of the most frequent examples to illustrate the disparity in coverage is the case of Natalee Holloway. Natalee, a blonde, white woman, disappeared in Aruba in 2005; her disappearance was a major focus of TV news for months, and at least two made-for-TV movies have been produced about the case. Of course, Natalee's disappearance deserved attention, as did her grieving family who are still hoping for some kind of resolution more than fifteen years later. However, mere weeks after Natalee's disappearance, LaToyia Figueroa, "five months pregnant and the mother of a 7-year-old," disappeared from her own hometown.[14] While both basic and cable news channels were airing nothing but Natalee, LaToyia's family were forced to picket "on a busy street corner to draw attention to her disappearance."[15] This same article also draws comparison between Evelyn Hernandez and Laci Peterson, both of whom were nine months pregnant and were discovered in San Francisco Bay within months of each other. So, why did the news media, especially the national news, focus almost entirely on Laci and not on Evelyn? According to Todd Boyd, professor of critical studies at the University of Southern California, there is an "unconscious decision about who matters and who doesn't.... [I]n general, there is an assumption that crime is such a part of black and Latino culture, that these things happen all the time.... In many people's minds it's regarded as being commonplace and not that big a deal."[16] Erin Bruno, the lead case manager for the National Center for Missing Adults in Phoenix, has another theory. As her office sends out thousands of press releases, they see that reporters are looking "for stories that they can identify with.... Perhaps they themselves are Caucasian" or are searching for "the 'damsel in distress.'"[17]

The disparity of coverage between Natalee and LaToyia and Laci and Evelyn restarted the conversation within the news industry as well as in academia, but, fifteen years later, that is all that has happened ... a conversation. Coverage of white female victims is still significantly higher than women of color, while statistics on coverage of members of the LGBTQ+ community are sparse. Following suit, fictional portrayals of true crime focus entirely on white victims. Perhaps, in the near future, a much-needed follow-up to this study will be possible but can only be accomplished with more television and films diversifying their true crime offerings.

In this project, each subject will be examined through the evolution of true crime media: print, big and small screen adaptations, and podcasts. After a short history of their story, how they have been portrayed in true crime will be analyzed. With the outliers of the study—the loved ones of the perpetrators or the perpetrators themselves—this analysis will show how popular culture has generally done them a disservice, if they were mentioned at all. In projects about Ted Bundy, it is shocking how few discuss Elizabeth Kendall, the woman he came home to after he brutally killed his victims. In other cases, pop culture has chosen to disregard history altogether for the sake of the story. Bonnie Parker, of Bonnie and Clyde fame, has been portrayed as psychotic as late as 2013, without any real historical fact to back it up. Without fail, more effort is spent to ensure the male perpetrators are shown faithfully than any of the women involved.

Even more outrageous is the treatment of women who have been the victims of crimes. As if it were not enough that they were killed in life, they have been frequently revictimized by aspects of popular culture. Films were made that barely mention the women, if at all. Women are relegated to bodies on the floor, while the male main characters are allowed to become fully-fledged individuals. One example is the documentary *The Staircase*, which shows Kathleen Peterson's deceased body on screen several times throughout its thirteen episodes, but little other attention is paid to Kathleen. To add insult to fatal injury, it is the names of the men involved who are talked about and remembered by true crime fans. Where possible in this analysis, the names of the offenders will not be named after the chapter introduction. Rather than give those men more attention, the focus will remain on the women while only referring to the men as the "offender" or the "alleged offender" if, as in one case, he was found not guilty in the criminal trial but liable in the civil trial.

True crime has been a popular and lucrative industry. From broadsheets with details of Mary Kelly in Whitechapel to detective comics to Lifetime movies, humans have continued to be fascinated by what we do to each other. Because of this, names like Jack the Ripper, Ted Bundy, and Richard Speck are infamous. However, how many know their victims' names? Their victims—all of them women—are lost to history to everyone except the most dedicated of true crime fans. One facet of pop culture, podcasts, is striving to correct this. This study will show pop culture's impact on the cultural memory of these women and how some elements of the media industry are working to undo decades of revictimization.

CHAPTER 1

Sabella Nitti

The 1920s were certainly not the beginning of true crime, but the dawn of the "Roaring Twenties" on January 1, 1920, ushered in an era in which crime changed along with society itself. Famously shown in films like *The Untouchables* and TV series like *Boardwalk Empire*, the decade began with the start of the Volstead Act, also known as Prohibition. Prohibition and the organized crime that flourished because of the illegal liquor trade, combined with the popularization of jazz music, helped the decade earn the nickname mentioned earlier, "the Roaring Twenties."

With so much attention on the glorious and glamorous aspects of the decade, few may know the uglier side, including the roles that racism and immigration played. Beginning in the 1880s, immigrants from Southern and Eastern Europe began to enter the U.S. in large numbers. By 1920, these individuals represented one of the largest waves of immigrants in American history. However, as they were often physically and culturally different from the immigrants from Western Europe, immigrants from countries such as Italy, Greece, Russia, Hungry, and other southern/eastern countries were deemed unwelcomed by large sections of America. One of the most glaring examples of America's racist immigration policies is the 1924 Immigration Law. This created essentially quotas based upon the estimated number of immigrants from that country already in the United States. Countries from Western European countries, such as Great Britain, France, and Germany, were highly favored over those from Southern and Eastern Europe. Immigrants from Italy, such as Sabella, were strictly limited and faced massive discrimination once they arrived.

Just the Facts

The first subject of this study is a victim, of not only the 1920s racism against immigrants from Southern and Eastern Europe, but also continuing racism throughout the 20th century. "Sabella" was born Isabella Maria

Travaglio outside of Bari in Southern Italy on March 14, 1879.[1] She married Francesco Nitti[2] when she was only fifteen and he was in his mid-twenties.[3] At 37, she arrived in the United States on the SS *Dante Alighieri* with two of her sons, now called Michael and Charles.[4] As was common at the time, Francesco Nitti had left Italy three years earlier with eldest son Vincenzo, who adopted the name James in the U.S. Known as chain migration, husbands, fathers, and/or eldest sons came to the U.S. first to establish residency, get a job, and begin to save money to bring over the rest of the family. Once Sabella and the younger sons joined Francesco and James, she had two additional children, daughters. The entire family lived on a farm on the outskirts of Chicago, in a small town called Stickney. Between the geographic isolation of Stickney and the economic and familial isolation of a woman in a farming family of the early 20th century, Sabella did not often have cause or the chance to leave her farm. By not venturing into English-speaking communities, she did not learn English and was limited to her native Italian dialect. This becomes a particular problem when she is brought to trial in Chicago.

Sabella's judicial nightmare began on July 30, 1922. One could easily say that her life had been a nightmare for decades leading up to July of 1922, but her dark path through the judiciary began when her husband disappeared. After weeks with no leads in the investigation of the missing person Francesco, Paul Dasso, the Cook County Deputy Sheriff, "drummed up charges of adultery and fornication against Sabella" and Peter Crudelle, a farmhand who was bunking in the family's shack while working on the farm.[5] They were taken into custody on September 14, 1922, and two weeks later, the police stopped looking for Nitti's body. Historians speculate that rather than marrying for love, Sabella and Crudelle married on March 7, 1923, to avoid additional charges of adultery. Two months later, both, plus Sabella's son Charles, were charged with murder when a body was found in a storm drain near the Nitti property.[6] Too decomposed for a visual identification, the body was identified by a ring as being that of Francesco Nitti.

The trial began on July 2, 1923, as the jury of twelve white men was chosen to decide the fate of Sabella, her son, and her new husband. Not only did her lawyer not speak her Bari dialect, but the primary lawyer, Eugene Moran, did not speak any Italian at all. As Emilie Lucchesi says in her book, the difference between Italian and Bari is the same as the difference between an English and a Dutch speaker. This stark difference in languages became all the clearer when Italian interpreters were brought in and no one was able to tell her what was going on, including when she was convicted and sentenced to hang after only two hours of jury deliberation.[7]

The public outrage at the death sentence was immediate, and much of

Chicago spoke out in support of Sabella. Mere weeks before her scheduled execution date of October 12, 1923, the Illinois Supreme Court stayed the execution and ordered a review of the case. In the time between her initial conviction and her review, Sabella's case was taken on by the "team of six," including Helen Cirese. The daughter of Italian immigrants, Helen was a rare woman in 1923—a lawyer who was trying to break into the field. She used the time to do what Moran did not do during the first trial—help Sabella learn English and give her a makeover. Fully aware that this trial was as much a beauty contest as a legal one, Helen brought in a hair stylist to cut and color Sabella's hair and made sure that Sabella ate regularly. With a few extra pounds on her bones, Sabella now looked like "someone's mom," someone closer to a woman that 1923 Chicago could identify with.[8] Helen's plan worked and Sabella and Crudelle both avoided the death penalty when, on April 14, 1924, the Illinois Supreme Court reversed the verdict and sent the case back for a retrial. Six months later, as the attention of Chicago was captivated by the Leopold and Loeb trial, all charges in the Francesco Nitti trial were dropped.

After her judicial nightmare was over, Sabella stayed in Chicago for a few years. She and her two young daughters moved into an apartment there, a far cry from the farm in Stickney.[9] As more proof that her marriage to Crudelle was one of convenience, their marriage ended soon after the pair were spared from the gallows. By the 1930 U.S. Census, she listed herself as a widow and continued to use the name Nitti.[10] Her third and final marriage was to Giuseppe Campobasso, whom she married on November 2, 1940. Within a year of her marriage to Campobasso, at the age of sixty-two, Sabella applied for citizenship and received it five years later.[11] She lived out her final eight years of her life in Los Angeles before dying on December 10, 1957, of acute coronary syndrome at age seventy-seven.[12]

News of the Day

Sabella was one of the many women who made up "Murderess Row" in the Cook County Jail. These women captured the attention of the Chicago press and Chicagoans for generations. While the rest of the women on Murderess Row received generally positive attention from members of the press, Sabella was criticized, mocked, and persecuted by them instead. Why was Sabella treated so differently than the rest? Sabella was the only immigrant. She was the only person on Murderess Row who, at the time, would not have been considered white by the racial definitions of the day.[13] Additionally, Sabella was the only person who was initially found guilty of the crime in which she was charged. It was only after a team of law-yers appealed her case that Sabella was able to walk out of jail. The other women, white and often wealthy, walked out with much more fanfare and much less time served.

The Chicago press was enamored with the women of Murderess Row. Dozens of stories appeared in the press of each woman who, after her arrest, was sent to the women's cellblock of the Cook County Jail. The stories typically focused on the women's glamorous or rich lifestyles. For Sabella, her life held none of the glitz and glamour of Belva Gaertner or Beulah Annan.

Some of the press attempted to provide relatively fair coverage of Sabella. In articles, she is described as a "disheveled Italian peasant"[14] or simply an "Italian peasant doomed to die on the gallows."[15] Amazingly, in comparison to the other coverage of Sabella, merely being called an Italian peasant is fair coverage. In the latter article, the unnamed author mocks Sabella's accent by quoting her as saying that her "two 'leetle babees' were taken from the custody of the neighbor woman who aided in her con-viction and placed into a children's home."[16] This was a common theme throughout the reporting on Sabella's case. As stated earlier, Sabella had been essentially sequestered on her family's farm for years with only her husband and children to talk to, so there was no reason to learn English. However, reporters took every opportunity to mention, or even mock, her accent or illiteracy.

One reporter who specifically targeted Sabella was Genevieve Forbes, who wrote for the *Chicago Tribune*. Even though it is the same paper in which the earlier, more even-handed treatment of Sabella appeared, Forbes's articles were not only extremely negative, but also full of bias and racism. In her article "Mrs. Nitti and Consort Given Noose Penalty," pub-lished on July 10, 1923, Forbes describes Sabella as a "dumb, crouching, animal-like Italian peasant."[17] Forbes continues, saying Mrs. Nitti "grew hysterical with the frenzied pleading of a cruel animal that has been cor-nered and tortured by a new kind of trap."[18] Doubling down on her ani-malistic metaphor, Forbes says that Sabella "was not the calm human who ... held her husband's head in her gnarled hands while her lover, twenty-three years her junior, pounded the sleeping farmer over the head with a six-pound hammer."[19] Describing the trial, the prosecutor, Milton Smith, urged the jury to forget that Sabella was a woman. Forbes, however, says that it was hard not to remember that Sabella "was a woman—a cruel, dirty, repulsive woman."[20] After these repeated slurs and slanders against Sabella, Forbes attempts to describe her as she sat in the courtroom in 1923. The descriptions used are incredibly problematic and only under-lined Forbes's overarching racism against Sabella. Forbes uses phrases such as "stubby fingers, where the dirt was ingrained into broken nail," "matted hair," and "stocky legs."[21] The final sentiment of the article further victimizes Sabella at the hands of Forbes. When describing Sabella after the verdict was read without her understanding a word of the English, Forbes wrote that Sabella "twisted her face in a grotesque angle of fear, and inferiority, and cruelty and hope."[22] Animalistic comparisons were, horrifically, not uncommon when discussing race during the 19th and 20th centuries. This, more than anything else, shows Forbes's racist nature. The other women housed in Cook County Jail were described as "sultry," "sensuous,"[23] "the prettiest murderess Cook County has ever known,"[24] or with "rosily tinted nails" instead of Sabella's dirty nails or "ugly" countenance.

A popular writer for the *Tribune*, Forbes wrote several additional articles on Sabella, each of them containing the same kind of racism and aggressively victimizing language. In an article published on July 7, 1923, Forbes calls Sabella a "seamy faced, weather-beaten peasant ... at home in a truck garden, but little used to the refinement of even the stiff wooden chair in which she hunches restlessly."[25] Less than a week later, Forbes attempts to make the ordeal more sordid by heightening the sexual relationship between Sabella and her then-husband, Peter Crudelle. The main thesis of the article from July 12, 1923, is not about Sabella at all, though— it is instead about the kind-hearted attempt of the "normal" women who shared the women's cellblock with Sabella, who rallied around her during the press attack, an attack perpetrated by Forbes herself. In a truly surreal experience, Forbes begins the article by calling Crudelle Sabella's "illicit lover," though there is no evidence that Sabella and Crudelle were having an affair before the death of her husband. As the crux of a letter Sabella's defenders wrote was the unfair and racist—though they don't put it in the exact same terms—treatment of Sabella, Forbes has resorted to "dog-whistles," terms or phrases that when used signal to only those who understand their true meaning—like a dog whistle. After calling her relationship, whatever there was, with Crudelle illicit, Forbes says that the waiting on the cellblock made "normal women out of the ladies behind the bars at the county jail yesterday."[26] The overt implication is that while the women who wrote the letter were "ladies" made into "normal women" by Cook County Jail, Sabella was neither. Forbes even goes so far as to call the women's affection for Sabella "primitive loyalty to a forlorn sister, down and out, and homely."[27] Not only can Forbes not help herself with one more jab at Sabella's personal appearance, but she also resurrects the word *primitive* once again. The article makes the authors of the letter appear to be Sabella's wonderful friends, who wanted to make it clear that she was not the "dirty, disheveled woman" that the press (Forbes) called her.[28] This article of July 12 is perhaps one of the most egregious written by

Forbes because not only is it continuing her attack on Sabella, making her a victim of racial prejudice and libel, but it is also perpetuating the white savior complex. While the article pushes Sabella down, the other women of the cell block are elevated as kind, helpful women who wanted to help a "poor, homely" immigrant woman in need.

Not only does this speak to the racist attitudes of the 1920s, but it also helped to establish the way Sabella has been treated for the last century. The musical *Chicago* was born in the halls of the *Chicago Tribune*. By the 21st century, *Chicago* has become a "$2 billion entertainment franchise featuring A-list celebrities, a hit, Tony-Award-winning Broadway musical, and an Oscar-winning movie."[29] Because of a musical based upon a play written by a *Chicago Tribune* reporter, the names Roxie Hart and Velma Kelly have entered the history books alongside the rest of the "true" crime cases of the 1920s. A quick Google search brings up the names Beulah Annan and Belva Gaertner as their real-life counterparts; Sabella has either been forgotten in favor of the more traditionally beautiful, native-born women or she has been manipulated by popular culture to remove the more "displeasing" elements of Sabella Nitti.

Books

In the last ten years, there have been several books written on the women who at one point or another served time at the Cook County Jail's Murderess Row. For the most part, however, these books unsurprisingly focus on Belva Gaertner and Beulah Annan. While Belva's and Beulah's stories cover hundreds of pages, Sabella's is told in a mere dozen. More than anything else, this shows how little historians and true crime writers have cared about the female side of Chicago in the Roaring Twenties.

The Girls of Murder City: Fame, Lust, and the Beautiful Killers Who Inspired Chicago (2010)

The earliest recent book on the women of Chicago is *The Girls of Murder City: Fame, Lust, and the Beautiful Killers Who Inspired Chicago* by Douglas Perry from 2010. Sabella is mentioned a few times, described as a "poor, rough-looking, middle-aged ethnic woman who spoke almost no English."[30] Perry treats Sabella well throughout the book, though she could be featured more heavily. He calls out the press of the time for treating her terribly, saying, "No reporter ever entertained the thought she might be innocent."[31] Overall, it is a fair treatment of Sabella, with one glaring problem—the title of the book, which presupposes that Sabella, like Beulah and

Belva (for whom there was overwhelming evidence), was a killer. Perry and his title do not give Sabella any presumption of innocence. The book, like *Chicago*, only allows the public to think that Sabella killed her husband.

Ugly Prey: An Innocent Woman and the Death Sentence That Scandalized Jazz Age Chicago (2017)

Perry's book had one additional positive outcome: it serves as the inspiration for the one book that places its sole focus upon Sabella Nitti— *Ugly Prey: An Innocent Woman and the Death Sentence That Scandalized Jazz Age Chicago* by Emilie Le Beau Lucchesi, published in 2017. Lucchesi has said that reading about Sabella in Perry's book inspired her to find out more about the trial and the woman. *Ugly Prey* finally gives Sabella the respect she deserves by spending hundreds of pages on her, including far more detail than any other pop culture iteration on Sabella's life in Italy and her life after she left Chicago. With this look at Sabella's journey from Italy to the United States, Lucchesi also examines the pervasive racism of the 1920s that afflicted Italian Americans. She describes Sabella as "everything that America reviled about these invading southern Europeans."[32] While describing Forbes's disgusting treatment of Sabella, Lucchesi also provides the necessary historical context, a combination that is often lacking from a treatment of Sabella Nitti.

Ugly Prey has no shortage of context for Sabella, acting as a counterweight to the rest of the iterations. Whereas nearly every mention of Sabella has described her physically, with many of those descriptions based on the court coverage by reporters like Forbes, Lucchesi describes Sabella as a "compact woman with a muscular frame built with a lifetime of work."[33] Rather than simply referring to Sabella as "not as glamorous" as the other women in the cellblock, this book supposes that "under different circumstances, it would have been easy to describe her as pretty."[34] Relying on photos from before and after Helen Cirese's makeover, Lucchesi describes Sabella as having "fine arched eyebrows and round, close-set eyes … a slender nose, a wide mouth, and a defined jawline."[35] This description is far more balanced and relatable to a reader than Forbes's description of a "dumb, crouching, animal-like peasant."[36]

In addition to the unique experience of having an entire book about Sabella, her life, her trial, and what happened to her after the charges against her were dropped, Lucchesi's book explores circumstances that people like Forbes and Judge David did not, and did not bother trying to, understand. One particular element of Sabella's life that Lucchesi outlines in her book is that of the "white widow," or the common practice in Italy in which husbands would leave their wives for long periods of time, sometimes years, to manage the family and homestead alone. According to *Ugly Prey*, Sabella was "a white widow for most of her marriage to Francesco."[37] Judge Davis "didn't know that Sabella had lived without her husband in Bari ... or how in the United States, she had lived for many years on the Nitti family farm with only other Baresi for company."[38] Lucchesi continues, saying that her own sons had the freedom to run around Chicago without constraints, learning English from Americans and Italian from other immigrants, while Sabella was "confined to the truck garden farm."[39] Not only is Lucchesi explaining that Sabella spoke a specific dialect, but she also explains why without calling her intelligence into question. In fact, while discussing Cirese's makeover, which included English language skills, Lucchesi points out how intelligent Sabella had to be to be able to learn a language without the normal reading and writing study aids.

After the obligatory discussion of the 2002 film *Chicago*, Lucchesi describes Sabella's life after the charges against her were dropped. As with the rest of her treatment of Sabella, Lucchesi gives her the attention and respect that is lacking in other iterations. During her publicity tour, she managed to meet one of Sabella's granddaughters, who told her that the woman described in the book was the woman she remembered.

Other Books

Two more books were written in 2019 that included the women of Murderess Row: *He Had It Coming: Four Murderous Women and the Reporter Who Immortalized Their Stories* by Kori Rumore and Marianne Mather and *Second City Sinner: True Crime from Historic Chicago's Deadly Streets* by Jon Seidel. As *He Had It Coming* focuses solely on five women, it has far more information on Sabella, her life, and her case. Rumore and Mather cover the same ground in their chapter as Lucchesi did in her book. In addition to the fair, balanced treatment of Sabella, the book included two articles, "'Chicago' on Stage" by Chris Jones and "'Chicago' on Screen" by Michael Phillips. These articles give background and information on the musical productions on stage and screen. While they do not include information about Ekaterina or Sabella, the background on the musical/movie is beneficial. However, *He Had It Coming* has the same problem as Perry's book—the title presupposes that the four women covered in the book, including Sabella Nitti, were murderers, calling them the FOUR murderous women of Chicago.

Second City Sinners focuses on true crime during this overall period in Chicago. While there is a section called "Murderess Row," it is far smaller than any of the other books on the subject. As with other iterations of coverage on Sabella, the problematic coverage begins right away. The subchapter on Sabella, titled "Dumpy," begins with Francesco's disappearance, and Sabella is not even mentioned until the second page. Seidel does make the distinction that it was Sabella's *"perceived* lack of beauty" (emphasis added) that mattered to people.[40] While he also discusses the language barrier between Sabella and the rest of the criminal justice system, there is nothing specific about her Bari dialect or the context for why she never had the means or the opportunity to learn English.

With the exception of the shining light of Lucchesi's treatise on Sabella, other books on Murderess Row sit on a spectrum. For some, the treatment of Sabella is cursory, with far more time spent on the more "glamourous" of the Chicago characters. For others, the treatment is far better, including much of Sabella's life outside of the trial and context for why Sabella was so misunderstood. However, regardless of where they sit on the spectrum, chapter or book titles in turn call Sabella "dumpy," a killer, or a "murderous" woman. Lucchesi's *Ugly Prey* is the only tome that offers a full examination of the woman who escaped the noose and whose memory has had to endure nearly a century of revictimization.

Movies

There have been a few films adapted from the play, and later, the musical based upon the crimes of the women of Murderess Row. As the source material, originally written by Maurine Watkins, concentrated heavily on the life and crimes of Belva Gaertner and Beulah Annan, there is little on any of the other women incarcerated alongside Belva and Beulah. While that can, on one level, be understood, it shows a lack of growth as the trials approach their centennial.

Chicago (1927)

The 1927 *Chicago*, the first film to be made from Watkins's play, is a silent film that focuses heavily on the character of Roxie Hart. Directed by the famous Cecil B. DeMille, the film was released only a few short years after Sabella, Beulah, and Belva found themselves together in Cook County Jail. Being so wholly focused on Roxie, the character based upon Beulah, there are few scenes of anyone other than Roxie, her husband Amos, and her lawyer Billy Flynn. The only scene where there are women who could even be interpreted as Sabella or Belva is a scene in the cellblock. Roxie is sitting on a table admiring her many press clippings. An older woman, presumably the matron as she is wearing a badge, is sitting next to her, clipping out articles and handing them to Roxie. A woman with dark hair, likely Belva, taunts Roxie with how her name has appeared in the papers more times than Roxie's. The other women in the scene are caricatures of female murderers. One had allegedly stabbed her husband and became fascinated by the discarded scissors on the table. Another rocked in a rocking chair while she pantomimed hanging a baby doll. The matron told Roxie that this woman was in prison for strangling her baby after "her man refused to give her a ring."[41] There is only one other woman, who appears older than the rest, like Sabella, but she is barely in a singular scene before she disappears again.

Again, it is unsurprising that this iteration of *Chicago* did not stray from the original text. Being so close to not only the creation of the Watkins play, but also the trials themselves, this film had no time to grow. With the 1920s attitudes towards Italian Americans, it is also not surprising that Sabella was not included in either the original text or the film.

Chicago (2002)

After decades away from the silver screen, *Chicago* returned with a bang (pun fully intended) in 2002. This film has played a "major role in the sustained interest in Chicago."[42] Directed by Rob Marshall, the screenplay was written by Bill Condon. Starring Renée Zellweger as Roxie Hart and Catherine Zeta-Jones as Velma Kelly, the film follows the story and musical book that Bob Fosse created and honed on Broadway in the 1970s. In this iteration, obvious advancement has been made since the 1920s. There are more women included in the background in addition to Roxie/Beulah and Velma/Belva. "Cell Block Tango," one of the soundtrack's most popular songs, gives a few women at least a moment in the spotlight, including a character based upon Sabella Nitti.

The film begins with roughly the same basic storyline centering around the case of Roxie Hart. After shooting her lover, Fred Casely, she ends up in Murderess Row at Cook County Jail in Chicago. While some of the 21st-century updates can be seen as Roxie makes her way through the cellblock, it is when "Cell Block Tango" is played that it becomes more evident. Not only is this where the character based upon Sabella is introduced, but it is also where the audience sees women of color play two characters. While a viewer in 2020 may see this as not enough, this would have shocked an audience in 1924 and for decades after.

The song features the famous phrase, "Pop. Six. Squish. Uh-uh. Cicero. Lipchitz." Sabella, considered the "innocent one" of the cellblock, is represented by the "Uh-uh" stanza. Right away, however, problems present themselves. Sabella Nitta, small in stature, with the olive complexion and dark hair of someone from Southern Italy, has been entirely manipulated into a lithe, blonde, Hungarian ballerina. As discussed earlier, Sabella's physical traits were a prime target of Forbes and other reporters. Nearly eighty years later, nothing has changed. One would have hoped that in the 21st century Sabella would have been offered up the respect of having an actor cast who is closer to her actual body type. One obvious defense of the film is that it was simply following the book from the Broadway musical and that the blame really lies with those who created the Hungarian character in the first place. If the film version had made such a drastic change to the original, it may have flopped. So, there is some small defense of the film production. However, regardless of where the blame lies, Sabella was victimized in the 1970s by the original writing of the musical and again in 2002 by the filming of the movie musical.

Not only is Sabella disrespected by the creation of this character, but also this character's name is only spoken twice in the film, during the scene where she is being taken to the gallows. It is only then that she is named Ekaterina Chtchelkanova by the reporter Mary Sunshine as she tells Chicagoans what is happening in the prison yard. For the rest of the film, the character is merely referred to as the Hunyak, a racial slur for a person of Hungarian origin, particularly an immigrant.[43] Again, while the film was somewhat bound by the original text of the musical, it was possible to do more than just name Ekaterina, and also avoid having nearly all the characters refer to her as a racial slur throughout the film. If Ekaterina had had any character development at all—just a few more moments of screen time—it could have been explained as the film's way to explore the racism of the 1920s in Chicago. Ekaterina could show how much hurtful racial slurs likely affected Sabella. However, with only a few moments of screen time, and even fewer where she is the focus of the scene, it seems far more likely that Ekaterina is merely an afterthought and not worthy of the attention.

Besides this obvious victimization of Sabella by transforming her into a lithe, blonde ballerina, the film character does have some important traits that give an audience a glimpse into an otherwise forgotten woman. While she appears in very few scenes, those scenes show a woman much like Sabella. The greatest characteristic is the lack of English-speaking skills. The only words of English that Ekaterina speaks other than "Uh-uh" is her speech during "Cell Block Tango." During the song, each singer gets her own verse, which most of the women use to describe how they killed their victims. During Ekaterina's verses—the only time she has a spotlight other than her execution—she sings in Hungarian. As she dances under a white light (the others dance under a red light denoting their guilt), she sings:

They say my famous boarder held down my husband while I chopped off his head. But it isn't true. I am innocent. I don't know why Uncle Sam says I did it. I tried to explain at the police station but they didn't understand me.[44]

This at the very least shows a character who, like Sabella, was forced to navigate the criminal justice system without anyone understanding her or being able to understand anyone else.

Ekaterina's final scene is her "final" scene—her execution. She is led out to the gallows, crying, with Roxie watching from a window. The executioner pulls the lever, dropping the door, and the camera focuses on Ekaterina's feet swinging against the cold grey of a Chicago prison yard. She gets that brief moment where the film focuses on her before she is once again used as a plot device for Roxie Hart. Roxie had earlier fired Billy Flynn as her lawyer, believing that her popularity would be enough to save her. After seeing Ekaterina executed, Roxie is now scared enough to follow Billy's plan, which gets her acquitted. Ekaterina's execution, while not only historically inaccurate, serves as a way for Roxie to be acquitted and find her own fame.

This iteration of Sabella, while being the best on the big or small screen, only proves that there has not yet been a good or decent portrayal of Sabella Nitti. She is relegated to a plot device or a background actor in the storylines of the other women of Murderess Row. Any person who is a fan of the musical, who can sing "Cell Block Tango" without a second thought, will likely only know Ekaterina's verse of the song and her execution scene. However, very few have heard Sabella Nitti's name or even that the Hungarian ballerina is based on an Italian-American woman who escaped execution to live a long life in Los Angeles.

Podcasts

Without the connection to the musical, it is unlikely that podcasts would have been tempted to cover any of the women on Murderess Row. True crime podcasts cover the gamut from fully researched through primary sources to those who rely on Wikipedia from which to pull their facts. Both are valid formats and extremely popular, but the spectrum means that cases that require deeper research through primary sources are covered less than those with Lifetime movies. Belva Gaertner and Beulah Annan both have Wikipedia pages, while neither Sabella nor Francesco Nitti have one. Given all of the facts, it is unsurprising, then, that there are only a few podcasts that even mention Sabella.

Of the seven podcasts that were returned after a search for all things "Sabella," "Chicago," "Murderess Row," or even "Belva and Beulah," the only ones that focused solely on Sabella were those that had interviews with Emilie Le Beau Lucchesi. On May 2, 2018, *Books on Law* released its interview with the author. Five months later, *Most Notorious*, a history podcast that features a different author each week, interviewed Lucchesi in its October 25, 2018, episode. In both episodes, Lucchesi, clearly on a publicity tour for the book, discusses Sabella's life and her experience in 1923. One of the important pieces that she brings up in the conversations is naming the treatment of Sabella as torture and terrorism. On *Most Notorious* Lucchesi explains that during her time in the prison, Sabella watched "horribly botched hangings" where the convicted women were "strangled to death."[45] Lucchesi also points out in both podcasts how important Helen Cirese's makeover was, and that this makeover did not simply involve hair and makeup. Between a hard life on the farm and months in prison, Sabella was too thin. Cirese helped Sabella put on weight so she "looked like someone's mom" or "looked like someone who belonged at the flower show," a woman to whom most Chicagoans could now relate.[46] On *Books on Law*, she also points out the hypocrisy of Sabella compared to Beulah. Again, concentrating on context, she points out that Sabella was considered a dirty woman because of the perception of Italian Americans. However, Beulah was arrested in her nightie after allegedly shooting her lover after they had consumed "a gallon of wine on a Tuesday."[47]

Outside of interviews with Emilie Lucchesi, Sabella gets mere mentions in podcasts, with one problematic exception. *True Crime Historians* bases large portions of its episodes on newspaper articles, with the hosts reading them aloud. While episodes with nothing but primary sources are something historians may support, there needs to be some kind of context to explain the documents. Episode 230, based solely on Sabella Nitti, is a perfect example. The newspaper articles in this episode, again, with no context, include those of Genevieve Forbes. Her incredibly racist descriptions of Sabella are read aloud with other articles without any explanation. Additionally, the episode name, "The Ugly Duckling Murderess," presents all of the same problems as discussed earlier. Referring to Sabella as both an ugly duckling AND a murderess, without any context, is irresponsible. A visit to the episode's webpage, an optimal place for such context, reveals none.

Conclusion

For nearly a century, Sabella has either been forgotten by history and pop culture or she has had her story manipulated until she is unrecognizable. Before the books written in 2010, very few had ever heard her name, certainly not anyone who watched any of the iterations of *Chicago*. Even with the books written in the last decade, only one offers advocacy of Sabella. She has been portrayed sometimes as an innocent woman executed in a cold Chicago prison yard or, in the recent books, lumped in with other killers, leading many to assume that she was guilty of killing her husband. Her story is included in one of the most famous musicals, turned into an Oscar-winning movie, yet she has been overshadowed by the "more glamorous" Roxie and Velma.

Nearly forgotten to history, Sabella Nitti is in real danger of fading entirely without anyone advocating for her. There are no podcasts or Murderinos who are trying to spread the word about her case and the injustice of the years she spent accused of her husband's death.

With the surge in true crime and refocus on women who have not received their proper attention, the hope is that advocacy will soon give Sabella Nitti the pop culture iteration that she deserves.

CHAPTER 2

Bonnie Parker

By the 1930s, the Great Depression had settled upon the United States. Generally understood to have begun with the Stock Market Crash on October 29, 1929, an economic downturn had been affecting groups, particularly farmers, for years before 1929. To make matters worse, those living in the middle of the country would have to face the grinding daily threats and years of economic depression combined with the worst drought the region had faced in decades. This was the world that Bonnie Parker faced, reaching adulthood as the Great Depression and the Dust Bowl tormented her home in Texas.

Just the Facts

Bonnie Parker is a rare woman in this project as she is both arguably the best-known woman in these pages as well as one of the only female criminals featured. Not only has Bonnie Parker's name survived nearly a century after her death on a Louisiana road, but also, she has been "memorialized" or, more accurately, been done a disservice by pop culture for just as long. While her name is said first in the duo of "Bonnie & Clyde," it is she who is lost to history in favor of the more daring and exciting Clyde Barrow. It may be said by some that, as a woman who committed crimes in several states throughout the Midwest and South during the Great Depression, Bonnie does not deserve the respect shown to many of the other women analyzed in this project. However, Bonnie is not on trial here. She is being examined in the same vein as other women—by how poorly she has been treated by popular culture over the decades since her death. Like so many others, Bonnie has also been the subject of podcasts in the 21st century's latest digital obsession with true crime. Remember, the question is, as with all chapters of this project, is this newest wave of true crime simply regurgitating the same exploitative history or is it advocating for an objective and full account of Bonnie's life?

Bonnie Parker was born to Emma Krause Parker and Charles Parker on October 1, 1910. Her mother said that Bonnie was "a beautiful baby, with cotton-colored curls, the bluest eyes you ever saw, and an impudent little red mouth."[1] While Cement City, outside of Dallas, Texas, was a hard life, especially after her father died in 1914, Bonnie did well. She was considered one of the best students in her high school, even winning a spelling bee.[2] But this talent was not enough to keep Bonnie in school when there was the possibility of marriage. She married Roy Thorton on September 25, 1926, though Roy would often leave her alone for his numerous stays in various jails.[3] Without a husband to rely upon, Bonnie had to support herself by working at Marco's, a local cafe. According to Go Down Together, a 2019 book on Bonnie and Clyde, it is possible that Bonnie may have considered supplementing her income with sex work. The book's author, Jeff Guinn, points out that if Bonnie did consider sex work, it wouldn't have been out of the ordinary for working-class women from her area of Dallas—"[I]f they were cute—and Bonnie was—they had to at least consider the option."[4]

It is thought that Bonnie first met Clyde in January of 1930 when Bonnie was only nineteen years old and still married to Roy. In fact, she never divorces Roy and is still Mrs. Thorton when she dies. Soon after their meeting, Clyde is arrested and sent to "The Farm," one of the more brutal prison farms in Texas. With both Roy and Clyde in prison, Bonnie had no choice but to wait. As Guinn puts it, "Her life was dwindling away in spirit-crushing tedium."[5] When Clyde was released from The Farm, he came for Bonnie and, together, they began a life of "full-time lawbreaking."[6] Various other members joined them over the next two years, including Clyde's brother Buck, and Buck's wife, Blanche. W.D. Jones and Henry Methvin also joined the gang, with Methvin ultimately causing the couple's downfall. The Barrow Gang, as the group was known until the 1967 film changed the public's perception of Bonnie and Clyde, robbed banks, stores, and gas stations all across the Midwest, moving as far south as Texas and as far north as Minnesota. There were occasional instances of kidnapping and eventually murders of both civilians and police officers.

Methvin, in exchange for a pardon, arranged with the Texas Rangers, including the famous Frank Hamer, to set up Bonnie and Clyde. Hamer—on the gang's trail since February 1934—finally caught up to it on a rural road in Bienville Parish, Louisiana, near Methvin's father's home. On May 23, 1934, Clyde slowed the car, with Bonnie inside, to speak to Methvin's father (also in on the ruse). When the car slowed and Methvin was out of the line of fire, the law enforcement officers opened fire, killing both Bonnie and Clyde. They were buried separately, against their wishes to be buried together, but the legacies of Bonnie and Clyde were not left buried for long as they were soon resurrected for entertainment.

News of the Day

It should come as no surprise that the newspapers of the day were full of stories of the Barrow Gang and its exploits. Often, though, the articles spent far more time on Clyde than they did on Bonnie. If she was mentioned at all, she was depicted as Clyde's "girl," "moll," or in one case, "the Bandit Queen." In several articles from the *El Paso Times* from 1934, there is no mention of Bonnie at all. Either Clyde's name is in the title of the article, such as "Barrow's Auto Found in Kansas,"[7] or he is discussed in the text of the article, called a "kidnapping gunman" in "Hunt Dillinger in Oklahoma."[8]

When newspapers did talk about Bonnie, the articles tended to use words like "gun woman,"[9] "woman companion,"[10] or in a demotion, "girl companion."[11] Bonnie is often called "a Dallas girl" or "Clyde's 'frequent companion.'"[12] Her aunt, Millie Stamps, had ensured that the press, especially the local Texas press, knew Bonnie's name, so leaving Bonnie's name out of the articles was not out of ignorance. Guinn refers to it as "Texas chauvinism," but one must wonder if it was limited to Texas. It is very unlikely that other southern states would have treated Bonnie any better than Texas in press coverage. She was described as "addicted to cigar smoking," though her family was clear how much she hated cigars. She only posed with the cigar for the famous photo and much preferred cigarettes. In the May 24, 1934, *El Paso Times*, a photo of Bonnie was published under the words "Bandit Queen Slain." The photo was from her time before she joined up with Clyde and a life of crime and shows her in costume with toy guns. The caption below states, "The guns shown ... were toys, but Bonnie learned to use real weapons with deadly accuracy, many officers are willing to testify."[13] On the very same front page, there was a similar spread on Clyde, with his photo and a small write-up, but that photo was recent, not from before his life of crime. So, why choose this photo of Bonnie? The only reason can be that she is dressed up like, well, like a "Bandit Queen." From the very beginning, the news media and popular culture were trying to twist and shape Bonnie to force her to fit their narrative.

Books

The True Story of Bonnie and Clyde: As Told by Bonnie's Mother and Clyde's Sister (1968)

Originally published under the name *Fugitives* in 1934, the book was reprinted in 1968 as *The True Story of Bonnie and Clyde: As Told by*

Bonnie's Mother and Clyde's Sister. There were no changes between the editions; both were written by Jan I. Fortune. The 1968 edition, published after the huge success of the 1967 Warren Beatty/Faye Dunaway film, shows the outline of two people vaguely dressed in 1920s clothing, holding weapons, with red dots on them to symbolize where Bonnie and Clyde were shot in 1934. Swirling script next to the outlines reads, "They killed ruthlessly, loved passionately, and went to their violent deaths together."[14] Without cracking the book, the audience has already been tainted against Bonnie. With the quote "they killed ruthlessly," anyone who picks up the book is already under the direct impression that Bonnie fully participated in the murders associated with the Barrow Gang. Once the book is opened, one finds wonderful primary sources inside. While Jan Fortune curates the testimonies of Emma Parker and Nell Barrow Cowan, they are nevertheless great insights into the world of Bonnie and Clyde. Emma Parker, Bonnie's mother, gives some details on what Bonnie was like as a child, describing her as a "bouncing ball of energy" who loved learning to act.[15]

In addition to telling Bonnie's story from her birth to her death on the dirt road in Bienville Parish in 1934, Emma Parker wanted to use this forum to at least attempt to set the record straight. She says, "I notice that newspapers and detective magazines state that the meeting occurred while Bonnie was working at Marco's Cafe; that Bonnie was seen often with Clyde in night clubs and speakeasies, Bonnie always smoking a big black cigar and paying all the bills."[16] Stating frankly that Bonnie met Clyde in a simple country kitchen, Emma Parker recognizes that "truth is never so interesting as a good, windblown yarn."[17]

Emma continues to fight against the media portrayal of her daughter through the rest of the book, recognizing within a year of Bonnie's death that someone had to fight to correct the record. After the Joplin, Missouri, raid, when the photos of Bonnie with the guns and a cigar in her mouth were discovered, the press latched on to them and printed them over and over. Emma says, "A cigar smoking gun moll made such lurid headlines, no paper would ever correct the story for me.... [and from] that day on, Bonnie was branded and nothing I could say would change it. It was one of the best stories which they used to make Bonnie seem tough, calloused, hard, course, and utterly beyond all human feeling."[18]

From the outside, the book appears to be much like the rest, looking to cash in on the legend of Bonnie and Clyde as quickly as possible, getting Emma's and Nell's stories within weeks of the deaths. However, once one delves into the text, what is discovered is a mother who is still defending her daughter and already recognizing the damage being done to Bonnie's reputation.

Movies

The Bonnie Parker Story (1958)

The first film studied for this analysis is also the one that strays the furthest from any historical fact. Directed by William Witney, written by Stanley Sheptner, and released on May 29, 1958, *The Bonnie Parker Story* portrays Bonnie as more of a 1950s bad girl than a 1930s "gangster moll," as the newspapers of the day called her. Bonnie is played by Dorothy Provine as a 1950s platinum blonde in poodle skirts (without the poodle). It is as if the costume designer, makeup artist and hair stylist on this film did not know or did not care that this movie takes place in 1932, as the title card at the beginning states. Not only do the production company/producers care so little about Bonnie that no one bothered to remotely get her hair or dress correct, but the first shot of Bonnie shows her getting changed. This unnecessary sexualization of Bonnie will continue without fail throughout the fictional versions of her story.

When her name is first spoken in the film, she is referred to as Duke Jepson's wife. This is the first verbal sign that this film is taking huge liberties with historical fact. As mentioned above, the name of Bonnie's husband was Roy Thorton, not Duke Jepson. Before one can comprehend this, the dialogue continues to demean Bonnie. One man in the bar says, "She's a real wild cat"; while the other says, "I like how they scratch when they get excited."[19] Again, Bonnie is hypersexualized for no reason. "Duke" gets 175 years in prison, which leads to Bonnie working in a cafe. A man called Guy comes into the cafe and begins to flirt with her. When he unties her dress, she flings hot grease at him, which seems like a reasonable response; however, when he later follows her home, she invites him in. It becomes clear that "Guy" is really supposed to be Clyde. From this night onwards, the two are together, with Bonnie disregarding the fact that "Guy" assaulted and stalked her.

After meeting this "Guy Darrow," Bonnie and Guy begin a crime spree that seems sporadic, much like that of Bonnie and Clyde, but this film begins to perpetuate the myth that Bonnie received pleasure from the danger and the action. Their first real robbery is a bar, and after leaving, it is Bonnie who goes back to shoot up the place, with no real reason. The next place they hit is a gas station, which was more in line with historical fact, but this Bonnie again shoots up the place and, this time, sets fire to the gas pump. As they drive away, Bonnie yells, "Kiss me, Guy!"[20] As their spree continues, Guy/Clyde seems content with their situation, and it is Bonnie who continues to push the Bonnie Parker Gang—as it is now known—to continue to rob. It is Bonnie who puts all of the men in danger and pushes them closer to trouble. She makes the choice to break her husband out of jail, which means that her gang is now made up of her husband and her lover. While this sounds far too risqué for a film made in the 1950s, it skirts a very strange line. Bonnie has clearly been made into a cautionary tale—an overly sexualized woman whose life of loose morals led her down a life of crime. To make it clear that it is Bonnie making the choice to have relationships, she places tacks around the bed to keep the men from coming into her bed without her permission. According to the morals of the 1950s, Bonnie is straying far from the "traditional" values expected by mainstream Americans, and therefore an audience would be far more accepting at the end of the film when Bonnie is killed.

In the final action scenes, Bonnie continues to mock and belittle the two men as they run from the law. When Duke and Guy are too afraid to put themselves in danger, she tells them, "I'm not chicken. If I blow up, give my share to the old ladies' home and you two can move in."[21] In a confusing conclusion, Guy/Clyde shoots Duke before Bonnie and Guy die in a shootout. In what may be the only piece that is historically accurate in the entire film, Bonnie Parker dies in a shootout.

In addition to Bonnie's hyper sexualization, Bonnie is the only character whose name is not changed for this film. All of the men involved have had their names changed—for what purpose, who knows—but Bonnie Parker's name is included in the title. Perhaps it was because the filmmakers did not feel the need to afford Bonnie Parker the same courtesy or privacy afforded the men. Bonnie is depicted as "a sleazy femme fatale who seduces a series of lovers into committing criminal acts."[22] This is the only mainstream film to feature Bonnie for nine years, until the much more famous 1967 version starring Faye Dunaway. For those nine years, it was entirely possible for people to have no knowledge of Bonnie except what they learned from this film—that Bonnie was a "kill-crazy criminal mastermind" while Clyde, or Guy Darrow, was the "love-struck minion" of the dangerous Bonnie Parker.[23]

Bonnie and Clyde (1967)

The epitome of the Bonnie and Clyde story, this film is the one that most think of first when mentioning Bonnie Parker. Directed by Arthur Penn and written by David Newman and Robert Benton, *Bonnie and Clyde* was first shown at a film festival in Montreal on August 4, 1967, before being released to a wider audience by Warner Brothers on August 14.[24] Warren Beatty, who stars as Clyde, bought the rights to the story and petitioned the Barrow and Parker families to use the real names in the film. Until this film, Clyde's name always came before Bonnie's and the gang was always referred to as the Barrow Gang—with an obvious emphasis put upon Clyde. As soon as this film was released, that all changed, with Bonnie getting top billing in name if not in any other respects.

As is becoming a pattern with depictions of Bonnie, this version is overly sexualized for no other reason than to add sex appeal to the movie. While it is hard to fault producers for that—as we all know, sex sells—why is that specifically Bonnie's job? The first shot of Bonnie in this film is of Faye Dunaway's red lips. She is clearly naked and in bed. As with the 1958 film, the hair is not quite right. Bonnie Parker's hair was closer to strawberry blonde, a far cry from the bleached blonde of the 1958 version, but also not the blonde bob that Faye has in this film. In all of the photos of Bonnie from this time, her hair was at least long enough to pull back into a bun that was common during this era, with some waves framing her face. Faye's blonde bob fits into the era but is not true to Bonnie. These are little details that may not seem important when compared to other elements of this project—however, Bonnie Parker has some of the most famous photos of the women included in this study. Even so, multiple films either do not care or did not bother to attempt to get the smallest details correct.

In the film, Bonnie meets Clyde as he's trying to steal her mother's car, and within an hour, she has helped him rob a store and run away with him. In the space of an afternoon, they get to know each other, and Bonnie becomes completely subservient to Clyde. He "reads" her and tells her all about herself—including the fact that she's not married in this iteration. By removing her husband, whom she never divorced before taking up with Clyde, this Bonnie becomes purer. The audience could imagine that this overly sexual woman was possibly still a virgin before falling into a life of crime. The very same day when she meets Clyde, she obeys even the simplest orders from him. While sitting at a table in a cafe, he tells her to change her hair, and she does.

Bonnie wakes up the next day on the floor of an empty house after a night of sleeping on car cushions. Clyde patronizes her while teaching her how to fire a gun by telling her that he is going to get her a "littler gun."[25] Their relationship continues throughout the film to be one of Clyde patronizing Bonnie. After Clyde kills a bank manager, they go to the movies, but Bonnie seems completely unperturbed by, and unfeeling toward, the death of this innocent man. Clyde is annoyed at having to explain the seriousness of the situation to her. He gives her an "out," a way out of this relationship that is still only weeks, if not days, old. She refuses to leave, instead saying that she likes the romance of it and that she "doesn't want a rich man."[26] With these few scenes, Bonnie is shown as easily manipulated and so desperate to be loved by Clyde that she is willing to overlook the senseless death of the bank manager.

While much of this can easily be seen as Clyde's patronizing Bonnie, this film also spends time infantilizing her. She is clearly a grown woman but throws tantrums at the slightest inconvenience. While on the run, the gang, composed of Bonnie, Clyde, Buck, and Blanche, is living in a house—a far cry from living out of their cars or camping in the woods. She has a roof over her head and protection from prying eyes, and yet Bonnie is unhappy. Throwing herself down on the bed like a child, Bonnie tells Clyde that she is bored and does not like living with other people. Later, Bonnie disappears in the middle of the night. While the rest of the gang are looking for her in a cornfield, Clyde finds her having some kind of tantrum, yelling, "I just want to see my mama!"[27] It is documented that Bonnie often voiced missing her mother and her family and tried to get back to see them as often as possible, but Bonnie running off in the middle of the night makes her appear all the more like a child who needs Clyde's protection.

Perhaps the most enduring legacy of *Bonnie and Clyde* is how the public's perception has changed since the film's release more than fifty years ago. In addition to changing the arrangement of their names, *Bonnie and Clyde* romanticized the couple. Rather than thinking of photos of the real-life couple, most people now picture Warren Beatty and Faye Dunaway. As Guinn points out, the film does get elements correct, such as Bonnie's poetic bent, but the film misses the mundane—of her life before Clyde, while Roy and Clyde were in prison, and while the gang were "camping in cars and dining on cans of cold beans."[28] Without the boring details, Bonnie was sexy, but a realistic sexy, not the dangerous sexy from the 1958 film. Bonnie was suddenly the glamorous woman she had always strived to be in life.

Bonnie & Clyde (2013)

Advertised as a miniseries event, this History Channel series of two episodes from 2013 promised a modern update to the story last told in 1967. Starring Holliday Grainger as Bonnie and Emile Hirsh as Clyde, it begins with the bullet-riddled car being towed through a residential neighborhood, with the bodies still in the car and hundreds of people desperate to get a look inside. A boy, one of many children who rush the car, pulls at the sheet, revealing Clyde's bloody face—thus leading to Clyde's voiceover of his origin story.

A large portion of this origin story is Bonnie and Clyde's first meeting. The voiceover claims that he saw Bonnie in a vision when he was younger. Clyde has several visions throughout the series, all warning him of dangers that awaited them, many of them ignored by this iteration of Bonnie. The voiceover also says, "Maybe if [Clyde] hadn't met Bonnie Parker, all [he'd] be known for is stealing chickens."[29] Given that Clyde had already been to prison before ever meeting Bonnie, it is difficult to understand this logic. As will be seen for the rest of this series, much of the blame for the gang's crimes is placed solely at the feet of Bonnie Parker. Their first official meeting on screen is when Clyde and his brother Marvin crash Bonnie's wedding to Roy Thorton.

Bonnie starts living a life, of a sort, with her husband. Roy ends up going to jail himself for unrelated crimes, and Bonnie has a desire to not only get out of Texas, but to start acting and go to Hollywood. While Clyde begins his life of crime, being sent to a chain gang, Bonnie has photos taken, only to have them rejected by Columbia Pictures. Upon receiving this rejection, Bonnie appears to have some kind of anxiety attack, and only her mother can calm her down. While anxiety disorders are incredibly common, it seems as if this production has lumped Bonnie's anxiety in with other mental illnesses. At various points through the series, Bonnie is shown having symptoms that suggest a variety of illnesses, none of which were ever diagnosed. Clyde has "honest-to-God visions" throughout the show, but he is never seen as "crazy"; but Bonnie's story is manipulated to make her less sympathetic and more of a loose cannon.

This portrayal of an unhinged Bonnie is reinforced in the scenes following Bonnie and Clyde's first real "date." Clyde comes to get Bonnie for a date, even though they have never really met in any real way,[30] because he has heard some gossip that she may have left her husband. What is fascinating is the lack of conversation about Clyde's clear stalker behavior. They go dancing at a speakeasy, but as soon as the police raid the place, Clyde runs and abandons Bonnie. She is arrested for being at an illegal speakeasy, and her name is listed in the local paper. In a further step towards confirming Bonnie's romanticism or possibly mental illness, she keeps and cuts out Clyde's picture along with her own and begins to scrapbook.

Bonnie and Clyde officially become partners in crime after Clyde gets released from "The Farm," a prison farm where he was repeatedly raped and assaulted by guards and other prisoners. The fact that this series does cover this is to its credit, as it is very rarely discussed at all in other iterations of their story. After he is released because his mother secured a pardon for him, Clyde offers to give up "criming" for Bonnie and offers her a life of marriage and children. Disappointed, Bonnie tells him that she wants some time for just the two of them. Clyde's voiceover comes in again to place blame at the feet of Bonnie. He says, "Bonnie never told me that one more job wasn't going to be enough—she let me figure it out on my own."[31] From this account, it sounds as if Clyde was waiting for Bonnie to tell him when their life of crime was over and they could settle down, but it was just never enough for her. All subsequent actions, including all the deaths of law enforcement officers, innocents, and Bonnie and Clyde themselves, are blamed on Bonnie.

While robbing a bank, Bonnie calls them "Bonnie and Clyde" to the people inside the bank. Afterwards, Clyde is pissed, not because she announced their identities while committing a crime, but because she said "Bonnie and Clyde" and not "Clyde and Bonnie." This seeming desire for attention and press only continues when Bonnie breaks into the home of a female journalist. Later identified as P.J. Lane, played by Elizabeth Reaser, she has written a few stories on the robberies. Bonnie is apparently so angry that she is only ever mentioned as "female companion" in these stories that she breaks into P.J.'s house. Given her earlier goals for a career in Hollywood, the series seems to be making Bonnie an attention seeker, and it does not particularly matter from where that attention comes.

During another bank robbery, when there does not look like a way out for both of them, Bonnie offers to get arrested so Clyde can run. One must wonder her true reasons for offering, given the way Bonnie has been portrayed so far. She tells Clyde that since she has no record, she will be able to talk her way out of any charges. Clyde, with multiple arrests and a long record, would likely receive a much longer sentence, so her logic is sound. However, at the trial, Bonnie takes the stand and plays the part of the woman led astray all too well. Placing all the blame on Clyde, she pretends to be a meek and timid woman who simply trusted the wrong man. At one point, she even acts faint and asks for a glass of water. After being acquitted, she happily tells her mother that it was all an act. So, was she arrested to take the fall for Clyde and true love, or was she arrested so she could once again be the center of attention and act as if she were on stage? Either way, this is further evidence of this series' manipulation of Bonnie Parker into a flippant and unstable woman, without any historical evidence to back it up.

Reunited, Bonnie and Clyde start committing crimes once again. It is not long before the series jumps at the opportunity to portray Bonnie's fictional mental illnesses. Following the Hillsboro job, where someone was killed during the robbery, Bonnie is reading a newspaper and appears to be very emotional over the man's death. Just when a viewer could appreciate that Bonnie is finally showing some human empathy, she shows her true colors by telling Clyde that she's "sore because they used my sophomore photo."[32] That's right, she was not upset about the man they killed; she was upset because the newspaper had used her sophomore class photo and she thought she looked stupid. Still, she cut out the photo and put it in her scrapbook, the same one with her childhood pictures and achievements.

Bonnie's obsession with fame is, in part, what led to the now infamous photos. Clyde steals a camera to take "publicity photos" that they send to P.J. Lane for publication. After sending the photos, there is an interesting dichotomy between a vision of Bonnie's and a vision of Clyde's. Clyde's visions, as discussed earlier, are often of dangers or even the future. This vision showed him their deaths, now including Clyde's brother Marvin and his wife, Blanche. While Clyde is seeing, or foreseeing this, Bonnie is having a different kind of vision entirely. Her vision is a fantasy of being on the stage, again her dream of achieving some level of fame and fortune. Then there is a montage of Bonnie as a ballerina on stage with shots of the Barrow Gang robbing banks. This Bonnie clearly equates the fame she received from criminal activity to the fame that she had once hoped she could get from being on the stage. This desire for fame again damns the gang when they are surrounded at a motel. Bonnie goes back, refusing to leave a box of her newspaper clippings, even though it puts her and the rest in danger. Because of this delay, small as it was, Clyde is shot in the arm, Blanche gets glass in the eyes and is effectively blinded, and Marvin is shot in the head. Once they are far enough away to stop, Clyde blames the entire debacle on Bonnie and throws her box of clippings into the fire. Soon after this, Bonnie and Clyde are forced to leave Marvin and Blanche behind. Bonnie tries to comfort Clyde, who is worried that Marvin is surely going to die, by saying, "Even if he does, people are gonna remember him." Incensed, Clyde shouts, "That's all you care about, isn't it? People knowing you're alive."[33] He calls himself a footnote in the story of Bonnie Parker, which is almost amusing given how often the situation is quite the opposite.

Now alone, Bonnie and Clyde get into their car accident where Bonnie is severely injured. The injury is the most severe of any of the iterations of Bonnie Parker, but still not nearly as bad as it was in history. Rather than the painkillers being needed for the burns that literally went bone-deep, this series seems to portray Bonnie as becoming addicted to them. The combination of her already-established mental illness and now her addiction to painkillers has only heightened her psychosis. While stopped on the side of the road, Bonnie and Clyde kill two motorcycle police officers. When one officer tries to crawl again, Bonnie limps forward and shoots him point blank in the head. She turns and says, "See how his head bounced, Clyde, just like a rubber ball."[34] To make matters worse, the murders occurred on Easter Sunday, and one of the officers killed was meant to be married the following week. His fiancée wore her wedding dress to his funeral. Bonnie's evolution into an entirely psychotic, deadly woman is now complete. The eyewitness who told law enforcement that Bonnie Parker shot the police officer was more than a hundred yards away, and it was more likely that Henry Methvin was the one who killed him. However, as Methvin was the informant who arranged the spot where Bonnie and

Clyde were killed, and a pardon for him was already in the works, it did not really work for Methvin to kill a cop on Easter Sunday.[35]

Seemingly knowing that the end is near, Clyde calls Methvin to arrange for a place to hide out while in Louisiana. Whether Clyde has had some kind of vision about this or not, it does feel like the series is implying that Clyde is setting up a suicide by cop. While driving the infamous car down the infamous road, Clyde looks like he knows he is driving to his death, while Bonnie is oblivious. He slows down and pulls to a stop at the right spot to be killed by the posse waiting for them. Instead of Methvin's father creating a ruse to make sure they stop, Clyde just rolls to a crawl and waits to be killed. Whether it is Clyde accepting the fate his visions had been showing to him all along or something else, one cannot help but see this, at least partially, as the only way he could stop Bonnie. The Bonnie created for this series, the severely mentally ill, and now morphine-addicted woman who craved fame so much that she was willing to kill for it, could only be stopped by being killed. Perhaps Clyde knew that.

In reality, neither of them wished to die on that road in Louisiana, nor was Bonnie a mentally ill woman who thoroughly enjoyed the mayhem the gang inflicted upon the country during the 1930s. As with many other iterations of this case, Bonnie is the person who is more easily manipulated by creative license to add excitement and sex appeal to an already exciting and sexy story. In the case of 2013's *Bonnie & Clyde*, it can easily be said that the series went far too far. Not only is this miniseries victimizing Bonnie, but it was produced by and aired on the History Channel, which is traditionally trusted for factual accuracy. While Bonnie is a criminal whose crimes should be discussed, she also deserves a fair treatment that includes not being portrayed as a madwoman who took fame in whatever way she could get it.

The Highwaymen (2019)

The latest of the films that covers the exploits of Bonnie and Clyde, *The Highwaymen* was released on Netflix on March 29, 2019. Directed by John Lee Hancock and written by John Fusco, this film, while based in the greater world of Bonnie and Clyde, focuses instead on the law enforcement officers who track them. Kevin Costner plays Frank Hamer, the real-life Texas Ranger who did work on the case during the 1930s. Frank Hamer does appear in several of the pop culture iterations of this case, but this is the one example where Hamer is the main character. Joining Costner's Hamer is Maney Gault, played by Woody Harrelson. Rather than being about Bonnie and Clyde, this Netflix original is instead more for older individuals who enjoy stories about aging lawmen.

Much like with other pop culture iterations, Bonnie Parker in *The Highwaymen* is almost a caricature of the historical figure. The first image of Bonnie—as a sexualized object—sets the tone for the rest of the film. She is sitting in a car reading some kind of *Photoplay* magazine, and when she moves that, there is a gun between her knees. When she gets out of the car, her foot is seen first, then her leg, then the camera scans upwards as she walks away. In fact, *The Highwaymen* sexualizes Bonnie so much that her face is not even shown until an hour into the movie.

Throughout the movie, Bonnie is frequently implied to be the weak link in the gang, or it is outright said by various characters. The only other main female character in the movie, Ma Ferguson, the governor of Texas, played by Kathy Bates, promises the press that they will capture "Clyde Barrow and his paramour."[36] Ma Ferguson does not even bother naming Bonnie, not perceiving her as a dangerous threat like Clyde. Hamer and Gaunt have a conversation about the possibility of shooting a woman, with Gaunt saying that he has "never shot a girl before."[37] Hamer recommends shooting Clyde and Bonnie will surrender. While it can be explained again by the older men's misogyny, including it in a 2019 film is also an indication that Bonnie is a weakness. She continues to be seen as one for Clyde throughout the movie. After the car accident that horribly disfigured Bonnie, burning her leg so badly that the bone could be seen,[38] the gang complains about how often they need to get "dope" for "the girl."[39] Hamer and Gaunt quickly figure out that they can track the gang by tracking the medicine. The clear implication is that Bonnie is the only reason that the gang was caught. Bonnie is even a weakness for a childhood friend—Ted, a local cop from Texas, who joined the posse to be able to identify her. In a few different scenes, other law enforcement officers look down upon Ted upon because he is "soft" on Bonnie.

Entirely one-dimensional in this film, Bonnie Parker is denigrated to the point that she exists only as a sexual being who serves as a foil to the Barrow Gang. Anyone watching the film cannot help but ask ... why? Even if the film is to attract an older audience, those who would be interested in seeing Kevin Costner and Woody Harrelson eating a meal in a car while listening to the radio—why create such a poor picture of Bonnie? There were not many other women in the film, but they were not treated with the same crazy creative license that was used for Bonnie. However, Bonnie, a woman and a criminal, is open for as much bastardization as they wish.

TV/Documentaries

Highlander

In *Highlander*, season five episode seven, there is the rare comedic depiction of a character based on a subject for this project. *Highlander*, a historical science fiction show, was a spinoff of the film series from the 1980s. The series, starring Adrian Paul as Duncan MacLeod, continues the story of immortals, a race of people who live forever and fight each other to become "the one," the last immortal on Earth. Over the seven seasons of the show, Duncan's life, all four hundred years of it, is shown through flashbacks as he lives in the modern age of the mid- to late 1990s. To the joy of historians, Duncan has met numerous famous people over his lifetime, or some of his immortal friends step in place of famous people.

The latter happens in "Money No Object," the seventh episode of season five, when Amanda, Duncan's longtime on/off girlfriend, becomes a Bonnie-like character. Amanda, introduced early in the show as a thief with a heart of gold, serves as a constant in Duncan's life and possibly his one true love throughout his many centuries. In this episode, which aired in syndication on November 4, 1996, Amanda has reentered Duncan's life and they run into another immortal, Cory, whom they knew in a former life. Cue the flashback to Missouri in 1926. Amanda and Duncan meet Cory while he robs an armored car in the middle of the day on a remote road. Amanda, a thief for centuries, is impressed by Cory's brazen robbery and is even further so when they catch up with him and Cory has given the money to a poor farmer nearby. The farming family tell their tale of woe— their crops died and the government "left [them] flat."[40] A fun montage with ragtime music plays, showing Cory and Amanda robbing banks and trucks across the Midwest, just like Bonnie and Clyde, except after each robbery, they are killed. Luckily, they are immortal, and Duncan is there to dig them both up after the police and authorities leave.

Included in this truly entertaining montage is a photo shoot, just like the one that Bonnie and Clyde did with the guns and the cigar. The biggest difference is that Amanda is holding a cigarette instead of a cigar. Elizabeth Ward, who plays Amanda, looks far closer to Bonnie than Faye Dunaway, at the time the most famous portrayal of Bonnie Parker. The costuming department, used to matching costumes to specific eras of history, was also better than that of the 1967 film.

While it is obvious that Amanda is supposed to be a Bonnie-like character, there is also a line in the episode that makes it clear that Amanda and Cory exist in the same universe as Bonnie and Clyde. After one of their escapades, Amanda asks, "How many times did you get shot?"

Cory answers, "More than Bonnie—less than Clyde."[41] This depiction of a Bonnie-like character, even in a world where Bonnie obviously already exists, is an interesting addition to this study. Without Bonnie's name being explicitly mentioned, except for that one quick one, the audience is able to fully understand the comparison that is being made. By placing Amanda in Bonnie's shoes, *Highlander* helps to remove some of the tarnish that other pop culture has placed on Bonnie's memory. Without defending Bonnie's actions or crimes, her cultural memory does not deserve to be treated as it has been by movies and other pop culture vehicles over the last ninety years. Amanda's playful nature and ultimate likeability adds some levity to Bonnie's memory and this project.

Podcasts

While it is common to find podcasts covering the infamous Bonnie and Clyde, it is far less common to find hosts who choose to cover only Bonnie. As has been her lot in life, since her death Bonnie has been considered only worth covering in connection to Clyde Barrow. Podcasts like *Stuff You Missed in History Class*, a prominent historical podcast, covered the couple in 2009, with a 27-minute episode that is closer to 20 minutes after ads. Nancy Grace, one of the biggest names in true crime, covered Bonnie and Clyde in a Valentine's Day special titled "The Love Crimes of Bonnie and Clyde." In her familiar manner, Nancy examines Bonnie and Clyde using clips from the PBS *American Experience* documentary.

A Parcast podcast, *Female Criminals*, spent two episodes on Bonnie Parker in April of 2018. Parcast, a network known for its many podcasts on historical topics, launched this series that year, with Bonnie Parker as its third subject. This is the only podcast that delves deeply into the history of Bonnie Parker as her own person, without placing her alongside Clyde Barrow. The hosts, Vanessa Richardson and Sami Nye, examine her childhood, referencing her talent as a student and her compassion, telling the story of Bonnie helping a disabled student in her class. Vanessa and Sami also discuss the abuse that Bonnie suffered at the hands of her husband, Roy Thorton. The show, which makes a point to clarify that while the hosts are not trained in psychology, they have studied it extensively and wonder if Bonnie's dependency on Roy had to do with her father's death when she was four years old.[42]

By episode two of the series, Bonnie has met Clyde Barrow and Vanessa and Sami continue to analyze the psychology of this female criminal. Instead of discussing the exploits of a pair of lovers on the run, they talk about how Bonnie missed her family and constantly fought with

Clyde about when she could see her mother again. There is also a conversation about Bonnie's anxiety and her attachment to Clyde because she was afraid of being abandoned. Rather than the typical romanticization of the relationship, *Female Criminals* is giving an objective look at Bonnie and why she acted the way she did.

Additionally, Vanessa and Sami give voice to the true impact of Bonnie's wounds suffered during the auto accident. Due to the horrific nature of the accident and the acid that spilled onto Bonnie's leg, she was in terrible pain for the rest of her life. This episode, with its concentration on the psychology of the subject, explores what effect the pain medications she was taking for her wounds would have had on her behavior and on her relationships with the rest of the gang.

Female Criminals does a wonderful job in examining Bonnie as a criminal but also as an individual with a unique psychology that has not been discussed in any real way. This psychology allows for insights into why Bonnie may have acted the way she did and a better understanding of the woman herself. Lastly, Vanessa and Sami explore the disrespect Bonnie has suffered from the beginning—from law enforcement, the press, and others. While on the run, former Texas Ranger Frank Hamer called Bonnie promiscuous to the press and told them that she had many sexually transmitted diseases. Not only were these accusations printed in the papers, but so were photos of Bonnie's naked body taken in the coroner's office after her autopsy.

Another powerhouse in the podcasting world, *Last Podcast on the Left*, released a three-episode series on Bonnie and Clyde in June 2019. Hosted by three comedians, Henry Zebrowski, Ben Kissel, and Marcus Parks, *Last Podcast on the Left* has over four hundred episodes on topics that range from true crime to the paranormal, aliens, conspiracy theories, and more. Relying heavily on Jeff Guinn's book *Go Down Together*, Marcus, the researcher on the podcast, goes through the history of the famous couple. In the first episode, as with most historical accounts, Clyde, about eighteen months older than Bonnie, is discussed first. In *LPOTL*, Bonnie is not discussed until fifty-one minutes into the first episode.

Following Guinn's book closely, by episode three Bonnie has been injured in the car accident. Where *LPOTL* differs from the other podcasts and the fictional versions of Bonnie Parker, is in the discussion of her injuries after the accident. Marcus tells the audience that Bonnie's leg healed "very badly" so that she was in a fetal position most of the time.[43] W.D. Jones, who appears in the 1967 movie, said that Bonnie could not use the bathroom unless he or Clyde carried her to the toilet.[44] Marcus is careful to warn listeners that Bonnie should not be turned into a feminist icon as she is still attached to a lot of crime, including murder. But Bonnie had no desire to murder anyone, and to the best of his research, she never killed anyone. Recent research, most by Jeff Guinn, proves that Bonnie was not responsible for the death of the motorcycle cop and that Henry Methvin was most likely the person responsible. However, as a pardon was already in the works for Methvin for his part in ending the crime spree, nothing worked if he was the one who killed a motorcycle cop on Easter, so Bonnie became the killer. As Marcus points out, if this murder was not suddenly laid at the feet of Bonnie Parker, she may have been sentenced to ten or fifteen years for her part in the Barrow Gang's crimes, but now she was destined to die. While less progressive than other podcasts, *Last Podcast on the Left* certainly gave Bonnie more attention over three episodes than she gets in films with her name in the title.

Conclusion

Bonnie Parker was one of the most infamous female criminals of the 20th century, and had she lived beyond that rural Louisiana road in Bienville Parish, she would have certainly been sentenced to at least a decade in federal and state prisons. Her guilt is not the question. However, her treatment by the press, law enforcement, and later, pop culture, victimized her by portraying her as a dangerous sexpot luring Clyde Barrow into a life of crime; or as an infantile blonde bombshell just along for the ride; or as a psychotic serial killer who can shoot a wounded police officer in the head on Easter Sunday.

The vast majority of coverage on Bonnie is entirely exploitative, hoping to take advantage of what the public knows about her crimes with Clyde for ticket sales. Bonnie's memory is manipulated to whatever suits the filmmakers at that moment without any thought to trying to do justice to the actual person. A few podcasts have strived to be simply informational—allowing Bonnie to exist without the decades of exploitation to color their coverage. With some informational podcasts, the next step would be to finally have a visual iteration of Bonnie that offers a balanced view of her.

With so many different types of "Bonnies" in pop culture, her cultural memory has been corrupted. The public has no idea who the real Bonnie actually was. All that they "remember" is what they see from the films like 1967's *Bonnie and Clyde* or 2013's *Bonnie & Clyde*. While it is easy to imagine that the only women who are victimized by popular culture are those who were victims in life, that is simply untrue. Pop culture can make a victim of any woman.

CHAPTER 3

Elizabeth Short

The decade of the 1940s, so deeply tied to the worldwide fight against fascism on two fronts, holds a place of honor in the 20th century. Those who fought in World War II went on to be heralded as the "Greatest Generation." With this kind of adulation, one might assume that crime bypassed this decade, but what lies beneath the shine of America's obsession with the Second World War is the noir best illustrated by Bogart and Bacall and the smoky alleyways of *The Big Sleep*. Noir, characterized by cynicism and fatalism and fallen women, was the perfect environment for a country trying to process what it had done and been forced to do during four long years of war.

The death of Elizabeth Short in Los Angeles in January 1947 captured that noir atmosphere and continues to capture attention in the 21st century. One rarely hears of this murder, better known by the moniker given to her by the newspapers, "The Black Dahlia," without immediately imagining detectives in long overcoats, felt hats, and the flash of the press's cameras. However, this crime, including something as simple as Elizabeth's name, has been manipulated from the start and through the decades by pop culture.

Just the Facts

Elizabeth Short was born in Massachusetts to Phoebe and Cleo Short in 1924. Five years later, after the Great Depression began with the plummet of the stock market in October of 1929, Phoebe and her five daughters were abandoned when Cleo Short faked his death. Leaving his car abandoned on a bridge, Cleo hoped, rightly, that the authorities would assume that he, like so many others, had leapt to his death.[1] Without the financial support of dual incomes, Phoebe worked several jobs and accepted public assistance. As with many in similar situations, Elizabeth "fixated" on Hollywood films and the escape they provide.[2] Going to the movies gave a respite from the constant concerns over money or a precarious living sit-uation, and in the case of Elizabeth, chronic health conditions. Plagued since childhood with asthma and lung issues, Elizabeth had to work harder to be the "lively girl" described by so many after her death.[3]

After years of believing Cleo to be dead, the Short family was shocked to learn that he was not dead but living in California. In his letter, he apol-ogized and asked for forgiveness and another chance. Phoebe refused to see him again, but when Cleo offered Elizabeth the opportunity to move to California in 1943, she jumped at the chance. This was partially for her health concerns; her doctors told her that the mild climate would be much better for her than the harsh winters of New England.

Elizabeth moved in with her father in Vallejo, California, in early 1943, but was kicked out only a few short months later. Without a place to go or a steady income, Elizabeth had to figure out a way to get both. As California was a hub of wartime activity, she was able to find a job as a cashier at the Post Exchange at Camp Cooke in Santa Barbara County.[4] While there, she was crowned the "Camp Cutie of Camp Cooke," a beauty contest for the base workers. Now known all over the base, Elizabeth, only 19, began to attract a lot of attention from servicemen. Like most of the women in the United States during the war, the women of Camp Cooke knew the increased workplace opportunities would disappear as soon as the emergency was over. Already familiar with poverty and the hardships of a woman alone in the world, after the war Elizabeth was among the thousands looking in the ranks for a husband.

Just before 10 a.m. on the 15th of January, Betty Bersinger packed her daughter Anne, three years old in 1947, into a stroller and started their day. Betty had errands to run, including picking up her husband's shoes, which took her through her Leimert Park neighborhood toward the more commercial shopping district. As she pushed the stroller along the 3800 block of Norton Avenue, she noticed something. Exactly what she noticed first has also been debated in Black Dahlia scholarship, but it was either "something white in the weeds"[5] or "the flies."[6] Whatever it was, she went closer and saw what she assumed, what most assumed, to be a store man-nequin.[7] Worried that the nude form would disturb any nearby children, Mrs. Bersinger went to the nearest houses, trying two doors before finding someone. Using the stranger's phone, she called the police, told them what she had seen, and continued on her day. The police logged the call at 10:55 a.m., commenting that the woman on the phone, Mrs. Bersinger, sounded "shrill."[8]

At 11:07 a.m., while Betty was back to her schedule and had likely for-gotten the store dummy in the field, a patrol car was dispatched. Patrolmen Frank Perkins and Will Fitzgerald went to the scene and quickly called for

Homicide. The same radio call that brought Sergeant Finis A. Brown and Lieutenant Harry Hansen to the scene also brought the press. At the end of the second decade of the 21st century, the press and the police generally had an adversarial relationship, with any cooperation seen merely as an outlier. In the 1940s, however, the press and police worked hand in hand. When a storm delayed the LAPD package containing Short's fingerprints from getting to the FBI for identification, the *Los Angeles Herald-Express* used its new Soundphoto machine to send the prints to its Washington, D.C., Bureau, which then sent them to FBI Headquarters. With this type of relationship, it is not surprising that the press was able to surround the body of Elizabeth Short and begin to take photos. Without a thought to trampling the crime scene or contaminating evidence, reporters circled the corpse, taking the now infamous photos of Elizabeth. The photos show Elizabeth Short's body, nude in the grass, cut in half below the waist. Her killer had made numerous cuts on the body, including wounds on the legs and breasts, and carved a cruel grin three inches on either side of her mouth.

The moniker "The Black Dahlia," infamous in true crime circles, sup-posedly came from a pharmacist in Long Beach. Elizabeth had "drifted" around the pharmacy in the summer of 1946. The pharmacist, Arnold Landers, Sr., told newspapers that she wore "black lacey things ... her hair was jet-black ... she was popular with the men who came in here, and they got to calling her 'The Black Dahlia.'"[9] Others have postulated that the name given to her by the newspapers referenced a film that had been released the previous year. *The Blue Dahlia*, starring Alan Ladd and Veronica Lake and written by famous detective writer Raymond Chandler, is a classic film noir—much like the case itself. It would not take much to imagine the grisly murder of Elizabeth Short as a plot point in one of Chandler's novels.

Pop Culture

As one of the most famous unsolved crimes in American history, the tale of Elizabeth Short has been the subject of a few different pop culture vehicles. The notoriety of the victim and the crime allows for writers to skip the exposition and get right into the story. With each iteration, very little has changed from the picture painted by the news media in the late 1940s. Elizabeth Short is always the girl, down on her luck, who makes choices that no "good girl" would make, and in the end, is the victim being blamed again and again for her death.

News of the Day

The press of the 1940s were only mere decades after the "Yellow Journalism" that helped to send the United States into a war with Spain in 1898. One of the major players in that phenomenon was William Randolph Hearst, whose papers were also instrumental in covering the murder of Elizabeth Short. That same yellow journalism, the manipulation of the facts to sell more papers, embellished Elizabeth's life, oversexualizing and revictimizing her for years after her murder.

One of the most obvious victimizations by the press was giving Elizabeth Short the name "The Black Dahlia." While it was common for the press to "rename" victims to embellish headlines, the situation was made worse because the name has endured for more than seventy years. In papers from all over the country, Elizabeth was referred to as the "Black Dahlia" or more simply, the "Dahlia," removing her identity altogether. This removal of her name, of her identity, to be replaced with a name chosen almost randomly, only heightens the insult.[10] By the 21st century, this "nickname" has often become the only name that anyone knows from this case. Of all the pop culture iterations found for this project, numbering in the dozens, only four do not include "Black Dahlia" in the title. Podcast hosts and content creators know that to get a 21st-century public to download a book or an episode, the words "Black Dahlia" should be in the title.

While the LA police department continued to search for Elizabeth's murderer, the press had to find ways to keep people buying copies of that day's edition. The easiest way to do that was to turn Elizabeth Short into a cautionary tale—a young woman who was killed because of her "dangerous" lifestyle, a real-life femme fatale. For a nation that was still struggling to readjust after the end of the Second World War, and where "traditional family values" were heralded as the foundation upon which to rebuild the country, the quickest way to manipulate Elizabeth into a "dangerous" woman was to portray her as overtly sexual or hypersexualized. Articles in newspapers across the nation described Elizabeth using phrases like "black-haired beauty,"[11] "playgirl,"[12] "attractive,"[13] "diminutive,"[14] and "man-crazy adventuress."[15] In an article published only three days after Elizabeth was found, *The Washington Post* wrote, "[W]hen her mutilated, bisected body was found in a vacant lot Wednesday morning, her jet hair had been hennaed and was just beginning to grow out its natural color."[16] If this were published before her identity was known, then a physical description in nationwide newspapers would make sense, especially given that Elizabeth's family was still on the East Coast. However, she is named as Elizabeth Short a few times in the same article, so these details about her hair were not about helping the police identify her. In fact, this is the second reference to her hair color, so this sentence is entirely unneeded and serves only to unnecessarily remind readers of *The Washington Post* of her looks and sexuality.

Several of the same articles paid far too much attention to Elizabeth's social and romantic life. Again, only three days after her body was found, an article was published in the *Los Angeles Times* that includes two quotes that make claims about her love life. Her father told the paper that Elizabeth had arrived in Los Angeles to live with him but spent "all of her time running around when she was supposed to be keeping house for" him.[17] In accounting Elizabeth's final weeks, another *Los Angeles Times* article says that she shared an apartment with several roommates from November 13– December 5, 1946, where "she was known as a girl with a different boyfriend every night."[18] One of those roommates, Linda Rohr, says Elizabeth "was always going out and she loved to prowl the boulevard."[19] While this article is titled "Black Dahlia's Love Life Traced in Search for Her Fiendish Murderer," the point of the article seems to be more about casting Elizabeth as promiscuous than trying to find her killer.

Books

Several books have been written about the murder of Elizabeth Short since her death in 1947. It would be impossible to cover all of them in this section, so a cross section was chosen to study how Elizabeth has been treated in print.

Black Dahlia Avenger (2003)

Steve Hodel, a former LAPD detective, published his book *Black Dahlia Avenger* in 2003 and reprinted it in 2012 with updated materials and "new findings." Since his first book, Hodel has published two additional books, *Black Dahlia Avenger II* in 2014 and *Black Dahlia Avenger III* in 2018. Hodel's investigation is interesting and thorough, but the element that has garnered the most attention is Hodel's ultimate conclusion that Elizabeth was killed by his own father, Dr. George Hodel.

Black Dahlia Avenger (2003) intertwines the stories of Elizabeth's murder and Steve Hodel investigating his own father for that decades-old murder. Unsurprisingly for a former homicide detective, the book reads a bit like a homicide file. Hodel gives a brief two-page background before beginning to talk about the investigation. As with much of the coverage, he often calls it the "Black Dahlia case" or the "Dahlia homicide" instead of the Elizabeth Short case or the Short homicide.[20] Chapter 11, "The Dahlia

Witnesses," lists testimonies of people who knew Elizabeth. Some of them offer up positive pictures of her; others are the same misleading or even blatantly untrue descriptions of Elizabeth.

Tucked into Chapter 29, titled "The Dahlia Myths," is Hodel's examination of Elizabeth's treatment by the press and in books. He does not include films, television, or documentaries, but his analysis of her "character assassination" proves that this is a standout work, made before this latest wave of true crime that has been so heavily influenced by fourth-wave feminism. Hodel says, rightly, that "from day one," with the beginning of the name Black Dahlia, Elizabeth's "real identity disappeared."[21]

He places the initial blame at the feet of the press, citing several instances of alluding to the myth of Elizabeth's possible lesbianism. After his accusation of the press, he begins his examination of what he calls "true crime experts" ranging from the 1950s to the 1990s.[22] In his 1954 book, *Ten Perfect Murders*, Hank Sterling wrote, "It's fair to say that her death was the result of her deplorable way of life."[23] Four years later, Elizabeth was called "a lazy girl and irresponsible" by Jack Webb in his book, *The Badge*.[24] Hodel skips several decades ahead, saying, "[B]y the 1980s, Elizabeth's character had reached rock bottom."[25] The 1986 book *Fallen Angels: Chronicles of L.A. Crime and Mystery* by Marvin Wolf and Katherine Mader gives this description of Elizabeth: "A pretty girl not too mindful about where and with whom she slept, a pretty girl desperate enough to pose nude for sleazy pornographers, a pretty girl descending into a private hell."[26] In 1989, author Steven Nickel published *Torso: The Story of Eliot Ness and the Search for a Psychopathic Killer* and, according to Hodel, made "even more starling claims."[27] Among these claims was the statement that "[f]or a time, [Elizabeth] operated as an expensive call girl with a flashy lifestyle ... but before long she degenerated into a common street prostitute hooked on alcohol and drugs, posing for nude photos to earn extra cash and occasionally living with a lesbian lover."[28]

At first glance, Hodel's book is a straightforward account of Elizabeth's murder—the facts combined with the suspect Hodel thought most likely to be the killer—his own father. However, his introspective analysis, what Hodel calls his examination of the "character assassination" of Elizabeth Short, is what sets this book apart from so many of the rest.

Movies

Who Is the Black Dahlia? (1975)

The first movie that centered itself entirely on the case was the 1975 made-for-TV movie *Who Is the Black Dahlia?* Starring Lucie Arnez as

Elizabeth Short, and Efrem Zimbalist, Jr., Tom Bosley, and Donna Mills, this vehicle presents a complicated view of Elizabeth and the crime. As with most of the pop culture on this case, it focuses heavily on the police investigation, but it does give more background on Elizabeth than the others covered below. What is strange are the random details of Elizabeth's life that have been changed. Creative license plus random factors have long been the cause for altering history for popular consumption; however, it is difficult to see exactly why these details have been changed. For example, the movie gives Elizabeth's hometown as Portland, Maine, not Medford, Massachusetts. This change of location achieves exactly nothing, but nevertheless it happens. Other names are randomly changed—Camp Cooke to Camp Clark and San Diego to Santa Barbara. In addition, Elizabeth is living with her grandmother in Portland, not her mother in Medford. Again, it is unclear why this would be changed, but it does make Elizabeth more sympathetic. Adding to that is the interaction with her father once she does make it to Vallejo, California. The only time Elizabeth is seen with her father on screen, Cleo Short is cold—telling his daughter (presumably his only daughter as none of her sisters are mentioned) that he did not intend for her to live with him in California.

As with the 2006 movie, the role of the police in this film is at the heart of the story. The names have not been changed, so the audience follows Harry Hansen and Finis Brown investigating the case. The Hansen played by Zimbalist is a little bit more sympathetic than the real man, at least, the real man as represented in the press and in interviews. The film ends with a straight-to-camera—almost confessional-like—Hansen, telling the audience that the crime scene still haunts him.[29] This is a departure from the Hansen quoted in Piu Eatwell's 2018 book, who called Elizabeth a "man-crazed tramp," indicating a lack of care about her case.[30] Zimbalist's Hansen does antagonize a 1975 TV audience by immediately victim blaming at the crime scene. Upon seeing the body, shot in such a way that the audience only saw her black hair and some unblemished skin, Hansen says, "Lady, what the hell could you do to make anybody that mad?"[31] Removing victim blaming has been one of the largest pushes in the altered storytelling of 21st-century true crime, spearheaded primarily by women.

Another large deviation from reality is the very first thing seen in the film. Rather than Betty Bersinger finding the body in a fairly neat field while pushing her daughter's stroller down a sidewalk, the film has a boy finding the body in a slightly seedy, overgrown area as he is out with his grandfather. Not only does this delete a woman from the narrative, but also it adds to the destruction of innocence that revolves around the Short case. By introducing this theme at the beginning, viewers are prepared for what is going to happen to Elizabeth Short.

The evolution of Elizabeth Short into this idea of the Black Dahlia is more complete in this film than in any of the other works. At 18, in her grandmother's living room, she is a bright and excited girl, ready for her move to California. After her father throws her out, she is accosted more than once by servicemen (between 1942 and 1943). Each time, the men begin by charming her, only to soon shift to suggesting sex and/or try-ing to assault her. Random men come to her rescue to stop the assaults, but assumptions are immediately made that she somehow invited those attacks. After the first assault, by a sailor in broad daylight in a park, he and her rescuer-turned-another potential assailant call her a "tease" and say, "She'll get hers."[32] The assumption after the second assault comes from a woman, setting up another theme of the film—women judging Eliza-beth with little to no evidence. While walking to Camp Clarke (aka Camp Cooke—she was walking because she got off at the wrong bus stop), she is offered a ride by a serviceman who pulls over. At first, she refuses, saying, "Walking doesn't cost anything," suggesting that this Elizabeth already knows the cost many men would extract if given the opportunity. He men-tions his Good Conduct Medal and charms her into consenting to a ride. He traps her between himself and the car, telling her that before going to the camp, he is going to take her to the "place where all the girls bed down."[33] She is again saved, this time by a couple who, when passing, saw trouble and stopped. After the serviceman leaves her there, the husband asks if she is okay. The wife—still in the car, not having bothered to get out—said, "Can't you see she is—girls like that are always all right."[34]

Scenes like these contribute to the evolution of Elizabeth from the optimistic girl to the survivalist player she became just before her death. To get a job at the camp, she tells the manager of the Post Exchange that she was not interested in the men on base—that she had not cared about men since her husband died in the war. Immediately after hearing this, the manager relaxes, becomes sympathetic and offers her the job. They appar-ently become friendly, having lunch together in the next scene, presum-ably many weeks or months later. He feels betrayed when, after he helps her get the "Camp Cutie" title, she leaves in the night. While he assumes that she has left because of the unwanted attention of the servicemen, the women in the exchange say, "She probably said no when she meant may-be."[35] Women in this movie are vicious to each other—every interaction that Elizabeth has with another woman other than her grandmother and the nice policewoman after her arrest in 1943, is antagonistic and demean-ing. The characters are pitted against each other in a way that is anachro-nistic to the way women pulled together on the Home Front.

While the film offers up what is perhaps a rose-colored glasses ver-sion of Elizabeth Short, it does seem like the most realistic journey for the woman to have made from Medford to Leimert Park. By the end of the film, she is so desperate for affection, she agrees to sleep with "Doc,"[36] but only if he tells her he loves her first.

True Confessions (1981)

Based on the book by John Gregory Dunne,[37] directed by Ulu Grosbard and starring Robert De Niro and Robert Duvall, *True Confessions* was released by United Artists on September 25, 1981. De Niro plays Monsignor Desmond Spellacy, while Duvall plays his brother, Detective Tom Spellacy. Set in 1948 Los Angeles, the film is primarily about the two brothers and their relationship; however, there is a subplot focused on the finding of a bisected body in an abandoned lot.

As an LAPD detective, Tom was assigned to the case. It is clear from the first moment the woman appears on the screen that she is supposed to be Elizabeth Short. The body is in the same basic positioning as Elizabeth, with the only change being that the legs were crossed to hide the genital area from the camera. The camera focuses on a rose tattoo on the victim's body, much like the tattoo on Elizabeth's body. Reporters milled around the scene, asking questions. One of the reporters told Tom that it "looked like a werewolf got to her."[38] This is significant because before the case became known as the "Black Dahlia case," it was referred to as "the Werewolf Killer" case. Clearly based on Elizabeth, her murder, and the case, the treatment throughout the rest of the movie of the victim, named Lois Fazenda, only further victimizes Elizabeth Short.

The abuse of the victim, and by extension, Elizabeth, begins while Tom is still at the crime scene. Both a reporter and Tom refer to the victim as a derogatory word multiple times, showing a huge lack of respect for the dead woman in front of them.[39] Instead of the "Black Dahlia," Lois is nicknamed "The Virgin Tramp" by the press. There are multiple headlines with this name shown on camera, and it is spoken aloud a few times. When Tom goes home after a long day, he turns on the radio to hear a news program report that the "Virgin Tramp" was known to "be a romance seeker."[40] Just like Elizabeth, Lois was given a name that stripped her of her identity while the press also made assumptions about her character. Other assumptions about Elizabeth made by the press also show up in *True Confessions*. Lois is referred to several times as a sex worker. In fact, Tom and his partner watch a porn film starring Lois in one scene to heighten this degradation of her character. There is also a mention that Lois traded sex as payment for her rose tattoo.

In addition to leaning heavily into the mythos of the "Black Dahlia" rather than giving any kind of real portrayal of Elizabeth Short, *True*

Confessions further revictimizes Lois by making her a subplot that only drives the storylines of men. It is her death that brings the brothers back together and forces DeNiro's character to face his life choices. However, she is merely used as a plot device without any character development of her own. In another eerily similar path to Elizabeth, the film is only interested in sordid details of her life and her death. There are no details of her life or anything that would allow Lois, and by extension Elizabeth, to exist as an individual.

The Black Dahlia (2006)

The case of Elizabeth Short was the basis for a noir fiction novel by James Ellroy, *The Black Dahlia*, published in 1987. Ellroy, whose mother was murdered when he was a boy, also wrote the famous noir novel *L.A. Confidential*. After *L.A. Confidential* was turned into a successful film in 1997, Hollywood turned its attention to *The Black Dahlia*. The film went through multiple rewrites over a period of eight years, with each rewrite being tailored for a new leading man. At various points, Paul Walker, Stephen Dorff, and Chris O'Donnell were slated to play the part that eventually went to Josh Hartnett. The film adaptation, starring Aaron Eckhart and Scarlett Johansson alongside Hartnett, was released to both critical and financial failure in 2006. Based on the Short murder, even putting her media moniker in the title, the film barely scratches the surface of the case and manipulates Elizabeth Short into a plot device and nothing more.

In a film called *The Black Dahlia*, one would expect to be introduced to the case of Elizabeth Short earlier than twenty-two minutes into the film. However, the first twenty-two minutes are spent introducing the audience to the two male main characters, Hartnett's Bucky and Eckhart's Lee, with some attention paid to Johansson's blonde bombshell, Kay. When Dwight and Lee are at another crime scene (where Lee takes part in some blatant murders of his own), they stumble upon the scene of Short. Other detectives are already surrounding the body, and the man in charge makes it very clear that all reporters should be kept away from the scene—a huge deviation from the facts of the case. When the reporters do show up, there are no women in sight—no Aggie Underwood to be seen. The camera hovers over the body and shows all the wounds in crystal-clear detail. Rather than an accurate reporting of the crime, this instead feels exploitative with lingering on the breasts.

Dwight and Lee visit Mr. Short, played by Kevin Dunn. There is no evidence as to what Cleo Short said to police when, or if, they questioned him, but the exchange in the film only further cements the idea of Elizabeth as a promiscuous woman. Mr. Short says, "They were all her boyfriends—long as they wore a uniform. See, Betty believed in quantity before quality."[41] Dwight, in surprise, asks, "Are you calling your daughter a tramp?" Mr. Short responds with, "I got five daughters. One rotten apple ain't so bad…. She just paraded Hollywood Boulevard in those black get-ups. I mean, who wouldn't get herself killed doing that?"[42]

Dwight and Lee follow separate investigations, with each becoming obsessed with Elizabeth in separate ways. Only Dwight refers to her as Miss Short, but most refer to her as the Dahlia, The Black Dahlia, or simply "that dead girl." During an interview with a former roommate of Elizabeth, Dwight hears insinuations that she may have been a lesbian. As he follows this line of inquiry, Dwight discovers that Elizabeth and another girl (underage) were forced to make a "nudie film" for money to survive. When he obtains a copy of the film, the entire squad sits down to watch it—no consideration given to either the victim of a brutal murder or to the underage girl on the screen. It is extremely disturbing that not one, but two different films with characters based on Elizabeth show her working in adult films. There is no discussion of either iteration being forced to engage in this as a form of survival sex work, which is the most likely form of sex work that Elizabeth may have been involved in—but has not been proved.

Short's promiscuity is further discussed when Dwight meets Madeline Endicott, played by Hilary Swank. Dwight first assumes that Madeline is a Dahlia wannabe but learns from her that it was the other way around—that Elizabeth was trying to look like Madeline. This quick statement hits a nerve for those aware of the facts of the case. Elizabeth's hair was listed in the autopsy report as dyed black with the roots growing out. Combined with this moment in the film, Elizabeth is manipulated into a woman who was altering her image to match that of a socialite. Madeline is a fictional character, but many do not possess the media literacy to separate the character of Elizabeth Short from the real person. Viewers have likely taken details from the movie and accepted them as true facts from the case.

At several points throughout the latter half of the movie, both Dwight and the audience forget about Elizabeth Short or that this movie is supposed to be about The Black Dahlia case. Especially after (spoiler alert!) Lee dies, both Bucky and Kay find solace in each other, and everyone forgets about Elizabeth Short. All of the women in this movie, the Dahlia, Kay, and Swank's Madeline, are plot devices first for Bucky and Lee and then, just Bucky. In the last half hour of the film, Bucky is so distracted by his new romance with Kay and cheating on her with Madeline that he has seemingly moved on from the case. He is reminded of it when he sees a painting in Madeline's house that reminds him of the smile carved in

Elizabeth's face. Finding a lead, he follows it all the way to the killer. Here again, the movie differs from reality by solving the murder.

In a rousing bit of exposition, the audience finds out that a woman killed Elizabeth. When Elizabeth called Madeline asking for money, Madeline's father offered Elizabeth money to "spend some time" with an old friend. Madeline's deranged mother was jealous of this, being in love with this old friend, and followed them to a shack in the shadow of the Hollywood sign and proceeded to mutilate and murder Elizabeth. Then the mother—the killer—shoots herself. Case closed, right? Dwight is seen reading a newspaper that calls the suicide an "accidental shooting."[43] Presumably, Dwight lives out his days with Kay and they lived happily ever after.

The ending is incredibly unfair to Elizabeth Short and the audience. Again, painting the murder as solved or even solvable alters the audience's perception of the actual crime. Likely, there have been more than a few people who, not bothering with additional research, believed that a): Elizabeth Short was a survival sex worker (if they are aware of the proper terminology); and b): a woman who in turn killed herself killed her. Even for those who can separate the fact and the fiction, this ending is extremely problematic. The Elizabeth of the film gets no justice. Her killer dies by a suicide that is covered up by the press and the police. No one is charged, by either the court or public opinion, for the crime. The killer gets an honorable death and maintains her social standing while the Dahlia remains a sad, cautionary tale for all new women to the City of Angels.

Television/Documentaries

Hunter: Season 4: Episode 13 (1988)

One of the first appearances of Elizabeth Short in a television show was in 1988, in the fourth season of *Hunter*. A typical detective show on NBC, it follows Sgt. Rick Hunter and Sgt. Dee Dee McCall, two members of the Los Angeles Police Department. Episode thirteen of the fourth season, titled "The Black Dahlia," aired on January 9, 1988, which the show argued was the 41st anniversary of the murder of Elizabeth Short. However, according to the official account, Elizabeth died no more than twelve hours before she was found, putting her date of death January 14, 1947, a full five days after the date set by *Hunter*.

The episode centered around the discovery of a new skeleton that was found during the demolition of a building built in 1947. After similarities between the new skeleton and Elizabeth Short were identified, a retired detective met with Sgts. Hunter and McCall, who were the current detectives assigned to Elizabeth's case. According to McCall, Elizabeth's case is "theirs until they retire."[44] Sgt. Doyle, the retired detective who originally worked the case, helped familiarize Hunter and McCall with details of the case. An actor was hired to portray Elizabeth in some scenes, but the crime scene photos look like the actual crime scene photos taken on January 15, 1947. Sgt. Doyle is also portrayed as a man still obsessed with the case after 41 years, with newspaper articles tacked all over his living room wall. Like the crime scene photos, the articles are genuine articles from 1947, with pictures of Elizabeth Short. Whether the production did not want to spend the money or did not have the ability to re-create the crime scene photos and the articles on Doyle's wall, having the camera linger so long on them brings the audience's attention to them specifically. By using Elizabeth's actual name and her likeness, the show is trying to capitalize on Elizabeth's image and the notoriety surrounding her murder.

When they close the case at the end of the episode, it is Sgt. McCall who places the handcuffs on the suspect—a man who killed both Elizabeth and the woman whose skeleton was found in the building foundation. However, McCall does not solve the case through superior detective skills; the killer attacks her in her home because, in his mental illness, he has mistaken McCall for Elizabeth. At the very end of the episode, a special message appeared on the screen saying that the case is still open and that the real killer has never been officially caught.[45] This lingering message does remind the audience (this episode and the rest of the series is streaming on Amazon Prime for a modern audience) that the case has not been solved, but the gesture does not make up for the TV show's blatant use of Elizabeth's name and likeness for its own purposes, especially when it was and is typical for a show to create fake articles to avoid the use of any real persons.

American Horror Story (2011)

The Black Dahlia—the character in season one of *American Horror Story* is not named Elizabeth Short until twelve minutes in—appears in the ninth episode, "Spooky Little Girl." Named *Murder House*, this season of *American Horror Story* centers around a Victorian mansion in Los Angeles. The audience is introduced to several ghosts that haunt the house, including a vengeful maid, a school shooter, and a doctor from the 1920s, who did Frankenstein-like experiments in the basement of the house. Episode 9 opens with a yellow cab pulling up to the walkway leading to the house, itself the main character of this season. It is clearly the 1940s when Mena Suvari steps out of a yellow taxi, dressed in a black suit, with a white dahlia pinned to her black hair. As she walks to the house, Elizabeth passes a prim mother with a teenaged son, who is wearing some of the most unfortunate headgear. The mother automatically reacts to Elizabeth, pulling her son closer as she quickens her pace. Without a word spoken, the audience sees that Elizabeth is dangerous.

In the 1947 incarnation of the Murder House, a dentist lives there, operating his dental practice out of the home. Those familiar with the Elizabeth Short case know that Short reportedly had horrible teeth, so it makes perfect sense for this fictionalized version to be seeking a dentist. The dentist, played by Joshua Malina, walks Elizabeth down the hall towards his office, asking her who had referred her to his practice. Elizabeth's lines are overtly sexual. Citing her friend, "Nabby Pierce," Elizabeth says, "You filled her cavity. She said you were very good."[46] Uncomfortable, the doctor begins to prep his instruments while Elizabeth says, "Nabby also said that you sometimes made special arrangements with girls who are a little short."[47] When the doctor continues to hesitate, Elizabeth purrs, "It really hurts, Doctor. I need you to fill it."[48] The implication is clear; Elizabeth is offering sexual favors for free dental work. The writers of this episode made the same assumptions about Elizabeth that the press did in 1947. Her "reputation" combined with no job could only mean that she used sex as a bargaining tool. It should be noted, again, that Elizabeth Short had horrible teeth, so bad that it was mentioned over and over. If this woman was trading sexual favors for basic needs, wouldn't her teeth look as good as Mena Suvari's in *American Horror Story*?

In case there were one or two viewers of *AHS* that were not familiar enough with Elizabeth's story to get it from the general look, she mentions the flower in her hair is a dahlia. And if that was not enough, the show cuts from her in the dentist's chair to a fictionalized version of Betty Berslinger finding Elizabeth's body in Leimpart Park. Given the desensitized nature of 2011 and the average fan of *AHS*, the episode shows far more than the newspapers did in 1947. This version is laid out in an identical fashion to Elizabeth Short, her body bisected with various cuts, especially the vicious smile.

Elizabeth next appears in present day, as a ghost, to interact with Dylan McDermott's character Ben. As a psychiatrist, Ben had been running a practice out of the home, much like Malina's dentist. Elizabeth presents herself as a possible patient, telling Ben that she "does things with men, things she shouldn't."[49] When Elizabeth tries to make an appointment, Ben asks for her name; here she is finally named Elizabeth Short. Without insurance, Elizabeth tries to pay for her therapy with sex, starting to unbutton her jacket. Ben, a man with his own massive issues, has a quick daydream of having sex with Elizabeth before snapping himself out of it to take a phone call … about his pregnant wife. Elizabeth steps out of frame and disappears.

She reappears in another fantasy of Ben's, where she is making out with the hot maid on the couch in his office. Ben pictures himself as a part of that tryst, with neither he nor Elizabeth understanding that she is a ghost. Rejected and confused, she sits alone on the couch where a ghost (yes, another one) consoles her. Here again, we see the vapid, vain Elizabeth. She tells Kate Mara's character, "I know it sounds selfish, but I must become famous. It's the only thing I've ever wanted."[50] Mara's character, Hayden, responds with, "Honey, don't you know who you are?"

Returning to 1947, the scene begins with the dentist raping an unconscious Elizabeth. Only when he is finished and ready to examine her teeth does he realize that he has given her too much gas and has killed her. Panicked, the dentist drags Elizabeth into the basement where he is confronted with the Frankenstein-like character, played by Matt Ross—another ghost! A renowned surgeon, Dr. Montgomery bisects Elizabeth and adds the cuts on either side of her mouth because "she looked so sad."[51] In death, Elizabeth becomes simply a plot point. Whether it is the dentist, Dr. Montgomery, or Ben, Elizabeth is merely a way for each man to take another step on his already laid path. None of the men involved in her death, or her realization of her death, pay any consequences. If the dentist is accepted as the killer, the audience knows that he must get away with it—the killer was never caught.

Back in present-day 2011, Elizabeth—now realizing what happened to her—is horrified. At least, she is horrified until Hayden mentions that the crime put Elizabeth on the front page of every newspaper in the country for two months. Elizabeth's face softens as her mouth forms the smallest smile. "I really did become somebody."[52] While it cannot be said with certainty, one would imagine that Elizabeth Short would have rather had her life and become famous in some other way. However, this episode of an incredibly popular show gives the impression that Elizabeth accepted that her vicious murder was the price she had to pay for fame.

James Ellroy's L.A.: City of Demons: Episode 1 (2011)

James Ellroy, famous for his noir novels set in 1930s and 1940s Los Angeles, hosted his own show for Investigation Discovery in 2011. Lasting only six episodes, the show blends information with the overblown and sensational. The first episode, titled "Dead Women Own Me," looks at four murders in LA during the 1940s and 1950s that have had a profound impact on his life. The first is the murder of his mother, Jean Hilliker, and the third and fourth murders are those of Stephanie Gorman and Lily Burk. The second in the episode is the murder of Elizabeth Short.

Ellroy says that his mother's murder brought him to the "woman known as The Black Dahlia."[53] Ellroy exclusively calls Elizabeth "Betty" or "Betty Short," a privilege that no other historian, host, or author took. While Ellroy shows Elizabeth the small respect of not calling her The Black Dahlia only, others interviewed do not use the name Elizabeth Short at all, or refer to it as the "Black Dahlia case" instead of the Elizabeth Short case. As Ellroy puts it in the episode, Elizabeth's[54] life "became dissected, scrutinized, hyperbolized in print."[55] He defends her with one breath; he slams her with his next by calling her the "sad, so eager-to-please-and-be-somebody girl from Medford, Massachusetts."[56]

The episode spends so little time on Elizabeth, one of four women in forty-four minutes. Yet, Ellroy's connection with Elizabeth's case is likely one of the reasons that people would have tuned in to the show in the first place. It is unsurprising that Ellroy treats Elizabeth as he does, but, produced in 2011, the show was just at the beginning of this latest true crime revolution. Perhaps if the show had been made in 2020, at the height of the wave of true crime, not only would all of the women have been better represented, but also Ellroy himself may have presented a more balanced portrayal.

Buzzfeed Unsolved: Season 1: Episode 4 (2016)

Part of the entertainment juggernaut, *Buzzfeed*, *Buzzfeed Unsolved*, or just *Unsolved*, premiered in 2016. Over the last eleven seasons, Ryan Bergara was joined by Shane Madej to cover mysteries, both true crime and supernatural. With the first episodes running less than ten minutes, episodes that are more recent are closer to the half-hour mark. They covered only three topics before covering Elizabeth's case, with her episode airing on April 1, 2016.

The episode is titled "The Chilling Mystery of The Black Dahlia," and over the next eight minutes, their treatment of Elizabeth does not improve. They do not refer to her by her name, only The Black Dahlia. Far more attention is paid to suspects than to anything else, even the finding of her body. There is no information about Elizabeth's life at all. She is merely a prop for the mystery. While this is not a network-supported show or a studio-produced film, this episode of *Buzzfeed Unsolved* has nearly 10.2 million views on YouTube. Reaching so many people, this series has a massive impact on viewers' perception of Elizabeth.

Three years later, *Buzzfeed Unsolved* revisited the case. Sponsored by the miniseries *I Am the Night*, this episode is three times as long as the original episode. With the additional time, the hosts do actually name Elizabeth Short and give some very basic information on her life. However, the episode unsurprisingly begins with the discovery of Elizabeth's body and spends more than half of the twenty-six minutes on George Hodel as the main suspect. As George Hodel is the main villain of *I Am the Night*, the sponsor of the episode, one must wonder if this was a contractual obligation of the hosts. "The Chilling Black Dahlia Murder Revisited" has 7.7 million viewers, meaning that it is entirely possible that nearly 18 million people have learned at least some of their information on Elizabeth and her murder from this YouTube channel.

I Am the Night (2019)

Seventy-two years after Elizabeth's body was found, the cable channel TNT began airing a miniseries titled *I Am the Night*, based on the autobiography of Fauna Hodel, the granddaughter of suspect George Hodel. The series' opening credits cleverly hint at the brutal violence done to Elizabeth, with shadows "cutting" across women's bodies, but one wonders just how many may have noticed that allusion, especially in this day of skipping opening credits. Heavily marketed as a "Black Dahlia-adjacent limited series," the six episodes do not even mention the words black or dahlia until the third episode.[57] Jay Singletary, a reporter and Korean War veteran played by Chris Pine, buys a crime magazine, and as he reads an article on Elizabeth Short, he realizes there are similarities between her murder and one that just occurred. Yet, no one says her name aloud. Her name is not spoken until the fifth and penultimate episode. The case, always referred to as "The Black Dahlia Case," is mentioned a dozen times, but Elizabeth Short's name is said less than five.

At the end of each episode of the series, photos of the real-life counterparts of the characters are shown. After episode three, a few photos of Elizabeth's body and crime scene are shown. The only words on the screen are "The Black Dahlia crime scene."[58] These are the only images of Elizabeth Short shown in the entire series, and she is not given the respect of being named.

If the miniseries were not marketed as one so heavily connected to Elizabeth's case, it would be entirely forgivable if Elizabeth was barely mentioned. If, as perhaps Fauna Hodel had hoped, this would be the telling of her story, those few mentions of Elizabeth would be enough. However, when the companion podcast is called *Root of Evil: The True Story of the Hodel Family and the Black Dahlia*, the series, directed by Patty Jenkins, should have shown Elizabeth and her memory the respect of better representation.

Podcasts

As the new wave of true crime began in the 21st century, the case surrounding Elizabeth Short was prime for coverage by numerous podcasts. As with any medium, true crime podcasts run the gamut from tabloid drivel to hard-hitting journalism. One of the most famous cases in American history, Elizabeth has been covered by several podcasts, including some of the most famous and an entire show dedicated to uncovering new information. The hosts of many of these shows strive to alter the perception of the victims of historical crimes—giving greater agency and attention to the women.

Of the podcasts that cover Elizabeth Short's murder, nearly fifty episodes were listened to for this chapter; many of them give a basic overview of the case. To entice downloads, hosts often focus on the grisly details of the crime and the many possible suspects. In these episodes, Elizabeth is merely a prop. The episodes typically begin with the finding of her body. For example, "The Black Dahlia—Elizabeth Short" episode of *True Crimecast* begins with the discovery of her body and does not improve from there. One of the worst offenders in the podcast coverage, one host only knew the name Black Dahlia, but not Elizabeth Short, and the other host had no knowledge of the case at all.[59] They also seemed uninterested in treating Elizabeth as anything other than a plot device, going so far as to say that her movements before her death were too difficult to follow, and if the listener wants to know everywhere she went (which may be important in determining what may have happened to her), "there are resources out there for you."[60] *True Crimecast* is not the only offender—another podcast spends only sixteen minutes of a twenty-minute podcast on Elizabeth.[61] *Killer Instinct* includes its coverage of Elizabeth Short in its 2019 Halloween series, along with the cases of the List family and the West Memphis Three. It is unclear why these cases were chosen for a curated Halloween event—none of them have a specific supernatural element about them. Again, this episode presents only general background information on Elizabeth before moving on to the more "exciting" details of her murder. Much like visual media coverage of Elizabeth, these podcasts are hoping to use the details of her vicious death to entice listeners and garner more downloads.

Happily, there are several podcasts that offer up a more introspective look at Elizabeth, both her life and how media and pop culture have manipulated her memory. One of the greatest examinations was in *Talk More About That*, episode 20: "Elizabeth Short—Part One." Released in April 2018, the first indication that this was going to be a different portrayal is that the title did not include "The Black Dahlia." Immediately,

Diana and Gina are paying Elizabeth the simple respect of naming her. This good start continues when they discuss how the coverage of Elizabeth's murder and not her life has tainted how the public perceives her. Elizabeth "becomes a caricature" and is no longer a real person.[62] The Elizabeth Short whom Diana and Gina discuss is the entire woman, or as they describe her, the "good, bad, and otherwise."[63] They do not want to make Elizabeth out to be a saint or a sinner, but given how poorly she is generally treated in the press, they both profess to wanting to "cut Elizabeth some slack."[64] Everyone has flaws, they say, and if the "press focus only on the flaws ... we'd all look terrible."[65]

Gina and Diana begin their background on Elizabeth with much of the same basic information used by the rest of the podcasts, but again, they add some much-needed context. For example, when they mention that Elizabeth dropped out of high school at fifteen, they also discuss that she went to school longer than some children did. By saying that, they were alluding to the point that during the Great Depression, not all children, especially in a family of five children, had the luxury of graduating high school. This helps a listener picture Elizabeth as a woman not only struggling with a difficult family life and the normal problems of high school but also with one of the biggest economic depressions in American history.

Talk More About That, along with a few other podcasts, has shed a more flattering light on Elizabeth's personal life, particularly her romantic life. Mark Shostrom, interviewed by Nic from *True Crime Garage*, not only offers a lot of wonderful information about Elizabeth but also clearly debunks all claims of sex work that have been levied against her since 1947.[66] Mark also uses different terminology that helps to reframe Elizabeth, moving away from the "yellow journalism" coverage. For example, Mark calls her "nomadic" in the post-war years, as many people were. Diana and Gina point out that, from their research, Elizabeth seemed to have a "very innocent outlook" on life.[67] Whereas she is described as a "party girl" or a "run about"[68] in another podcast, this reframing of Elizabeth as "innocent," "naive," and "looking for human connection"[69] allows a listener to picture a young woman who was looking for love after losing her fiancé during the war. As the hosts of the podcast *Morbid* also mention, even if there was truth in stories that she was going to parties and dating a lot, Elizabeth "was 22" and they say, "Do your thing, girl."[70] Many of the female hosts do mention just how young Elizabeth was at the time of her murder and how, while she may have made some poor decisions, it certainly did not mean that she deserved what happened to her.

Additionally, one of her roommates is quoted on the podcast as saying that if Elizabeth were not going out on dates, she would not be eating because she could not afford it. As Diana and Gina point out, Elizabeth was another woman hustling to survive in Los Angeles. Karen and Georgia, the hosts of *My Favorite Murder*, also reclassify Elizabeth's behavior in the months leading up to her death. A massive amount of press ink was used in discussing Elizabeth's dating habits with the word "tease" used over and over. Georgia makes it very clear, once and for all, that there is no evidence of prostitution. Yes, Elizabeth went out with men and she did it to eat—"That's what it's like when you come to LA to be an actress really, so, that's not prostitution."[71] Mark Shostrom also defends Elizabeth, saying that any argument that the way she dressed may have had anything to do with what happened to her "is just disgusting."[72]

This latest female-driven wave of true crime, represented primarily by podcasts, allows Elizabeth to finally have some level of amateur psychoanalysis that interprets all aspects of her life, including the trauma that she endured. Again, Diana and Gina of *Talk More About That* offer up a validating conversation about the debilitating traumas that Elizabeth went through in her life. Not only did she have to live through the Great Depression AND World War II, but also both events took men from her life. Her father faked his suicide, only to reappear later, and when she traveled to California to live with him after years apart, he kicked her out when she would not keep his house and cook his meals. Then, just a few years later, after Elizabeth met Matt Gordon during the war, he was killed in the final months of the war. As Diana and Gina point out, Elizabeth developed into a "person with multiple traumas" and cannot be looked at through a "typical nuclear family lens."[73]

This new lens allows for a reinterpretation to combat decades of victimization of Elizabeth Short. Instead of relying on 70-year-old newspaper articles for their impressions of Elizabeth, some podcast hosts are instead using their own instinct to examine her life and her case. *Talk More About That* ends its two-part series on Elizabeth with its hosts wondering whether the case will be solved, or whether it should be. While they do wish to get resolution for Elizabeth, they also do not want to give the offender, whoever he was, the notoriety because the more the public (and pop culture) speak about the offender, the "less we recognize that there was a real person that was a victim here."[74]

Conclusion

Elizabeth Short is one of the most consistently exploited women in this study. Even in a lot of the informational coverage, those content creators use the name that has replaced her own. Hoping to capitalize on notoriety surrounding the case, documentaries, films, and podcasts include her "nickname" in their titles without any kind of inclusion of Elizabeth's real name. For decades, details of her murder were used as audiences would easily know it was about Elizabeth's case, and yet again, no one spoke her name.

It is only in recent years, and on rare occasions, that advocacy for Elizabeth has begun. Instead of solely focusing on how she may have been murdered,[75] podcast hosts strive to present Elizabeth as a whole person. Additionally, these advocates are trying to combat more than seven decades' worth of aspersions against Elizabeth's character by attempting to look at her with objective eyes. While her killer may never be found, perhaps after decades of exploitation and victimization by pop culture, Elizabeth's life will be more known than her violent death.

CHAPTER 4

Marilyn Sheppard

The 1950s is often an area of divergence in historical study, when historians are forced to not only combat ignorance, but must also face off against decades of consensus memory. Used as a weapon in the Cold War, American history was smoothed to erase tension, revolt, and anything else that may have lessened the United States in the eyes of the world. Because of this, the 1950s is often perceived to be an idyllic time. To the public, this decade evokes images of poodle skirts, Elvis, and *Leave It to Beaver*.

Whether because of this whitewashing or because this decade truly had less crime than the rest of the century, it was more difficult to find a subject for this study. Another reason is the unfortunate position it finds itself in—between the Second World War and the Swinging Sixties. In true crime terms—and in terms of this book—it falls between Elizabeth Short and Sharon Tate. There is one case that does stand out, both in terms of coverage of the case at the time and also the popular culture treatment of the story over the next decades. While some know the name of Dr. Sam Sheppard, few know that of Marilyn Sheppard, his wife and the victim of the brutal crime of which he was accused.

Just the Facts

Marilyn Reese was born on April 14, 1923, in Cleveland, Ohio, to Dorothy and Thomas Reese.[1] She attended Cleveland Heights High School, where she met Sam Sheppard,[2] before going to Skidmore College in Saratoga Springs, New York.[3] While at Skidmore, she did not excel at her classes but did focus a lot of her attention on her relationship with Sam. After a year away at college, Marilyn returned to Ohio to marry Sam and become "a good doctor's wife." According to Thomas Neff, author of *The Wrong Man: The Final Verdict on the Dr. Sam Sheppard Murder Case* (2001), "a good doctor's wife" in 1954 had to be "an attractive, cheerful helpmate who could run the household like a quartermaster, manage the children, and make life easy for her ambitious, hardworking husband."[4] Before he graduated medical school, she became a good "medical student's wife," which included the additional tasks of quizzing him on information from his classes, typing up his notes, and essentially serving as a teaching aide.[5] It was not until he graduated from medical school and established himself as a doctor that they were able to begin their family, with their only child, Samuel R. Sheppard, born in 1947.

At the time of her death, the Sheppards lived at 28924 Lake Road in Bay Village, a suburb of Cleveland that was situated twelve miles outside of the city. According to the *Akron Beacon Journal*, residents of Bay Village were "youngish between 30 and 40" and were "moderately well-to-do."[6] Part of the town sits along Lake Erie, which allows for residents to boat, swim, and waterski. The Sheppards were among the prominent families in Bay Village, especially in the medical community. Sam, his father, and both his brothers were doctors. Together, the Sheppard doctors built the Bay View Hospital, the same hospital where Sam was taken to be treated after Marilyn was found dead.

On July 3, 1954, Marilyn Reese Sheppard was found bludgeoned to death in her bed. According to his statement to the police, Sam fell asleep on the sofa while watching a movie with Marilyn and some friends. He awoke to Marilyn's screams and ran upstairs, only to be confronted by an intruder. He was knocked out and when he came to, he chased someone outside and onto the beach, only to be knocked unconscious again. At 5:40 a.m., the neighbors received a call from Dr. Sheppard asking for help. Mr. and Mrs. Sam Houk came into the Sheppards' home to find Sam disoriented and with blood on his clothes. Mrs. Houk walked upstairs to a "fearful sight."[7] Marilyn was on the bed, clearly dead, "her face 'unrecognizable from a mask of blood coming from wounds in her head.'"[8] As this was a homicide, an autopsy was performed and determined that she "had been struck no fewer than 27 times" or more.[9]

As with every suspicious death, law enforcement looked first at the intimate partner. In this case, however, there is some criticism that police focused too quickly on Marilyn's husband. Within hours, detectives Robert E. Schottke and Patrick Gareau told Bay Village Chief of Police John Eaton: "You don't have to look any further. Sam Sheppard is your man."[10] For several weeks, as the police continued their investigation, this case received a massive amount of press coverage, but this was more than the average press attention. The Ohio newspapers covering the case made accusations of police incompetence and "family protection," which incited a backlash resulting in thousands of letters and phone calls to the Bay Village police.[11] In response, the Bay Village City Council passed a resolution asking for the Cleveland police to take over the investigation.

Soon after, Sam Sheppard was arrested and charged with first-degree murder.[12]

He spent twelve years in prison before being granted a second trial by the United States Supreme Court due to the pretrial publicity. During this second trial, Sam was acquitted, in part because of his new defense counsel, F. Lee Bailey. He married again and, for a short time, regained his doctor's license before losing it due to malpractice and becoming a wrestler.[13] When he died in 1970, it was first thought to be because of the heavy drinking habit he had developed since being released from prison, but the official cause of death was Werknicke's encephalopathy or thiamine deficiency.[14]

In the mid–1990s, Marilyn and Sam's son, Sam "Chip" Sheppard, began a campaign to clear his father's name. With the new technology of DNA, the hope was to be able to exclude Sam from the evidence found on Marilyn and maybe even find the real perpetrator. This campaign included suing the Cuyahoga County coroner to prove Sam's innocence. Sam's body was exhumed in the fall of 1997 under a court order, and samples were taken which "excluded [Sam] as a donor."[15] Two years later, Marilyn's body was exhumed to get "clean DNA" samples from Marilyn and her fetus as part of an effort by "the state's office to defend itself" in Sam R. Sheppard's lawsuit.[16] After more than two months of testimony and three hours of deliberation, the jury found Sam R. Sheppard's claim that Sam did not kill Marilyn was not strong enough to prove innocence. The case was dismissed, leaving it essentially in the same place as it had been before Sam R. Sheppard began his campaign in the mid–1990s.

News of the Day

Given the amount of press coverage on the case, the amount of attention paid to the Sheppards is not surprising. What is surprising only to newcomers to true crime is that the attention has been hugely disproportionate towards Sam, even though Marilyn is the victim. At even the most basic level—the number of times their names are mentioned—Sam outstretches Marilyn. In an article in *The Cincinnati Enquirer* from April 30, 1955, Marilyn's name is mentioned twice while Sam's is mentioned four times. There are other points in the same article when Marilyn is simply referred to as "his wife" or "his murdered wife."[17] In every article examined for this project, Marilyn's identity is entirely tied to her position as Sam's wife, something that is to be expected for a wife in 1954. There is some variety as Marilyn is called the wife of a suburban doctor,[18] the "31-year-old sport-loving wife of an osteopath,"[19] or the "31-year-old blonde wife of an

osteopath neuro-surgeon."[20] That last description is particularly problematic given that Marilyn was a brunette. The only individualist descriptor
that is used by any of these articles is "sports-loving." Every other piece is
either a physical descriptor or has something to do with her relationship
with Sam. Occasionally, journalists mentioned the Sheppards' son, Samuel
"Chip" Sheppard,[21] or the fact that Marilyn was expecting the couple's second child, but that was rare.

Sam's portrayal in the press was much different from that of Marilyn. He had a huge amount of coverage where he was called handsome,
popular, a high school athlete, and a very talented doctor. Marilyn, on the
other hand, was rarely mentioned. If she was, her descriptors were all in
reference to her position as Sam's wife. Marilyn was described as being
"more tolerant than the average wife,"[22] but more often than not, her only
descriptor was simply "pretty." Even when describing the murder scene,
an article in the *Lancaster Eagle-Gazette* still used the word pretty, saying,
"[T]he tooth chips were found in the blood-soaked bed of Mrs. Marilyn
Sheppard, 31, whose pretty face framed by light wavy hair, was chopped
almost to pieces."[23] It is appalling that, while describing her body at the
crime scene, a reporter still needed to call Marilyn pretty. According to
the press, Marilyn had nothing outside of her marriage to Sam—she was
not even described, as many would imagine for a woman in the 1950s, as
a mother. Marilyn's only achievement, as anyone would see in the press of
the day, was marrying a prominent doctor.

Books

Mockery of Justice: The True Story of the
Sheppard Murder Case (1995)

Written in the midst of the renewal of the Sheppard case, *Mockery of
Justice* provides a disturbing look at Marilyn, especially given that Sam
Reese Sheppard, Marilyn Sheppard's son, wrote the words. It is clear how
Sam R. Sheppard felt about the case as he wrote the book with Cynthia
Cooper. He stresses that "mistakes are made" and "the system errs."[24] He
also pointedly attacks the pop culture portrayals of the case. As early as
page four, Sheppard writes, "[A]s if the notoriety at the time of trial were
not enough, a popular 1960s drama had kept the story before the public
eye."[25]

As with the beginning of most of the coverage of this case, the book
delves into the history of Sam and Marilyn Sheppard. *Mockery of Justice*
mentions that Marilyn was her middle name and that her first name was

Florence, but that she had dropped it "as a bit flat."[26] There are a few nuggets of information that had not been seen anywhere else, which makes sense given the intimate connection with the case. During high school, Marilyn spent summers with her grandparents at a cottage at Mentor-on-the-Lake, a "distant suburban town that had one of the few accessible swimming beaches on the East Side."[27] Marilyn particularly loved that area because she was a good swimmer.

The Rev. Alan Davis was a friend who remembered Sam and Marilyn from their time at Roosevelt Junior High School. In his recollections in the book, Davis remembers Sam very well while Marilyn is barely remembered at all. Sam is described as "the gracious successful athlete, the popularity contest winner, the darling of the Sheppard family, a do-right fellow at the vortex of a large circle of friends," and "dreamily attractive, with hazel eyes, and Hollywood poster-boy looks."[28] The only mention that Marilyn gets is "she was good at sports too and readily pledged into fashionable sororities."[29]

Sam R. also gives a unique perspective into the Sheppards' marriage, having seen it firsthand for the first seven years of his life. He and Cooper state quite frankly that Dr. Sam[30] had affairs. Not only do they believe the affairs are a foregone conclusion, but also that Marilyn knew about them. When talking about them, she "described the situation to his friends, not in anger, but with a calm distance."[31] This problematic portrayal of Marilyn continues as her son and his co-author make judgments about Marilyn's mental health and sex life. Marilyn's mother died in childbirth and she herself had a difficult birth with Sam R. *Mockery of Justice* uses this to explain Marilyn's lack of interest in sex, even going as far as saying that she was afraid of sex after giving birth. It only gets worse from there. In the same paragraph, the authors say that Marilyn was trying to "revive her sexual desire and, at least for the time, excused Dr. Sam's dalliances."[32] Not only does this blame Marilyn for Sam's affairs, but also it also overly simplifies what Marilyn was going through.

The poor attention continued after the murder and as the trial commenced. As previously discussed, very little of the press focused on Marilyn. *Mockery of Justice* briefly discusses one article in *The Cleveland Press* that highlights Marilyn Sheppard but does so in a hugely insulting way. The article was called "But Who Will Speak for Marilyn?" and was published on October 12, 1954. While *Mockery* should be commended for mentioning that article, all goodwill immediately vanishes when it says, "It [is] hard to imagine the same impact from 'But Who Will Speak for Florence?'"[33] Within two pages, this book, written by the victim's son, has defended Dr. Sam's affairs, blamed the affairs on Marilyn, blamed Marilyn for her own trauma and complications after Chip's birth, and insinuated that no one would have cared about his mother's death if she had not decided to go by her middle name.

With two authors, it is unclear how much Sam R. Sheppard wrote versus Cynthia Cooper, which certainly would change the interpretation of the text. Regardless of how much Sam R. wrote, he still had some level of creative control over the project. Marilyn's son read the paragraphs about Marilyn "having problems with sex" and still agreed to the book's publication.[34] While certain allowances should be made for grieving family members, especially in cases that attracted such huge press attention for decades, that is no excuse for such irresponsible treatment of Marilyn Sheppard.

The Wrong Man: The Final Verdict on the Dr. Sam Sheppard Case (2001)

Given the 1997 exhumation of Sam, the 1999 exhumation of Marilyn and the increased interest in the case due to the son's civil litigation, there was a lot of attention both in print and on screen on the Sheppard case. James Neff, a former *Cleveland Plain Dealer* reporter, is now the assistant managing editor for investigations at Philadelphia Media Network. He grew up in Cleveland, not far from where Marilyn was murdered, "believing Sheppard's guilt" and wanted to reexamine the case with the "plain facts."[35] Neff's investigation comes to the same conclusion as Sam R. Sheppard's, with a convincing case for Richard Eberling as the likely killer over Dr. Sam Sheppard.

The Wrong Man: The Final Verdict does give far more information on Marilyn than any other source available. Not even Wikipedia has an entry for Marilyn for something as simple as a birthdate. It is also here that the "sports-loving" comment gets some context. Marilyn and someone named Nancy bowled together on the Bay Village ladies' afternoon bowling league while the children were in school.[36] While the book does give a lot of added information, the interpretation of Marilyn leaves much to be desired or, in some places, is downright disturbing.

Beginning with Marilyn and Sam's courtship, the portrayal of Marilyn is problematic. Neff writes that Marilyn "snagged a local sports hero."[37] To prove his point, Neff spends more than half a page on Sam's extracurricular activities, including racing, competing, football, track and field, basketball, being a local DJ, and serving as class president for his sophomore, junior, and senior years of high school. After all this detail, there are two sentences on Marilyn stating she "also had many extracurricular activities."[38] He clearly has access to their school records, or at the very least, some kind of histories that tell him what the Sheppards were doing while in high school. Yet he spends more than twice the amount of time on Sam versus Marilyn. A look at the sources does redeem Neff a bit. There are a few sources from Marilyn's point of view: her report card and letters from Marilyn to Sam. However, the vast majority of the sources are those not from Marilyn's point of view. There are eight distinct sources in the chapter on Marilyn and Sam, but there is a note that unless otherwise noted, all information came from a handwritten autobiography by Sam Sheppard to help with his defense in 1954.[39]

That may be easily dismissed, but there are more examples that further damn Neff's portrayal of Marilyn. Again, Neff gives the most information of her time at Skidmore, her only time away from Sam, but his interpretation paints her as a shallow and careless girl. She failed Spanish while also getting a D- in European history "at a time when it seemed likely that friends and relatives would be dragged into battle overseas."[40] Graciously, he does mention that she earned Cs in all of her other courses other than horseback riding and dance. He has managed to turn grades from her first year at college, when many are adjusting to life away from home for the very first time, into a treatise on the Second World War. Marilyn was likely going through a difficult year: her first year at college and away from home and Sam for the first time combined with the entry of the United States into the Second World War. It would be understandable for anyone to get less-than-stellar grades under those circumstances. To shame Marilyn for those grades is bad enough, but to make it seem like she could not be bothered to learn European history before her friends and relatives would soon be fighting and dying is disrespectful and irresponsible.

The skewed account continues throughout the book as Neff describes Marilyn and Sam's married life. While Sam was in medical school, Marilyn "typed his reports, drilled him from lists of questions and answers from his classes, serving in effect as a teacher's aide."[41] In addition to helping him as a tutor and academic secretary, she worked part-time as an assistant in a research laboratory. Neff does her the service of calling her a breadwinner, especially with the $50 per month that her father sent the couple, but that is the only credit that Marilyn gets for keeping the family afloat while also helping Sam pass medical school.

After Marilyn gave birth to their son, she "slipped into a postpartum depression."[42] A copy of *Every Woman's Standard Medical Guide* from 1948, the year after Marilyn had Sam, includes nothing about postpartum depression or any of the hormonal shifts that occur after giving birth.[43] The only thing that it does say is that a "sensitive, anxious woman" might develop "bad nerves," thereby putting the blame on the woman herself instead of simply explaining the cause for the depression.[44] According to Neff, "From Sam's point of view, Marilyn had lost interest in having sex" and it bothered him so much that he "complained about it to other medical teams."[45] Given everything known about Sam, that sounds completely believable, but Neff elaborates and complicates the situation. In what seems like a defense of Sam Sheppard's dissatisfaction with his sex life, Neff says, "[U]nlike Victorian mothers, who were expected to tolerate sex only for reproduction, postwar wives such as Marilyn were expected to enthusiastically enjoy sex and in fact insist on conjugal satisfaction."[46] He is not exactly wrong here; however, one must wonder how many 1950s wives were expected to be enthusiastic about sex within weeks of giving birth. Marilyn's labor was described as difficult. Beyond that, her mother and a newborn brother died after an extremely difficult birth. Marilyn was likely going through some level of post-traumatic stress disorder in addition to her postpartum depression. It does not matter whether it is Sam or Neff; no one should blame Marilyn for taking time to process her mental health issues, not in 1954 nor in 2001.

By chapter six, Neff's focus has moved entirely on to the trial and Marilyn is again relegated to random mentions or gory details. The intimate details of her life are forgotten and she is only "useful" by being a body. As with all the pop culture depictions of the story, Marilyn becomes a plot device for the overall story of Dr. Sam Sheppard.

The Fugitive[47]

The Fugitive is an interesting situation for this project as the original production (and thereby all subsequent remakes) was not based on the Sheppard case; however, popular memory believes that the TV show and the film were, in fact, based on the case. Given that many in the general public believe, if they have any knowledge of it at all, that Dr. Richard Kimball is based on Dr. Sam Sheppard, this has superseded any original intent of the content creators.

The Fugitive (1963)

Roy Huggins created the first telling of Richard Kimball as Sam Sheppard in 1963. Produced by QM Productions and United Artists Television, it starred David Janssen as Dr. Richard Kimball. It aired on ABC from September 1963 until the finale in August 1967, with a total of 120 episodes over four seasons. The series was nominated for a total of five Emmys and won for Outstanding Dramatic Series in 1966. David Janssen also won a Golden Globe in 1966 for his role as Richard Kimball.[48]

In this incarnation, Richard Kimball is a doctor, specialty unknown, who was convicted of murdering his wife. The pilot opens with Kimball on a train with a police escort only for the train to derail, giving Richard the chance to escape. Each episode is 51 minutes in four acts of Kimball on the run from Lieutenant Gerard.

Helen Kimball, the fictional version of Marilyn Sheppard in all incarnations, does not appear until episode fourteen of season one, titled "The Girl from Little Egypt." The episode begins when Ruth Norton, a "beautiful airline stewardess," hits Richard with her car following a breakup with her boyfriend after finding out he is married.[49] The danger is apparent as police and emergency services, exactly the type of people he strives to avoid, now surround Richard. While dozing in and out of consciousness, Richard's flashbacks show the audience its first glimpse of Helen Kimball. She is in a hospital bed, slowly waking, when Richard tells her that their child was stillborn and that, to save her life, the doctor had to perform a hysterectomy. No one says the word, obviously due to 1963 censors, but it is clear that Helen will not be able to have children. She is seen again at eleven minutes into the episode when she and Richard are preparing to leave for a party. Richard brings up the prospect of adoption, but Helen refuses to listen to him, saying that she would never be "its mother." The last time Helen is seen is in a pool of blood when Richard finds her dead. Added up, Helen is on screen a total of three minutes and forty-seven seconds.

For those nearly four minutes, Helen, and by extension Marilyn, is not portrayed in a great light. There is no sensitivity for Helen going through the massively traumatic event of losing a child, nor any for her hysterectomy. Richard is the sympathetic character as he is the one who suggests adoption and wants to move past the loss of their child. Without any of the context for what a woman like Helen would be going through, she is shown to be drinking to excess and combative with Richard. While it ultimately makes sense that Richard Kimball, the main character of the show, would be the sympathetic character in any scene, Helen is done a disservice by first only being in two episodes in the entire series and second, by being so two-dimensional. As many people closely connect *The Fugitive* with the Marilyn Sheppard case, Helen Kimball is forever tied to Marilyn in public consciousness. If Helen is portrayed as a shrill drunk with emotional problems, the audience is going to make those same assumptions about Marilyn. Sadly, the situation does not get better for Helen/Marilyn in the next incarnation of *The Fugitive*.

The Fugitive (1993)

This version of *The Fugitive* was released in American theaters on August 6, 1993, and stars Harrison Ford as Richard Kimball and Tommy

Lee Jones as Sam Gerard, the U.S. Marshal tasked with finding Kimball after he escapes. Ford's Kimball is a respected Chicago vascular surgeon whose wife was found brutally murdered after he came home to find an intruder in their bedroom. After having a fight with this "one-armed man," Kimball is arrested, tried, and convicted in a quick montage all before the movie hits the half-hour mark. As the title suggests, the majority of the film follows Kimball on the run as he tries to prove his innocence, all while being chased by one of Jones's signature characters. As the final credits roll, Gerard and Kimball sit in the back of a police car while the real killers are being driven away in another car. Kimball has been vindicated and he and Gerard have seemingly been able to meet as equals. Justice has been served ... or has it?

Helen Kimball, played by Sela Ward, is central to the plot of *The Fugitive*, as Richard needed to be wanted for a crime before he could actually be a fugitive; however, she is only on screen for roughly six minutes. Those are a generous six minutes as they include parts of the trial where the prosecution plays Helen's 911 call that implicates Richard, and the opening credits. Sela Ward is the third billed actor in those credits after Harrison Ford and Tommy Lee Jones, yet she only has six minutes of screen time. This is a massive indictment of how pop culture treats both women and female victims. To be third billed when it has nothing to do with alphabetical order is typically a big deal, but it is completely overshadowed by the fact that she is barely in the movie and most of that is in the first twelve minutes. Of the mere minutes that Helen is on screen, 75 percent of it is in the first twelve minutes of the film—the time it takes for Richard to be arrested, tried, and convicted of Helen's murder. She is only seen again in dream sequences and for no more than a minute at a time. Both Sela Ward and Helen Kimball are disrespected in a film that would not have happened without the character of Helen.

Of the time she does spend on the screen, most of that is spent dying. The film opens with shots of Chicago at night with flashes of Helen being killed by the "One-Armed Man." When the audience sees Helen for the first time, she is fighting for her life, her face contorted in fear. The first and only noise that she makes in this entire scene is a gasp as she is killed. The next time that Helen is seen, she is dead, motionless on the bedroom floor. She is further dehumanized by the negative camera effect. It is used to give the audience the sense of crime-scene photos being taken, but instead it just removes anything that might have reminded anyone that Helen is a real person. A close-up of her face is completely unrecognizable—the dehumanizing complete.

The movie tries to redeem itself with a flashback to earlier in the night, before Helen was killed and Richard was arrested. Richard enters the room, the charming doctor hero making his way to Helen, talking and shaking hands. He rescues Helen, who is surrounded by a group of admirers. For the first time, Helen is alive and happy. The Kimballs appear to be a happy and loving couple with the limited information of Helen staring adoringly at Richard as they drive home from the charity benefit. In this short scene, Helen has half of her lines, all eight of them, before Richard is called back to the hospital to assist in surgery. This gives the One-Armed Man the opportunity to find Helen alone in their apartment and kill her.

The rest of Helen's lines in the film come in the 911 call, which is played in court during Richard's trial. Here again, the audience must watch Helen die on screen. Much like the repeated telling of Marilyn's death in the contemporary press, Helen's death is played over and over again—with most of the 911 call mentioning her husband's name. Earlier scenes erase her features and now they have erased her voice by only giving her sixteen lines in 130 minutes. When Helen is given a voice, her words are always about her husband.

Helen appears twice more in the film, rounding out her six minutes of screen time. Both appearances are dream sequences: once when Richard has fallen asleep in the woods after escaping the U.S. Marshals and again when he is asleep in his crappy basement apartment. It is the first of these dreams that is the most disturbing. The first few flashes of Helen are overtly sexual. From Richard's point of view, the audience sees Helen rising above him wearing one of his shirts. Then they move so Richard is hovering over her, kissing Helen softly. Abruptly, the scene shifts and Richard is giving Helen CPR on their bedroom floor.

Not that Helen was given much of a chance, but there is absolutely no detail of her life in the film. At no point during any of the conversation at the charity benefit, nor in the car, does anyone mention anything about Helen's life. There is nothing that appears in the Kimballs' apartment that could hint at Helen's interests or a life she had apart from Richard's. Neither in the initial investigation nor in the manhunt did any of the law enforcement officers do any kind of victimology on Helen. She is absolutely a one-dimensional character that exists only as a plot device to further her husband's story. Sela Ward could be completely removed from the film and it would not change. There may be slightly less sympathy for Richard Kimball if he were not seen cradling his dead wife's body, but Helen is only there to further his story, nothing more.

Unfortunately, the same could be said for Marilyn Sheppard. Sam Sheppard, just like Richard Kimball, was a rich and respectable doctor. While neither man was particularly well known outside of their immediate circles before their wives were murdered, both quickly became infamous. Marilyn, like Helen, was often forgotten in the story, rarely mentioned in the news accounts.

The movie reaches its climax as Richard Kimball finally finds the One-Armed Man and the real reason behind Helen's death. Unsurprisingly, it was all because of Richard. The One-Armed Man was sent to the Kimballs' apartment to kill Richard because he had stumbled upon medical fraud. Dr. Charles Nichols, a man Richard had considered a friend throughout the film, had been falsifying drug test results to the FDA. The One-Armed Man, a former police officer named Sykes, was sent to kill Richard to prevent him from reporting the fraud. Sykes killed Helen instead and, since Richard was convicted of Helen's death, the outcome was still the same. Richard was discredited, the drug was approved, and Nichols made millions.

As if Helen's death was not already disturbing enough, it is made worse by the fact that she is killed only because Richard was not home. He was the true target. This further solidifies the idea that Helen does not have any existence outside of her relationship with Richard. Sykes did not want to kill her specifically, not that this ever entered into anyone's mind at all at any point in the movie. And it was not a case of a stranger invasion. Helen was killed as an accident—as an afterthought. In both the fictional world of the Kimballs and in the scripts, Helen is merely a plot device in her husband's story.

The Fugitive (2000)

In the third and final incarnation of *The Fugitive* triad, the television remake premiered on October 6, 2000. Starring Tim Daly as Richard Kimball and Myketi Williamson as Lieutenant Gerard, it lasted for one season of twenty-three episodes. This was the hardest of all to find for this study, and so only the pilot is examined for its portrayal of Helen. The 2000 remake follows the same basic format as the 1963 show with some of the 1993 film peppered in. It is the best portrayal of Helen, which is not saying much.

The pilot begins much like the others, with Richard being transported to prison by Gerard, but by car instead of train this time. After a crash, Richard escapes and the flashbacks begin. At a few places online, Helen's name is listed as Helen Ross-Kimball. It is not mentioned in the episode, but this does present a very clear difference between this Helen and her predecessors. In the short flashbacks, she is on screen for a total of one minute and forty seconds, the shortest of all the versions of Helen, but she is the most progressive. She and Richard do seem to have the most loving relationship, as they are shown joking, making love, and jogging.

During their jog, they discuss a future that involves buying a house, getting a dog, and having a baby. Richard points out that the money for the house would come from Helen's money, which is revealed later to be an inheritance from her mother. Their relationship appears to be on good and equal terms, which is more of an insight than is seen in any other incarnation of *The Fugitive*. This Helen also has sixteen lines, the same amount as Sela Ward in the film, in her one minute and forty seconds on screen, giving her a line every eleven seconds.

The rest of season one is incredibly difficult to find, as it has not been released on DVD nor is it available on any streaming platforms. Relying only on sites like IMDb, it is known that Helen appears in a total of four episodes, or in 17 percent of the total episodes. That is far better than the Helen in the 1963 series, who appears in a total of three episodes, or only 2.5 percent of the 120 episodes of *The Fugitive*. While it is far less screen time for the most prominent woman in the series, Kelly Rutherford's Helen is the superior Helen Kimball.

My Father's Shadow: The Sam Sheppard Story (1998)

With the attention the case received in the 1990s, it was prime for a made-for-TV movie. *My Father's Shadow: The Sam Sheppard Story* aired on November 17, 1998, on CBS. In the version watched for this project, the title sometimes was listed as *Death in the Shadows: The Sam Sheppard Story*. It begins well, with Marilyn on a beach with a young Chip. If Marilyn is the first person seen on screen, one hopes that she will continue to be a prominent part of the production. However, those hopes are quickly dashed.

Marilyn playfully chases Chip back to the house where she interacts with a very creepy handyman. The audience is then introduced to Dr. Sam Sheppard, performing surgery while flirting with a nurse and openly discussing his sex life. Given this behavior, it is not surprising when Marilyn is unhappily waiting for him when he is late getting home. The rest of the night follows Sam's story: friends come over and they watch a movie, and Sam falls asleep on the bed. He wakes to Marilyn's screams and that is the last time Marilyn appears in the movie.

The rest of the movie is entirely about Sam R. "Chip" Sheppard and his fight to exonerate his father. There are two different timelines: one of Chip in the "current" period of 1998 where he's fighting the court to exonerate Dr. Sam, and another of young Chip as he grows up dealing with the ramifications of being the child of Dr. Sam Sheppard. This is clearly a movie about a man's very complicated relationship with his father, who was in prison for a major portion of Chip's childhood. While allowing Chip to tell his side of the story is cathartic in its own right, it certainly does not give Marilyn any kind of respect.

It takes thirty-five minutes (without commercials) before Chip reframes his mission from just proving his father is innocent to also finding out who really killed his mother. How it took that long for him to understand that proving that Dr. Sam was not the killer also meant bringing justice to his murdered mother is inconceivable.

Chip, aka Sam R. Sheppard as he has been known in later life, gets frequent "visits" from the ghost of his father or is suffering from some serious psychosis causing him to see his dead father. These visits push Chip to keep fighting. What is interesting is that Chip never gets a visit from Marilyn. He was seven when she was killed, old enough to have plenty of memories of her. If he was truly searching for his mother's killer, why did he not get a "visit" from Marilyn? Even one visit would have brought her back into the narrative, reminding both the audience and Chip that Marilyn was also a victim in the case. So much time is spent in this movie to show Dr. Sam Sheppard as a victim that many viewers may have forgotten Marilyn. Obviously, if Dr. Sam did not kill his wife, his life was ruined by the case, but so often, the murder victim is forgotten. This film only further perpetuates the trend of forgetting Marilyn Sheppard in the larger narrative of Dr. Sam Sheppard.

Podcasts

Marilyn Sheppard's case has been the subject of a few podcasts, but it is common for the episodes to be listed or referred to as the "Sam Sheppard case," with little on Marilyn. With few exceptions, Marilyn exists only as a minor character in the story of her husband.

True Crime Garage episode 10, "Dr. Sam Sheppard," was released on January 10, 2016. The hosts Nic and The Captain give a basic overview of the case, including a nice discussion on whether Sam actually killed Marilyn, but there is no real discussion on Marilyn. *My Favorite Murder*, with hosts Karen and Georgia, covered the case on episode 55, "Let's Hear Your Podcast," released February 9, 2017. Georgia covered the case, again with the basic facts. Towards the end of the conversation, Karen and Georgia discussed the misinformation or lack of information about the case. They made the point that there are many facts of the case that the general public do not know, possibly because of the way this case exists inside pop culture. They specifically named *The Fugitive*, both the show and the film, as "clouding" the history of the case in the mind of the public.[50] Particularly when a case has such a famous film or show attached to it, the general public will likely have a very skewed opinion of the facts of the case. *Hollywood Crime Scene*'s November 22, 2019, episode compares the case to *The Fugitive*, a common theme for this particular podcast—again, basic details with little information on Marilyn Sheppard. It is difficult to judge these podcasts for this omission as it has become clear just how little information there is on Marilyn to begin with.

Unsolved Murders, a Parcast podcast, has two episodes named "Dead on the 4th of July—Marilyn Sheppard." Released in the summer of 2018, most of the information on Marilyn is in the first episode with the second episode covering Sam's trial. As this series is part of a more professional podcast network with several shows focusing on history and true crime, the production value and research is superior to other podcasts on Marilyn. Far more time is spent on her background, such as the time she spent with an aunt and uncle after her mother's death, which was not discussed anywhere else. The show also gives attention to Marilyn's activities that had nothing to do with her murder: teaching Bible classes at the local Methodist church, bowling, golfing, and ballroom dancing.[51] The title of the show itself reinforces the idea that Sam Sheppard did not kill his wife, something decided by the courts but not by the public. While all of the other podcasts discussed whether Sam killed Marilyn, *Unsolved Murders* immediately establishes that Marilyn's death is still unsolved. This combined with the additional information on Marilyn as a person makes *Unsolved Murders* the best podcast coverage of the Marilyn Sheppard murder.

Conclusion

Marilyn Sheppard is the case of a woman who has been almost entirely superseded by either her husband's notoriety or the fictional retellings of her murder. So many people would easily recognize *The Fugitive* or the "One-Armed Man" or even Dr. Sam Sheppard. But how many would recognize Marilyn's name?

A major factor in this is the sheer lack of coverage of the woman at the center of this crime and, when she is covered, the lack of justice to her memory. In books about the case, little thought is given to her mental health difficulties or any other traumatic issues Marilyn may have been facing. She was blamed for her husband's extramarital affairs. Then she was forgotten, only to be remembered as details in an autopsy report. This coverage tends to be informational with a dash of exploitation, particularly, as always, in the death scenes. There is no advocacy for Marilyn, not even from her own son, who chooses instead to defend his father and forgets the possibility that if his father is innocent, his mother's death has gone unsolved for sixty years.

Fiction has failed Marilyn as well. Appearing no fewer than four times in overt roles, Marilyn (or Helen Kimball) barely shows up before she is killed. Moreover, when she is killed, it is only to further her husband's storyline. Marilyn Sheppard is in danger of being forgotten, and Murderinos must do better.

CHAPTER 5

Sharon Tate

The 1960s opened as a decade full of optimism and hope as the Kennedy administration signaled youthful change to the nation. Those who participated in sit-ins and marched for civil rights hoped the new decade would bring real systemic change as they were happy to leave the 1950s behind. Women, feeling the crushing oppression of centuries of misogyny, reignited the flame for women's rights. However, the decade that began with such hope quickly turned sour with assassinations, violent protests, and ultimately ended in a horrific crime that has continued to fascinate audiences for fifty years.

Just the Facts

On opposite coasts of the United States in August of 1969, one event epitomized the hope and promise of the decade that had begun to decay, while another signaled the death knell of not only the 1960s but also served as a sign that the Old Hollywood of Normand and Turner was most definitely dead. While hundreds of thousands of people gathered in Woodstock, New York, on August 15, 1969, police were frantically seeking those responsible for the deaths of nine people in the hills of Los Angeles.

The deaths of Sharon Tate, her unborn child, Jay Sebring, Abigail Folger, and Wojciech Frykowski are arguably the most infamous cases covered in this study. Murdered in the house that Sharon and her husband, Roman Polanski, were renting on Cielo Drive in Los Angeles, these five are some of the most famous victims in American history. However, they are rarely mentioned beyond an initial naming, as the real focus is on who killed them. The murders are often referred to as the Tate murders, but the focus is almost exclusively on Charles Manson and/or on his Family.[1] Sharon Tate has been historically marginalized, diminished, or outright ignored by the media, both historically and in current interpretations in the 21st century.

Born in Texas in 1943, Sharon Tate seemed destined for a life beyond that of a child of an Army officer. As a child, she was entered into pageants, winning Miss Tiny Tot in Dallas at six months old and Miss Richland, Washington, at 16.[2] While her father was stationed in Italy, Sharon was cast as a background actor and became certain that this was the life she wanted. After Sharon graduated high school, her father was transferred back to the United States to San Pedro where Sharon began hitchhiking to nearby LA. During a 1963 audition for *Petticoat Junction*, she was introduced to Martin Ransohoff, a producer, who allegedly told her, "Sweetie, I'm going to make you a star."[3] With his help, Sharon booked guest-starring roles on *Petticoat Junction*, *The Beverly Hillbillies*, and two films produced by Ransohoff.

Her first feature role was in *Eye of the Devil*, starring Deborah Kerr and David Niven, in 1965. It was filmed in London, where Sharon first met Roman Polanski. Ransohoff convinced Polanski to cast Sharon in his spoof horror movie, *The Fearless Vampire Killers*.[4] In both films, Sharon had less than a dozen lines. Her primary job, as was unfortunately normal for many women in the film and television business, was to look pretty for the camera. By the time of filming of *The Fearless Vampire Killer*, Sharon and Polanski were lovers and wed on January 20, 1968.

After the premiere of Polanski's *Rosemary's Baby* in June of 1968, the couple moved into the house at 10050 Cielo Drive. Record producer Terry Melcher, son of Doris Day, needed someone to take over his unexpired lease. They signed the rental agreement on February 12, 1969, and moved in three days later.[5]

Sharon made two other films before her death, *Valley of the Dolls* and *The Wrecking Crew*. Many of the critics of the day seemed to agree that Sharon simply had not been given any roles that would "bring out whatever acting ability she may have had."[6] However, after her marriage to Roman, she put her career in second place. While her marriage was far from perfect—Roman was widely known to be having multiple affairs fairly quickly after the wedding—she put all of her energy towards being a wife, and after she learned she was pregnant, being a mother.

On the evening of August 8, 1969, four members of the Manson Family—Tex Watson, Susan Atkins, Linda Kasabian, and Patricia Krenwinkel—broke into 10050 Cielo Drive and proceeded to murder the four inside the house and Steven Parent, who was killed in his car in the driveway after visiting the caretaker. The following night, the four were joined by Leslie Van Houten and Steve "Clem" Grogan to kill grocery chain executive Leno LaBianca and his wife Rosemary. Family members were not arrested until December 1969 when they were linked to an unrelated homicide of music teacher Gary Hinman. While in jail awaiting trial, Susan Atkins bragged about killing Sharon and the others. She and the other Manson Family members were soon indicted on additional charges relating to the murders of August 9 and 10.

Members of the Family were tried for their crimes through the summer and fall of 1970. Vincent Bugliosi, an assistant district attorney, prosecuted the case and went on to write *Helter Skelter*, arguably the most famous true crime book of all time. The defendants were all found guilty and sentenced to be executed but were saved when the California Supreme Court declared capital punishment unconstitutional. The sentences of all Family members were commuted to life in prison.

In the fifty years since the deaths of Sharon, her unborn child, Jay, Abigail, Wojciech, Steven, Leno, and Rosemary—Charles Manson and Susan Atkins have died in prison. Tex Watson, Patricia Krenwinkle, and Leslie Van Houten remain imprisoned. Five decades have passed but the public remains as obsessed with this group and their crimes as it was in 1969. Manson is so ubiquitous that his entire name is not needed—just Manson. It has become shorthand for crazy cult leaders who manipulate followers to carry out homicidal actions. It would be difficult to find someone who did not have even the smallest awareness of Manson and his Family living in the desert. However, it would be far easier to find someone who could not name all, or even any, of the Family's victims. Sharon has become a footnote in Manson's story, both in history and in popular culture. As with footnotes, she is rarely examined and often misrepresented … if she is mentioned at all.

News of the Day

As one of the most famous crimes of the 20th century, the "Tate Murders" as they became known, were heavily covered in newspapers across the United States as soon as the bodies were found. Given that Sharon was the most famous person murdered in the house, she was featured prominently; however, she was still often written about in relation to the men in her life. In an article in the *San Mateo Times and Daily News Leader*, Sharon is identified as one of the victims at the beginning of the article before the focus turns to Sharon's husband. The sentence referencing her husband, Roman Polanski, gives his latest directing credit—*Rosemary's Baby*—and describes how he was "renowned in the industry as the master of suspense and the macabre" before mentioning that he was reportedly in Europe at the time of Sharon's death.[7] Only at the end of the article are any of Sharon's personal details or acting credits included. Even when Sharon is found murdered, her husband and his credits were featured above hers.

Another theme that can be found in the news articles published after Sharon's death is the continued oversexualization of her. An article in the *San Francisco Examiner* describes Sharon as "a pregnant honey-blonde actress who played sexy parts in movies" and "a beautiful blonde."[8] In many of the articles, they clearly list what Sharon was wearing when she was found, naming it as either a "bikini nightgown"[9] or a "bra and panties."[10] In none of the articles did they describe what any of the other victims were wearing when they were found; only Sharon was singled out. As if the murder of five people by a mysterious desert cult was not salacious enough, news reporters felt the need to oversexualize Sharon.

Books

Unsurprisingly, the vast majority of the books published about the death of Sharon and the other four victims focuses almost entirely on the offenders. They dig deeply into the background of each of the offenders while giving very little background on Sharon, Jay, Abigail, Wojciech, or Steven. One outlier is the book published by the Tate family in 2012, more than forty years after Sharon's death.

Restless Souls: The Sharon Tate Family's Account of Stardom, the Manson Murders, and a Crusade for Justice

Titled *Restless Souls: The Sharon Tate Family's Account of Stardom, the Manson Murders, and a Crusade for Justice*, the book was written by Alisa Statman and Brie Tate. In the introduction, the reader is introduced to the Tate family, specifically Patti Tate, Sharon's sister. Statman was Patti's domestic partner before her death and worked with Patti's daughter Brie to write this family memoir. After Patti and Alisa moved in together, Patti became increasingly frustrated "over the constant inaccuracies and misportrayal of her family in the media ... so together [they] wrote her autobiography in an attempt to ease her mind, set the record straight, and fulfill her parents' goal of sharing their important personal stories as well."[11] After Patti died from breast cancer, plans to publish the memoir were postponed but were picked up again once the family agreed this book was a way to honor not only Sharon but Patti as well.

As with so many other projects, *Restless Souls* begins with the Tate family finding out about Sharon's murder. However, from there, the book offers perspectives from Sharon's family members: PJ, her father; Doris, her mother; and Patti, her sister. One unique perspective that the book gives is the photos included in the middle of the book. Instead of the one headshot that typically accompanies the grisly crime-scene photos, the glossy pages are filled with several shots of Sharon as a child and with the family contributors to the book. While not directly a treatment of Sharon, *Restless Souls* gives the Tate family a voice after so many years.

Given that so much of the telling of Sharon's story ends with her death, *Restless Souls* also illustrates the impact of Sharon's death on the family. Sharon's mother, Doris, became a victims' rights advocate for the rest of her life. She was crucial to the passage of Proposition 8, the Victims' Bill of Rights, in 1982, which allowed for victim impact statements. Doris became the first Californian to give an impact statement while speaking at the parole hearing of one of the offenders responsible for Sharon's death. After Doris died from a brain tumor in 1992, Patti took up the mantle, working for victims' rights and to keep Sharon's killers in prison. Seeing this story in *Restless Soul* allows a reader to get just a glimpse of how Sharon's death affected those closest to her. Rather than merely an informational view of Sharon, the book is advocacy, not only for their lost sister, aunt, and daughter, but also for the rights for all victims.

Movies

Helter Skelter (2004)

Starting chronologically first is *Helter Skelter*, a made-for-TV movie that aired on CBS on May 16, 2004. This is one of the first in a wave of renewed interest in the case in American pop culture. Before 2004, there had not been a project on the Manson Family murders since 1989.[12] In the decade that followed, there were six movies and television shows, all ushered in by *Helter Skelter*. Based on the best seller by Manson trial District Attorney Vincent Bugliosi, the movie focuses on Linda Kasabian, a—or possible the—crucial witness who testified against Manson and the Family.

Perhaps the most famous phrase associated with the Tate/La-Bianca murders, *Helter Skelter* is the name of two different movies, one in 1976, seven short years after the murders, and this one in 2004. The over-exaggeration and overacting common in made-for-TV movies are evident. Even so, the cast is a veritable who's who of the early 2000s. Jeremy Davies, who, a year later would join the cast of *Lost*, plays Manson. Clea DuVall is Linda Kasabian, arguably the main character of the film. As with many of the films discussed in this project, there are many good female characters, but the subjects of this study are not among them. Sharon Tate is in a few scenes of the movie but is neither faithfully portrayed nor given the attention due to the most famous of the victims.

Given that the district attorney who tried the case in 1971 wrote the book, it is not surprising that the focus would be on the court proceedings. Linda Kasabian was a crucial element in getting a conviction, so making her the focus is also entirely understandable. However, it is surprising the lack of time or attention that was paid to Sharon Tate. It joins the ranks of nearly all other projects that place little attention on the victims while nearly idolizing the killer or killers. Charles Manson is elevated to a master manipulator as he gets Linda and others to give up their old lives, embrace his image of the Helter Skelter, and eventually kill in his name. Linda is given a chance to evolve throughout the movie as she quickly regrets her choice to join the Family. We see her struggling with being a mother and a daughter and trying to decide to do the right thing and go to the police. She is shown in prison, where she professes to Bugliosi that any punishment she received was fine because she deserved to pay for her sins. Linda comes across as a hugely sympathetic character, proving that far more attention was paid to the woman who stood outside the house on Cielo Drive than the woman who died inside.

An actor named Whitney Dylan plays Sharon in this film. In another hint as to the seriousness with which the film took Sharon, Dylan is the 18th entry on the cast page on IMDb. It is heartening at the beginning of the movie that we are given the chance to see Sharon as a person, but nearly right away, problems arise. Her makeup and hair are closer to the 1990s than the 1960s. The rest of the cast's hair and makeup is generic late 1960s, but Sharon stands out and not in a good or even intentional way. Once one can get beyond those choices, one can focus on the character herself. An overly romanticized version of Sharon calls Roman and there is no mention of any marital infidelity on Roman's part. In fact, it is Sharon whose fidelity is questioned. On more than one occasion, she defends her relationship with Jay Sebring, making Roman another kind of victim.

As the Family begin their attack at the house, the focus remains on Linda. She runs away, towards the car, only hearing the screams of the victims. Wojciech and Abigail are murdered in the yard, so she sees them killed and allows more of a connection with those deaths. Sharon is killed in the house, but Linda only hears her screams to save her baby. The next time Sharon is seen, she is in the morgue for her autopsy. This is the only project that shows the postmortem on Sharon Tate, further cementing her place as a victim and corpse rather than an actual person.

It is clear that, in this film, Sharon Tate is merely a plot device—a victim that had to be killed in order to get to a trial where Vincent Bugliosi and Linda Kasabian can persuade a jury to convict Manson and his followers. Like many plot devices, Sharon in *Helter Skelter* lacks any real development or attention to detail that would show any respect to the woman who died on August 9, 1969.

Wolves at the Door (2017)

This film is a contender for the worst movie on the Manson Family killers and the deaths of Sharon Tate and others on August 9, 1969. Clocking in at a minimal 72 minutes, *Wolves at the Door* feels more like a student film rather than a feature film by New Line Cinemas. Movie critic Mark Kermode called *Wolves at the Door* "not only the worst film released in 2017, but the worst he had seen in several years."[13] Other critics joined Kermode, giving the film a 0 percent rating on *Rotten Tomatoes*. Critics called the movie "shamelessly exploit[ative]," "bland and uninteresting," "a deeply distasteful mess," and "a repellent, misconceived, and pointless film."[14] The cast is populated with actors not completely unknown: Katie Cassidy, best known for her role on CW's *Arrow*, and Elizabeth Henstridge, part of the ensemble cast of ABC's *Marvel's Agents of Shield*.[15] Nevertheless, the film falls far from the mark for anything resembling a fair treatment of Sharon Tate.

The film's distribution was one sign that shows the lack of support given to it by the production company. Whether the production company did not care or, after seeing the film, didn't want to waste money on a certain flop is unknown, but it does offer evidence that few took the film seriously. It was released first on October 21, 2016, in India. Six months later, it was released in Germany and the United Kingdom. It was finally released in the United States, but only on DVD, in April of 2017. This kind of distribution schedule, combined with the running time, damns the movie to the discount bargain bin.

Strangely enough, the film does stand out in its treatment of Abigail Folger. The only woman who is treated less fairly than Sharon is Abigail. In most cases, Abigail is lucky to be named at all. In a few movies, she is named, but sometimes only with a nickname, thus denying her proper recognition. Henstridge's Abigail seems to be the main character of this story, far more than Cassidy's Sharon. Over the course of the 72 minutes, it is revealed that Abigail is leaving Wojciech and Los Angeles to go back to her family in Boston because she felt like "things just aren't right in LA." The audience is only vaguely aware that Roman is not in town, learned from a quick phone call Sharon had in the nursery. There are no other real details learned about Sharon.

Abigail gets a phone call from her mother, has a meaningful conversation with her boyfriend about moving on, and she is the last victim to be killed by the Family. During the attack, the men are dispatched rather quickly. Here the film has dispensed with the facts of the crime. Jay is stabbed on the sofa instead of Wojciech. Wojciech is attacked outside and shoved in a shower before being killed in the bedroom. That leaves the two women alone against the attackers. Sharon does little to fight back, choosing a passive path of locking herself in a bathroom—timid compared with Abigail's actions. Abigail does hide in a hallway closet but then escapes into the living room. When she finds the door blocked, she makes her way into the kitchen, where she is injured by broken glass that littered the floor. Abigail pulls a three-inch piece of glass from her hand and gets out of the house. Once outside, she is stabbed by one of the attackers, but instead of being stabbed multiple times as actually happened, Abigail runs away again. Despite the deep stab wound to the stomach, she scales a high fence and makes it to the road. It is not until after she flags down a car that she and the audience realize that the people in the car are members of the Family and coming to finish her. While dramatic, one has to wonder how this actually plays into the facts of the case. Abigail Folger was found in the yard with multiple stab wounds—the forensics fairly certain that she was killed at that spot. So, did the killers transport her body back up the hill and position it in the yard? To the same point, given that all the victims were killed in places other than their final location, did the killers reposition all of them before writing PIG on the door and leaving? The flagrant disregard of any of the historical facts could be one of the prime reasons for the movie's 0 percent score on *Rotten Tomatoes*.

Given that the Manson Family murders are often referred to as the Tate/LaBianca murders, it seems strange that the main characters are neither the Manson Family nor Sharon Tate. While it is great that Abigail Folger is getting some fair, if almost entirely fictional, attention for once, Sharon is once again shown as a two-dimensional person without any depth. She is seen solely as a victim—of losing her best friend to Boston, of murder, and of false and irresponsible movie making.

Above and beyond the treatment of Sharon, the film did not make any effort at any kind of historical accuracy. There are a few unique pieces from the night of the murders that make their way into all fictional accounts. Jay Sebring's white pants with blue vertical strips are always present. This is the only common historical point *Wolves at the Door* meets. Other easily recognized markers are the overall layout of the living room, aka the crime scene, and the American flag blanket that lay over the back of the sofa. None of these were in *Wolves at the Door*. The look of the house in the film is completely different. It is possible that the budget forced producers to use whatever location they could secure, but it is strange to miss something as simple as a blanket on the back of a sofa.

The Haunting of Sharon Tate (2019)

Released on April 6, 2019, *The Haunting of Sharon Tate* is the first of two movies released in 2019 centered around the Manson Family and the murders on Cielo Drive. With the 50th anniversary of the murders, there was likely hope to capitalize on this milestone. It quickly left the theater and found its way to DVD and digital release. It is listed on *Rotten Tomatoes* with an 18 percent critics' score. Critics quoted on the site describe the movie as "deserv[ing] the instant obscurity for which it is certainly destined," "failure of imagination and morality," "exploitative, cheap, and genuinely insulting," and "unfathomably bad."[16]

The Haunting of Sharon Tate was an obvious choice for this project, especially given that it features the subject of this chapter in its title. Surely, a movie called *The Haunting of Sharon Tate* must give a fair and balanced portrayal of Sharon. Unfortunately, it became clear very early that the critics were very accurate in their reviews. Like many of the other recent projects about the Manson murders, *The Haunting of Sharon Tate* attempts to make the telling of the events into a horror movie. As the murders of Sharon and her friends are easily some of the more horrific crimes of the 20th century, it boggles the mind that any filmmaker would feel the need to amplify the events to make them even scarier.

It begins with Sharon Tate, played by Hilary Duff, speaking to the camera. At first, and second, glance, Duff is a great casting to play Sharon. The modern actor does look a bit like Sharon and the hair and makeup only enhanced this. However, Duff's performance feels rushed and lacking commitment. The fact that Duff spent only two weeks filming the 94-minute movie only proves the point. Duff's Sharon is speaking to the camera in 1968, telling the audience about a dream that she had where she saw herself and her friends being brutally murdered. This nightmare, which Sharon reportedly did have roughly a year before the murder, establishes the film's premise as more supernatural than true crime.

Cut to a year later and Sharon is now pregnant and returning to her rental house on Cielo Drive. Her relationship with Jay Sebring is roughly the same as in all the projects examined for this work, but Abigail Folger and Wojciech Frykowski are established as irritants or even enemies. Upon coming back to her house, Sharon wanted to be alone with her thoughts before the baby arrived, but this version of Abigail and Wojciech are houseguests that refuse to leave. This constant irritant serves to accelerate Sharon's mental breakdown. Given the audience's assumed knowledge of the Tate/LaBianca murders, we share Sharon's fear that something might happen to them, just like in her premonition. Her friends, primarily Abigail and Wojciech, but also Jay to an extent, think Sharon is bordering on crazy. At various points, they blame it on her pregnancy or lack of sleep. The consensus is that Sharon is merely a hysterical woman who keeps freaking out at the slightest gust of wind. She screams, "Do you think I've gone mad?" and "I'll show you crazy ... these people are a threat to me and my baby." While we know that Sharon is right, her portrayal only hurts the image of women in true crime. One of the more important ideas to come out of the wave of true crime that began in 2016 is that women should trust their instincts—most notably in *My Favorite Murder*'s catchphrase, "Fuck Politeness." If this version of Sharon had simply fucked politeness and listened to her instincts, perhaps she would have been able to survive this fictional telling. As it is, any woman watching this film sees so-called friends second guessing their friend and making her feel like she is losing her mind.

The end of the film adds another layer to an already convoluted story. At various points during the attack, Sharon finds herself in the caretaker's trailer with Steven Parent.[17] During one of the visits, he takes one of the many reel-to-reel tapes dropped off at the house by Manson. Parent plays the tape backwards, perhaps a nod to playing "Revolution 9" backwards, and tells Sharon about subliminal messaging. She buys into this completely, believing there is some larger conspiracy that may even involve Abigail and Wojciech.

As the attack by the Family intensifies, an audience that is familiar with the facts of the case gets increasingly confused. As Sadie Mae Glutz, also known as Susan Atkins, is prowling around the house, she is attacked and drowned by Wojciech. A few minutes later, Tex Watson is injured but still bent on killing. He limps and crawls towards the group, only to be beaten by Steven with a shovel and finished by Sharon and a shot to the head. After a long lingering shot of the Hollywood sign—one wonders if there is a Hollywood ending for such a terrible story. The group, hand in hand, begins walking away from the house, but Sharon stops and slowly heads down the driveway. Slowly, the audience sees police and crime-scene tape. Sharon looks mournfully at the driveway where the camera shows five bodies covered with white sheets, one of them clearly pregnant. It is then that you realize that Sharon and the others are merely ghosts. As she walks back to the group, she is carrying something in her arm—possibly her baby. The group walks off down the road, together for eternity. It is a fun ending of a horror movie but only further invalidates Sharon Tate as a real person. What better way to invalidate a person than to literally make her ephemeral—a ghost? In this final scene, Duff's Sharon is invisible to all who surround her—just like Sharon is nearly invisible or a pale imitation of the real woman in all iterations in pop culture.

Once Upon a Time in Hollywood (2019)

The second of two films featuring Sharon released in 2019, *Once Upon a Time in Hollywood* is the best representation of her that has ever been produced. Written and directed by Quentin Tarantino, this film was released on July 26, 2019. It stars Leonardo DiCaprio as Rick Dalton, a washed-up actor who happens to live on Cielo Drive, and Brad Pitt as Dalton's long-suffering stuntman, who now serves as the chauffeur and general house manager. Margot Robbie stars as Sharon Tate, in a role that, while less prominent than DiCaprio's and Pitt's, is the most significant female role in the film.

This film is set apart from the rest with one simple fact: this was the first film where the script and the portrayal had the approval of the Tate family, specifically, Sharon Tate's sister Debra. A cursory review of projects covering the murders of Sharon and the others produces a list of nearly two dozen entries in IMDb. *Once Upon a Time in Hollywood* is the first that has portrayed Sharon in a way that her family was comfortable supporting the project.[18] In addition, Debra gave interviews leading up to the release praising Robbie's performance, saying it was the first time in fifty years that she had heard her sister's voice. When they heard this, most people smiled warmly but did not consider what this really meant. Imagine what it must be like to have not only lost your sister in a horrific manner, but to then have dozens of poor imitations paraded across the big and small screens. Debra and the relatives and loved ones of every other person discussed in this book have to relive the worst moment of their lives every time a film or a show plays on television.

Beyond the endorsement of the Tate family, *Once Upon a Time in Hollywood* sets itself apart in other ways. The first is apparent from the moment Robbie's Sharon Tate appears on the screen—the film shows a Sharon who is not yet pregnant—the only example of this seen in the pop culture examined for this study. Throughout the first hour of the film, Sharon is a happy woman, partying with her husband and friends, and not yet pregnant. By all accounts, Sharon was overjoyed to be pregnant, but this film allows an audience to see her as a whole woman, not just a woman made more vulnerable by pregnancy. Rather than simply a victim, Sharon is seen dancing with Mama Cass and Michelle Phillips at a party at the infamous Playboy Mansion. It is not until deep within the movie that we see a pregnant Sharon, allowing the character to evolve into pregnancy and the audience to see her go through the natural progression.

One of the more heartwarming portions of the film is when Sharon does get to see one of her films at a theater in Hollywood. After ordering books for her husband, she sees a theater is playing *The Wrecking Crew*, a Dean Martin movie where Sharon plays a comedic sidekick to Martin's

Matt Helm. A Rat Pack version of the James Bond franchise, the Matt Helm films offered up a campy romp. *The Wrecking Crew* was released in February 1969, which falls in line with Robbie's Sharon seeing the film before she was pregnant. As she asks for a ticket, Sharon self-consciously admits that she is in the movie and that, yes, she was also in *Valley of the Dolls*. After happily taking a photo for the theater, she finds a seat, pulls out an enormous pair of glasses, and slips them on. Every peel of laughter visibly boosts Sharon. After a quick flashback showing her training with Bruce Lee, there is a scene in the film showing the same fight scene, and Sharon is elated when the audience surrounding her cheers. This scene in the dark movie theater gives yet another facet to an increasingly complex Sharon Tate.

Sitting in that theater seat, Sharon is incredibly relatable, something that—again—is rare in pop culture. She is a woman with a profession—one in which she takes great pride. In training with Bruce Lee, she took her craft seriously, seeing opportunity in a campy comedy. By seeking out and being elated by the fictional audience's reaction, her self-consciousness is revealed to modern-day audiences, as well as her desire to be taken seriously in the movie industry. Some of her earlier career opportunities came because of her connection to Roman, but she was obviously dedicated to making her own way, without the nepotism of her husband.

In a very interesting twist, Tarantino elected not to alter the scenes of the original 1969 film, *The Wrecking Crew*. At other points in the film, DiCaprio is superimposed onto *The Greatest Escape*, allowing this modern actor to occupy the same space as other actors in 1963. But Tarantino did not choose to put Robbie into *The Wrecking Crew*. Sharon Tate continues to exist as herself.

This scene also provides the image of an imperfect Sharon. Between the almost comically large glasses and the dirt on her feet that she propped up during the film, Sharon is a woman just like the rest. She is a woman who is vain enough to hide the fact that she needs glasses. She is a woman who enjoys taking off her shoes at any opportunity. While these may seem like small and inconsequential details, they are important steps in the continuing humanization of Robbie's Tate. In many of the iterations of Sharon, the audience mourns her murder, but it's because of the loss of a heavily pregnant woman who begs for the life of her child. She is never seen as a person outside of her role as a mother and, unfortunately, as a victim. Sharon in *Once Upon a Time in Hollywood* is a fully formed woman: vain and self-conscious, passionate and friendly, a woman who wears glasses and has dirty feet. Never before has Sharon Tate been able to simply exist on screen as a woman.

In the most crucial contribution of this film, Sharon does not die in *Once Upon a Time in Hollywood*. Through the first two hours of the film, one waits for what we all know happened in August 1969. Seeing Sharon as such a vibrant woman made that wait all the more anxious. Hearts were heavy as members of the Manson Family drove up Cielo Drive. Even as DiCaprio drunkenly stumbled into the road to yell at the Family for their engine as it idled loudly at midnight, the mood in the theater was still ominous. However, the Family turned its attention on Rick Dalton. As a TV star they had known as children, Dalton represented people who "taught [them] to murder." After a true Tarantino fight scene, the audience sees the Family dead and the entire Tate household still alive and healthy. Brad Pitt's Cliff knew enough to implicate Manson and the rest of the family, which insinuates that not only does the Tate household survive, but so do Leno and Rosemary LaBianca, who were murdered the next night by other members of the Family.

As the flashing lights and sirens fade down Cielo Drive, a very alive Jay Sebring greets Rick Dalton. Sharon calls down on the intercom and invites Rick up to the house. The last shot of the film shows Rick being welcomed by Sharon and her friends. A familiar script swoops across the screen: "… Once Upon a Time … in Hollywood." Tarantino gives us a fairytale ending to this horrific era. Tarantino, a director widely known for graphic violence, released a film with little violence and altered history to omit some of the most famous murders of the 20th century. In doing this, he has produced one of the most comprehensive representations of Sharon Tate.

Following the release of the film in the summer of 2019, reviewers criticized the film for its oversimplification of the women, specifically Sharon Tate. Aisha Harris, writing for *The New York Times*, said, "Tarantino got it mostly wrong when it came to the women who populate his script."[19] Harris continues by calling Robbie's Sharon a "gazelle in a nature documentary—she hardly speaks, but does dance and walk and drive around Los Angeles a lot in slow motion, the camera lingering on her presence in her natural habitat."[20] This review is not wrong when compared to other women in historical dramas, but it is wrong when Robbie's Tate is compared to all other portrayals of Sharon over the last fifty years. *Once Upon a Time in Hollywood* gives the most human, independent, empowering portrayal of Sharon Tate, allowing the audience to see her as more than a victim and as a full-fledged person for the first time in cinema history.

Television

Aquarius (2015–2016)

Aquarius marked David Duchovny's return to network television after thirteen years, playing Detective Sam Hodiak, a World War II veteran and LAPD officer. In the pilot, he is partnered with Officer Brian Shafe, combining Sam's old-school ways with Brian's longhaired, "hippie" undercover work. In addition to their various cases, all interesting in their own right, Sam is pulled into the world of Charles Manson through the missing daughter of an old flame. Emma, the daughter, has become disillusioned by the lives of her Republican parents and runs away to join the Family. Grace, Sam's ex, asks Sam to find her daughter, bringing Sam in contact with the infamous manipulator.

As the first season focuses entirely on events before the August 1969 murders, there is no mention of Sharon or any of the other victims. The second season, however, is a different story: the first scene of the first episode is the Tate/Polanski house on Cielo Drive. Throughout the second and final season, there are frequent flash-forwards to the night of August 9, 1969. Emma, now pregnant and fully mesmerized by Manson, repeatedly watches in horror as the others kill Sharon and the other victims. While these scenes offer further dimension to Emma, Sharon is barely one-dimensional.

There are only a few scenes that show Sharon alive at all, and they tend to be incredibly predictable. According to official accounts, the night of August 9 was one of the hottest of the summer, and Sharon, who was nearly full term in her pregnancy, had complained that she was uncomfortable. Most films and shows have Sharon expressing this sentiment at some point. In *Aquarius*, it was as she was lying on her bed with Jay Sebring in the moments before the killers came into the home. This is the only time that we see Sharon as more than a victim, but it was mere moments. The only other time Sharon is seen alive or speaks is when she is being murdered and she is begging for her life. She is not even named until the second episode. As the flashes take place at the beginning and end of episodes, it is easy for the audience to ignore or even forget where Manson's manipulation is headed.

For the majority of the time Sharon is on screen in *Aquarius*, she is little more than a piece of furniture in the room. Other characters move around her body as they would a table or a chair. She is a set piece that lies there as other characters evolve and develop. Emma, horrified at what is happening, stares as Sharon is murdered. Brian arrives at the scene and, upon looking at the victims, relapses and shoots heroin while still sitting next to a pool of blood. In one scene, Brian stares at the sofa as Sharon's body blinks in and out of the scene; Sharon is just a delusion, a part of Brian's drug-induced haze, and less than a person.

In one last insult, as she is being murdered, the closed captioning reads "Sharon screaming." But the person being murdered on screen is Abigail Folger, not Sharon Tate. Sharon could not be honored by being correctly named, not even at the moment of her death.

Aquarius takes its place at the lowest rung of Sharon Tate interpretations, refusing to give her any agency or even allow her to exist as a person. None of the characters give her any of the respect that is offered to other murder victims on the show. As with a typical crime procedural, there is a crime, usually a murder, in each episode. The victims are named, they are respected, and their crimes are solved. In one episode, Sam cradles a woman as she dies from stab wounds. But Sharon, another stabbing victim, is barely given the respect of a name, let alone the human kindness of being comforted as she died.

Podcasts

As with the other media, the murders of Sharon Tate, Abigail Folger, Jay Sebring, and Wojciech Frykowski have been a frequent topic of true crime podcasts. It's common practice for movie studios to offer enticements to podcasts to cover a crime that is the subject of a soon-to-be or newly released movie. This was certainly the case in the weeks surrounding the release of *Once Upon a Time in Hollywood*. Between that promotion and the 50th anniversary, there is an abundance of podcasts on the August 1969 murders.

Podcasts like *Redrum Blonde*, which published a three-episode series on the case, do offer at least some insight into Sharon and her life outside of being a victim. The indication of this series that sets it apart from the others is simply the title—"Sharon Tate: Parts One, Two, and Three." Of the many podcasts listened to for this project, the vast majority on this case have a title that is more related to the offenders than Sharon. Having three episodes titled after Sharon is unfortunately a unique characteristic of podcast coverage. The first episode of *Redrum Blonde's* series, dropped on July 23, 2019, contains a background on Sharon, as well as her husband, and how the five victims knew each other. While it would be wonderful to have an entire episode on Sharon herself, having this is still more than what is offered by other podcasts.

A few cover the murders only tangentially or without any real analysis of Sharon or the other victims. *Haunted Family's* 47th episode, titled "Charles Manson and the Tate/Labianca Murders," starts much like *The Haunting of Sharon Tate*, with Sharon's dream of the murders. A paranormal podcast, the hosts home in on the supernatural element of Sharon potentially predicting her own death. Other than that, the only other real information on Sharon, besides the details of the murder, was that she was pregnant and married to Roman. Sharon's name is in the title, but she is dealt with only superficially.

Two other podcasts have dedicated more episodes and time to covering the details of Charles Manson, the Family, and the murders. *Hollywood & Crime* had a spinoff series entitled *Young Charlie*. Over the course of six episodes, the Wondery podcast network simultaneously examines the life of Charles Manson before creating the Family and the crimes of that Family. Right away, this means that any time given to all the victims is halved. Sharon is not even mentioned until 5 minutes and 38 seconds into the first episode. Before the investigating officers knew about Manson and his Family, various motives were investigated. *Young Charlie* lists the possible causes: drugs, sexual orgies, jealous rage. Sharon's sex life—the possibility of her having an affair with Jay—was mentioned as a possibility. Jay's sex life was equally questioned. While these are normal lines of inquiry, there is no mention of Roman's infidelity. The victims were blamed by the police for their deaths and are being blamed still by continuing to perpetuate this line of thought.

With each subsequent episode of *Young Charlie*, there is less and less information on the victims. By the end of episode two, Sharon is referred to only as Roman's wife, not by name. She is not mentioned again until episode four and only as Sadie aka Susan Atkins describes the murders.

The popular podcast *You Must Remember This*, known to do series on classic Hollywood, did one called *Charles Manson's Hollywood* in May and June of 2015. The host, Carina Longworth, did two episodes with a focus on Sharon Tate, but each of those also included a man. The seventh episode in the series focused on Sharon and her relationship with Jay Sebring. Backgrounds on both of them were given. Sharon was called "really, really, really" good looking, but also covered were an alleged rape of her as a teenager and an abusive relationship in the early 1960s after she moved to LA. After this quick overview, Carina moved on to Jay and then began to discuss the romantic triangle of Sharon, Jay, and Roman. The next episode centered on Sharon and Roman's relationship. While *You Must Remember This* does discuss Sharon more than any of the other podcasts, it is problematic that Sharon is only discussed in the context of her lovers. Surely, she is worthy of an episode entirely to herself, but she is not ever given that honor.

Conclusion

The murders of Sharon Tate, her unborn son, Jay Sebring, Abigail Folger, Wojciech Frykowski, and Steven Parent not only signified the end of the 1960s for many, but also have provided exploitation fodder for more than fifty years. From the start, people were fascinated by the Manson

Family, and that fascination quickly turned into a market for books, films, television series, and podcasts. In almost all of them, Sharon either was simply a plot device in the story of the Family or manipulated into the victim of a slasher film.

Informational treatment of Sharon includes only the most basic facts of her life before immediately transitioning into the gruesome details of her death. There are far more iterations of Sharon that fall into the exploitative category, particularly movies that wish to capitalize on the name Sharon Tate and the Manson Family murders, such as *Wolves at the Door* and *The Haunting of Sharon Tate*. The only iteration that can be fully categorized as advocacy is a book written by Sharon's own family members. A movement to place Sharon at the forefront of this story has not yet begun. Perhaps now that Manson has died and the other offenders are beginning to die, the focus will finally shift to the victims. In the near future, hopefully Sharon will begin to get the attention that she has been denied for five decades. Not only does that attention need to include more than simply the basic details of her life, but pop culture iterations that offer a Sharon Tate who is a fully-fledged woman and not just the victim of a slasher film.

Chapter 6

Patricia Hearst

The tumultuous 1960s, even with violence, both foreign and domestic, that plagued Americans, still felt vaguely optimistic as the country rolled into the 1970s. However, the war continued to drag on, and, when the Rolling Stones attempted to recapture the magic of Woodstock at Altamont Racetrack, a man was killed by the biker gang that was hired as security.[1] Not only did the 1970s have a deep sense of apathy and disillusionment, but it was also the beginning of what some refer to as the Golden Age of serial killers and serial crimes. Because of this, two women from the 1970s have been included: one who was kidnapped into a life of crime and one who found herself unknowingly living alongside a serial killer for years.

Just the Facts

Patricia Campbell Hearst, better known as Patty Hearst, holds a unique position in this project as neither history nor public opinion can come to an agreement on whether she was a victim or an offender. From the beginning of her tale, when she was kidnapped in 1974, there were those who said she was being coerced or even brainwashed. There were competing voices, equally as loud, that swore Hearst was a willing participant of any and all actions of the Symbionese Liberation Army (SLA). Given this mystery, the story of Patricia Hearst[2] has been a prime target for pop culture. Numerous iterations have attempted to answer the question of whether Patricia was brainwashed or not, or whether her account of her ordeal was simply a story to play on the sympathies of a jury, a governor, and a president.

Patricia Hearst was born in 1954 to Catherine and Randolph Hearst. The granddaughter of publishing tycoon William Randolph Hearst, Patricia was raised with both wealth and comfort that only the Hearst name could bring. As a young woman in the early 1970s, she sought to find her own way, apart from her family name and legacy. She attempted to do that at UC Berkeley, studying art history while living with her boyfriend, Steven Weed.

On the night of February 4, 1974, Patricia was at home in her apartment with Steven, when members of the SLA knocked on the door. Four members pushed into the apartment and beat Steven badly, asking both of them for their "safe." Without a safe in the apartment, the SLA instead took Patricia, throwing her into the trunk of a car before taking her back to their hideout. After 57 days in captivity, where she was kept in a closet, Patricia joined the SLA, either under coercion or as a survival measure. In the eighteen months she spent with the SLA, she participated in illegal activity before hiding with a few of its members in Pennsylvania and finally making her way back to San Francisco mere weeks before she was arrested in September of 1975. Her trial began in January of 1976, where she was eventually found guilty of bank robbery and using a firearm during the commission of a felony. Sentenced to seven years, Patricia was freed from prison by a commutation from President Jimmy Carter issued in January 1979. Her story was finally complete when she was given a presidential pardon from President Clinton on the final day of his presidency in 2001.

News Coverage of the Day

While most of the press covered both the kidnapping and the trial, the press of the day proved an interesting and intriguing conundrum. Hearst Publishing, which owned several papers at the time, had direct influence over some news coverage and indirect influence over other coverage. With this kind of possible tainting of the journalism, most of the news coverage has been set aside. There were two articles, however, that did stand out as interesting portrayals of Patricia Hearst.

Rolling Stone published a two-part series written by Howard Kohn and David Weir called "The Inside Story." The first part was published in the October 23, 1975, issue while the second part was published in the November 20, 1975, issue. This "inside story" offers up an interesting primary insight into how Patricia was being reported on at the time of her arrest. One huge source of information for this series seems to have been Jack Scott, a reporter who was attempting to write a book on the SLA. Several paragraphs before even discussing Patricia's kidnapping, Kohn and Weir spend time on Scott and his ordeal with trying to get his book contract. Kohn and Weir write, "On February 4, 1974, while Patty Hearst was being kidnapped, Jack Scott was confronting his own private crisis."[3] Scott had been trying to get a contract with Doubleday, but his editor had insisted he get more information from people involved in the movement. The insider information that Scott chose came from members of the SLA, and more time was spent on Scott and his journey than Patricia and hers. After the police confrontation where six members of the SLA were killed and Bill and Emily Harris and Patricia left Los Angeles, they spent a lot of time with Scott as they traveled across the country. Scott also stayed with the group in Pennsylvania for a time, using his savings as the group's primary source of income. A huge amount of time is spent on Scott and his time with the group, even though the series is described as an inside look at Patricia Hearst. The original artwork that accompanied the articles was exclusively of Patricia, and yet Scott and his interaction with SLA members were a major focus of the series.

When Patricia is discussed in this series, it is through a problematic lens. After describing her kidnapping by SLA members, Kohn and Weir write, "Even in those first terrible moments Patricia Campbell Hearst managed to summon up the daring and arrogance that had been her style through 19 years of her life as an heiress to the Hearst fortune."[4] While daring is complimentary, the word arrogance is problematic, especially given that this was the section describing Patricia's traumatic kidnapping. Her portrayal as a spoiled, rich heiress continues as the authors explain that Patricia's parents "had provided every indulgence, tolerated her dope smoking, her sneaking out to rock concerts at San Francisco's Fillmore auditorium and her faded jeans."[5] In addition to the jaded view of Patricia, this is also a strange and conservative opinion for a magazine such as *Rolling Stone*.

At various points in the series, the authors describe Patricia's treatment at the hands of the SLA. While every other iteration of Patricia's case refers to the space that she was kept in as a closet, this article refers to it as a "closet-sized room."[6] The implication that the space was, in fact, a small room instead of a closet allows *Rolling Stone* readers to believe that her treatment by the SLA was less harmful than it actually was. To further confuse the matter, later in the same article, the space is described as "a small 'isolation chamber' approximating a San Quentin 'hole.'"[8]

Additionally, the authors made declarative statements such as "[s]he lost track of time and didn't feel like eating" and "[s]he was not raped or starved or otherwise brutalized."[9] This take on Patricia's treatment by the SLA is unique. By stating that "she lost track of time and didn't feel like eating," it puts the indisputable weight loss that Patricia experienced as entirely her fault rather than the fault of her captors.

The statement that Patricia was not raped is the first of many comments about her body and whether she engaged in consensual sex with SLA members. Having already established for *Rolling Stone* readers that, according to their sources, Patricia had not been raped, Kohn and Weir describe every sexual encounter as consensual, saying that she "began sleeping with 23-year-old Willie Wolfe, whom she called Cujo."[10] In the second part of the series, Steve Soliah, a new member of the SLA, is introduced and is described as a close friend and lover of Patricia.[11] Soliah is described as "full of smiles and hugs ... had a full beard and golden hair to his shoulders [and] [f]riends called him a big teddy bear."[12] In those two sentences, Soliah gets better treatment by the authors than Patricia does. Even after being arrested, he was considered Patricia's boyfriend as fellow inmates were asking him for favors, "figuring that as Patty's boyfriend, he must have influence somewhere."[13]

Rolling Stone's two-part series, published between Patricia's arrest and her trial, is heavily skewed against Patricia and in favor of the SLA. While Patricia is referred to as Randolph Hearst's "spoiled brat," Bill Harris, who took over for DeFreeze after the latter's death, was called by his SLA name of General Teko several times throughout the series. Showing Harris the respect of calling him by his chosen name and yet not showing Patricia similar respect of even mentioning the possibility of abuse and torture is irresponsible. Perhaps it can be explained by Kohn and Weir getting the majority of their information from Scott and likely did not have access to Patricia during her time in holding as she was awaiting trial.

Published in the *Los Angeles Times* on December 12, 1978, the article "Patricia Hearst's Torment Is a Disgrace" was written by Louis Jolyon West, a psychologist who was appointed by Judge Oliver Carter to examine Hearst prior to her trial. Written three years after West was appointed in 1975, he explains that he worked with Dr. Margaret Thaller Singer to spend 40 hours in "direct examination" of Patricia and "more than 200 hours reconstructing her entire life history, studying all of the government's documents and other data relating to her, interviewing various informants, and reviewing pertinent medical and psychological literature."[14]

This article sets itself apart from the rest of the news coverage not only by discussing Patricia's case from a psychological perspective, but also by categorizing her trial and treatment as a "disgrace." During the trial, there was a lot of discussion from Patricia's defense team about the possibility of Patricia being brainwashed or the victim of "coercive persuasion" at the hands of the SLA. Drs. West and Singer both had experience working with branches of the military and were considered experts on coercive persuasion.[15][16] West reports that before Patricia was kidnapped, she "had been a normal, healthy 19-year-old college student with a stable life situation and a responsible orientation to society."[17] Additionally, they found that she had "no predisposition whatsoever toward crime, antisocial activity or revolutionary politics."[18] This is an interesting addition to the coverage of

Patricia. As discussed later, part of the modern conversation of Patricia is whether she was particularly vulnerable to coercion—whether she was, as some put it, "depressed" and "susceptible" to brainwashing. But here, West is saying that Patricia was, in their expert opinion, "normal and healthy."

With their experience with military veterans who had experienced similar coercion in the Korean Conflict, Patricia's doctors recognized a similar "prolonged period of torture" that Patricia endured that "induced … a psychiatric illness of the type known as traumatic neurosis."[19] When Americans, including the 12 jurors in the courtroom, were trying to determine whether Patricia was guilty of the robbery of Hibernia Bank in 1974, West and Singer were confident that she only participated in the robbery because of the coercive persuasion. Much like the treatment of American prisoners of war during the Korean Conflict, Patricia was exposed to "continual threats against her life and person, coercive interrogation, pain, sexual assault, humiliation and isolated confinement to a tiny closet while constantly blindfolded for 57 days and nights."[20] Not only did this impact her psychologically while she was held captive, but she "still showed marked psychiatric symptoms … including impaired concentration, constricted awareness, poor intellectual functioning with a loss of more than 20 IQ points, patchy amnesia, incapacity to make meaningful plans, and severe loss of autonomous personal identity."[21]

In this article, West makes what is probably the strongest argument for Patricia being the victim of brainwashing, also known as coercive persuasion. However, one must wonder why this was not only published in a newspaper, but in December 1978. The researcher can see two major issues with this article. The first is that a court-appointed doctor wrote an article about a patient, including details of the patient's diagnosis and case history, and published all of it in a national newspaper. An article from 1989 by Gerald Higgins titled "The History of Confidentiality in Medicine" points to ancient Greece and the Hippocratic Oath for the roots of patient confidentiality.[22] The American Academy of Family Physicians has a history of patient confidentiality that is dated 1979, only a year after West's article.[23] Regardless of the beginning of patient confidentiality, one must wonder about the ethics of a doctor printing such details in a national newspaper.

The first issue could be explained by the second issue—the possible collusion with the Hearst family. In December of 1978, the Hearst family had spent the last two years trying to get Patricia out of jail. After being found guilty, she was sentenced to seven years in prison for the bank robbery. The Hearst media machine was activated to convince whoever could possibly help them, including Governor Ronald Reagan and President Jimmy Carter. So, the question becomes, was West's article a part of this?

The end of the article includes a plea to Carter for a pardon, saying, "Patricia Hearst poses no threat of any kind to society ... [b]ut further incarceration clearly poses a terrible threat to her."[24] So, if the Hearst family, or possibly even Patricia herself, gave West permission to write the article, the problem of patient confidentiality is negated. However, the problem then becomes that the doctor has lost his partiality by becoming a part of the mechanism to get Patricia out of jail.

While the article offers some very interesting insights into Patricia Hearst's psychological case before and after her kidnapping, one has to wonder what was the motivation behind the publication? Was there collusion between West and the Hearst family to get Patricia out of prison? Was the article part of a plan? And if so, how much did Patricia know/have a say? On the surface, the article feels like a supportive effort on behalf of Patricia, but was this yet another manipulation of her experience by some of those whom she trusted during her trial? Whether or not the article had a national impact, Patricia's sentence was commuted by President Carter on February 1, 1979, six weeks after the article's publication.

Books

Patty's Got a Gun:
Patricia Hearst in 1970s America (2008)

For such a well-known case, there have been surprisingly few books written on Patricia and the events surrounding the SLA kidnapping. Patricia herself wrote a book in 1982, titled *Every Secret Thing*, telling her story only a few years after being released from prison. Of the few books on the case, William Graebner's book *Patty's Got a Gun: Patricia Hearst in 1970s America* is the most interesting. Part history and part psychology, this treatment wonders if Patricia was "a victim, of duress or fear of what the defense labeled 'coercive persuasion,' or had she taken up with the SLA willingly, decided to be a different person, chosen a new life?"[25] Graebner takes the question a step further by pondering how the era factored into Patricia's treatment by the courts. He says that if she had been arrested and tried in 1965, "she would surely have been acquitted, judged to be nothing more, and nothing less, than the unfortunate victim of kidnapping, rape, and physical and mental torture."[26] However, if a decade was added and Patricia was tried in 1985, she would "surely have been convicted, steamrolled by the Reagan revolution, judged to be just another person who had failed to take personal responsibility for her acts."[27] While many admit that the era in which a woman lives has a profound impact on how she is/

was treated, this is the first instance of someone pointing out how Patricia's circumstances were unique to the mid–1970s.

Patty's Got a Gun also examines how Patricia's image has been manipulated from the beginning. From the moment of her disappearance, it became clear to everyone that her motives were … unclear. Without any certainty, Americans obsessed over the case for months "to project their values, ideals and concerns onto the persona of Patty Hearst and interpret her conduct as they saw fit … so she became, for one person or another, or one group or another, a terrorist, a misguided sixties radical, a woman with a gun, a rich bitch, a victim of sexual abuse, a confused [and] frightened girl, a bored woman awakening to a life of risk and purpose, a veteran of a new and nasty kind of war, a brainwashed zombie, a survivor."[28] This interpretation of Patricia is academic and objective, far more so than any other iteration. There is no sense that Graebner has any preconceived ideas about Patricia, nor is he trying to convince an audience of his stance. In this book, he provides a wonderful and completely objective examination of Patricia and the trauma she experienced in the mid–1970s.

Movies/TV

Patty Hearst (1988)

The only fictionalized account of the Patricia Hearst kidnapping and trial is a 1988 film simply named *Patty Hearst* starring Natasha Richardson. In addition to its unique standing as the only fictionalized version, this film is the only one that seems to be fully authorized by Patricia. In addition to it being based on her autobiography, Patricia promoted the film during her 1988 interview on *The Larry King Show*. Outside of the trial itself and her campaign for commutation, the autobiography and the promotion of this film are Patricia's largest contributions to the overall historiography of the story.

Natasha Richardson, in preparing to play Patricia, perfected Patricia's voice, so much so that the researcher was unclear as to whether it was actually Patricia in the opening voiceover or the actor. During the voiceover, she describes herself to the audience as a college student but also a strong woman who "never doubted my ability to handle the unknown."[29] Her depiction as a "normal" college student continues into the next scene at the apartment that she shares with Steven Weed. She is shown gossiping on the phone and doing her homework—all things that Patricia is not shown doing in any other iteration watched for this project. After introductions, Patricia is immediately kidnapped by the SLA. *Patty Hearst* allows Patricia, for a few moments at least, to be a "normal" girl, to walk through a college campus, to talk on the phone with a friend, or to do homework at the dining room table. Just those few moments humanize Patricia in a way that is supremely important for viewers to be able to see her as a human being and fully sympathize with her on the rest of her journey.

Those "normal" few moments are shattered when the SLA burst through the door. (It is at this point that the movie begins its quick descent into the ridiculous. There are many elements of this film that are terrible, but the researcher will attempt to overlook those and concentrate solely on the portrayal of Patricia.) The members of the SLA attack Steven Weed and carry Patricia out to their car, throwing her in the trunk. Once back in their safe house, she is thrown in a closet, bloody scrapes on her knees visible. All of the iterations talk about Patricia's 57 days in this closet, but this film gives the audience an idea as to what it may have been like for her. The entire montage takes place from inside the closet. When the SLA members open the door, the camera is looking up at the SLA members, as if the camera is Patricia and the audience is locked in the closet with her. After the first few interactions, the framing of the SLA members changes and the lighting behind them becomes stark white. This only increases the fear and alienation that Patricia, and by extension the audience, feels in the closet.

During this initial period, the film also shows Patricia being broken down psychologically. Again, this is something that the documentaries and the podcasts all discuss or mention, but this film shows specific scenes that, even with some ridiculous dialogue, allow insight into what Patricia went through. When she had to go to the bathroom, they screamed at her, "If you gotta pee, say you gotta pee. If you gotta shit, say you gotta shit."[30] She is forced to go to the bathroom with at least one member of the SLA watching. She is also forced to bathe with at least one member of the SLA in the room with her. In the bathing scene, Natasha Richardson is shown fully nude in the bathtub, further driving home the vulnerability Patricia found herself in during this stage of her captivity.

The montage slowly shifts, again illustrating the shift in Patricia's captivity. Members of the SLA, particularly the female members, start showing affection towards her. While also telling her that the FBI was going to come into the safe house and shoot her, they asked her questions like, "Don't you have sexual feelings?" They brushed her hair and washed her clothes for the first time since her kidnapping. The SLA members refer to Patricia as their "pet chicken," telling her that no one wants to ring her neck. By the time Patricia is asked to "join or be let go," she sees only one choice—joining her captors. In many of the iterations of the Patricia Hearst case, the primary question is always whether she was coerced into joining the SLA or whether she joined of her own free will. What *Patty Hearst* provides is a path between the two. Natasha Richardson's portrayal shows a Patricia who is deeply affected by the weeks of conditioning by the SLA, but also aware enough to recognize that when her captors told her they were going to let her go, that meant that, if she chose not to join them, she would die. So, rather than an either/or, this one specific scene shows an astute Patricia who does what she needs to in order to survive.

Soon after Patricia makes the decision to join the SLA, she is told that sex is a revolutionary act, but SLA members cannot go into the streets to find partners, so they must do this revolutionary act with their comrades. Patricia is shown into a large room where members were having sex while she is told that it is "not camaraderie" to say no to sex if another member "requests" to have sex with you. As a newly minted SLA member, she can "fuck any man or woman here," but that also means that any man or woman could fully expect to force Patricia into sex as well. This again answers a question asked by many both during and in the years since the Hearst trial. One of the most damning pieces of evidence against her was the testimony that Patricia had been sexually involved with Willie Wolfe, also known as Cujo, one of the SLA members. Members of the jury, and the public, wondered how someone who was supposedly a victim could enter into a consensual relationship with Wolfe.[31] However, if, as part of her conditioning, Patricia was taught that she was not allowed to say no, then saying no could mean the removal of her position as a comrade, which, in turn, would end in her death.

The final scene in the closet shows Patricia at the end of her psychological rope, shivering and muttering to herself. Clearly broken, she chants things like "I can't do this anymore" and "Just shoot me, okay? Just shoot me!"[32] It is at this point that she is ready for her "reeducation." The head of the SLA, Donald DeFreeze, also known as Cinque, played by Ving Rhames, takes her out of the closet. While Cinque crows about the propaganda coup of having control over Patricia Hearst, the group chooses a new name for Patricia—Tania.

For the majority of Patricia's time as Tania, the film follows the Hearst autobiography closely. She is seen recording the tapes that are sent to both the press and to her family, but with members of the SLA, specifically Cinque, telling her what to say. When they are in the car on their way to the Hibernia Bank, Cinque forces Patricia to practice her speech, telling her, "Fuck it up and you're dead."[33] Once inside the bank, Patricia appears timid and unsure during the robbery. At several points over the next several months of her life—and several moments of the film—Patricia seems to be looking for some way to escape her situation. Whether it is while she is in the van outside of the sporting goods store or while Cinque is trying to get her to recruit more members by saying, "Smile Tania; people don't recognize you unless you smile," Patricia looks continuously apprehensive.

As with every telling of the Patricia Hearst case, Richardson's Hearst crosses the country with Bill and Emily Harris after six members of the SLA are killed in a confrontation with LA police.[34] She quickly ends up in an apartment in San Francisco with another activist, Wendy Yoshimura.[35] When FBI agents come through the door with guns drawn, Patricia runs for the door before being stopped by more agents coming through the back door. This is an interesting departure from the way most people tell the story. In every other iteration, Patricia is said to have been running toward a room full of guns to defend herself and Yoshimura. There is an obvious personal interest in showing herself as running for a door rather than a room of guns. However, she more than anyone else would know where she was running on that day of her arrest.

There is also a split second within this arrest that proves to be incredibly telling. When the agents come through the back door and confront Patricia, they call her Patty. At that moment, there is a single second of a short-circuiting. The imagery tells the audience that as soon as "Tania" is called Patty again, her brainwashing is literally short-circuited for the first time in eighteen months.

After being arrested, Richardson's Patricia begins her long journey back from Tania to "Patty." Lawyers obtained for her by her family argued on her behalf, beginning their brainwashing defense. An unnamed lawyer says that if this was a military court martial, much like the argument of West, brainwashing would be an accepted defense and Patricia would be home within a day. Her memory is described as "Swiss cheese" during yet another montage of "shrink" interviews.[36]

The film ends with Randolph "Randy" Hearst visiting Patricia in prison. Now wearing her prison uniform, Patricia is a fully realized person at last. Gone is Tania and Patricia is back. She tells her father that she wants to use the media to "confront people's prejudices" about her.[37] She continues:

> I was forced to have sex with my captors so people think I'm a whore. See, people fantasized about me so long, they thought they knew me. When I finally surfaced, the person, the real story, I was inconvenient. But I'm here and I'm going to let them know it too. I made it worse hiding from the press. I let people keep their fantasies. I hope to let people see the real me, to demystify myself. No one wants to accept that their mental state is so fragile. Not me—just don't lock me in that closet. I finally figured out what my crime was. I lived—big mistake—emotionally messy. Pardon my French, Dad, but fuck 'em.[38]

This speech sounds as if it came directly from Patricia Hearst and not from the lips of Natasha Richardson. One must wonder if Patricia had been holding this in since 1976 and took the opportunity in 1988 to finally tell the world what she had been thinking.

The film has some glaring problems, the lack of overall quality being at the top of that list. There is obviously a possible, even probable slant in the telling in Patricia's favor. However, the seal of approval from Patricia Hearst makes this film and this version of her story an important one. For that reason alone, *Patty Hearst* cannot be ignored.

Documentaries

The Radical Story of Patty Hearst (2017)

In 2017, CNN[39] announced that it would be airing a six-part documentary called *The Radical Story of Patty Hearst*. Based heavily upon the book *American Heiress* by CNN legal correspondent Jeffrey Toobin, *The Radical Story of Patty Hearst* includes interviews with several people who were involved, including Steven Weed, Bill Harris, and the police officers and FBI agents who worked the abduction and bank robbery. Most notable is the absence of Patricia Hearst or any of the Hearsts. At the beginning and end of each episode, a disclaimer appears, alerting viewers that Patty Hearst and her family refused to be interviewed or participate in the series. While it is explained that Patricia does not do many or any interviews, especially about her kidnapping or trial, her absence is glaring. The producers used an interview from when Patricia appeared on *The Larry King Show* in 1998 almost as a stand-in for a modern-day interview.

Right from the beginning, the documentary starts with the question as to whether Patricia is "America's most famous crime victim" or "is she America's most famous turncoat?"[40] This language automatically sets up a dichotomy that Patricia must be one or the other. By immediately establishing that Patricia must be either an innocent victim or "the most famous turncoat," which is a bold statement for a country that includes Benedict Arnold in its history, the audience has this either/or in their mind for the entire six episodes of the documentary. Any person tuning in or queuing it up to stream is not given the chance to judge Patricia, which means that Patricia is not given the chance to be judged on the merits of the argument.

As with many documentaries, the first episode gives background on the Hearst family and Patricia's childhood. Within minutes, Patricia is called a princess and a rebel—again setting her up in a dichotomy of an either/or rather than allowing audience members to decide for themselves. The narrator states, "If any family in California was royalty, it was the Hearsts, which made Patty in her own little way a princess."[41]

Other than Jeffrey Toobin and the narrator, the only person who is speaking about Patricia outside and before the kidnapping is her fiancé, Steven Weed. In the first episode, "The Kidnapping," Steven describes the night when Patricia was taken by the SLA. In addition to the salient facts, Steven describes running outside, after being beaten by the SLA members who came into the house, to try to find help. As with any firsthand account, there is always the chance of alterations, but this is a dramatically different story from the one told in the podcasts that cover the story.[42]

Other than the story from Steven Weed, the only other account of the kidnapping in the entire miniseries is from Bill Harris, one of those who burst through the apartment door that night. Of those who kidnapped Patricia Hearst, only two are still alive and only one of them was interviewed for this series. Bill Harris is arguably the most substantial interview subject, with a hefty amount of screen time. When he tells the story of Patricia's kidnapping, which she has described as an extraordinarily traumatic event, Harris has a smile on his face. Even if a series is looking for primary sources, what does it mean to have a kidnapper tell the story of the kidnapping?

Harris's involvement in the documentary series continues to raise questions throughout the rest of the six episodes. In episode two, "The Captive," Harris describes Patricia's 57 days in a closet of an SLA safe house by saying she "interacted admirably" with people he still describes as comrades forty years later. While Patricia reported that the tapes given to the press were words given to her by the SLA, Harris makes it clear that she wrote all of those messages. He repeatedly states that her life was never in any danger. Whenever possible, he attempts to put responsibility with Patricia. He makes it very clear that Patricia chose to have sex with Willie Wolfe. After this portion of his interview, a statement appears on the screen that makes it clear that Patricia "strongly disputes Bill Harris's claims. She claims that she was raped and tortured by her captors."[43] While it is good that the documentarian(s) have included this statement, even with Patricia refusing to participate, this one-time refutation of Harris's claims is not nearly enough to counteract the several different instances where Harris not only says things but also makes faces and gestures that show his ambivalence towards the case.

In the same episode, Harris again puts the responsibility of Patricia staying with the SLA with Patricia. Most accounts of the case show that the SLA offered Patricia a choice, to join to leave or to join to die, depending on the telling. However, according to Harris, Patricia staying with the SLA was "never anyone's idea until she said it."[44] Without much thought,

Harris has easily dismissed the 57 days that Patricia spent in a closet. Even in the best circumstances, she is still the victim of an abduction where she was held for nearly two months in a closet. To see Bill Harris not only dismiss the claims against the SLA but put all of the blame onto Patricia is disgusting. Whether one believes that Patricia was brainwashed or not, this kind of victim blaming is irresponsible to have on a mainstream cable news network.

Harris's character assassination of Patricia continues into the third episode, "The Robbery." Beginning with the robbery of Hibernia Bank, the episode continues through the confrontation with LA police where six SLA members were killed. Yet again, Harris attempts to remove all responsibility from any members of the SLA, living or dead. According to Harris, Patricia not only volunteered for the bank robbery but also volunteered for the assault team. He continues, saying, "Patricia's performance in the bank robbery only solidified what we suspected about her. Somewhat of a revolutionary savant. We kidnapped a freak! ... People freeze in certain situations. She did not freeze. She was spectacular.... We weren't making her do anything against her will."[45] In the same breath, Harris admits to the kidnapping while also putting all responsibility for the robbery with Patricia. Not only was she not brainwashed, but also the SLA happened to kidnap a "revolutionary savant."

In the final two episodes,[46] *The Radical Story of Patty Hearst* concentrates on the arrest and trial of Patricia, bringing the story to a conclusion. In episode five, "The Conversion," Patricia is with the Harrises as the rest of the SLA had died in a fiery confrontation with the Los Angeles Police Department. The remaining members, Bill and Emily Harris, Patricia aka Tania, and a few other recruits they picked up during the "lost year," began a bombing campaign against law enforcement agencies in California. During his interview, Bill Harris dances around the conversation, coming dangerously close to implicating Patricia in the bombings while making very sure that he is protected against prosecution.

After detailing her arrest in 1976, the documentary spends considerable time on the issue of brainwashing. F. Lee Bailey, one of Patricia's attorneys, describes Patricia as "broken" and that it took "months [for Patricia] to be able to return back to society where she wasn't afraid of the SLA."[47] However, Harris chimes in to say that yes, Patricia was brainwashed, but she was brainwashed by her lawyers, not by the SLA. When asked if the SLA had any kind of brainwashing training, Patricia's attorneys said yes and Harris said no. Mirroring the larger conversation about whether Patricia was coercively persuaded, one group of individuals in the episode was convinced she was and another group argued that she was not.

Those same groups argue whether Patricia was raped by members of the SLA:

> Specifically, Willie Wolfe. Even with Patricia's own account and her lawyers' support, Harris insists that there was never any rape within the SLA. Rather than use the word rape, he says that Patricia used "the 'r' word."[48] The episode delves into whether Patricia was raped; whether she was ordered to have sex or coerced; or whether it was consensual. While this is a part of every conversation of the Patricia Hearst story, this smacks a bit more of victim blaming than a straightforward discussion. Not surprisingly, much of this is because of the interview of Bill Harris. His strongest argument against Patricia's accusation was that the SLA was made up of "strong women" and "they wouldn't have let Patty get raped."[49] Once again, Harris puts the responsibility with the women of the argument—if not Patricia, then the other women of the SLA who would or should have protected Patricia. At no point in his account do the men of the SLA bear any of the responsibility for any of these events.

The final episode of the documentary, "The Verdict," does cover Patricia's verdict, as well as her commutation and eventual pardon. However, it also covers the eventual arrest of the other SLA members for the Crocker Bank robbery and the murder of Myrna Opsal. In the final episode of a documentary bearing her name, a huge chunk of the time is spent on the conviction of Bill and Emily Harris and Kathy Soliah. At several points, Bill is resentful and angry at Patricia. He attacks Patricia's privilege, saying, "It's really good to be rich and powerful … even though she participated in bombings, bank robberies, etc.—she wants a pardon in addition to her commutation."[50] He tells the camera that everyone, meaning all of the SLA members, suffered, "maybe Patty least of all."[51] His entitled and extremely out-of-date opinions on both women and Patricia populate all episodes of the series. With such a clear resentment against the subject of the series, it begs the question—how could Harris be remotely trusted as a source?

CNN's *The Radical Story of Patty Hearst* introduced many people to the story of Patricia Hearst and the SLA. However, relying so heavily on the interviews of men like Steven Weed and Bill Harris provides a skewed perspective of Patricia and her experience. Without any input from Patricia herself or any of her family, it is difficult to get any kind of balanced treatment of the story.

Guerrilla: The Taking of Patty Hearst (2004)

Another documentary that attempts to provide an account of the Patricia Hearst story is *Guerrilla: The Taking of Patty Hearst*, released in

2004. Other than the basic information included in every telling of this story, *Guerrilla* is very sympathetic to the SLA. At various points during the documentary, clips are shown from 1938's *Robin Hood* starring Errol Flynn. The clear implication is that the documentary believes the SLA to be a modern-day Robin Hood with men like Cinque standing in for the folk hero. Skipping Patricia's trial completely, the documentary essentially ends with the death of the six SLA members in the house during a confrontation with Los Angeles police.

While the title implies that the documentary will focus on Patricia Hearst, a more accurate title should at least include the SLA. It seems to the researcher that the documentarian(s) were attempting to capitalize on Patricia's name, much like the SLA were in 1974, wanting to draw attention to themselves with the Hearst name.

Podcasts

As a companion to *The Radical Story of Patty Hearst*, CNN released a companion podcast called *Patty Has a Gun* in January and February 2018. Over seven episodes, interviews with Jeffrey Toobin and others provide additional information for anyone who saw the documentary and wanted more. While it does offer some interesting insights, and it does have a few redeeming points, *Patty Has a Gun* makes many of the same mistakes as the accompanying documentary. The name itself proves problematic as it further puts the spotlight onto Patricia. The cover art is the infamous photo of Patricia as Tania with the beret and machine gun. Rather than choosing a photo that portrays her in a neutral circumstance, the podcast chose arguably the most controversial photo of Patricia Hearst.

The first episode, titled "The Kidnapping," which dropped on January 26, 2018, already gives a deeper understanding of Patricia than the documentary. Several pieces of history of the 1970s, such as the more than 2,000 political bombings every year and the very different media culture, give context to the Patricia Hearst story. Toobin, offered up as an expert on the case, gives his opinion on why he believes the case is still popular—that it is a "drama and a mystery" and that Patricia had become a symbol of the decadent ruination of the country.[52] It is also Toobin who further puts the Hearst fortune in context for the listeners. While many other podcasts make comparisons between the Hearsts and the Hiltons, Toobin rightly says that the wealth of the Hearsts is closer to the modern families of Gates, Zuckerberg, and Bezos.

The second episode, "Inside the SLA," released on February 2, 2018, again offers a new tidbit that was entirely missing from the documentary.

When discussing the question of whether Patricia had been raped or had consented to sex with Willie Wolfe, the podcast acknowledges that "in modern definitions—there was no way she could have consented."[53] In all of the conversations in the documentary, at no point was the modern understanding of consent discussed.

Much of the rest of the podcast closely follows the rest of the documentary—from the "birth of Tania" and the Hibernia Bank robbery to the arrest and trial and ending with her commutation and pardon. When asked if Patricia gives interviews, Toobin mentions that she does not give interviews and had declined to give any to CNN for the documentary or for his book. While a title card said the same thing in the documentary, the podcast conveys that information a bit easier. Without the interviews from Bill Harris, the podcast also feels more balanced and less misogynistic.

Beyond *Patty Has a Gun*, several other podcasts have covered the story in one way or another. However, only a few have delved with any kind of actual detail. Once again, the Parcast Network has a show called *Hostage* that covers the subject of this chapter. *Hostage* is hosted by Irma Blaco and Carter Roy, the latter being one of the more popular hosts on the podcast network. In the first of the three-part series, Blanco and Roy give background on the SLA, including the death of school superintendent Marcus Foster. Once the SLA decided on a political kidnapping, they pored over newspapers, and according to *Hostage*, it was Bill Harris who chose Patricia. This is the first real discussion of Patricia in the episode. The conversation on her background does not begin until twenty minutes into the forty-five-minute episode. Her childhood was described in much the same way as before, as a bubble that Patricia lived in, separated from the rest of the "real" world.

Here, Blanco and Roy delve into a conversation about Patricia's mental health. Few others have discussed her mental health before her kidnapping, only bringing that up after her arrest. While all hosts of the Parcast network shows make it clear they do not have psychological training, they have researched their individual topics thoroughly. In this episode, they describe Patricia's mental health before the kidnapping as "going downhill."[54] According to Blano and Roy, Patricia was dreaming of running away and had even considered suicide. She was feeling weak and vulnerable, meaning that she was the perfect target for the SLA—she was controllable. As with the 1988 film, this further helps to support the claims of Patricia Hearst that everything she did was a result of coercion.

In the second episode, the similarities between their version of the story and the 1988 film continue. Patricia was verbally abused by DeFreeze, and SLA members spent hours outside of her closet door reading propaganda literature to her. They were only giving her two small meals a day, and, by the time she was let out of the closet, her weight had fallen below one hundred pounds.[55] *Hostage* names both DeFreeze and Wolfe as those who had raped Patricia but made the point that even though the SLA would have seen this as consensual, Patricia had no choice and could not have refused.

The third and final episode of this series highlights the period where the FBI "stopped trying to find a fugitive and started trying to catch a criminal."[56] Blano and Roy state clearly that the SLA chose the name Tania for Patricia, a point that few podcasts make. While it seems inconsequential where the name came from—the SLA or Patricia herself—it speaks to Patricia's willingness, or lack thereof, to participate in the SLA. If she chose the name herself, then it would be difficult to refute her role in the organization. However, if the SLA chose the name for her, as *Hostage* and Patty Hearst say, it is further supportive of the coercive persuasion. They mention coercive persuasion yet again towards the end of the episode. The hosts end the series with the thought, "Patricia Hearst—whatever you think of her—is a true survivor."[57]

Other podcasts, such as *White Wine True Crime!* and *Hollywood Crime Scene*, are less formal in their production and telling of true crime. Therefore, their episodes on Patricia Hearst and her kidnapping are far less formal than one produced by CNN or those produced by the Parcast Network. *Hollywood Crime Scene* (*HCS*) does not begin on a good note as the hosts say that they "love stories of super rich freaks."[58] Both *HCS* and *White Wine True Crime!* (*WWTC*) compare Patricia to Paris Hilton, the granddaughter of Conrad Hilton and reality show star. While elements of the comparison are valid—rich, white women who were living off of the family name and family money—there is an inherent problem with the Hilton comparison. As Toobin points out in *Patty Has a Gun*, in comparison of family wealth, the Hearsts were closer to the Gateses, Bezoses, or Zuckerbergs. While many people know of the name Hilton, the level of family wealth is more abstract. However, when someone says Zuckerberg, that gives a modern audience of 2022 the ability to more fully realize the kind of wealth that Patricia's family had and why she was targeted by the SLA.

HCS also covers the interesting twist that provided Patricia's case ammunition during the fight for commutation. After her conviction, Patricia, her family, and her legal team were all fighting to have her sentence commuted by California Governor Ronald Reagan or President Jimmy Carter. One of the people helping the case was Representative Leo Ryan, who in 1979 went to Jonestown in the Republic of Guyana and was killed by members of the People's Temple. Soon after, more than nine hundred members of the People's Temple were found dead, most by their own hand, after having followed their leader Jim Jones to Guyana. As *HCS* says, the massacre at Jonestown put brainwashing into an entirely new light.

WWTC, much like *HCS*, is an informal, comedy true crime podcast. As such, their hosts are not striving to be informational; however, the hosts' opinions of Patricia Hearst are so negative that any person who is a casual listener may be automatically predisposed against Patricia. The hosts, Kari and Caitlin, and guest-host, Rachael, utter phrases like "Patty Hearst is such a fucking moron," "I really don't like her as a person," and "she's really stupid ... just really dumb."[59] When discussing why Patricia was taken by the SLA, where other podcasts have simply mentioned that SLA members were looking for someone who was accessible and well known, *WWTC* calls Patricia "low hanging fruit on the heiress tree" before asking, "How did they know she was going to be a dumbass?"[60]

The hosts of *WWTC* also attack Patricia's appearance as well as her voice in the recordings that were delivered to the press during the kidnapping. One host calls Patricia very plain and the others sigh in relief, saying they were "glad [she] brought it up."[61] While she "felt like an asshole," the host is disappointed when rich people look normal.[62] It's unclear exactly at what moment Patricia was looking "very plain" for their tastes—whether it was trying to live as a normal college student in the 1970s when beauty tastes were far different than they are now, or after she had been arrested after her kidnapping, or while she was in prison. Regardless, this commentary on Patricia's physical appearance again prejudices an audience against her for nothing more than "looking plain." In the same vein, the hosts comment on the tapes that Patricia recorded, calling her "so dramatic" before adding, "fuck you, Patty Hearst."[63]

As with documentaries and films, the treatment of Patricia Hearst by podcasts runs the gamut. While some, like *Hostage*, offer impartial observations about Patricia's mental health that provide new insights into the case, others merely tear Patricia down or simply make fun of her. If, as many of the new wave of true crime podcasts profess, the ultimate goal is to uplift the victims and women, then Patricia Hearst's story falls far short. Only occasionally is she given objective treatment without judgment or beratement.

Conclusion

After her sentence was commuted in 1978, Patricia Hearst married and had two children. After more than half a decade of trauma and imprisonment—first at the hands of the SLA and then in the California prison system—she embraced her passions. She raised her children, starred in several John Waters films, and began her successful career raising show dogs. In the 21st century, Patricia Hearst has retired from public life, but her place in public memory is still in flux. As with many cases in true crime, questions remain that are still debated; however, these questions all center around Patricia's character. While Patricia has given her official account of the events, documentaries, historians, and podcasts all call that account into question.

The range of examination of Patricia runs the spectrum from informational to advocacy. While some, especially podcasts, may begin as informational treatments, they quickly evolve into exploitative by attacking her actions or even calling Patricia harsh names without any objective consideration. Interestingly, the exploitative coverage crosses all media and all demographics. As with previous chapters, it has been less likely that women would exploit another woman, but there are female content creators who treat Patricia horribly. Happily, a few podcasts advocate for Patricia. These podcasts not only offer more detail about Patricia's life, but also examine her life, kidnapping, and ordeal with as much of an objective nature as possible.

Pop culture still needs to discuss whether Patricia is a victim or a villain—a survivor or a terrorist. In the midst of this discussion, Patricia herself, or her character, is left a smoldering pile after repeated attacks. Pop culture has continually victimized Patricia Hearst, simply by making her relive her most traumatic experience for the last forty-five years.

CHAPTER 7

Elizabeth "Liz" Kendall

Just the Facts

Before introducing her, an important point about Elizabeth Kendall is needed. This is not the name that she was born with, nor is it her married name. Her first name is Elizabeth, or Liz, but Kendall is a name chosen by Liz to maintain some anonymity during Theodore Robert Bundy's many trials and subsequent press. While some press and pop culture coverage have respected her choice to remain anonymous, others have included her real name, against her wishes. This project will respect her wish and only use her pseudonym of Elizabeth Kendall. Some sources included in the notes may give away her real name, but any inclusion of her actual name is unintentional.

Born at the end of the Second World War, Elizabeth Kendall grew up in Utah, the daughter of a "successful Utah doctor."[1] Before her older brother was born, Liz's mother was a nurse. The family was based in Ogden, Utah, about thirty miles north of Salt Lake City.[2] Not surprising for Utah, Liz's family was Mormon, but she describes them as "Jack Mormons," or "people who were Mormon in name but didn't follow all the church's rules."[3]

Through high school, Liz dated a boy named Ben, whom she was determined to marry as soon as they graduated. Her parents insisted that she needed a college education, but Liz told them "they would be wasting their money, because all [she] wanted out of life was to marry Ben and start having babies."[4] Liz's parents, however, won the fight and she went off to college. Her four years were not without bumps, both academically and personally. After her marriage ended she was on her own with her daughter and a semester left to finish her degree. Liz, along with Angie, her "friend since junior high school," decided to move to Utah, but first Liz had to "stay around long enough to collect [her] degree."[5]

In 1969, Liz and her daughter Molly moved to Seattle, Washington, to begin their new life. She began looking for a job, but knew that with a degree in business and family life, she was most likely going to get a job as a secretary.[6] Being comfortable on a college campus, the University of Washington was her first choice, and she ended up working as a secretary at the medical school. On September 26, 1969, Liz and Angie decided on a night out at the Sandpiper Tavern in the University District.[7] It was at this tavern that Liz met Theodore Robert Bundy. They danced, drank, and talked before going back to Liz's house. According to Liz, they slept in her bed together without having sex on that first night. When she woke the next morning, her bed was empty and she found Ted in the kitchen with Molly in her high chair and Ted making breakfast for them.

News of the Day

A search of Newspapers.com for Liz Kendall or Elizabeth Kendall for the timeframe of 1974–1989, the time of the offender's first arrest to his execution, results in fewer than sixty articles. Most of them are articles published in 1981 after Liz published her memoir, *The Phantom Prince*. Either in book reviews or as a reason to bring the offender's story back to the headlines, they use the author's pen name. In an article written in *The Salt Lake Tribune* on October 25, 1981, the author, Con Psarras, names Liz only as "Ms. Kendall" or "the author."[8] Psarras goes further, describing Liz's book not as a love story but "an account of how Ms. Kendall survived her love for the offender."[9]

However, other articles, written the year of the offender's execution, included not only details of Liz's life, but also her actual name. Written two days before the offender was executed, "Authors Try to Make Sense of Bundy" was published by the *Tallahassee Democrat*, less than three hours from the prison where the offender spent his last years. George Thurston writes on three books that best cover the life of the offender, including *The Phantom Prince*. Thurston's treatment of Liz is problematic from the beginning as he includes her real surname as if it was her middle name. The inclusion of her real name means that her anonymity has been destroyed. To describe Liz's relationship with the offender, Thurston says that she "knew Bundy for several years" and described herself as "Bundy's lover and fiancée for more than six years."[10]

"Trail of Death: Bundy Killed," was written by Salim Jiwa for *The Providence* in British Columbia in February 1989, when the offender was executed by the state of Florida. In an effort to connect the offender's crimes to British Columbia, Jiwa and Royal Canadian Mounted Police Staff Sgt. Fred Bodnaruk use Liz's book to find accounts of the offender traveling across the Canadian border. Calling Vancouver a "favorite playground" of the offender, Jiwa namedrops *The Phantom Prince* and Liz Kendall's name.[11] Right after introducing the book and Kendall's name, Jiwa gives her married name, saying that Liz had chosen to use the pseudonym "because she had by then concluded that her lover of nearly eight years was a vicious killer."[12] From the moment that Jiwa introduces her real name, he does not use her chosen pseudonym again. The one spot of respect that he shows her, that others will not, is that he gives her the credit of being "among the first people to report her suspicions about Bundy to Seattle police, after she heard they were looking for a suspect named Ted and she saw a composite drawing of the suspect."[13]

While this section typically refers to news of the day, in this case, the 1970s, it would be incomplete without including the recent journalism on Liz. As discussed later in this chapter, 2020 saw the release of the Amazon documentary *Falling for a Killer* and the release of the updated version of *The Phantom Prince*. With so much attention being paid to Liz and her story, she began to appear in news stories again. This time, there was a noticeable lack of respect for her choice of a pseudonym or desire for anonymity. For example, *The U.S. Sun* includes her real name in a bolded subheading in a larger font than the rest of the article.[14] *Women's Health*, in an article called "Who is Ted Bundy's Ex-Girlfriend, Elizabeth 'Liz' Kendall, From 'Falling for a Killer'?" starts this unmasking of a sorts from the very beginning. The first subtitle of the article simply states, "For starters, Liz Kendall isn't her real name."[15] After an introduction, the next subtitle includes Liz's real name, in a larger and bolded font than the rest of the article. The exact same thing happens in an article titled "Who Is Ted Bundy's Ex-Girlfriend Liz Kendall? Here's What You Need to Know," written for *Good Housekeeping*. Her real name is disclosed in the very first paragraph and again in large bold letters in the middle of the page, highlighting it.[16] The list of online articles published in 2019 and 2020 that out Liz's real name is lengthy and comprehensive. In some cases, like an article published on May 3, 2019, on *Refinery29*, her real name is included in the title.[17]

The treatment of Liz in the news media is a fascinating look at how those closest to an offender can be treated, not just during a trial or in the years immediately following the crimes. It has been more than fifty years since Liz walked into that bar and met the offender and more than thirty years since his execution, and yet her life is still deeply impacted. If she is still using her real name, the name that she tried to hide throughout the 1980s by adopting a pseudonym, that name is now heavily compromised. With the new wave of true crime focusing on offenders like this one, Liz is thrust once again into the spotlight. By including her real name alongside her alias, the media and pop culture are not only disrespecting her wishes but also potentially putting her life in danger by shining a light on details of her life that she is trying to keep hidden.

Books

As discussed above, *The Phantom Prince* is a fascinating primary source for a study on Liz Kendall. It is, in fact, the way that the world was introduced to Liz Kendall, Liz's pseudonym to protect herself, daughter Molly, and their family from additional unwanted attention. This alone makes the book an invaluable resource. Liz wrote this book in 1981 as a catharsis and as an attempt to provide for herself and Molly after their lives were turned upside down following the offender's trials. Published eight years before the execution of the offender, by the beginning of the latest true crime wave of the 21st century, the book had been out of print for years. Those that wished to know Liz's thoughts on her life during that time had to try to find a copy on eBay or from a library. It represents a pre-served moment in time of Liz, attempting to sift through the ruins of her life.

What adds to its value in this study is the updated version that was published by Abrams Press in 2020. The new edition includes a new pre-face, a new afterword, and an epilogue written by Molly, Liz's daughter, who is telling her story for the first time. Liz begins the new preface, writing in May 2017, having learned online that a "new Ted Bundy movie was being made."[18] After doing a quick search that garnered more than twenty thousand hits, she found news "about 'my story' being told in a new Ted Bundy movie."[19] Stunned, she asks, "[H]ow could they tell my story without ever speaking to me?"[20] After three decades of having films made about her life, by 2017 Liz was done with having no say. Continuing with her insight in the filmmaking process of *Extremely Wicked*, Liz says, "[A]fter getting off on the wrong foot initially, the collaboration we had with the film was a good one."[21]

During her and her daughter Molly's experience working with the production of *Extremely Wicked*, Liz says they "decided it was essential" that they tell their own story as they experienced it, leading to the updated edition of *The Phantom Prince*.[22] This self-exploration also motivated Liz to participate in *Falling for a Killer*, a documentary produced by Amazon and directed by Trish Wood. As discussed later in this chapter, this documentary series is one of the most comprehensive and well-rounded treatments of not only Liz, but of all women involved in this case.

The preface and afterword provide enormous insight into Liz's state of mind fifty years after her first meeting with the offender and thirty-five years after the original release of *The Phantom Prince*. Liz notes that when she wrote the original text, she still "cared deeply for Ted" and it "took years of work" for her to accept "who he was and what he had done."[23] This clarity continues into the afterword. Liz admits that, as she reread the original book, there were pages she "felt like ripping out" because they made her so uncomfortable.[24] Liz admits that revisiting *The Phantom Prince* after so many years is her chance to write a "more clear-eyed version" of the statements she wrote in 1981.[25] One significant change is to the statement that originally read, "The tragedy is that this warm and loving man is driven to kill." With the help of time, therapy, and introspection, she says now that the same statement should read, "The tragedy is that this violent and manipulative man directed his murderous rage at innocent young women to satisfy his insane urges."[26]

Now that *The Phantom Prince* is not only back in print, but also with Liz's additions that have come with decades of retrospection, the book offers one of the best insights into Liz as a person—not a character in a film or a faceless name in a documentary. With the additions, readers can see just how much she has grown since first writing the book in the year after the offender's Florida trial.

Movies

As the offender is considered one of the most prolific killers in American history, there have been several pop culture iterations based upon his life. The ones chosen for study in this chapter are those that include characters based upon Liz. As discussed earlier, most of them do change the character's name to protect Liz's identity, but this is not the case for all. There are other movies, documentaries, or shows that cover the case but do not include Liz. For example, *Bundy: A Legacy of Evil*, released in 2009, focused entirely on the offender without any mention of Liz at all, therefore it is not included in this study.

The Deliberate Stranger (1986)

Based on the book *Bundy: The Deliberate Stranger* by Richard Larsen, published in 1980, the TV movie was broadcast on NBC in May of 1986. The book was turned into a script by Harper Anderson and was directed by Marvin Chomsky.[27] Larsen, a reporter for the *Seattle Times*, interacted many times with the offender during his time working for Dan Evans's governor's campaign in 1972. He then went on to cover the offender's various trials for *The Seattle Times*. Having met the offender several times,

Larsen provides an insider's look at the story but does not have the same insight into Liz. The portrayal of Liz will be covered, but first, a few comments on other elements of the film.

The Deliberate Stranger holds the unique position of being the only pop culture iteration produced before the offender's execution. The offender's lawyer, Polly Nelson, in her book *Defending the Devil*, said that he had no interest in seeing the movie.[28] The film, running three hours and five minutes, aired over two nights and starred Mark Harmon as the offender. Casting in these projects has been a controversial point of several iterations of this offender, particularly with *Extremely Wicked, Shockingly Vile, and Evil*, produced in 2018, which cast former Disney star Zac Efron as the offender. *The Deliberate Stranger*, however, creates a pattern of casting handsome stars in this role, especially considering that this movie aired the same year Harmon was named *People*'s Sexiest Man Alive. The film frequently compares the offender to a "young JFK" or calls him "Seattle's answer to JFK."[29] By casting Harmon and Efron, both projects were trying to use attractive actors to convey the charming and attractive nature of the offender, thereby helping viewers understand why and how Liz spent so much time in a relationship with him.

As the film begins, a brown VW Bug drives through Seattle with a male voiceover telling viewers that "for most, it ended in Miami in 1979 ... [but] it didn't end for the families, husbands, and lovers of the victims. This is dedicated to them and to the few men who didn't give up."[30] The offender is clearly in the VW Bug, his car of choice. And in addition to this known killer driving happily through the streets, there is a male voice honoring the men attached to the case—the police officers, husbands, lovers (male only), and presumably fathers of the victims. While all of those men absolutely deserve this honor, this is ignoring the women who were involved with the case—as law enforcement, mothers, sisters, friends, classmates, and lovers (without the heterosexuality presumption). There were at least two female police officers in different jurisdictions who worked on the offender's case, and this voiceover overlooks them entirely by dedicating the film to "the few men who didn't give up."

The Deliberate Stranger begins a long tradition of changing Liz's name entirely. Most of the fictional films about the offender that feature a character based on Liz change her name, but one wonders whether this is to protect her identity or to have the freedom to further manipulate a character that is so clearly based on Liz. This iteration is renamed Cass and Molly Kendall is renamed Jenny. The first introduction of Cass comes after the offender finishes driving under the voiceover. He arrives at her apartment and often adopts a condescending tone with her while showering Jenny with attention. Overall, the character of Cass is portrayed as a timid woman who is more afraid of losing her boyfriend than the possibility that he may be a killer. When she asks him if he is cheating on her, he gets defensive and calls her a "rejected little girl."[31] After this verbal attack, Cass shrinks back and says, "You're right—it's me—it's me. It's just that [that other girl] I can't compete with that."[32] There is no evidence that Liz was suspicious that the offender was cheating on her, and this scene only shows Cass, and by extension, Liz, as a weak-willed woman who is clinging to her man, regardless of what he does.

At various points, the film flies close to the truth by allowing Liz to shine through in Cass, but those moments are quickly muted. While in the offender's bathroom, she finds plaster of Paris, the same material the "Seattle Ted" had been using to trick women into thinking he was injured. Worried, Cass calls the police, just as Liz did in real life, and just like Liz, Cass was told that the police had checked out the offender and removed him from the suspect list. While the film deserves some credit for actually having Cass call the police, rather than a friend of hers, as with some of the iterations, her desperate hope that maybe, just maybe, he is innocent, counteracts that credit.

The next time his guilt is questioned is when a friend brings it up while she and Cass are at work. When the coworker asks if Cass has considered that her Ted is THE Ted, Cass shifts into a defensive denial mode. Cass yells, "You make me sick!" while she mixes her yogurt. Deflating, she says, "I just miss him so much. I wish I could see him. I wish I could touch him."[33] Not only does this make Cass seem desperate for the offender's attention and love, but also the film immediately cuts to the offender picking up a hitchhiker. By putting those two scenes together, the film is hammering home the offender's crimes while also making Cass look like a lovesick fool to be this in love with the man who was committing these crimes.

This point continues to be made when Cass and the offender are preparing for a trip to Utah to visit Cass's parents for Christmas. A friend, watching her pack in her bedroom, she asks again if Cass has called the police. Cass admits that she did call once but hung up. The friend, who, according to IMDb is called Bobbi, but whose name is lost in the film, asks Cass, "Why didn't you talk to me before?"[34] Pausing her packing, Cass tells her friend that she cannot believe it is possible, that "every time I talk to him, he's so wonderful."[35] Even as Bobbi shows genuine sympathy at Cass's situation, all that Cass can do is talk about how wonderful the offender is. Immediately after this, Cass, Jenny, and the offender spend a warm and happy Christmas with Cass's parents in Utah. There is a scene where the family sings Christmas carols with the offender playing the piano. Jenny brags to her grandparents that the offender was going to be her dad one day. When all of these factors are combined—Cass's almost blind devotion to the offender, the amount of camera time dedicated to the offender's crimes, and the scenes of a happy family—this creates a picture of Cass as a woman who may, like the audience, know about his crimes and stays with him anyway.

After this happy Christmas, things begin to unravel pretty quickly for the offender, and by extension Cass. The male police officers make a big show of finally matching Seattle Ted to Utah Ted, and Mark Harmon's face finally appears on their computer match. Cass gets the nerve to go to the police station and speaks to a female police officer as the film finally acknowledges the female law enforcement officers who worked on the case. This step in the right direction is a strange one though as Cass admits many things to the officer, who goes unnamed, that seem entirely out of character. During their interview, Cass talks about a time that the offender strangled her during sex. But the very strange part of the conversation comes when she admits that she has been studying the times and dates of the crimes and has been comparing them with the offender's movements. Cass goes from yelling at a coworker in the middle of a lunchroom to creating her own murder board to track her boyfriend's movements and match them to the disappearances of women over multiple states? This feels more like an overcorrection—an attempt to try and fix Cass, perhaps over a sense of guilt over the film's treatment of Liz.

The film ends with the offender going to prison and, since the film aired three years before his execution, there was no coda. There was no final act for Cass and Jenny—no resolution for them. Any viewers in 1986 or since are left with the impression that the woman who was with him during his crimes and stood by him during his trial was lovesick and hugely devoted to him up until his conviction. While the film was praised for its faithful portrayal of the offender, Liz's life was left open to manipulation as it was written as the character of Cass. With only a handful of years between the most traumatic events in her life and the release of this film, Liz was likely retraumatized by this telling and by seeing herself as Cass. Liz has spoken openly about her struggle with low self-esteem, and seeing Cass as the first pop culture interpretation of her trauma would send anyone into a spiral. Unfortunately, for Liz, unflattering portrayals would continue to come for decades.

Ted Bundy (2002)

The next film that includes a version of Liz is 2002's *Ted Bundy*, written by Stephen Johnston and Matthew Bright and directed by Bright. With an estimated budget of $1.2 million, the overall worldwide gross was a mere $68,716. Unsurprisingly, the film has a 41 percent on *Rotten Tomatoes*, a score determined by reviews of movie critics. It stars Michael Reilly Burke as the offender and Boti Bliss as Lee, the character based on Liz.[36] This film spends far more time on his crimes with a much more violent lens than some of the other iterations. By doing this, it not only shocks the viewer with the brutality of the offender's crimes but also colors the viewer's interpretation of Lee, and by extension—Liz.

Lee is introduced in an entirely disturbing way. The offender follows a random woman home, where he watches her undress and masturbates in the bushes. After being caught by a neighbor, who recognizes the offender, he leaves and calls Lee, his clothes still wet with the water the neighbor threw on him to make him leave. Lee, already in bed, answers the phone and knows immediately that it is him. This implies that not only does he call frequently but also that she is used to answering his calls, regardless of the hour. They meet, presumably the next day, at the park, where he plays with Lee's daughter. In the same scene, Lee wistfully says, "One day maybe I won't have to share you with so many women."[37] While it's clear that Lee is talking about the other women he was seeing in addition to Lee—that apparently their relationship was not yet exclusive— it's a strange statement while he is still playing with her daughter. Some may interpret her words as a jealous reaction to her own daughter.

In addition to showing much more of the violence than other films, especially *The Deliberate Stranger*, which was bound by TV censors, *Ted Bundy* is also more sexually explicit than other films on the subject. In a few explicit sex scenes between Lee and the offender, the actor playing Lee was topless. This literal stripping down of Lee serves to further victimize her. In the middle of sex, the offender wants to try a new position, one that she calls dirty. Lee is clearly uncomfortable, but when she refuses, he begins to strangle her. Once he finally releases her, rather than being outraged or even calling the police, Lee apologizes to him. In the next sex scene, he convinces her to agree to be tied to the bed. It quickly becomes clear that he is not pleased with the situation and he yells, "Can't you just lay there and pretend to be dead?!"[38] While still lying there, tied to the bed, she says, "I love you, Ted; I'll do whatever you want!"[39] Even while naked and tied to the bed, Lee is telling him that she will do whatever he wants, including pretending to be dead.

Once the offender is arrested, Lee finally seems to figure out that her boyfriend is the killer of the women in Seattle and Utah. There is nothing in this film about Lee calling or going to the police station with concerns. There are no scenes of Lee finding plaster of Paris or crutches in his apartment. Any of Liz's intuition that the offender may have been THE Ted is missing from the character of Lee. Lee is seemingly blindsided by his arrest. Sitting alone at her kitchen table, reading his letters while crying, she does not want to see him. However, when she sees on TV that he may have a girlfriend, she immediately goes to the prison to visit him. Again, this only serves to make Lee, and by extension Liz, appear to care only about whether or not he's cheating on her. She goes to the prison and, instead of asking whether he has committed the crimes of which he is accused, she only asks if he is cheating on her.

As the first film made after his execution, *Ted Bundy* is able to show Lee trying to deal with what she now knows, but also the execution. Coincidentally, these are the only scenes where Lee is included after going to the prison to ask him if he is cheating on her. The first shows Lee waking up from a nightmare, obviously upset, and crying, "How could I have ever touched him?"[40] Knowing Liz's struggle with guilt and self-image after the offender's arrest, viewers may appreciate seeing this in the film. However, most viewers do not know this context, so this only further shows to those viewers a version of Lee who is blaming herself for being involved with a killer. The next, and last, scene of Lee in the film comes just after his execution. Staying with the violent and brutal nature of the movie, the preparation for and the actual execution is shown in gruesome detail. After the brutal execution, a series of reaction shots are shown, including Lee's. Sitting on a sofa, next to a man whom the viewer can only presume is her husband, they are watching news coverage of the execution. Shaking her head, she says, "I can't believe it. I was with him for years. Who was Ted Bundy?"[41] Once again, with the context of reading Liz's book, especially with the 2020 update, this could be interpreted as Lee still dealing with trauma. It could be easily believed that, even after fifteen years, Liz was trying to understand who the man was and how she could have loved him. However, this context is missing—this is perhaps the greatest crime against Lee/Liz. Without the context, Lee looks like a woman who is still obsessed with him and still trying to figure him out, even after his death.

Deeper context and deeper character development would have allowed the audience to understand Lee as a person instead of a secondary character. The exact same scenes would have been much more powerful and provided a far more faithful portrayal of Liz.

Extremely Wicked, Shockingly Evil, and Vile (2019)

The most recent, and controversial, film about this offender is named after words spoken by the judge in the Florida case, who called the offender's act "extremely wicked, shockingly evil, and vile." This film was directed by Joe Berlinger and premiered at the Sundance Film Festival in January 2019. Heavily based upon *The Phantom Prince*, the screenplay was written by Michael Werwie. Depending on where one looks, sometimes Liz is included as a writer on the project, and sometimes she is not. The film was sold to Netflix, where it premiered on May 3, 2019.

While it should have received attention for being the first film to be told largely from Liz's point of view, most of the critical and popular attention surrounded the casting of former Disney star Zac Efron as the offender. As discussed earlier, this was not the first time that a man celebrated by pop culture to be "attractive" was cast to play this offender. Even Efron himself was concerned about the possibility of his public persona "glorifying" the offender and his crimes. His portrayal was generally praised; however, the film itself received mixed reviews.

For a film that is meant to be from Liz's point of view and based upon her memoir, *Extremely Wicked* does not spend nearly enough time on Liz herself. It even begins with a lie, with Liz visiting the offender in prison, something that never happened. After he escaped from prison in Colorado, she never had contact with him again. From there, a flashback takes the audience back to Seattle in 1969 as Liz begins her new life in Washington state. She meets the offender and the night goes much as Liz tells it in her book. After the romantic moment they had over breakfast the morning after, there is a montage of what would normally be a happy family—days in the snow, birthdays, and warm memories. This montage sets up one of the large problems with *Extremely Wicked*—viewers may be tempted to forget that the man on the screen is a notorious serial killer. Combining original news footage with the home movies featuring Efron makes it all the more difficult to separate the two.

Liz is "reintroduced" after the offender is arrested in Utah. After he returns from Utah, she slaps him. When he tries to explain his arrest was because he ran a stop sign, she yells, "How many stop signs did you run?"[42] He charms her into believing him, and when the trial begins she is there, sitting right behind him. When they are at home, they seem to have a "normal" relationship, drinking, listening to music, and dancing. Liz's "normal" drinking escalates after his conviction and subsequent escapes. After getting a call at work from Colorado authorities, she goes home and pours herself a very large drink. By the time the offender is on trial in Florida, Liz is clearly battling her addiction to alcohol. As this is an important part of Liz's journey that is rarely discussed, much less mentioned in movies, it is great to see it included here. There is a scene, shown after the offender's conviction, in which Liz throws all her alcohol bottles away before hugging Joanna. Symbolizing Liz's step toward sobriety, its inclusion is powerful, but, knowing Liz's story, this one scene falls short. The same can be said of Liz trying to find her way through the trauma of finding out her boyfriend is a serial killer. There are a few scenes that show

Liz both depressed and enthralled with the Florida trial. What is missing is the fascinating story of how she managed to survive all of this and come through the other side, sober and healthy. At the very end of the movie, there are a few lines of text saying, "Liz and Molly still reside in Washington state. Liz has been sober for decades."[43] Again, it is great that this is finally being included; however, it is far too little. With the inclusion of just a few scenes and a couple of lines, Liz's trauma and ordeal trying to wade through the trauma is minimalized.

At the end of the movie, viewers are told it is now 1989, and viewers familiar with the case know that was the year of the offender's execution. Liz is shown in what looks like a manager position at her job, hiring more women in her department, when she gets a letter from the offender. She goes to the prison to see him and the film returns to the very first scene. Liz repeatedly asks him if he actually did what was accused of, and he repeatedly says he is innocent. Frustrated, Liz yells, "All these years you've had your hands around my neck—release me! You need to release me, Ted!"[44] Not only did she never visit him in prison, but she also never received this final letter. In *Falling for a Killer*, Liz's daughter Molly admits to burning the final letter from the offender before her mother could read it. Molly did admit this to Liz at some point before the filming of the documentary. Additionally, and more troubling, Liz's declaration implies that she requires the offender to give her permission to move on. While it would be great to believe that her declaration is a metaphor for how much her relationship with the offender strangled the rest of her life, that subtext is not there. What is on the screen is Liz begging for a serial killer to release his perhaps literal stranglehold on her.

Extremely Wicked, Shockingly Evil, and Vile can be credited with bringing much-needed attention to Liz Kendall, even if it falls far short of giving her story justice. In addition to reminding the true crime community that Liz exists, the movie also prompted Liz and Molly to revisit *The Phantom Prince* and participate in the *Falling for a Killer* documentary. The initial shock of "her story" being told without her input signaled to Liz that she needed to tell her story herself. Without *Extremely Wicked*, two of the most significant iterations in Liz Kendall's story may not have been made.

TV/Documentaries

Ted Bundy: Mind of a Monster

As previously stated, many episodes on this offender do not include information on Liz, and, therefore, were not included in this study.

However, this smaller documentary was included because not only did it cover Liz, but it also removed a lot of agency from Liz and her story. Aired on August 18, 2019, on Investigation Discovery, this two-hour documentary attempts to delve into the psychology of the offender.

One of the people interviewed in this documentary is a woman named MaryLynne Chino. She says she met the offender in September 1969 when he met a friend of hers; the famous photo of Liz and the offender appears on the screen. Chino describes them as a "threesome in Seattle, Washington."[45] She continues telling her story, saying that she was the friend with whom Liz talked about the famous Ted sketch. With Liz "distressed because she didn't want Ted to find out," Chino claims she was the one who called the police to report the offender and inquire about his VW Bug.[46] Police told her that they were looking for a bronze VW, not a beige one. She told Liz and "they were relieved."[47]

This is contradictory to all other evidence presented in the history of this case. Liz herself admits that she called the police on several occasions before going to the station to speak with the police after the offender's arrest. If corroboration is needed, there are interviews with the police officers she spoke with, talking about Liz's bravery. Additionally, there are some recordings of interviews that were done with Liz at police stations. With this preponderance of evidence, all that this episode does is remove the strength and bravery from Liz. Investigation Discovery is an incredibly popular true crime cable channel. It would be very easy to imagine that many people could watch this and get much of their knowledge of Liz from it. Therefore, they may get a very wrong idea that someone other than Liz called the police, not once, but multiple times, putting not only her relationship but also her life in danger.

Conversations with a Killer (2019)

After nearly a decade off the screen, the offender reappeared in 2019. Whether it was the thirtieth anniversary of the execution or the latest wave of interest in true crime is unknown, but several iterations have appeared in the last couple of years.[48] While the cause of this revival of a sort is unknown, one of the first "new" documentaries is well known—*Conversations with a Killer.* Not only is this different because of the decade in which it was produced, but it was produced for Netflix, the streaming service. Premiering on January 24, 2019, the thirtieth anniversary of the execution, it was directed by Joe Berlinger, the same person who directed *Extremely Wicked, Shockingly Evil, and Vile.* The four episodes are comprised of audio interviews and archival footage of the offender edited together with interviews with those who knew him, those who survived him, and those who hunted him. While Liz is discussed, she did not agree to be interviewed for this documentary.

While there are four episodes of *Conversations with a Killer*, only two of them deal with Liz in any real way. The name of the documentary comes from taped conversations reporter Stephen Michaud had with the offender from the 1980s while he was in a Florida prison. Michaud and others said that he enjoyed talking about himself more than almost any other topic. It is during this conversation about himself, giving his own backstory, that most of the discussion of Liz occurs. The documentary describes her as a woman who "fell madly in love," while he calls her "somewhat meek."[49] He continues, saying their relationship had issues because they did not have a lot in common and that he was "terribly jealous of her."[50] Descriptions of Liz in this first episode almost entirely come from the offender himself. Considering his crimes against women and his documented abuse of Liz, any information coming from him has to be immediately questioned for its validity. By relying so heavily on these tapes, giving credence to his words, this documentary allows for the dismissal of Liz and her overall role in this story.

In the second episode, the documentary redeems itself a bit by including Liz's voice. A few short interviews of Liz from the 1970s are aired, including an interview with police. Beyond this, the narrator mentions Liz going to the police with her concerns. The first step in the right direction is hearing Liz's own voice—literally allowing her to speak for herself. Having any coverage that does not come directly from the offender also begins to make up for episode one. Further proof of the war between episode one and episode two is the coverage of Liz's interview with the police. Whereas Liz is described as "somewhat meek" in the first episode, she is heard going to the police because her instincts were telling her something was off—instincts that were eventually proven right. While this episode is better than the first, not enough is done to counteract the words of the offender. People tuned in to hear about his crimes directly from the offender's mouth; how much attention would they pay to any other voice?

One must wonder why there is so little attention paid to Liz, especially given that this is the same director of the film that attempted to tell the story from Liz's point of view. Perhaps it is that lack of attention that prompted Berlinger to make *Extremely Wicked*, but how many true crimes fans would or did watch them both? Given the negative press surrounding *Extremely Wicked*, it seems more likely that those interested would have gravitated towards *Confessions of a Killer*. In doing so, they would entirely miss any real discussion of Liz.

Ted Bundy: Falling for a Killer (2020)

As mentioned above, in addition to cooperating with *Extremely Wicked* and contemplatively updating *The Phantom Prince*, Liz decided to participate in this series. Produced by Amazon Studios and directed by Trish Dash, Liz writes in *The Phantom Prince* that she was interested in the project because of "its emphasis on the viewpoints of many of the women involved in this tragic story."[51] She praises the crew for providing "a calm and safe environment to talk about a difficult subject."[52] She also makes the point that she continues to use her pseudonym, Elizabeth Kendall, to "spare Molly's father's family name [from] further association with Ted's crimes."[53] This strongly makes the point that, even while her real name is readily available, Liz is still dedicated to using her pseudonym. Her reasoning is not only to continue to protect her own anonymity, but also to protect her daughter and the family of her ex-husband. The documentary series respects her wishes, referring to her only as Liz or Elizabeth Kendall.

Over the five episodes in the series, the documentary focuses on the women who "fell" for the offender, meaning they either fell for him romantically or fell for his murderous ruse. Given that this is the first time that Liz has agreed to give several in-depth interviews about her life, including her time with the offender, she is one of the main threads through the series. Significantly, the entire series begins with an interview with Liz. Putting Liz before anyone else, especially the offender, which is what many other documentaries have done, supports its claim that *Falling for a Killer* put the stories of women before all others. The narrator continues, calling out the retelling of the story over and over again; many times, the story was told by men. Liz tells the viewer that this is her story, "from beginning to end."[54]

Liz describes her background and her life before she met the offender in Seattle. Much of this information can also be found in *The Phantom Prince*, but Liz expands on this by talking about the beginning of her alcoholism. Mentioning the shyness that she describes in the book, she says that she began drinking in college to deal with the shyness and to try to be more social.[55] She references the drinking again when describing the night she met the offender. After meeting him, she was too drunk to drive home, so he brought her home. While this is a common occurrence, especially for young people, it is a pattern for Liz that will only continue to worsen. She continues to talk about her addiction throughout the series, an addiction that only got worse during the trauma of living with Ted.

Molly Kendall is introduced in the first episode, also in her first ever interview. She describes meeting the offender on that first morning after Liz brought him home and how he taught her how to ride a bike. She says that he read her favorite book to her. She "thought he was delightful" and she "trusted him 100 percent."[56] While this was her impression as a child, as an adult Molly wonders if the offender merely used her as "part of the plot to get her mother."[57] As time passed, the offender became more inappropriate with her. Molly tells a story of playing hide and seek with him and when she found him, he was naked under the blanket. He said that he was only naked because he could become invisible but his clothes could not. As she told the story in 2019, she admitted that she did not tell Liz about it until years later.

Liz's suspicions about the offender started at the end of the second episode, when the sketch from Lake Sammamish came out.[58] After the sketch is published in Seattle area papers, Liz takes it home and compares it to every photo of Bundy that she had in her albums. In episode three of the series, the offender had moved to Utah to go to law school. Soon after that, Liz describes getting a phone call from an old friend who told her that she did not want to scare her, but "it's happening down there in Utah."[59] This prompts Liz to call the police for the first time. Taking some of the photos that look close to the sketch, she met with officers with the Kings County Sheriff's Office. After being told the detective would check it out and hearing nothing, Liz called and followed up. She describes that call as if "the detective couldn't remember who [she] was."[60]

The escalation of her suspicion continued the longer time the offender spent in Utah. Concerned, Liz tried to keep up with the latest news of the "Utah Ted." While reading about the kidnapping of Carol DaRounch, who was abducted in Salt Lake on August 16, 1975, Liz read Carol's account of the brown VW Bug. "Borderline hysterical," she called the police again.[61] She described the detective's response as basically "why are you calling now?" Feeling frustrated, she asked her father to get involved because her father had contacts in the Utah police departments. Liz also felt that her father would be taken more seriously by the police as a man than she would as a woman. However, when she asked her father to go to the police, he scolded her, saying, "If you're wrong, you're going to ruin Ted's career."[62] As Liz sits in whatever set was prepped for her interview, she contemplates this, perhaps for the first time in decades. She says that, as a parent herself, she "would be calling the next day"[63] if her child had asked her to go to the police. Still contemplative, Liz calls the memory "traumatic."[64]

After this traumatic encounter with her own father, going to the police felt like a nonstarter for her. However, a glimmer of hope came to Liz when she spoke to the offender's landlord. The landlord mentioned that she had spoken to a female police officer, and Liz hoped that a female officer may finally listen to her. Kathleen McChesney,[65] also interviewed in *Falling for a Killer*, was the first female officer in Kings County, and she tells the camera how brave she thought it was for Liz to "turn in [her] partner."[66] Liz continues to meet with Kathleen after the offender's arrest, providing the police with information. She also begins to seek help to deal with her issues resulting from the trauma of dating a man arrested for multiple disappearances. Liz tells the camera that, while he was in jail, the offender began to write letters "right away," and she began drinking "a lot to shut [her] mind up."[67] Her therapist insisted that she make a choice between her past with the offender and a future without him. Not yet ready to break away, Liz says she recommitted to the offender and told the police she would not continue to cooperate with the investigation. "I can't explain it," Liz says. I "look[ed] at his face and thought, this man is not a killer."[68] Kathleen reappears on the screen and speaks thoughtfully on "why people stay." After decades in law enforcement, she is able to say that it is "very unfair to judge why people stay in relationships that are unhealthy. … It has to do with hope; they hope the person they love hasn't done the thing they're charged with."[69]

This inclusion of the crucial relationship between Liz and Kathleen continues to prove the importance of *Falling for a Killer* in the telling of Liz's story. For the first time, Liz has someone in law enforcement who believes her and is able to give her purpose, even for a little while. At a time when many police departments—local, state, and federal—were considering allowing women into their ranks, Kathleen proves why female officers are crucial to law enforcement. Kathleen not only praises Liz's bravery for turning in her partner but also helps the audience understand why Liz stayed with the offender. Liz's decision to stand with him during a large part of the trial is one of the biggest reasons people cannot understand her story. However, having Kathleen's support will go a long way in helping those same individuals understand and hopefully will help restore Liz's reputation.

In the final episode, covering the years between the offender's conviction and his execution, Liz and Molly discuss their long road to rebuilding their lives. Liz says that she was not able to start the process until he was in prison in Florida. She began seeing a new counselor, who was helping her. However, she was still deep in her addiction to alcohol. The counselor told her that he would not see her anymore if she continued to drink. So, she got into a recovery program and got sober.[70] Liz says that she spent years "working, working, working to rebuild" her life.[71] Much like the update to *The Phantom Prince*, this offers the audience insight into not only what Liz is like today, but also how she got through unimaginable trauma. She had to completely rebuild her and her daughter's lives. While trying to do that, she has had to deal with movies, documentaries, and now podcasts monopolizing on her life. At the end of *Falling for a Killer*, Liz declares that this "is the end of [her] participation" in anything to do with the offender.[72] Having finally said her piece, she is ready to put the subject to bed.

One final note on *Falling for a Killer*: in addition to its wonderful treatment of Liz and Molly, the documentary also sets a new standard for how to properly represent women and victims. Interviews were done with as many friends and family members of the women killed by the offender as possible. While interviewing those who knew victims is not out of the norm, these interviews tell the audience about who the women were before their lives were taken by the offender. As discussed in other chapters, one of the most important areas of emphasis created by the latest wave of true crime is humanizing the women and reminding audiences that victims were friends, students, and daughters long before they were victims. *Falling for a Killer* does exactly that for each of the victims. One can only hope that other documentaries take heed and follow in Trish Dash's footsteps.

Podcasts

With the overall "popularity"[73] of this offender, the case has been the subject of several podcasts. To stay with the purpose of this study, only episodes that discuss Liz will be included. However, searches on several podcast apps for episodes on Liz, using her pseudonym or her real name, garner no results. The only episodes where Liz is discussed in depth are ones where the hosts are doing an analysis of *Extremely Wicked*. Several episodes on the offender were listened to, but they included only basic information on Liz. For example, in *True Crime Brewery's* episode "Surviving Ted Bundy," Liz is described as "nice" and "shy," but also "not beautiful like Stephanie," the offender's first serious girlfriend in Washington.[74]

Unsurprisingly, few podcasts treat Liz well and with respect. And unsurprisingly, the *Morbid* podcast does a wonderful job at discussing Liz and examining her treatment by *Extremely Wicked*, while also showing her respect. In the first episode, "Episode 5: Ted Bundy Part 1," Alaina, one of the hosts, makes clear that Kendall is her alias. Alaina continues, saying, "I do know her real name, but I'm not going to use it. If you want to know it, you can find it."[75] Alaina and her cohost, Ashleigh ("Ash"), recognize that Liz's real name is not a national secret—one can easily find it with a quick Google search. However, the *Morbid* podcast is making the clear choice to respect Liz's privacy by using her alias and pseudonym.

Almost exactly a year later, in May of 2019, Alaina and Ash released their review of *Extremely Wicked*. Liz's book had been out of print for years. Alaina jokes that she found a copy on eBay for hundreds of dollars, but that was too much for her budget, so she managed to find an eBook online. Using that as their source, Alaina and Ash discuss Liz's story. Unlike so many podcasts, they begin with Liz talking solely about the offender. Once they establish Liz as a person, something very few other iterations have bothered to do, their analysis of the Netflix film begins.

Again, they rely on *The Phantom Prince* for Liz's story and compare it to the film. While there are numerous sources that depend on the offender's version of the story, *Morbid* is ensuring that Liz's voice is heard loudly. Given that the film is supposedly from her point of view, comparing it to the only time Liz actually told her story herself is the only way to see how well the film did. They quote the book often, which is even more impactful as the book was out of print at the time the episode aired. As discussed earlier, Liz in the film does not call the police on the offender. Alaina and Ash discuss this, wondering why there is not a build-up of Liz realizing that her boyfriend is THE Ted. Watching Liz get more and more suspicious, which she writes about in *The Phantom Prince*, would make the film much more exciting as well as suspenseful.

In addition to wishing for greater representation and respect for the Liz character, Alaina and Ash point out their biggest issues with the film, most of them revolving around how Liz was presented on screen. At various points, their analysis indicates the film made Liz appear "too naive." They take umbrage with the portrayal of a Liz that is "pretty convinced that he's innocent" throughout the movie, when in real life, she was "super not."[76] Beyond going to the police several times with her suspicions, she "found a ton of shit that pointed to him being the killer," including crutches and casting material.[77] *Morbid* goes a step further than even the best coverage, noting the time that Liz had the offender's landlord let her into his apartment to look for further evidence. She was worried she was going to be caught, grabbing only a box of cancelled checks and taking them to the police.[78] This additional detail provided by Ash and Alaina helps to solidify the image of Liz as a woman who did more than any character in a movie to take down one of the most notorious killers in American history.

In their concluding thoughts, the *Morbid* podcast hosts discuss the character of Liz visiting the offender on death row in the film. As it is portrayed in the film, she seems to be obsessed with him, needing some kind of closure from him. As *Morbid* points out, she was happily married ten years later and did not travel to Florida's death row.

Two Girls One Murder!, in a minisode review of the movie, does better than some, while not living up to the high standard set by *Morbid*. The hosts criticize the film for not showing enough, or even any of the abuse endured by Liz—saying those times are "just as important as the times that he was charming" because it shows that he "wasn't relentlessly charming."[79] Throughout the episode, they discuss that the film should have shown more of the physical, emotional, and psychological torment that Liz went through during her entire relationship with the offender. However, they also make the point that perhaps a reason the film did not, or could not, delve deeper was because it "had to be gentle with it because true crime is not just for hardcore fans anymore."[80]

After *Morbid*, other podcast reviews of *Extremely Wicked* fall short in their portrayal of Liz Kendall. Director Joe Berlinger, interviewed on *You Can't Make This Up*, uses Liz's real name. He describes the film as showing how a serial killer "[gaslit] the woman he dated for seven years."[81] This again supports the false storyline that Liz had no idea that the offender was committing any of his crimes. As *Morbid* points out, not only was she suspicious, but she also took direct action to try to find evidence against him. Episode 63 of the podcast *Crime Culture* states the show's disappointment with the film, not because of Liz's treatment but because it was told from her point of view, which made it "less gory" and, therefore, disappointing.[82] Not only that, but later in the episode, one of the hosts goes further by saying they didn't even really "get" that it was supposed to be from Liz's eyes and that the producers "were just being too precious with the violence."[83]

When this project began, it was unclear whether there would be a sufficient amount of podcast episodes that even mention Liz to complete this analysis. Before the release of *Extremely Wicked*, there were few podcasts that even mention her for more than a few sentences. After the release of the film, several episodes talk about Liz, but the treatment of her runs a spectrum of well researched and respectful to disregarding Liz as a disappointing or minor player in the "Ted Bundy" show.

Conclusion

Liz Kendall is one of the lesser-known women of this project. If known at all, she was only ever known as "Ted Bundy's girlfriend." She has spent the last fifty years not only coming to terms with her relationship with the offender, but also achieving and maintaining her sobriety. She has also spent fifty years avoiding or answering questions about her relationship with the offender, torn between wanting to set the story straight and wanting to put the story to rest.

The offender, one of the most prolific killers in American history, has been the subject of the media since soon after his arrest and conviction. Given Liz's years with him, characters based on her appear in most of the iterations. While manipulations of the true Liz, those characters can still be categorized as informational. The only true exploitation of Liz comes in the utter disrespect shown to her by multiple outlets that choose to use her real name instead of her chosen pseudonym, which was meant to protect her family. What is incredibly interesting about pop culture's coverage of Liz Kendall is the advocacy that has occurred in recent years. With the production of *Falling for a Killer* and the reprinting of *The Phantom Prince*, Liz, along with the offender's victims, is finally getting increased attention. Rather than a documentary focused entirely on an offender, *Falling for a Killer* offers an example on how true crime can turn the tables and advocate for victims, even if the offender has already been convicted and executed.

CHAPTER 8

Kirsten Costas

The 1980s were a decade full of contradictions. While the rich got richer and men like Donald Trump built real estate empires, many others fell into poverty and were kept there by the recession of 1987. With so much emphasis on class in America, it is no surprise that a murder in California that served as a class commentary captured America's attention.

Just the Facts

At the height of this decade, high school student Kirsten Costas was preparing for the summer before her junior year. Her parents, Arthur and Berit Costas, moved to Orinda, California, from Oakland to find a safer community with "good schools" for Kirsten and her younger brother, Peter.[1] Orinda, just half an hour outside of San Francisco, was described as a "perfect town ... a crime-free environment" and a community whose address announced to the world that its residents had "arrived."[2] This was the town that Kirsten was born into, with her father an executive at the 3M Corporation and her mother a stay-at-home mother. Berit, her mother, described Kirsten as "the energy of the house ... always listening to music, making phone calls, dancing. She was full of life."[3] Kirsten attended Mira Monte High School, where many of the students displayed their parents' wealth with BMWs, the "most popular car" at the school.[4]

In addition to her studies, Kirsten had an active social life and extra-curricular career. *Ladies' Home Journal* describes her as being part of the "loud crowd" or "the clique that counted."[5] Just a few months before her death, she was asked to join the Bob-o-links, or Bobbies, an "elite sorority-like organization ... of the best looking, most popular girls in school."[6] She was also a member of the varsity swim team and had, soon before her murder, become a member of Mira Monte's cheerleader squad. This membership in the cheerleading squad becomes a defining factor both in Kirsten's life and in her memory. Her friend, Jessica Grant, quoted in *Ladies' Home Journal*, said that "cheerleading [was] taken really seriously" at Mira Monte.[7] Applicants had to write essays to explain to the judging panel what they could add to the school, and parents had to agree to spend $500 on uniforms and sleepaway cheerleading camp.[8] A panel of twenty experts judged the applicants, and the newest members of the squad were announced in an "Academy Awards–type ceremony where outgoing cheerleaders pluck names from envelopes, giving the winners kisses and flowers."[9] As one of the winners, Kirsten was described as a perfect cheerleader.

She had much to look forward to when, on the night of June 23, 1984, she was stabbed to death on her own front lawn by Bernadette Protti, another 15-year-old student at Mira Monte High School. On June 21, the offender had called Kirsten's mother, telling Berti that Kirsten was needed for a special dinner for the new members of the Bobbis. When Kirsten came outside to meet her secret ride, she found the offender at the wheel of her family's Pinto. Disappointed at who was in the car, Kirsten allegedly expressed her dismay but got into the car.[10] For some unknown reason, they pulled over into a church parking lot. At various times, the offender says they stopped so that Kirsten could smoke a cigarette or smoke marijuana. Whatever the reason, when stopped, the two fought. Kirsten ran away from the Pinto and found herself on the porch of Alex and Mary Jane Arnold, complete strangers. When Alex Arnold opened his door, he saw Kirsten and "behind her, another girl who, looking about fifteen, [was] 'lurking out [on] the path.'"[11] Kirsten told Arnold that her friend "got weird on her" and asked if she could use their phone.[12] Her parents were not home—they had gone out with Kirsten's younger brother—so the call went unanswered. Arnold offered her a ride and kept watch as a Pinto followed them all the way back to Kirsten's house.

As Kirsten walked from Arnold's car to her front door, the offender ran from the Pinto with a knife in her hand. She testified later that the knife was in the Pinto because her sister often made her lunch, which included chopping vegetables, in the car during her lunch breaks. Kirsten was stabbed multiple times before the offender ran off. Searching for help, Kirsten made her way to neighbor Arthur Hillman's house, asking for help. First responders arrived and transported Kirsten to the local hospital, but she was declared dead within an hour of her attack.[13]

Contra Costa County law enforcement spent weeks investigating Kirsten's murder, with a suspect list that included Nancy Kane Mark and Bernadette Protti. Nancy, referred to as "Heather" in the *Ladies' Home Journal* article to protect her identity, had shed her "preppy" identity for one she later called "New Wave."[14] Considered by many to be an outsider, Nancy was immediately suspected. Police, however, confirmed her alibi and moved on to the offender. She gave an initial statement saying she was babysitting the night of the murder, but on December 11, she was called back in to meet with police and FBI who were assisting with the case.[15] After her interview, law enforcement was confident it was her but needed a confession, which they got the following day.

Three months after the arrest, the offender's trial began. When asked why she had killed Kirsten, she said:

> I have a lot of inferiority feelings—and I really have bad feelings about myself. I lost for cheerleader. I didn't get into the club I wanted to. I didn't get on year-book. So, I don't know, I just felt bad.... [Kirsten] just sort of put me down.... I remembered one time on the ski trip we were on together. I mean, we don't have a lot of money and we can't afford a lot of nice ski stuff, and I just had this really crummy pair of skis and some boots, but, you know, I was having fun anyway. Kirsten made some comment about them, and it just seemed like everyone else was thinking that, but she was the only one who would come out and say it.[16]

On April 1, 1985, the offender was sentenced to between one and nine years in the California Youth Authority. Under California law, it was the maximum sentence as she was a minor and had to be released by the age of twenty-five. She was released in 1992 and changed her name.

Given that this case involves teenage drama, cheerleading, and murder, it was only a matter of time before the story of Kirsten's murder was translated to the small screen. However, a surprisingly small number of iterations of the case have been made. Even with the small number, Kirsten has been revictimized in the years since her murder. She has been made the ultimate "mean girl" who "had it coming" or merely became known as "the cheerleader" in "The Cheerleader Murder."

News of the Day

As with many women examined in this project, news articles covering Kirsten Costas appeared only after her murder on June 23, 1984. In addition to details about the investigation, the articles include quotes from Kirsten's friends and family, describing who she was in life. These are the only impressions of her, a few words in each article, which allow anyone to remember Kirsten as something other than a victim. Given that the primary pop cultural iterations of Kirsten have been an incredibly problematic film from 1994 and its remake, the news stories are the only remotely unbiased accounts of Kirsten to combat the "mean girl" depiction.

To ensure the most accurate and least corruption of information, the search was limited to California newspapers. In the days and weeks following Kirsten's murder, numerous interviews were conducted with those closest to her. She was described as an "all-American girl" to *The Californian,* a paper local to Salinas, 187 miles away from Mira Monte.[17] Guy Schultz, a neighbor, told the *San Francisco Examiner* that Kirsten was "a popular student who excelled in swimming, skiing, and dancing."[18] In the same article, another friend, unnamed, said that Kirsten was "good at everything" and "did not have a boyfriend, nor was she particularly interested in dating."[19] This last part directly contradicts the portrayal in the 1994 film of the character based on Kirsten, who not only has a boyfriend but also toys with the idea of cheating on him. Another article from the *San Francisco Examiner* includes a portion of Kirsten's funeral service. The Rev. James F. Little said, "She had a will of her own ... but she was kind and loving and always reaching out. She loved to dance; I hope you can hear the joy and see the dancing of Kirsten. She loved to swim; I hope you can hear splashing water."[20] Again, this contradicts the pop culture iterations of Kirsten. Other than cheerleading, characters based on her are not shown to play any other sports. At no point in *Death of a Cheerleader* does she "bring joy to the lives" of anyone.

While these articles do offer invaluable insight into Kirsten before her murder, they must be taken with a grain of salt. Few would wish to speak ill of the dead in print; fewer would do so of a 15-year-old murder victim. However, even with the cloud of grief hanging over these words, they ring truer to who Kirsten was than the made-for-TV movies that aired decades after her death.

Movies/Documentaries

As stated above, there have been surprisingly few presentations of this case. Whether it is the case that has entered into the popular consciousness or the film version of the characters, some version of Kirsten Costas exists in the memory of anyone who lived through the 1980s or watched Lifetime movies in the 1990s. What also makes this case, and its pop culture portrayals, unique is that the second film is a remake of the first. The first was made in 1994 and the second, twenty-five years later. Even with few iterations, Kirsten is revictimized by the portrayals, made into a mean girl who is far from the truth.

A Friend to Die For/Death of a Cheerleader[21] (1994)

While Kirsten was killed in 1984, the first film did not appear until a decade later. It was not unusual in the mid–1980s to see TV movies "ripped from the headlines," but the film was made and released during a high point of true crime attention in the early 1990s. Prompted by the trial of the Menendez brothers in 1989 and the murder of Nicole Brown just four months before, *Death of a Cheerleader* premiered on NBC on September 26, 1994. Given that the offender had just been released two years earlier—and to avoid liability—a title card appears before the start, stating that the names, locations, and certain events had been changed. That is to be expected with these films, but the movie follows the real events so closely that it is easy to make the connection, even without doing the requisite Google search.

It was directed by William Graham, and the screenplay was written by Don Bronson, with additional credit given to Randall Sullivan, as he wrote the *Rolling Stone* article on which the film was heavily based. The principal cast is made up of Tori Spelling as Stacey Lockwood (Kirsten), Kellie Martin as Angela Delvecchio (the offender), and Kathryn Morris as Monica Whitley (Nancy Kane Mark), with Valerie Harper as Mrs. Delvecchio. The film begins with Stacey, aka Kirsten, going to the Arthurs' door and asking for help. Just after she is stabbed, the camera shifts and the words "Ten Months Earlier" appear on the screen. Clearly now back before the horrible crime, the audience is on a journey to find out how the "pretty blonde girl" is killed. However, this immediately presents a problem. In both this and the 2019 remake, blonde actors were cast for the character based on Kirsten even though she had dark hair. In addition, the actors cast to play the offender both had shortish dark hair while Bernadette Protti had longer blonde hair. While casting of films is often a complicated process, and actors may be cast because of their talent rather than their looks, it is conspicuous that both films made similar casting choices. By casting a blonde actor as Stacey/Kirsten, it not only makes her one of many blonde California girls, but Angela's contrasting dark hair makes her look more like the outsider. Many were surprised when the offender was arrested because they thought it was she who was just like all the other blonde California girls. Switching the physical characteristics of the two main players is a significant alteration that subtly influences any audience watching it. It becomes quickly clear that the main character of this film is not Stacey aka Kirsten, but Angie, the character based upon the offender. As with nearly all the true crime entertainment ever created, it has been determined that the person deserving of the attention is the killer, not the victim.

Having flashed back ten months, the students are beginning their school year. For Stacey and Angie, it is the beginning of their sophomore year. Angie, clearly an outsider, is determined to become yearbook editor, cheerleader, and a Meadowlark—the film's version of the Bob-o-links. Her "normal" friend, Nina, tries to warn her that the editorship of the yearbook is a popularity contest and the Larks "aren't for people like us."[22] Angie is unfazed and tries to gain favor from the "in-crowd," including Stacey. However, Stacey is nothing like the Kirsten described by her friends and family. When Angie approaches Stacey and her group of friends, Stacey mocks her openly and in front of everyone. Given the look of malice on her face and the way she looks around for attention after her barbs, it is clear that Stacey is attacking Angie purely to be cruel.

This behavior that seems out of character for Kirsten[23] continues in Stacey when the scene changes to the high school's attendance office, where Stacey and Angie both have jobs. It is apparently their job to help the office workers with tardy students and process notes from doctors or parents. While they are supposed to share the work, Stacey is too busy gossiping or goofing off to get any work done. Angie, on the other hand, is shown working diligently at her desk. When Stacey's boyfriend comes into the office, she asks Angie for a "favor." Since she is such a good writer, could she forge him a note so he is not in trouble? Happy to do anything for Stacey, Angie does what she asks. Not only is Stacey shirking her duties, but she is also asking her coworker to forge notes for her boyfriend. There is also an implication that if she is willing to break the rules once, she has done it possibly several more times for him or even herself, allowing them to skip school. Knowing Kirsten's dedication to not only her school but also service, it seems unlikely that she would be so willing to circumvent school rules. By portraying her fictional persona as someone who would, the movie gives the audience a very different idea of who Kirsten was as a person.

Soon after this, the high school announces that there will be a ski trip but that the cost for each student will be $75.[24] Angie, whose family is from a lower socio-economic situation than most of the residents of this town, is clearly worried about being able to afford this trip. Cue the completely expected montage of Angie doing odd jobs around town to earn money: babysitting, washing cars, and, best of all, scraping paint off the outside of a house. Again, the film is spending most of its time on Angie while there are huge chunks of time where Stacey is not even seen. When she reappears, it is in the van on the way to the ski trip. Sitting in the back with her friends, she talks about ditching her boyfriend to go to a dance with someone else. So, in addition to breaking the rules for this guy, she is also not even faithful to him.

Stacey's "mean girl" behavior continues once they reach the ski lodge. With sleeping arrangements more like barracks than a hotel, all of the female students are in the same large room with bunk beds. Stacey goes to Monica's bunk and grabs her diary out of her bag. Holding court, she reads the diary aloud to the entire group while Angie is the one trying to work up the courage to tell Stacey it is not nice. In the diary, Monica wrote that she would "rather kill herself than be friends with Stacey."[25] Without missing a beat, Stacey says that would be a real "contribution to society."[26] The next morning, Stacey is the first to make fun of Angie's hard-earned ski outfit by saying, "Nice clothes, Angela. Where did you get them, a thrift store?"[27] Her behavior on this ski trip is the most damning evidence of how much Stacey differs from Kirsten and how much Kirsten's memory is tarnished by this film.

There is one grain of truth to this character assassination. During her conversations with law enforcement, the offender said that Kirsten had "said something" about her skis while they were on the trip. Given that Kirsten was a 15-year-old, it is possible and even probable that she made a comment about the offender's skis or her outfit. While she may have said something, perhaps even hateful towards the offender about her ski clothes and/or equipment, there is no evidence, hearsay or otherwise, that indicates that Kirsten was anything close to Stacey in her behavior. As quoted in the various newspapers following the murder, people described Kirsten as good, kind, loving, and joyful. Those words do not match the character seen in *Death of a Cheerleader*.

More offensive behavior by Stacey continues up until the night of the murder. Even without the flash-forward, no one would be surprised when Angie arrives to pick up Stacey. After forcing Angie to explain the ruse, Stacey makes her pull into the parking lot of the church, saying she needs to "fortify [herself] for this."[28] According to the offender's account of the night, Kirsten wanted to pull into a parking lot to smoke before going to the party. Kirsten's friends insisted that she did not smoke cigarettes or take drugs. However, by explicitly making it a joint that Stacey pulled out of her purse, not only is the film supporting the offender's account of the night, but it is also implying that Kirsten smoked pot.

Soon, the audience is again forced to watch the stabbing death of Stacey, and by extension Kirsten. It is rough when a film makes one watch the death of a real-life victim once, but in some cases, like this, it is exponentially worse to watch it twice, especially with the less-than-stellar acting of Tori Spelling. What is just as offensive is how quickly the film refocuses back on Angie. Stacey only gets to be the main character in the movie about her murder for mere moments. Angie is shown struggling with what she had done, all while winning at life. A football player makes a pretense to come into the attendance office to talk to her. She is seen later, working as a peer counselor, wearing a letterman's jacket. Angie is even shown as a candy striper, working at the hospital, where a nurse says she is the only one who can calm a patient.

Finally, Angie becomes the prime suspect of the investigation. Knowing her time is up, she confesses to her mother by writing it in a letter and then, strangely, going to school. During the trial, the majority of the Larks show up in support of Stacey, but one, a girl who had known Angie when they were younger, has a realization. She tells a friend, "I've been thinking about it—I never really liked her—I was just scared of her."[29] This friend, Marley, with this speech confirms suspicions that Stacey not only bullied people like Angie but also people within her own friend group. In the same act that sees Angie convicted of Stacey's murder, Stacey competes with Angie as the true antagonist of the movie. With so much malice written into the Stacey character, and the statement from the beginning that this is a true story, it is surprising that the Costas family did not sue for defaming Kirsten. The character based heavily on Kirsten is a deeply flawed, hateful person who battles with the killer for the worst person in the movie. With the popularity of the cast and with films of this sort in the mid–1990s, it was no surprise when it became the highest-rated TV movie of 1994—which means that a large television audience tuned in to watch a highly adulterated version of Kirsten Costas that revictimizes her with each showing.

Deadly Women: "Deadly Delinquents" (2012)

After the release of *Death of a Cheerleader* in 1994, there were nearly twenty years before another account of Kirsten's death appeared on television again. This time, it is on Investigation Discovery's *Deadly Women* program. Aimed at capitalizing on the true crime wave, which was in its infancy, the show is like the dozens of other shows on that channel. With narration and dramatic reenacting, the murder of Kirsten Costas is covered in the eighteenth episode of season four, "Deadly Delinquents," along with two other cases.

Each episode has a theme and covers multiple cases, though it does strike a sour note that, in 1994 Kirsten's story was worthy of an entire TV movie, but in 2012 it does not even deserve all of a thirty-minute episode. With so little time to dedicate to Kirsten, there are fewer instances of open disrespect than in *Death of a Cheerleader*. There are, however, a few glaring errors. Beyond the overdramatic nature of the entire episode, there is open hostility between Kirsten and the offender, much more than what students testified to at the trial and in the press. Additionally, in the reenactment of the attack, "Kirsten" is wearing a little black off-the-shoulder dress. It is very sexy for anyone, but especially for a 15-year-old who thought she was going to a dinner with her service-oriented sorority. Judging from pictures of Kirsten printed in the press after the crime, it seems very unlikely that she would be wearing that. Therefore, *Deadly Women* chose that dress to further sexualize a 15-year-old victim in the same scene where she is brutally stabbed to death.

The revictimization by *Deadly Women* comes in a two-pronged attack. First, the sheer lack of time spent on her at all and the lack of time spent on her outside of the crime. Kirsten is only known as a victim, with little said in the episode of the person outside of the crime. Second is the sexualization of Kirsten, done decades after her death. While the short time in this episode may not seem impactful, it is more likely that "average" true crime fans would stumble across this episode on Investigation Discovery before they would find a TV movie from 1994. This may be their first, or only, entry into the life, and case, of Kirsten Costas. If that is the case, it does her a great disservice.

The 1980s: The Deadliest Decade (2016)

Investigation Discovery revisited the case four years later in a series called *The 1980s: The Deadliest Decade*. The name is diminished somewhat as the channel also has a series called *The 1990s: The Deadliest Decade*. Nevertheless, the third episode of the 1980s is titled "The Cheerleader Murder" and again endeavors to tell the case of the murder of Kirsten Costas.

After describing life in Orinda as "the more you had, the better," the episode moved on to Kirsten.[30] Calling her athletic, the narrator said she was a member of the baseball team, though it was far more likely he meant softball as baseball is traditionally only a male sport in American high schools. Even with this mistake, this gives Kirsten more credit for her athleticism than previous iterations. Kirsten is also described as "cute" and "naturally tan," as those interviewed concentrate on her physical appearance.[31]

Unsurprisingly, the episode covers much of the same territory as "Deadliest Delinquents" from 2012. However, there are a couple of points where "The Cheerleader Murder" sets itself apart. The first, and most important, is the inclusion of Nancy Kane Mark. While there are characters based on her in all iterations, this is the first time she appears on camera to give her point of view. In 1994's *Death of a Cheerleader*, the character of Monica is based on Nancy and occasionally appears on screen, but there is nothing of her after the death of Stacey. In "The Cheerleader Murder" Nancy describes what her experience was like before and after Kirsten's death.

Nancy describes herself as once belonging to Kirsten's friend group, with long blonde hair and preppy clothes. However, before their sophomore year, she needed to change her look to better fit who she really was.

In the episode, she describes it as "New Wave," with black hair and black clothes.[32] Her new look made her very much an outsider at Mira Monte and, according to Nancy, a target for ridicule. Given that her new look and attitude was at odds with much of the student body of the high school, she faced bullying that only increased after Kirsten's murder. Many students at the school automatically considered her a possible suspect. She was ostracized and berated until she switched schools to try to find some peace. The police had cleared her of any suspicion as she had an alibi corroborated by multiple people, but that did not matter to her classmates.

In *Death of a Cheerleader* (1994), as discussed above, Stacey treats Monica (the character based on Nancy) very poorly, but Monica disappears from the film after the murder. There are hints, some outright, that some of the Larks consider Monica to be the killer, but all of the intrigue occurs without the actor on screen. After Stacey's murder, Marley and Angie stop by a locker that has been graffitied with the word "killer." This is the only scene where it is explained that Monica had been teased so mercilessly that she needed to find a new school to escape. Nancy's interview in "The Cheerleader Murder" gives clarity on what she went through during that difficult time in her life. The episode may not forge any new territory for Kirsten; it is worth mentioning for its treatment of Nancy Kane Mark.

Death of a Cheerleader (2019)

Twenty-five years after the original, and thirty-five years after the death of Kirsten, Lifetime released a remake of *Death of a Cheerleader* on February 2, 2019. Written by Caitlin Fryers and directed by Paul Shapiro, it stars Sarah Dugdale as Kelly Locke, the character based on Kirsten, and Audrey Peeples as Bridget Moretti, the character based on the offender. This version is set in Colina, California, in 1985, where the girls go to Hollybrooke High School. For the most part, the film follows the same path as the original. Kelly Locke is a blonde "queen bee" of the high school, while Bridget Moretti strives to become yearbook editor, cheerleader, and a Bobbie. Bridget stabs Kelly and eventually confesses to the police at the end of the film. However, there are a few key differences between the two versions that deserve discussion.

In this updated version of the film, the character based on Kirsten, this time called Kelly, is still a "mean girl," but is less so this time, with additional context. Kelly Locke is once again played by an actor with long blonde hair rather than the shortish brunette hair that Kirsten had before her death. She is still mean to the offender's character, now named Bridget. The most glaring example of this still revolves around the ski trip. However, rather than insulting her in front of the entire group, Kelly calls Bridget's skis "crummy" while they're alone.[33] While still mean, this is far less offensive than humiliating Bridget in front of the entire Bobbies.

Additionally, there are a few scenes in this version where Kelly's mother is shown pressuring Kelly to keep her grades up, get on the cheerleading squad, and work hard. Before the cheerleading tryouts, Kelly is seen working on her routine, alone in the school gym. Bridget is also shown working on her routine, but it is in her family's living room, in her school clothes. Kelly is in athletic gear, working up a sweat, trying to get her routine perfect. It is unknown if Kirsten's mother pressured her this way, but showing the character based on Kirsten working hard for what she achieved adds an important layer to the movie, and to Kirsten. In the original 1994 version, Stacey was not shown to work for any of the things she had. This scene adds the very real likelihood of Kirsten having to work hard for all that she earned, including the swim team, dancing competitions, and softball. The pressure from her mother and her hard work for her achievements helps to transform Kelly into a more real, more complex person rather than the two-dimensional Stacey.

The 2019 version of the film also gives a much better treatment of the character based on Nancy Kane Mark, this time called Nina. Following the theme of exploring mother/daughter relationships, when Nina makes the decision to change her look to better fit her identity, she and her mother have a heart-to-heart. Her mother jokes of the importance of going to a hair stylist instead of coloring her hair at home. Nina fully embraces her new look but immediately gets backlash from the school. After Kelly's murder, Nina gets the full brunt of suspicion from the student body and the community. Not only is she bullied at school, but also police are shown executing a warrant at Nina's home. Again, the mother/daughter theme comes back when Nina and her mother sit down and make the decision for Nina to leave Hollybrooke High and go to another school where she could start over.

While 2019's *Death of a Cheerleader* is, in many ways, the same movie as the 1994 version, these differences are important ones. Kirsten's character is now layered, shown working hard to earn what she wants. She also has less malice and more context for her drive than Stacey, the similar character in the 1994 version. The addition of the fully fleshed out character of Nina, based on Nancy Kane Mark, also makes for a welcome update to the older version. Given all this, there is still a lot of room for improvement. There has yet to be a fictional version of Kirsten's story that has not had to go through the Lifetime treatment of over-dramatization. There has yet to be a version where the character based on the offender is not considered to be the main character of the film.

Podcasts

In the realm of podcasts, Kirsten Costas has received the same treatment as she has in film and television—too few episodes and not enough coverage of Kirsten herself. Of the eight podcasts that have been found to have released an episode on something connected to this case, few break any new ground that brings greater justice for Kirsten in this realm of pop culture.

With most episodes, there is merely a comment here or there that gives Kirsten preferential treatment over the offender. In *Our True Crime Podcast*, episode 34, not only do the hosts call Kirsten "not the typical blonde," which was more than either of the TV movies established, but they also call out the police for victim blaming when they asked Kirsten's friend what had she done to make the offender do this.[34] *Once Upon a Crime* gave Kirsten the respect of pointing out that by the time of the trial, it was all about the offender and everyone "seemed to have forgotten about the dead 15-year-old and her grieving family."[35] The hosts of *Fatal*i*teas* tried to imagine what Kirsten must have gone through that final night—the fear and confusion.[36] Even with each of these having these small moments, the rest of their episodes cover much of the same terrain. One cannot help but wonder how many episodes average true crime fans would listen to; if they only listen to one of these, they will only get part of the story.

The other podcast episodes that appear after a search for Kirsten's name cover the two films. Specifically, two episodes of the same podcast, *Lifetime Uncorked*, each covering each version of the film. The podcast, hosted by Patrick Serrano with the help of his friends, breaks down movies made and/or aired on Lifetime. Patrick and friends covered the 1994 version in season two of the podcast, which dropped in June of 2018. Much of the conversation centered on the "90s-ness" of the movie, even though it was supposedly set in 1984. The second episode, season four episode five, from February 2019, covers the 2019 version of *Death of a Cheerleader*. In this episode, there was more discussion on the responsibilities of the production and the network as to how they depicted a story based on real life. During their discussion, Patrick and his guests talk about how Kelly (the character based on Kirsten) is not "necessarily mean, she just had some moments."[37] They continue, saying, "Lifetime was like, 'we have to be careful here—are we responsible for showing people bullying and then they get murdered?'"[38] It would have been nice for the conversation to have continued into how Lifetime may have manipulated the truth of Kirsten's story, but this is an interesting avenue of thought. *Lifetime Uncorked* also mused on what the movie would have been like if the choice had been made to bring the story into 2019 rather than keep it in 1984. If social media were a part of the story, how much of an impact would that have had on Kirsten/Kelly and the offender/Bridget? While 2019's *Death of Cheerleader* did not do that, Patrick and his guests do suppose that they considered how they needed to update the portrayal of bullying since 1994 to include more modern sensitivities.

Conclusion

Kirsten joins women like Sabella as some of the lesser-known subjects of this project. Her murder is more likely to be known by its pop culture iterations "The Cheerleader Murder" or "that Tori Spelling movie murder." Even thirty-five years later, there has not been a fair and objective iteration of her death. Instead, the coverage has only exploited her death for not one but two Lifetime movies.

As with some of the earlier women discussed, the circumstances surrounding Kirsten's death are heightened for viewing audiences. Details concerning all involved have been manipulated, but each iteration exploits Kirsten's death in the most gruesome way possible. Only with podcasts does the treatment of Kirsten's life and death venture into the informational. This informational coverage only means that details of her life are included and the iteration is not overtly exploitative.

One hopes that, as with the visual media, Kirsten soon receives an updated and fairer treatment by the podcasting world. Most glaringly missing are substantial attention paid to her before her murder, and the majority of overall coverage paid to her and not the offender. Perhaps this cannot happen without more information on who Kirsten was before her murder. Unlike many of the other women covered in this project, there are no large books or documentaries on Kirsten. Whatever the path that leads to a better, more even-handed depiction of her story, hopefully the opening of that path will appear soon and Kirsten's tale will get the telling it deserves.

CHAPTER 9

Nicole Brown

The 1990s ushered in the era of twenty-four-hour crime coverage with cable news joining network news and, of course, the founding of Court TV, airing for the first time in 1991. This, combined with some of the most high-profile cases of the 20th century, created the environment in which many modern Murderinos were born. In addition to names like Menendez and Dahmer is the name of one of the most famous women of the 1990s, who still captivates people today.

Nicole Brown is at the center of one of the most famous cases of the latter part of the 20th century, and, while central as one of the murder victims, she is simultaneously overshadowed by the person who most likely killed her. Hosts of constant news coverage and infotainment had a celebrity in O.J. Simpson and used this to keep their audience rabid for more. In the process, Nicole and Ron Goldman, the other victim who died on the night of June 12, 1994, were mostly lost. In every subsequent telling of the story—in books, documentaries, and several fictionalized versions of the case—Nicole continually is revictimized by the press, by pop culture, and by O.J. himself.

Just the Facts

Nicole Brown was born to a German mother and an American father in Frankfurt, West Germany, on May 19, 1959. The Brown family moved to California, where Nicole first attended Rancho Alamitos High School before graduating from Dana Hills High School in Dana Point, California, in 1977. In the same year, when Nicole was 18, she met O.J. Simpson while working at The Daisy. Many of the histories of Nicole's story refer to this as a "nightclub," while O.J. refers to it as a "diner." A YouTube clip titled "The Daisy 1970s" shows more of a cafe with a sandwich board out front. According to *Raging Heart: The Intimate Story of the Tragic Marriage of O.J. and Nicole Brown Simpson* by Sheila Weller, The Daisy was an exclusive nightclub in Beverly Hills, but the owner, Hansen, was planning to open the venue for lunch. He knew Nicole from her time working in a shop down the street from The Daisy and hired her to work this new lunch shift.[1] While this is a tiny detail in the larger story of Nicole Brown and her eventual murder, it is interesting that it seems to be disputed. Depending on the true nature of The Daisy, a person's interpretation of Nicole can be drastically different. While a woman's place of employment should not color the public's interpretation of her, it does happen. An 18-year-old woman working at a cafe will be seen differently than an 18-year-old woman working at a nightclub.

Regardless of the circumstances of their first encounter, Nicole and O.J. began dating in 1977, when Nicole was 18 and O.J. was 30 and still married to his first wife, Marguerite, who was pregnant with the couple's third child. Soon, Nicole quit her job at The Daisy to be O.J.'s girlfriend full-time. He and Marguerite divorced in March of 1979, and in February 1985, O.J. and Nicole were married. They had two children together, Sydney, born in 1985, and Justin, born in 1988. During their marriage, there were numerous domestic disputes and abuse calls to the Los Angeles police, including one where, after being arrested, O.J. was sentenced to community service and therapy, which he was able to do by phone. Six years after getting married, Nicole made serious plans to leave O.J. Their divorce was finalized on October 15, 1992, and Nicole was looking forward to her life after O.J.[2] While they did reconcile for a brief period in 1993, Nicole was "very excited" to finally move into her house on 875 South Bundy Drive in January 1994.[3]

From here, the story typically jumps directly to the night of June 12, 1994; however, Sheila Weller includes June 7, when Nicole called the Sojourn Shelter for Battered Women in Los Angeles. She was seeking help. She told the person at the shelter that she was being stalked and that her ex-husband, O.J. Simpson, was the person stalking her.[4] Five days later, Nicole and her friend, Ronald Goldman, were brutally killed outside of her South Bundy Drive house. LAPD quickly looked toward O.J. for the murders, leading to a police "chase" in the infamous white Bronco.[5] After hours of driving, O.J. appeared back at his house where he surrendered himself to the police.

The "Trial of the Century"[6] lasted until October 2, 1995, when O.J. was declared not guilty of the two murders. There have been no additional investigations or arrests made in the more than twenty-five years since their murders. Not only have there never been any further investigation or arrests, but also there has been a plethora of popular culture produced since 1994 to take advantage of the public's fascination with the case. Unsurprisingly, pop culture's portrayal of Nicole began almost immediately.

News of the Day

Given the fame of the offender and the later spectacle of the case, it is not surprising that articles appeared the day after Nicole's and Ron's bodies were found. As with many of the women examined for this project, Nicole's treatment by the California newspapers was hugely problematic. In nearly all of the articles, across multiple newspapers, headlines not only do not mention Nicole's name, but only refer to her as the alleged offender's ex-wife, or worse, his wife, even though they had been divorced for more than two years.[7] This pattern of not using Nicole's name continues throughout the body of the articles. While the alleged offender's football and acting career is discussed in several places, reporters could not be bothered to write Nicole's name more than once.[8] In an article in the *Los Angeles Times*, Nicole's name is not mentioned until the fourth paragraph … in an article about her death.[9]

This trend of ignoring Nicole almost entirely will continue through not only the trial, but also for the next twenty-five years. It is only in the last few years, with the latest wave of true crime attention, that public memory of Nicole has begun to shift.

Books

The Run of His Life: The People V. O.J. Simpson by Jeffrey Toobin

First published in 1996 by Jeffrey Toobin, a staff writer for *The New Yorker* in the mid–1990s, *The Run of His Life* is a *New York Times* best-seller as well as the basis for the 2016 FX/Ryan Murphy vehicle by the same name. The edition consulted for this project was reissued in 2015 as a tie-in with the FX series. Toobin, now CNN's chief legal consultant, graduated from Harvard Law School in 1986, giving him an expert legal perspective on the case against this alleged offender. Given Toobin's legal career and concentration on the legal proceedings, there is relatively little on Nicole in the 458 pages of the book. She has dozens of entries in the index, but most of them are either having to do with the crime scene or the trial itself, and then only in passing. However, the few passages in the book show a lack of interest in the life of Nicole Brown combined with the general lack of understanding of coercive control.

While providing some background on Nicole and the alleged offender's life, Toobin analyzed Nicole's affidavit in the 1992 divorce proceedings.

As will be discussed at length later, Nicole was under the alleged offender's control from very early in their relationship, when he insisted that she quit her job to "be his girlfriend." When describing this in her affidavit, Nicole pressed for both child and spousal support, "stressing her complete financial dependence" on him.[10] However, Toobin characterizes this in a problematic way, saying, "Nicole had many years earlier made herself a hostage to O.J.'s fortune."[11] This phrasing places all the blame at the feet of Nicole. Rather than placing the blame with the alleged offender, who isolated Nicole and kept her from working and making her own money, this misleading wording reduces any sympathy the reader may have for Nicole.

This lack of understanding continues two hundred pages later, when Toobin was describing the defense strategy of Christopher Darden. Calling Darden's argument "a kind of California psychobabble," Toobin dismisses what is now recognized as the prevailing behavioral language explaining relationships like these. "'He stripped her of her self-esteem,' Darden said. 'He was so controlling that he attempted to define her identity. He attempted to define who she was.'"[12] In Toobin's analysis of this, he described Simpson's coercive control as "what others might call Simpson's generosity."[13]

While it can be hoped that much of this could be a sign of the times, as the book was published only a year after the verdict was handed down, there are no perceptible changes in the 2015 edition. One must wonder if Toobin has thought to revisit the issue of coercive control over the last twenty-five years and whether it may change his interpretation of Nicole.

If I Did It: Confessions of a Killer (2007)

If I Did It: Confessions of a Killer is an infamous book, written by the offender himself, but eventually published by the family of one of his alleged victims. In need of money, the offender wrote a manuscript that became essentially a confession. The Goldmans, who won a civil suit against the offender and are owed a significant amount of money, won the rights to the manuscript. Once they had the rights, the Goldmans, primarily Ron's father Fred and his sister Kim, had to decide what to do with it. They decided to publish it, making the "if" in the title so small on the cover that the title ends up reading *I Did It: Confessions of a Killer.*

The final version that ended up on the bookshelf included not only the original manuscript, but also sections written by the Goldmans, by the ghostwriter who helped the offender in writing the manuscript, and the lawyer who helped the Goldmans in their case. It is incredibly interesting to read the Goldmans' justification for publishing the manuscript, specifically, "to pull the veil off the issue of domestic violence."[14] Hoping to honor Nicole, Fred writes, "If one woman can see herself as Nicole and get out of that situation before she is killed, then we will have done our part."[15] While incredibly noble, publishing the manuscript also means publishing not only the offender's horribly skewed opinions of Nicole, but also a graphic description of her death. There is nothing in the book outlining *all* of the facts of the deal over the manuscript, but one cannot help but wish for an annotated version of the original manuscript. If the offender's words were marked, corrected, and sourced with accurate information, Nicole's memory, as well as Ron's, would be offered far better protection.

As no such annotation exists and the manuscript is printed without alteration (other than the articles before and after the manuscript), Nicole's treatment is terrible. The alleged offender uses words such as "whined" or "snapped" to describe how she spoke to him.[16] Describing Nicole as "venomous, full of rage and anger,"[17] the offender chastises Nicole for "whining about getting older and how much she hated it, how much it depressed her."[18] He accuses her of spending time with drug addicts and sex workers on multiple occasions.[19] He accuses Nicole of harassing him, calling his home on multiple occasions and even threatening him. All of this comes before he describes how he and an offender named Charlie go to Nicole's Brentwood home and murder her.

This is the offender's opportunity to, in his mind, finally defend himself against all of the slander against him over the years since the rumors started swirling about abuse. To the Goldmans, it was an opportunity to punish "the killer" while also advocating for women who may find themselves in situations like Nicole, perhaps saving lives in the future. However, for Nicole, this book only offers up terrible accusations against her without anyone offering up a defense for Nicole.

Movies

The O.J. Simpson Story (1995)

The first pop culture iteration was also the first made-for-TV movie covering the murder of Nicole and Ron Goldman. Premiering on Fox on January 31, 1995, it was filmed in 1994, but the network waited until after the jury had been sequestered before airing it. While the movie does hint strongly at the alleged offender's guilt, the movie aired a full ten months before the not-guilty verdict. This is also the only movie released before 2020 that includes Nicole as an actual character in her own story. Jessica Tuck plays Nicole, who, even though she is not named for the first eight minutes, ends up getting significantly more screen time in this movie than any other pop culture vehicle.

As the film begins with the discovery of Nicole's and Ron Goldman's bodies, just like every other film/show/podcast, expectations were low for a fair portrayal of Nicole. However, about ten minutes into the movie, the first flashback takes the audience to 1977 when the alleged offender meets Nicole. The Daisy is clearly a nightclub and Nicole is a sassy server with awesome crimped hair and who is cracking jokes at the customers. Already, she has more personality and life behind her than any other history of Nicole Brown. While the portrayal may not be as accurate as anyone would have liked, the audience still gets to see Nicole as a living, breathing person who smiles and cracks jokes and is far more of a fully developed person than any other iteration.

After the initial meeting, Nicole agrees to go out with the alleged offender, first meeting at the stadium, where she can see him being sympathetic with a sick fan, then next, for a walk in a park. When Nicole asks him about his marriage, he quickly explains it away by saying not to worry—that his marriage is almost over. While true to life, the film says nothing about Nicole being just 18 while the alleged offender is more than a decade older than she is ... and married. As Nicole is rarely shown, or when she is, she is shown in her last years, the age difference between the two is rarely discussed. The actors who played Nicole and the alleged offender, Jessica Tuck and Bobby Hosea, respectively, do have a similar age difference, but it is never overtly discussed.

Two years later, their relationship had progressed to the point where Nicole was openly attending events with him, even though he was still technically married. Here the film again stands out among the scripted television. In this scene, when they get back to their hotel room after attending some charity event, Nicole tells him that she wants to go back to college. When she tells him that she would like to study photography, he waves her desires away, telling her, "I can hire a photographer to teach you what you need."[20] Called "coercive control," which will be covered in greater detail later in the chapter, this behavior forced Nicole to rely solely on him. It is seen again later in the film when, after they are married, Nicole starts to make plans to become an interior decorator. He immediately goes to some of his friends to ask them to hire Nicole, with the rationalization that "if I get her a few clients, she wouldn't have to go professional."[21] While not as visually abusive as fists and bruises, this kind of control over Nicole was just as destructive. The O.J. Simpson Story is the only scripted vehicle that even mentions this. As discussed on the podcast Real Crime Profile, coercive control is a huge part of Nicole's abuse and must be told to be able to understand the whole story. It is significant that the film that was made in 1994, before the trial even truly began, includes this. It begs the question—why was this film more willing to include this behavior in 1994, when coercive control was far less likely to be considered abuse, than a miniseries produced in 2016, a full year after coercive control was criminalized in places like the UK?

Back in the "current era" of the investigation, in 1994, the police bring up the separate 911 phone calls as they focus on the alleged offender as their prime suspect. As the investigation narrows in on the history of domestic abuse against Nicole, the film again flashes back, this time to the only instance O.J. received any punishment for beating Nicole. While getting ready for bed, she confronts him over his cheating. Dressed only in a slip and a bra, Nicole is chased around the bedroom while he beats her. The first hit is off camera, leaving the audience to imagine that the beating was all going to be off camera, but the next dozen punches are clearly on screen. Tuck's Nicole manages to escape the bedroom and run outside. This was during one of her 911 calls, and the police were arriving as she ran towards them, still in her underwear and now with her face bloodied. O.J. is arrested but sentenced to community service and therapy, which he was able to do over the phone. While O.J. is sitting at a table on a golf course joking about his "punishment," Nicole arrives and sits, seemingly ready to reconcile with her abuser. Between in this scene and a later scene when Nicole is in therapy, the audience of *The O.J. Simpson Story* gets some insight into the nature of the question, "Why did she stay?"

The film was not aired until after the verdict, and, by that point, Nicole had become a footnote in the trial for her murder. More than twenty-five years old at the time of this writing, the made-for-TV movie has no ratings or reviews that can be found. One hopes that the unusually fair treatment of Nicole would help any audience gain perspective on the abuse she suffered at the hands of the alleged offender and her murder, but more likely, just like Nicole, the movie was overshadowed by the sensationalism of the trial.

The Murder of Nicole Brown Simpson (2020)

This film, released in January 2020, came out in the midst of the writing of this project, leading to the hope that there would finally be a modern iteration of Nicole Brown that would ensure she was treated fairly and not once again revictimized. Alas, that did not happen with *The Murder of Nicole Brown Simpson*. In a strange twist of fate, this film was directed by Daniel Farrands, the same director of *The Haunting of Sharon Tate* covered in Chapter 5. The unfortunate question now becomes, is there a true crime conspiracy hell-bent on revictimizing some of the most famous victims of the 20th century with some of the worst true crime films of the 21st century?

Beginning with Nicole's 35th birthday party, the film puts Nicole front and center (she turned 35 on May 19, 1994). For the first time, Nicole is the central player, both as a character on screen and in the title. It gives viewers hope—unfortunately, a false hope—that this film would be better than the others. Instead of enjoying her birthday party, Nicole, played by Mena Suvari,[22] walks to the window where she sees the ominous white Bronco parked outside the restaurant. She is also seen in therapy, talking about her destructive relationship with the alleged offender and the control that he had over her. Again, there is a sense of hope that this film may be finally addressing the coercive control and other issues surrounding this case that have been so long ignored. However, this hope is quickly and firmly dashed within the first half hour.

Nicole's famous friends, Faye Resnick and Kris Jenner, are featured in the film, but it is the relationship between Nicole and Faye that causes concern. During the scene at the restaurant, Faye kisses Nicole on the lips. Nicole shrugs it off as Faye's drunken behavior, but later when they are in Nicole's condo, there is clearly a relationship between them. Faye is attempting to convince Nicole to allow her to stay for the night, while Nicole says she does not feel like it tonight. The only evidence this relationship exists comes from Faye's tell-all book. There does not seem to be any additional information taken from Faye's book, so why take this and put it into the movie? The only conceivable reason is to make it more exciting with a lesbian storyline.

After this failed tryst with Faye, Nicole meets a house painter/handyman working next door. She asks him to take a look at her condo, which she is trying to get ready for her and her children to finally be able to move on from the alleged offender. Within a day or two—the timeline is not clear—Nicole sleeps with Glen the handyman. Again, the viewer might feel hopeful that Nicole has met someone new and is able to have a fulfilling relationship in the weeks before her death. She wakes to find the bed empty and finds him downstairs, naked and talking to himself, clearly mentally ill. Nicole runs upstairs to get away from him and calls 911. When the police arrive, there is some obvious animosity towards Nicole. While taking her statement, the officers comment on what she is wearing (a silk robe) and her "history of calling 911," and imply that she has a type and may have been asking for this. Nicole calls them on each of these insults, obviously fed up with the bias the police department has against her. When they call her Mrs. Simpson, she yells that her name is Brown. This feels like an empowering moment, until one pauses the film and remembers that its name is *The Murder of Nicole Brown Simpson*. How empowering is it to have Nicole insist that her name is now Brown only to have the name of the movie include her married name?

After this dangerous encounter with Glen, Nicole starts to see him everywhere she goes. She sees him following her around a shopping mall only two days before the murder. The creepy stalker-movie vibe only increases from here—changing the movie from a vague true crime movie into a slasher film. This shift signals the loss of any dedication to the facts or to history. Nicole tries to find out more about this Glen from her neighbor who originally hired him—turns out that neighbor is now missing and presumed dead. Glen goes to a bar, meets a woman who calls him Charlie, and kills her in a parking lot. Now that Glen/Charlie is a fully fledged serial killer, it becomes clear that the film is setting him up as a foil for the alleged offender.

On the night of the murder, Nicole takes her children to Sydney's dance recital, and the alleged offender makes his first appearance. For the few minutes that he appears on screen, he seems to be calm and rational, far from the alleged offender that is seen in any of the other iterations of this case. He calmly asks Nicole to be able to see the kids and she screams at him that he will never lay his "fucking hands" on her again.[23] Right after this confrontation, he runs into Glen and calls him "Charlie." Clearly, they know each other and the alleged offender knows him as his killer alter ego.[24]

Nicole and her children go home after that last famous dinner at Mezzaluna. In another confusing turn, the film gives Nicole a lovely moment where she is seen singing lullabies to her children in German, as she was known to do every night. After tucking Sydney and Jason into bed, Nicole goes downstairs to find a news story about Glen, now known as Glen Rogers, playing on the television. Obviously freaking out, she runs to lock all the doors and turn on the alarm, but this is the moment when Ron Goldman shows up with the glasses that Nicole's mother left at the restaurant.

The attack comes out of nowhere and is entirely expected. This scene is the worst portion of the film as it explicitly shows the deaths of Nicole and Ron. Ron is stabbed repeatedly on screen while screaming. The killer lifts Nicole up and slits her throat. This is the only time known to the researcher that Nicole is killed on camera. Dropped to the stone sidewalk, she bleeds out while gasping for oxygen. To see Nicole die on screen, and in such a graphic way, is the epitome of revictimization. This film has turned what most in the true crime community consider to be a huge miscarriage of justice into a slasher movie.

After the murders, the movie turns into a strange hodge-podge of real and filmed footage. Real footage from the crime scene, with Nicole's and Ron's bodies lying on the sidewalk, is shown just seconds after the fictional versions of their deaths. Their bodies are not blurred or protected in any way. Nicole's October 911 calls are also played over the credits, another exploitation of her pleas for help against her abusive ex-husband.

One of the loudest criticisms of this film is the suggestion that O.J. did not commit the murders. Glen is known to be Glen Edward Rogers, also known as the Cross Country Killer and the Casanova Killer.[25] Rogers, still in prison, is suspected and/or convicted in the stabbing or strangling deaths of one man in Ohio and four people in California, Mississippi, Florida, and Louisiana. In a documentary, Rogers's brother claims that Glen killed Nicole, while his family stated that he had been working for Nicole in 1994. Other than these accounts from the Rogers family, there is no evidence that Glen Rogers had anything to do with Nicole's murder. However, Farrands's introduction of this character turns Nicole into a "terrible judge of character ... [as] a subtle bit of victim blaming."[26]

TV Miniseries

The People v. O.J.: American Crime Story (2016)

Created by Ryan Murphy, famous for Glee and American Horror Story, American Crime Story spent its first season on the trial of the alleged offender. Much like American Horror Story, American Crime Story presents a completely different story from season to season. With a limited number of episodes and just one season, Murphy was able to tell a concise story and reignite the country's interest in the case.

News began to buzz when Murphy—already a big name in Hollywood—announced that his new show was going to focus on this case. There were frequent casting announcements, with Cuba Gooding, Jr., cast as the alleged offender, Sarah Paulson as Marcia Clark, John Travolta as Robert Shapiro, Courtney B. Vance as Johnny Cochran, and Sterling K. Brown as Christopher Dardin. David Schwimmer was cast as Robert Kardashian and Selma Blair as his ex-wife, Kris Jenner. But who wasn't cast? Nicole Brown. It is only if one looks far down the show's expanded cast list that Nicole can be found at all. She was played by Kelly Dowdle and only in three of the total ten episodes of the series. In one of those episodes, Dowdle is listed as "voice, uncredited."[27] If the title was not enough to point to the focus on O.J., the fact that Nicole is barely visible in this series shows how little attention was paid to the victims.

In the first episode of the series, "From the Ashes of the Tragedy," Nicole is named fairly quickly once her body is discovered. She is not named again until Marcia Clark and Gil Garcetti[28] are in the district attorney's office discussing the crime scene photos. Nicole is mentioned as being "practically decapitated."[29] As part of her initial investigation, Marcia pulls the file on any police reports that include Nicole's name. She is outraged to find eight 911 calls and a stack of medical reports. "All that battering before an arrest," she said. This is the extent of the miniseries' attention to the abuse of Nicole. A subject that was handled so well, or at least discussed at length in the 1995 movie, is barely a footnote in a ten-episode miniseries.

For the next few episodes, Nicole continues to be a footnote in her own murder case. In episode two, her name is only mentioned when the charges against the alleged offender are read aloud. During Nicole's funeral in episode three, Kris Jenner berates Robert Kardashian for taking O.J.'s side. Kris, one of Nicole's best friends, seems to be one of the only people in the miniseries who cares about her or is even genuinely upset over her death. As Selma Blair's mascara runs down her face, Nicole becomes human for the briefest of seconds—a woman who had friends who wanted to cry at her funeral.

Another one of Nicole's "friends," Faye Resnick, damages the good impression of Nicole in the very next episode when she attempts to sell her tell-all book to the highest bidder. In a throwaway line, Faye stresses that Nicole was a good mother but quickly begins to give salacious details of a life that Nicole may or may not have lived. Faye, played by Connie Britton, alleged that Nicole did a lot of cocaine and was known for her "Brentwood hellos," a term for waking a man with oral sex.[30] She also tells her potential editor that Nicole and the alleged offender "had hot sex," which was "a problem for O.J. after they broke up because he knew she needed it all the time."[31] None of these things are necessarily bad nor do they mean that Nicole was a bad person. Even though it becomes very clear that Faye's objective is to "sell a lot of books … in a completely non-exploitative way," this undermines any goodwill paid to Nicole. Yes, viewers will have the sense to give Nicole the benefit of the doubt and understand that Faye is simply trying to get paid. However, it is difficult to remove the mental image of a "Brentwood hello" in connection with Nicole after this episode.

The next time that Nicole is treated with anything more than a throwaway line is the final episode of the miniseries, titled "The Verdict." This episode gives the audience what they have been waiting for over the last nine episodes. The alleged offender is found not guilty of the murders of Nicole and Ron Goldman. After the verdict, Marcia is understandably heartbroken and says, "Everyone wants justice for victims' rights…. I never doubted that … until this."[32] While the producers have insight into the day of the verdict, some creative license was taken to create or re-create conversations lost to history. It is within one of those, a conversation hoped to be true to life, that Marcia says, "After all they heard, after all they know, a man who beat and beat and terrorized his wife until he just snuffed her out … and they let him go—for reasons that have nothing to do with those two people."[33] Marcia Clark seemed to be the only person—or was at least the only person shown by the show—who recognized the pattern of abuse that led to Nicole's death. In this short speech, she also voiced the true causes of the not-guilty verdict, which had nothing to do with whether the alleged offender actually murdered Nicole and Ron.

The episode and the miniseries end with a "where are they now" montage—a perfect end to a 1990s homage. The last frame shows Nicole and Ron with their birth and death dates. It was surely meant to honor them, but one cannot help think that it would have been a greater honor to have included either one of them in any other part of the miniseries.

While it should not be surprising that a show called the *The People v. O.J.* would focus solely on the alleged offender, the title also implies that the miniseries would give a detailed examination of the case. In the show's defense, it did that—to a certain extent. Viewers got a behind-the-scenes look at the defense and prosecution, but the one side of the case that was missing was the defense of the victims, Nicole and Ron. There were a few fleeting mentions of the abuse Nicole suffered for more than a decade before her murder in 1994, yet there was no mention of the coercive control that plagued her life while she was married to O.J. Her name is barely mentioned over the ten episodes. It is disappointing in 2016 that a show would be produced that pays so little attention to the victim and so much attention to the perpetrator, especially considering that a movie made twenty-two years earlier did such a better job (but by no means a great job).

Documentaries/True Crime Shows

O.J.: The Lost Confession

The murders of Nicole Brown and Ronald Goldman have also been the subject of many documentaries, especially with the twenty-fifth anniversary coinciding with the latest waves of popularity in true crime. One of the most interesting true crime shows covering the case was called *O.J.: The Lost Confession*. Airing on FOX in March of 2018, the show was considered to be a ratings failure, with only 4.4 million viewers—"less than half the number that tuned in to watch ABC's revived *American Idol*."[34] The show revolved around an interview that O.J. did with journalist Judith Reagan in 2006. Deemed too controversial to air in 2006, FOX instead presented the interview as a panel discussion. Hosted by Soledad O'Brien, the panelists included Judith Reagan; Christopher Dardin, part of the original prosecution team; Eve Chin, Nicole's childhood friend; and Jim Clemente, former New York City prosecutor, FBI profiler, and one of the hosts of *Real Crime Profile*. As the title suggests, FOX implied that the 2006 interview had been lost and this was the first time in a decade the world would see a potential confession by the alleged offender. Right away—Nicole is again forgotten. Between the title and the possible confession, it is about getting at the man, not about getting justice for Nicole and Ron.

The panelists quickly make up for this as they begin to talk about the case and about Nicole. One of the first questions Soledad asked was to Eve about Nicole as a person and about their relationship as friends. This is one of the only true insights into Nicole's life before meeting the alleged offender. There was the typical "she was born here and grew up here," but Eve allows a deeper view into this life. Almost immediately, she begins to tear up, more than twenty years later, when speaking about Nicole. In this short moment, all of Eve's thoughts were about Nicole as a mother. She said that Nicole was "an amazing mom" and she "would have loved seeing her kids growing up."[35]

Halfway through the show, Jim Clemente joins and you can immediately see his contempt for the alleged offender and his treatment of Nicole. The discussion revolves around the time after Nicole had left him and was actively dating. Jim points out that there is a very clear double standard at work. The alleged offender made it very clear that it was okay for him to "get some," as Jim put it, but it was not okay for Nicole to have a sex life with anyone other than him. This is mirrored in *The O.J. Simpson Story* from 1995, which includes a scene where Nicole is on a date that has ended on the sofa in her condo. Even though Nicole and her date were just talking on the sofa, the alleged offender barges in and breaks up the date.

The third act of the show is the "confession," where the alleged offender gives a hypothetical description of what happened on the night of June 12, 1994. He frequently reminds Judith that this is all hypothetical, just as protection for himself. While placing some of the blame on a killer named Charlie, he also places himself at the scene on the night of the murders. The producers chose to play significant portions of this "confession," essentially forcing everyone involved to relive the night of Nicole's murder. For all of the important moments of the show—giving voice to Nicole's friends and bringing attention to the brutal domestic violence—this detracts from that. The overall tone and exploitative nature of the show drew intense criticism from the entire entertainment world. *Entertainment Weekly* called it "the programming equivalent of finding your meth-addict buddy on the floor of his apartment, face-down in a puddle of his own sick."[36] Even Bill O'Reilly, on sister channel FOX News, called the special "indefensible and a low point in American culture."[37] A review in *The New York Times* was slightly more charitable by saying that, while "morally horrifying, it was also gripping and an important piece of cultural history."[38] Gayle King, host on *CBS This Morning*, and Oprah's bestie, specifically had a problem with his hypothetical retelling of the murder. King makes it clear who are the victims of a show like this—the families of Nicole Brown and Ron Goldman—saying, "I just think that is pretty disgusting.... And if I was the Goldman family, Nicole's family, it would make my blood boil."[39]

FOX's ploy to beat the juggernaut of *American Idol* did not work. While the American people were, and likely always will be, obsessed with the deaths of Nicole and Ron, only 4.4 million tuned in to watch this. Its few interesting points—the insight from Nicole's childhood friend, the participation of Christopher Dardin, and the expertise of FBI profiler Jim Clemente—could not compensate for the exploitation felt through the entire presentation. Nicole is there, but so is the alleged offender, and the spotlight is unfortunately always on him. There is no closure that anyone watching may have hoped to find.

True Crime with Aphrodite Jones

As with other cases in this project, true crime writers like Aphrodite Jones have focused on this case. The second episode of her show, *True Crime with Aphrodite Jones*, calls the alleged offender "one of the most troubling characters of the 20th century," "infamous," and "an American icon."[40] Again, the suspected murderer in this case is highly inflated while Nicole is all but forgotten.

The one aspect of this episode that differentiates this from the many other documentaries on the case is the modern perspective. When the show aired on Investigation Discovery in 2011, the alleged offender had already been arrested for armed robbery in 2007. Jones compares the 911 call in the 2007 case in Las Vegas to the 911 calls involving Nicole. By making this comparison, Jones strengthens the argument that this violence is a pattern of behavior for the alleged offender that has been going on for decades. While Nicole is still in the periphery, it does allow for greater understanding of Simpson's overall violence towards her and towards anyone who challenges him.

Podcasts

With the breadth of knowledge and information available, podcasts have been quick to cover the case. Dozens upon dozens of podcasts have episodes on the alleged offender, but as with the other aspects of pop culture, few have given Nicole the attention she deserves. Of the more than two dozen episodes listened to for this project, Nicole's name appeared in the title of a few. The hosts/producers knew that it was the name of the alleged offender that would get the downloads.

As with other subjects of this project, *Real Crime Profile* stands out as a voice for Nicole Brown and Ron Goldman. The hosts, former New Scotland Yard behavioral analyst Laura Richards, former New York City prosecutor and former FBI profiler Jim Clemente, and *Criminal Minds* casting director Lisa Zambetti, began their podcast in 2016 with several episodes on *Making a Murderer*[41]—those six episodes were followed by an intensive look at the case through the lens of *The People v. O.J. Simpson*. While the *RCP* series takes each episode of *The People v. O.J. Simpson* one by one, this first one is an overview during which Laura, Jim, and Lisa condemn the miniseries. Right away, they make the point that the victims are completely absent. The miniseries takes a perspective that is very "O.J.-centric," but to understand the case, viewers have to understand how Nicole and Ron lived.[42] Nicole is completely absent, until later, "when she's just trashed by the defense."[43] All of the hosts, but specifically Jim and Laura, both of whom have spent their careers working with the families of victims lost to violence, were outraged for the families. Jim, who was an FBI profiler at the time, did not work the case but did see the crime scene photos while working with the famed criminalist Dr. Henry Lee. He describes the photos as some of the most brutal he had ever seen before, raging, "How dare the defense and the media disrespect the victims by concentrating on anything other than these victims?"[44]

In episode two of their analysis (episode eight of the podcast), the hosts announce they are making the conscious decision to "take a break from what's covered in the series."[45] In what is now *RCP* tradition, the show wanted to spend significant time on Nicole and Ron. In episode eight, they began a deep examination of Nicole's life. As a daughter, mother, and sister, Nicole was described as the rock of her family. With so much attention paid to her relationship with the alleged offender, the fact that Nicole had family members—parents, a sister, children—is often lost in the bigger story. Inevitably, O.J. does enter Nicole's life, but *RCP* brings up the power imbalance of an 18-year-old entering a relationship with a man 12 years older. Beyond that, by the time they met, he was a famous football player who was already on his way to transitioning to Hollywood. Familiar with how this kind of power imbalance can lead to things like coercive control and abuse, Jim and Laura again offer insight into how Nicole entered into this relationship already off-balance.

Episode two plays the now infamous 911 call that has been played in nearly every podcast, show, and every other type of media covering this case. Nicole placed the call on October 25, 1993, while living in her condo in Gretna Green, after her divorce from O.J. He was trying to break down the door while screaming at her. *RCP* plays portions of the call while the experts analyze the response of the 911 dispatcher. There is an enormous amount of victim blaming as the dispatcher asks things like "what did you do?" and he's "just harassing you?" The dispatcher, a woman, asks all the wrong questions, something that Laura would know about intimately, as she came upon the DASH risk assessment checklist, DASH standing for "Domestic Abuse, Stalking, and Honour Based Violence." Nicole is clearly afraid and can be heard sobbing on the call. While this call is played over and over, few ever talk about the poor way that the call was handled.

The three hosts are very clear that absolutely nothing good came from this case, but they admit that if anything at all did come from this, Nicole was able to give a face and a name to domestic abuse. When the photos that her sister took after the 1989 abuse—which got the alleged offender his only real "punishment"—hit the media, it started a conversation on what domestic abuse looks like.

Their deep dive into the victimology of Nicole continued into episode three of their *People vs. O.J.* series (episode nine). Called a "bonus episode," Laura and Lisa (Jim was not on this episode) wanted to examine two letters by Nicole badly enough to interrupt the podcast schedule. One letter was read in the criminal trial, where the alleged offender was found not guilty of her murder, and the other was used in the civil trial, where he was found legally responsible for the deaths of Nicole and Ron.

The first letter, used in the criminal trial by the defense team, was primarily to convince the jury that Nicole was in love with the alleged offender, and to disprove the accusations of abuse. This blatant victim blaming was countered by an 85-page dossier and testimony by an expert on battered women who then kill. Laura points out that this is not the case for Nicole. Nicole was not a battered woman who killed. Laura continues by saying this is not even battered woman syndrome; it is "murdered wife syndrome."[46] The overall conclusion of this first letter is that it took Nicole and her relationship with O.J. completely out of context.

The second letter, used in the civil trial that the families of the victims brought against Simpson after the criminal trial was over, paints an entirely different picture. In this letter, written to the alleged offender, Nicole tells him that she considered their marriage a huge mistake. She says that the last time she trusted him was at their wedding ceremony. Nicole gives an account of the times she was terrified and terrorized by the alleged offender. She describes her pregnancies, when he coercively controlled her, including trying to control what and how much she ate. Laura suggests that this case, with this kind of evidence, should have been presented as a domestic violence murder instead of a "straight-forward" murder case. Nicole herself, as Laura and Lisa present, was preparing a file on the alleged offender. She kept diaries for fourteen years and kept them in a safety deposit box. These diaries list eleven particular incidents, including financial abuse, part of coercive control. This letter and this analysis by Laura and Lisa not only give Nicole's side of the story more weight but also give Nicole agency. Rather than the pop culture revictimization, *RCP* is giving Nicole back her power, twenty-five years after her death. She not only was able to endure this torment, but she carefully documented the abuse while also raising her children and trying to get on with her life. This is the Nicole the *RCP* presents.

In the final episode of their series, Laura, Jim, and Lisa cover the finale of the miniseries. Their most poignant comment concerns the photos of Nicole and Ron at the end of the episode. Laura asks if "there's anything more symbolic of them being footnotes than that…?"[47] As with many of the cases covered by *RCP*, their goal is to make sure that victims are no longer footnotes in their own murder cases. With this podcast and series such as this on miniseries, documentaries, and cases in the news, the people at *Real Crime Profile* are at the forefront of ending this revictimization by popular culture.

The handling of Nicole by other podcasts falls more on a spectrum between progressive on one end and total revictimization/forgetting on the other. One podcast that comes closest to *RCP* is *You're Wrong About*, hosted by Michael Hobbes, a reporter for *The Huffington Post*, and Sarah Marshall, a writer for *The Believer* magazine and *Buzzfeed*. The premise of their podcast is to attempt to dispel commonly held misconceptions about true crime cases. Sarah wished to cover this case to "do right by Nicole."[48] Part of her argument is that the huge spectacle surrounding the case caused Nicole to be forgotten, and Sarah wanted to do her part to correct this.

The two episodes on Nicole were part of a much larger series about the case, including episodes on Marcia Clark and Paula Barbieri, the alleged offender's girlfriend in the months leading up to the murders and during the trial. Using the source *Raging Heart: The Intimate Story of the Tragic Marriage of O.J. and Nicole Brown Simpson*, Sarah tells Michael about Nicole's childhood, first in Germany and then in Southern California. As with *RCP*, *You're Wrong About* presents Nicole as a whole person with a life before and outside of the marriage that she shared with the alleged offender.

One stark point *You're Wrong About* makes that few others do is how young Nicole really was when she began dating and moved in with the alleged offender. Nicole moved out of her parents' home when she turned 18, and she met the alleged offender five weeks later. As Sarah and Michael discuss for several minutes, Nicole had five weeks of living with her room-mate like a "normal" 18-year-old before she began the relationship that most likely ended her life.

In the second episode about Nicole on *You're Wrong About*, the hosts delve into the same letter discussed by *RCP* from the civil trial. This coverage of the letter that so clearly lays out the coercive control is yet another indication that this podcast is on par, only without the expertise of professional profilers, with *RCP*. Sarah and Michael also analyze Faye Resnick's tell-all book, making fun of Faye for clearly taking advantage of her friend's death. As they discuss, yes, Nicole did take part in a nightlife that would not be too extraordinary for a woman who had had her entire life controlled since she was 18, but they also describe a Nicole whom no other outlet has mentioned. After her final breakup with the alleged offender, Nicole spent some nights just hanging out with her friends Jeff and Mike, "watching *Melrose Place* and wearing sweatpants."[49] Sarah and Michael paint a picture of a perfectly normal 35-year-old woman moving on with her life. The normality of Nicole is yet another aspect of her life that gets lost in the drama of her murder, the trial, and the acquittal of her accused murderer.

In one of the most surprising turns, the two-part series on Nicole ended with the hosts saying they did not know how to end the episode. What is incredibly important is that they chose not to go over the murder or the trial. While nearly every other iteration of Nicole Brown has been a prelude to talking about the trial of the alleged offender, *You're Wrong About* makes it a point only to discuss Nicole's life and not her death. The only time her murder is mentioned is when Sarah, the primary researcher on this case, explains that it was only after doing the research into the escalation of domestic violence that it seemed incredibly likely that O.J. was the killer.

Two episodes of *Two Ghouls One Grave* cover the murders and the trial—episode 34, "The Murder of Nicole Brown Simpson and Ron Goldman," and episode 36, "The Trial of O.J. Simpson." Episode 34, as the title suggests, has far more information about Nicole and Ron. One interesting point made by the hosts, Meg and Joe Grim, is how so many have slandered, or revictimized, Nicole and Ron by trying to make their relationship something other than the platonic friendship that it was. Episode 36 asks a very important question that still remains unanswered: "If O.J. was truly innocent—why wasn't there any investigation into who the 'real' killer(s) were?"[50] Where was any kind of justice for the victims?

The rest of the episodes listened to for this project either barely mention Nicole or perpetuate her revictimization. *True Crime Garage*, hosted by two men who go by Nic and The Captain, did a series on the case in 2016. The first episode began with the October 1993 911 call, but without the same detailed analysis that *RCP* gave; it just exploited Nicole's terrified call for help. As with many of their episodes, they gave a detailed overview of the night of June 12 with some basic facts on Nicole and Ron, but nothing more than that. In the second episode, Nic and The Captain have a discussion on the phrase "battered husband" in the letter the alleged offender wrote before leaving for the Bronco chase. They wondered whether Nicole ever "came at O.J."[51] In the very same year that *RCP* is discussing coercive control and Laura has created the DASH Risk Checklist for first responders in the UK, these two hosts are wondering if the abuse in Nicole's relationship was a two-way street. Not only is this incorrect, but it gives some listeners the ability to explain away the abuse of Nicole. Similarly, the podcast *Conspiracy Asylum*, in the episode titled "O.J. Simpson" from May 30, 2019, calls Nicole an actor or a "would-be" actor.[52] The hosts, a married couple, split the topics by gender, with the wife covering anything having to do with Nicole. They were also self-aware enough to admit that, while they were not particularly proud of covering the killer as the main topic instead of the victim, it was because the killer in this case is just so much more interesting.[53]

Conclusion

It has been more than twenty-five years since Nicole's murder, and there still has not been a conviction for the two murders committed on the night of June 12, 1994. The alleged offender, while found not guilty in October of 1995, was found civilly liable for Nicole's and Ron's deaths. After not just one, but two trials, one criminal and one civil, the public knew enough of the details to be ripe for pop culture to take the reins.

In any kind of informational coverage of the case, where the facts are told in a straightforward manner, it is the offender who receives far more attention than Nicole. News coverage, books, films, and podcast episodes almost exclusively have titles that feature the offender's name and not Nicole's. Opposite of the situation of Elizabeth Short, where only her media name is used to garner sales and downloads, Nicole's name appears nowhere. It is only the offender's name that is used to attract the audience. Rather than rely on Nicole's name recognition or even educate the public on her, project after project continues to add to the library of the offender.

As is becoming clear, most of the women selected for this project have been victims of pop culture exploitation, and Nicole is no exception.

Between films that, much like those of Sharon Tate, turn Nicole into the victim of a slasher film, and books that turn her into a drug-addicted sex worker in the weeks before her death, it can be difficult to find any truth of the "real Nicole." One would hope that this would change over time, and yet one of the films most guilty of exploiting and victimizing Nicole was released in January 2020.

Once again, it is podcasts that have begun to turn the tide and advocate for Nicole two decades after her death. By examining both documentaries and what those documentaries are leaving out of Nicole's story, podcasts like *RCP* are adding terms like coercive control into the discussion. During the trial, many people were becoming more educated on domestic abuse. However, the subject is now known to be incredibly more nuanced, and experts like Laura Richards help audience members to better understand Nicole's life leading up to her death.

While there are a few standouts advocating for Nicole,[54] the vast majority of coverage is still either exploitative or informational. It is unknown what it will take for a fair depiction of Nicole to be produced. Perhaps the popularity of true crime combined with increased awareness of domestic abuse might spark interest in a movie about Nicole that allows her to appear on screen as she appeared in life—a daughter, a friend, a mother, and a woman long before she was ever a victim.

CHAPTER 10

Kathleen Peterson
and Teresa Halbach

The first decade of the 21st century has long been used to suggest a vastly different world from that in which earlier authors or screenwriters lived. Movies from the 1950s imagined the 2000s as a futuristic utopia (or dystopia) that moviegoers could not relate to in any way. In some ways, these writers were more prophetic than not. Cell phones, internet, and the dependency on computers would be alien to people who considered television the most technologically advanced thing in their houses. With TVs that only received three channels that stopped broadcasting at 11 p.m., they certainly could not have imagined the sheer possibilities at our fingertips with Netflix.

Launched first as a DVD delivery service in 1997, Netflix began offering tens of thousands of titles as part of its streaming service in 2007. By 2019, Netflix had hundreds of millions of paying subscribers with millions more sharing those subscriptions. The streaming service offers both original and non-original content, including a plethora of true crime options. In addition to changing the way video content is delivered to customers, Netflix has forever altered the way people watch content. By having all the content available at once, the practice of "binging" all of the episodes as quickly as possible began. Binging content, true crime or not, affects our interpretation of the media. Watching eight or ten episodes over the course of a weekend immerses people in the stories without the benefit of additional narratives. There is not the same opportunity to hear multiple versions or other perspectives on a case. Additionally, documentaries were released at times of rapidly changing news coverage and social media. Huge online communities sprung up following the release of documentaries, all with different ideas on the cases. It becomes increasingly difficult for individuals to sort fact from fiction, only adding more confusion to the entire case. This chapter will examine the impact of these documentaries on streaming platforms and how that altered the interpretations of the women involved.

Two documentary series, covering the prosecution of two crimes that happened in the 2000s, exploded onto Netflix and, arguably, served as a catalyst for this newest wave of interest in true crime. The first, *The Staircase*, centers around Michael Peterson, a man convicted of the death of his wife, Kathleen Peterson. Kathleen died at the foot of the stairs in their home in Durham, North Carolina, on December 9, 2001. *The Staircase* was not released in seasons but in installments. The first episodes were released as a series on BBC4, with additional updates released until all thirteen episodes were put on Netflix in 2018. The second documentary series, *Making a Murderer*, focuses on Steven Avery and his nephew, Brendan Dassey, who were convicted of the murder of Teresa Halbach in March and April of 2007, respectively. The first season of the documentary dropped on Netflix in December 2015 with the second season following in October 2018. Within months of their respective release, each was the subject of numerous podcasts, articles, and online discussions. Across the various platforms, one theme emerged … where is the voice of the victims?

◇◇◇

Kathleen Peterson

Just the Facts

There is little that can be found out about Kathleen beyond the basic details of her life. Nearly all of the information about her comes from her sister Candace Zamperini. Candace is a fixture on all the documentaries and podcasts to advocate for her sister. Kathleen was born on February 21, 1953. After attending college, she became the first woman to attend the School of Engineering at Duke University. She met and married Fred Atwater and, after years of trying, conceived and had her daughter, Caitlin. Divorcing Atwater after learning of an affair, she soon met and moved in with Michael Peterson. They married in 1997, blending a family of five children. Kathleen had Caitlin while Michael had his two sons, Clayton and Todd, and two adoptive daughters, Margaret and Martha.

By this time, Kathleen was a vice president of marketing at Nortel Networks. Her sister describes her as hardworking and resourceful, garnering a prominent position in Durham, North Carolina, society. As a vice president, Kathleen was the family's breadwinner. Michael, a writer, had a few successful novels, but by the early 2000s, he had no money coming in and the family had to rely almost exclusively on Kathleen's salary.

On December 9, 2001, Michael Peterson called 911 to report that Kathleen had fallen down the stairs in their Durham home. After telling this to the dispatcher, he hangs up, only to call back a few minutes later to ask them where they are. Emergency responders arrive on the scene only to pronounce Kathleen dead at the bottom of the home's back staircase. When the police arrive, Michael tells them that he and Kathleen had been drinking wine poolside before she came inside just before midnight to get some work done before going to bed. He stayed by the pool, smoking a cigar in the December chill. He claimed that when he came inside, he found his wife at the base of the stairs, bloody and not breathing.

Peterson was arrested by Durham police and was indicted in Kathleen's murder on December 21, 2001. Shortly after he was released on bond in January 2002, Peterson began being filmed by a documentary film crew, but more about this later. With a trial lasting more than a year, Peterson was not convicted of first-degree murder until October 10, 2003, nearly two years after the death of Kathleen. The case appeared closed until a complaint arose against blood expert and criminalist Dwayne Deaver with the South Carolina Bureau of Investigation. He was found to have misrepresented evidence, leading to the false imprisonment of at least one individual. Due to this development, other cases, including the Peterson case, were reopened in 2011. Michael Peterson was released on December 16, 2011, after more than seven years in prison. Bound over for a retrial, Peterson was monitored and on house arrest. Finally, in 2017, Peterson agreed to sign an Alford plea, which is a guilty plea in which the defendant admits that the state has sufficient evidence to convict him for voluntary manslaughter. During the Alford sentencing hearing, Candace read a victim's impact statement, speaking for her sister one last time.

News of the Day

In the weeks following Kathleen's death, she was the subject of dozens of newspaper articles. As has become unfortunately unsurprising in this project, Kathleen is both overshadowed and passed over in favor of coverage of the offender. After the initial few weeks, particularly when Michael became the focus of the investigation, Kathleen is nearly absent altogether from articles about her own death.

On the day after Kathleen was found at the base of the infamous staircase, the first article appeared in *The News and Observer* in Raleigh. Showing the clear bias towards the offender, the article is titled "Wife of 1999 Mayoral Candidate Found Dead."[1] Her treatment does not get any better in the body of the article. In the very first sentence, she is referred to as "[t]he wife of Michael Peterson."[2] Immediately after this, he is described as the man "who ran unsuccessfully for Durham's City Council this fall."[3] Kathleen's name is not actually mentioned in the article until well after the offender's. She is described as a Nortel Networks "employee" and not the director of information services that she was at the time of her death.

Kathleen is minimized in many other articles about her own death as reporters put emphasis on the offender and his career. In "Death of Wife of Ex-Candidate Under Scrutiny," yet another article that describes Kathleen solely as the offender's wife in the title, Kathleen is described as "a busy mother of five and director of information services at Nortel Networks."[4] While they are finally getting her corporate title correct, the reporters put her more traditionally feminine and acceptable role of mother before her corporate job. Additionally, this sentence comes after three different sentences describing Michael's career as a novelist, a columnist, and a politician. Any real background on Kathleen didn't appear in an article in *The News and Observer* until five days after her death, when Aisling Swift mentions that she was born Kathleen Morris Hunt in Lancaster, Pennsylvania.[5]

There was one article that stood out among the many that disrespected Kathleen. Appearing the day after the offender's conviction on October 10, 2003, "It Wasn't Just About Mike Peterson" was written by Ruth Sheehan. Echoing the words of District Attorney Jim Hardin, Sheehan says, "Really, the trial wasn't only about Mike Peterson."[6] Hardin told the jury that "Kathleen was crying out for justice ... and they listened."[7] Sheehan describes Kathleen's grave and the roses and wind chimes placed there by Kathleen's sisters. Calling the chimes' sound both eerie and mournful, she says it is a reminder that "even on a day of verdict and reactions, of analysis and water-cooler chatter—at the center of it all, still, is the late Kathleen Hunt Peterson.... May she rest in peace."[8] This is the only article that offers up any kind of respect for Kathleen or remotely recognizes that Kathleen got lost in the spectacle of the trial.

Books

Written in the Blood: A True Story of Murder and a Deadly 16-Year-Old Secret That Tore a Family Apart

Considered to be one of the best books on the death of Kathleen, *Written in the Blood* by Diane Fanning was first published in 2005, with a reprint in 2018. Fanning, who has written fifteen true crime books in her career, has also appeared on *20/20*, the *Today* show, and *Deadly Women*.[9] Her book on Kathleen was Fanning's fourth true crime book.

As with so many other iterations of Kathleen, *Written in the Blood* begins with her death and the offender's call to 911. From there, the book follows the familiar path of tracing the offender from the 911 call to what turned into the just the beginning of his legal troubles. Sixty-seven pages into the book, Fanning opens a chapter entirely on him. Flashing back to his childhood, the search begins for some kind of explanation of his actions. Subsequent chapters focus on Elizabeth Ratliffe, Kathleen Peterson, the offender multiple times, and the offender and Kathleen together.

Kathleen's first chapter does not begin until page 157, giving more than one hundred and fifty pages to the alleged murderer before focusing on the woman whose photo is on the front cover. Beyond this issue, this chapter gives the best background on Kathleen. Starting in the 19th century, Fanning offers a history of the Hunt family (Hunt was Kathleen's maiden name). Given that most iterations of Kathleen barely mention anything more than her birthdate before jumping to her death, this is beyond impressive. This pattern continues as Fanning follows Kathleen to college and to the School of Engineering at Duke. Her attendance at Duke is a detail commonly included in Kathleen's biography, but *Written in the Blood* also includes specific classes that Kathleen took and meeting her first husband. The same chapter offers insight into her marriage to Atwater; giving birth to Caitlin; and her career at Northern Telecom, more commonly referred to as Nortel.[10]

Fanning's coverage of the Petersons' financial situation before Kathleen's death is also unparalleled. If the family's finances are discussed at all, they may include the fact that Kathleen's success at Nortel led to $1 million in stock options, and sometimes the iterations also include that the family was experiencing financial difficulties. Fanning, on the other hand, takes it so much farther. In addition to the Nortel stock options "valued at over $1 million," the combined household income for 1999 "from salaries, rental properties, and military benefits was $276,790."[11] However, within months, the stock prices plummeted and "Nortel began its optimization program, a fancy phrase that meant they were downsizing and laying people off left and right."[12] Rather than simply stating that the family was having financial difficulties, *Written in the Blood* tells readers that "Kathleen's huge nest egg had shrunk to a value of less than $900,000" by the end of 2000.[13]

Written in the Blood, while offering background into the offender and coverage of the case itself, also gives readers the best background information on Kathleen Peterson. For the first time in the research for this project, outside of perhaps the descriptions by her children, Kathleen becomes a fully formed person, with hopes, dreams, anxieties, worries, and fears. While not the only book on the death of Kathleen Peterson, *Written in the*

Blood is considered the quintessential book on not only her death, but also her life.

Documentaries

The Staircase

The world outside Durham, North Carolina, learned about Kathleen Peterson when parts of the documentary later known as *The Staircase* began to air on a variety of platforms in 2004 and 2005. American audiences were able to watch the original eight episodes on the Sundance Channel in April of 2005. Those original eight ended with Peterson going to prison for the death of Kathleen. Additional episodes were filmed in 2011 and 2012 when Peterson was freed, bringing the episode count to ten. A full thirteen episodes were released on Netflix in 2018, achieving the widest release of the documentary. Over the last fifteen years since the release of the original episodes, millions of people have watched, often multiple times. True crime fans have their theories on who killed Kathleen, but other than controversy over her manner of death, few actually talk about Kathleen Peterson. With *The Staircase* as their primary source of information, it is not surprising at the lack of attention paid to the woman who lost her life on that back staircase.

From the opening of the first episode, it is clear that Kathleen is merely a plot point in the story of the offender's arrest, trial, and journey back out of prison. Kathleen is only mentioned a few times outside of her role as the victim. The offender or the children occasionally speak about her warmly while reminiscing, but there is not the kind of grief that one would expect from a family who had lost their matriarch.

One of the subtle but powerful ways the documentary continues to victimize Kathleen Peterson is the use of crime scene video and photos. It is expected, in a crime documentary, to see re-creations of crimes and/ or the scenes of crimes. It is also expected to see crime scene photos, but it is typical that those photos are blurred in post-production to protect the memory of the victim. However, in *The Staircase*, unblurred photos of Kathleen are shown in several episodes. They first appear in the first episode as the defense team strategizes in a bland conference room. David Rudolf and his team discuss alternative theories of her death while they, and the camera, examine stark photos of Kathleen's dead body. The photos return in episode two, completely unblurred, further victimizing Kathleen by showing her lying at the bottom of the infamous staircase. It's not unusual for a defense attorney to examine crime scene photos, nor is it strange for the prosecution team to show those photos in court, which they do in episode four, but it is unusual to have unaltered photos shown over and over. By not altering the photos, the filmmakers are showing Kathleen less respect than the editors of *Dateline* or *American Justice with Aphrodite Jones*, both of which blurred Kathleen's body in all footage and photos from the crime scene. One would imagine that a documentary that has full cooperation from the victim's family would want to show Kathleen the respect of not showing her body in a heap at the bottom of the stairs.

Not only does the family not request the photos to be blurred, but also the staircase is not cleaned in the months and even the year following Kathleen's death. It is not even cleaned when the jury pays a dramatic visit to the crime scene during the trial. Now, obviously, this could possibly be explained by Peterson getting arrested fairly quickly, and there may be court orders preventing the family from cleaning the blood that reached nearly eight feet up the walls. However, this is never articulated by anyone on the documentary. Neither the family members nor the defense team nor the documentary crew explain why the blood is never cleaned. How did no one involved in the making of eight episodes feel the need to explain why Kathleen's blood still stains the walls? How did the offender, who "whispers Kathleen's name in [his] heart," walk by that blood every day as he lived in the house during the yearlong trial? Additionally, the family has breakfast meetings and birthday parties mere feet from the crime scene. How did David Rudolf, Michael's high-priced attorney, not want to clarify how the courts were forcing his client to live with such a horrific reminder of the worst night of his life? The offender and David Rudolf can possibly be explained away, but not the filmmakers. It is clear that unfettered access to the Peterson family has given the filmmakers sympathy for the aging author. There are so many filming and editing choices that flatter the offender while leaving Kathleen as a forgotten acquaintance. The unblurred photos and seemingly blasé attitude towards Kathleen's blood are only a few, but are some of the most obvious ones.

Viewers see more photos of Kathleen in death than of her in life. There are a few photo montages in the original eight episodes of *The Staircase*. They move quickly, all showing Kathleen Peterson smiling, tricking the viewer into thinking only of happy families and begging sympathy for the offender. Less than half of the photos chosen for these montages have Kathleen alone or with anyone other than him. One cannot help but wonder if the photos were chosen specifically to portray the offender as a grieving husband instead of showing Kathleen as a vibrant woman. One of the most frequent photos shown is of Kathleen and the offender on their wedding day. He is standing above her as she sits on the main staircase of their house.[14] Again, the subtext guides the viewer to the opinions supported by the filmmakers. He is standing over Kathleen while she looks up at him, an adoring look on her face. A wedding photo should show a couple celebrating the commitment they are making, but this photo appears to show the offender's dominance over Kathleen. It is especially ominous when, if we take the events as presented by the prosecution—which said that he stood above Kathleen and hit her repeatedly—he is taking the same stance ... standing above her while she is positioned at the bottom of a staircase. This is a deep dive on a single photo in a documentary that exists over thirteen episodes, but that photo is shown more than any other photo, and the comparison quickly becomes clear.

Throughout the documentary, it seems as if no one is advocating for Kathleen ... no one but her sister Candace. Candace, who readily admits that she supported the offender until she read the autopsy report, appears only a few times. When she is on screen, she is typically portrayed as an emotional or even an unstable woman. As his family members rallied behind him, they became so focused on proving that he was innocent and ignored that, if their father was innocent, their mother's (or stepmother's) murderer was still out there. Candace seemed to be the only person who was concerned with trying to ensure that Kathleen's killer did, in fact, pay for the crime. In various other interviews that Candace has given in the years since the initial release of the first eight episodes, she has appeared much more rational and composed, implying editorial bias on the part of *The Staircase*. In the final episode of the documentary, Candace reads a victim's impact statement to the court. Not only was this the first time that Candace was able to confront the offender in the years since the death of her sister, but it was the culmination of everything she had been working towards. The offender had signed the Alford plea, which is a guilty plea in the eyes of the court. He had admitted, however reluctantly, that he had killed Kathleen. Candace could finally have closure after fourteen years. However, the footage that "aired" on Netflix shows Candace almost insanely screaming at the offender and the defense team, even yelling at David Rudolf, on their way into the courthouse. Candace is clearly situated by the filmmakers as the "villain" of the piece. It is telling that the antagonist is Candace, Kathleen's sister, another woman, and not the person who killed Kathleen.

Many of the choices made in the documentary may not be those of the director, Jean-Xavier de Lestrade, but instead the film's editor, Sophie Brunet. According to Lestrade in a 2018 interview with the *L'Express*, a French news weekly, Brunet "fell in love" with the offender, but "she never let her own feelings affect the course of editing."[15] That is a noble claim, but Lestrade has no way of knowing if it is actually true. The questions surrounding the photos of Kathleen could be explained by the offender's affair with Brunet. In the same article, Lestrade says that the relationship between the two lasted for at least fifteen years. Given that the relationship allegedly ended in May 2017, soon after he signed the Alford plea, that would mean that Peterson began seeing Brunet in 2002, while he was on trial for the murder of Kathleen. There was likely little footage filmed or little footage for Brunet to edit before they began their relationship. It would not be outrageous to suggest that most, if not all, information about Kathleen has been interpreted through the lens of the offender's new girlfriend. There are no episodes free of Brunet's influence. She even appears on camera in a 2011 episode, sitting with Peterson's family while the judge decides whether Dwayne Deaver's blood evidence constitutes the need for a retrial.

From beginning to end, Kathleen Peterson does not get a fair treatment by *The Staircase*. Huge swaths of episodes do not even mention her name. Between the narcissism of the offender, the skewed storytelling, and the partial editing, *The Staircase* not only tells only his part of the story, but also assumes his innocence from the beginning. The defense team insists that Kathleen died as result of a fall, even after the medical examiner ruled the death a homicide. To make their argument, claims were made against Kathleen that only further denigrate the viewer's opinion of her. Their explanation, made over and over, had Kathleen drinking throughout the evening and being so drunk as she tried to go up to bed that she fell and died. Michael states on more than one occasion that it was common for Kathleen to drink excessively. The picture painted is one of a woman who potentially had a problem with alcohol abuse. However, in the autopsy report, her blood alcohol content was 0.07 percent, which in North Carolina is not above the legal limit to be able to drive. If Kathleen was a woman who enjoyed a few glasses of wine in the evening, a 0.07 percent BAC would not be enough to have her stumbling around to receive the seven blows to her head. While, on the surface, this claim serves to offer an alternative explanation, the subtext is far more nefarious. Kathleen is continuously portrayed as an alcoholic, possibly to explain her fall, but could it not also be a way to further pry out sympathy for the offender? If he could convince everyone that she was, in fact, an alcoholic, he could suddenly have a much more convincing story to tell as the poor, supporting husband.

Other Crime Shows

The Staircase is, by far, not the only documentary or crime series that has covered the case of Kathleen Peterson. True crime has long been fascinated by whether she was killed by her husband or by other means.

The first time this researcher learned of this case was on an episode of *Forensic Files*, often the original entry into true crime for many Murderinos. In season 11, episode 22, "A Novel Idea," the story of Kathleen Peterson aired on Court TV on December 13, 2006. As this episode aired in 2006, it ends with the offender's conviction and does not include any of the later appeals or Duane Deaver's discredited forensics. Kathleen is treated well by *Forensic Files*, something not necessarily expected from a show that had been on the air since 1996. Crime scene photos were aired, but her face was blurred out, which was more than *The Staircase* did. Peter Thomas, the host of *Forensic Files*, has one line at the beginning of the episode that gives Kathleen more respect than she got in entire episodes of *The Staircase*. Thomas asks, "Which partner was the most accomplished? It was hard to tell with them." It is often mentioned that Kathleen was the vice president of Nortel Networks, but it is rare that this is given the same attention as his writing career.

Kathleen also got good coverage on the *Dateline* special "Down the Back Staircase," which aired on NBC on April 7, 2017. She is called a "top business executive" in a segment on her life before she met Michael. It describes her getting her master's degree from Duke and that she appeared on the cover of the magazine of the School of Engineering. Again, most of this came from her sister Candace, her advocate through more than a decade of the case.

The third episode of *True Crime with Aphrodite Jones* begins with a heavy focus on the offender. Aphrodite Jones, a crime writer, interviewed him in 2010, in the midst of the appeal process. She describes Kathleen as a "well-paid executive at Nortel Networks ... who worked day and night to keep the mansion and lifestyle going."[16] As the years ticked by and more shows outside *The Staircase* covered the case, more attention was paid to Kathleen's professional life and her total financial support of the family. The offender did have a few popular novels, but his last novel, *Charlie Two Shoes and The Marines of Love Company*, was published three years before Kathleen's death. If, as per usual, the offender got an advance for the book, then the last income he made was more than four years before her death. Aphrodite Jones makes the point that Kathleen was potentially going through a traumatic life event. She was stressed that she would be laid off, and there were "tensions bubbling under the surface when she die[d]."[17] Not only does this prove that the Petersons did not have the picture-perfect marriage that was portrayed in *The Staircase*, but it also gives Kathleen much-needed depth as a person.

Podcasts

In a world where podcasts have exploded over the last few years, it requires something unique for a podcast to stand out. *Real Crime Profile* has that in the qualifications of its hosts and the manner in which they cover documentaries. Since its premiere in January of 2016, the show has covered several true crime series, such as *The Staircase, Making a Murderer, Escape from Dannemora*, and *The Keepers*. Jim Clemente is a former New York City prosecutor and a former FBI profiler. Laura Richards is a former profiler with New Scotland Yard. Lisa Zambetti is the casting director for *Criminal Minds*, a long-running show on CBS that focuses on the Behavioral Analysis Unit of the FBI. While Jim and Laura give profiling insight into cases like *The Staircase* murder, Lisa gives industry insight into documentaries and series covering true crime.

Real Crime Profile (RCP) began covering *The Staircase* with episode 140, "Her Name Was Kathleen Peterson: Discussing the Staircase." The focus on Kathleen as the most important person in this story is evident, even before the episode starts. *RCP* has covered numerous true crime documentaries and with each one, the hosts attempt to shift the focus back onto the victim by creating a hashtag with the victim's name—in this case #HerNameWasKathleenPeterson. Right away, this podcast series has given Kathleen more respect and more of a voice than the entire thirteen episodes of *The Staircase*.

In its first episode on *The Staircase*, *RCP* immediately indicates its intention to focus on Kathleen and advocate for her. The three hosts call out the problems they saw in the documentary. The first of these issues is that the documentary only ever refers to Kathleen's death as a death and never a murder. While this could be seen as objectivity, the offender goes on trial for murdering Kathleen, so it does seem strange for the documentary never to utter the words murder or homicide. As the hosts point out, this only further proves that, as with many documentaries, *The Staircase* has a perspective. Despite any claims to the contrary, *The Staircase* does not have complete objectivity, especially as the crew began filming seven short weeks after Kathleen's death.

As former FBI and New Scotland Yard profilers, Jim and Laura approach the case as they would have during their profiling career, with victimology. Stating that there was not nearly enough about Kathleen in the documentary, *RCP* stepped in to offer up more insight into Kathleen's life. In addition to wanting to learn as much about Kathleen as possible as part of victimology, the *RCP* hosts also make the point that this deep dive into her life is their way of "giving her voice back."[18] Not only do they mention that Kathleen was 48 at the time of her death, but they also talk about her family and the financial struggles she was facing. Laura especially points out the struggles that Kathleen was facing in December 2001. Not only were there "five children in that house" but her "job was important to her" and she was worried about losing that job.[19] A particular point of discussion is how Kathleen took in four children who were not her own. Kathleen's compassion in the family she was building with the offender is not explicitly mentioned in *The Staircase* or by anyone else. The audience can only hope to infer it when Margaret and Martha call Kathleen "Mom." *RCP* also discusses Kathleen as the family's breadwinner, combatting much of the press around the offender's career as "best-selling author."

It would be difficult to cover *The Staircase* and not discuss Michael Peterson, but *RCP* gives the most information on Kathleen and keeps her a part of the conversation. Jim, Laura, and Lisa discuss not only the documentary's treatment of Kathleen, but of the other women involved in the case as well—most noticeably Candace, Kathleen's sister and most profound advocate during the offender's trials, who gave multiple impact statements. *RCP* praises Candace's work and wonders if her statement was included in the documentary. While more than 650 hours were recorded and only eight hours edited together, it is possible that there was not room for Candace's statement. However, given the clearly skewed nature of the documentary, it seems more likely that Candace was left out on purpose.

In their final episode on the series, the *RCP* hosts address how *The Staircase* manipulates Kathleen and her memory. Beyond all of the problems discussed in their previous episodes, Jim, Laura, and Lisa make it clear that this series is "Kathleen's story through the prism of Michael."[20] To them, "showing a few photographs [of Kathleen] doesn't cut it."[21] In addition to this final critique, they examine the fifteen-year relationship between the editor, Sophie, and the offender. As Jim and Lisa have spent years in the entertainment industry, they sound genuinely puzzled how "on-screen talent," particularly in a documentary series, would ever meet the editing staff.[22]

Dozens of other podcasts have covered *The Staircase* and the offender, especially since the 2018 Netflix release of the entire documentary. Most notably, *My Favorite Murder*, one of the most famous true crime comedy podcasts, discussed it in their first ever episode and again for their 100th episode. Others include *True Crime Garage*, *True Crime Brewery*, *You Can't Make This Up*, *White Wine True Crime!*, and the *Double Loop Podcast*. These and others all delve into the case, but true to form, rarely discuss Kathleen. The hosts may give the basic details of Kathleen's life, her job, and where she went to school, but then switch immediately to Michael and the horrific crime. Rarely, if ever, does Kathleen get the credit and attention she deserves.

◇◇

Teresa Halbach

Just the Facts

As with Kathleen Peterson, there is little information about Teresa Halbach available to the casual internet researcher. When you Google her name, the first page of results is related to the two men convicted of her murder, but not to Teresa herself. The Wikipedia page for Steven Avery, one of the men convicted and the main "character" of Netflix's *Making a Murderer*, is the very first result. Viewers of the documentary recognize her name, could possibly pick out her picture, and many only know that she died in 2005 after visiting Avery's salvage yard. Those who want to find more information will be sorely disappointed in the internet as there is not even a Wikipedia entry on the woman who lost her life in October of 2005.

Researchers of Teresa Halbach are at the whim of documentarians and popular opinion, which focused entirely on Steven Avery. All of the information known about Teresa is the same that has been repeated by nearly every outlet reporting on the crime and/or the criminal. Teresa was born in Kaukauna, Wisconsin, on March 22, 1980. Described as a bright and energetic girl, she studied abroad while in college and enjoyed photography. After graduating college, she began working for *Auto Trader* magazine. She had an ex-boyfriend and a brother. Presumably, she had other family members as others appeared on camera with her brother Mike, but they were not named in the documentary. And that is it. Some inferences can be made about her life from the ten episodes of season one, but one has to study the episodes closely. When Teresa is missing, her brother and ex-boyfriend coordinate a search party that seemingly has dozens of people participating, meaning that she had dozens of people who cared about her. But Teresa is not given the time to become a full-fledged person and certainly is not given the respect of learning anything more than the fact that she died.

News of the Day

The press coverage of the disappearance and death of Teresa Halbach can be divided into two different groups—before and after she was connected to the offender. Before the connection to the offender, the news stories focused entirely on her disappearance. They list what she was wearing when she was last seen, state she had no history of mental illness or criminal record that would lead anyone to believe Teresa left the Manitowoc area, and directed listeners where to call if anyone had any information on her disappearance. It is clear that her family and friends were extremely worried about her and hopeful they might still find her. However, as soon as the police announced the connection, that focus shifted quickly and dramatically to the offender.

More than a decade after Teresa's death, an article appeared, giving at least a little attention to Teresa. Written by Jess Commons for *Grazia*, "Who Was Teresa Halbach, the Real Victim of Making a Murderer?" was published after the first season of the series dropped on Netflix. Commons writes, "In the ongoing debacle over whether or not you believe that Stephen (sic) and Brendan are innocent or both, she should be the real focus of the case."[23] More detail is offered in this article than in any other iteration of Teresa, including any visual portrayal of her. In this article, readers learn that Teresa grew up on a dairy farm near Green Bay and had two brothers and two sisters. Commons describes her study-abroad experiences while attending the University of Wisconsin. The article also includes quotes from her friends. Teresa is described as "a very energetic, spontaneous person" by Kelly, a friend since preschool.[24] These details Commons contends were left out of the documentary series. The article includes a quote from a *Vulture* article in which Laura Ricciardi, one of the filmmakers, says that they invited the Halbach family "to participate in the film … but they decided not to participate."[25] While this is an entirely fair reason as to why the Halbach family did not have a huge presence in the series, it does not explain why the documentary did not use the same basic information that Commons includes in this article.

Books

Several books have been written on the case, but all are exclusively on the offender, his case, and the documentary. Books written by members of the offender's pre- and post-conviction legal teams, such as Jerome Bunting and Michael Griesbach, only mention Teresa occasionally. Like with so much of the coverage of her murder, Teresa is simply a plot device in the story of the offender. Only one book gives any sort of real attention to Teresa, but that attention, found in prosecutor Ken Kratz's *Avery: The Case Against Steve Avery and What* Making a Murderer *Gets Wrong*, is problematic. Vilified in the documentary, Kratz uses this as a platform to tell his story. The third chapter of the book, titled "The Victim," is only eight pages long while the chapter dedicated to the offender is twice that length. Before the chapter even begins, the name dehumanizes Teresa—making her only "The Victim." Kratz points out that the documentary did not have much detail about Teresa but negates this by saying, "That's fine: the series wasn't about Teresa."[26] He tells the reader that the book is, in part, "dedicated to her memory," but the book is actually dedicated to his son. While it is entirely normal for Kratz to dedicate his book to his son, this dedication to Teresa feels incredibly hollow.

Kratz does include some details on Teresa's life, setting his book apart from the others on this case. He calls her "a charming, funny young woman … an avid traveler, a long-distance runner."[27] Going a step beyond the normal fact about her photography, Kratz mentions Teresa's portrait business in Green Bay and that she "had a knack for photographing children."[28] He mentions that she was "especially close with her sisters" and that since her "breakup with Ryan Hillegas, her high school sweetheart, Teresa had not been in a serious relationship."[29] The chapter then turns with the line, "Teresa, it seemed, had caught the eye of one man, divorced, with five children, a criminal record, and a girlfriend who drank too much"—the offender.[30] With this line, only three pages into the chapter titled "The Victim," the chapter shifts the focus to Teresa's relationship with the offender. Teresa the person disappears and, for the majority of the chapter and for the rest of the book, she becomes the victim and a plot device in the offender's story and Kratz's attempt at redemption.

In the final pages of the book, Kratz states that he has "specific goals for this book."[31] His two goals included wanting to flip the public narrative to when "cops and prosecutors in the case were still generally considered the 'good guys'" and the hope that the book would "shed some light on why Avery killed Teresa, a question that, to this day, over eleven years after the murder, remains unanswered."[32] These goals shows that, while he did include some information about Teresa, Kratz did not see the continued advocacy of Teresa as one of his goals.

Documentaries

Making a Murderer

Season one of *Making a Murderer* premiered on Netflix on December 18, 2015. Netflix had begun releasing original content in 2013, but by 2015, most of that content had been fictional. *Making a Murderer* was one of the first true crime documentaries to be released in this new format. All ten episodes of season one were released on December 18, giving the audience the ability to binge-watch a true crime documentary for the first time. Many true crime fans have credited *Making a Murderer* with being their entry into the true crime genre. This true crime obsession was only heightened by being able to binge all the episodes in one sitting. Moving from one episode to another in such a way did not allow the viewer to absorb the information from each episode before another began.

It becomes clear right away that this documentary is focused entirely on the alleged offender. He is introduced as a wrongly convicted and newly freed man in Wisconsin. The entire first episode centers around the assault of Penny Bernstein, which occurred in 1985. The offender was identified, charged, and convicted of this crime before being exonerated in 2003 due to a negative DNA match. While there are photos of Penny after the assault, there are no photos of her before the assault, no pictures without the bruises. Penny is only known in the context of her assault. She picks the offender out of a photo lineup, and he is convicted for the crime. This is only the first instance of a woman's story being completely overshadowed by the offender's story.

The second episode of the first season gives Teresa Halbach adequate attention, if only they had continued to treat her with such respect for the rest of the documentary. The episode begins with a voicemail from Teresa, giving her a voice for the first time in the show. It is followed by a home video of Teresa talking to the camera about what the future may hold for her. Unfortunately, that is the extent of Teresa being presented as someone other than a victim. For the rest of the documentary, both seasons, Teresa is only mentioned in terms as a victim, if she is mentioned at all.

In that same episode, with only twenty-five minutes left, Teresa disappears, with her last known location being Avery's Auto Salvage. There is news footage of Teresa's family searching for her and interviews with family members, including her brother Mike, who steps forward as a spokesperson for the family. During the family scenes, Teresa is at the center of attention, but that is the only time that Teresa is the focus of the documentary. Teresa is at the heart of this case, literally and figuratively. Yet, there is absolutely nothing about her or her life after that second episode.

As the offender is the subject of the documentary, it is obvious that he should be the central character. The film crew had clear and open access to the Avery family, which would explain the amount of time spent on him and his story. However, that still does not justify the near dismissal of Teresa. When asked about the disappearance of Teresa, the offender says, "We're all victims."[33] The Manitowoc County Sheriff countered with, "There's only one victim in this case—Teresa."[34] For the rest of the documentary, Teresa is only mentioned in passing, specifically during the trial.

Just like with many of the other subjects in this project, the most screen time Teresa gets is as the subject of an opening argument. The woman who was shown talking about her hopes for her future at the beginning of episode two is reduced to a pawn for lawyers. During the trial of Brendan Dassey, the offender's nephew and suspected accomplice, there were moments when Teresa was referred to simply as "the victim."[35]

Season two of *Making a Murderer* dropped on October 19, 2018, with an additional ten episodes. The first episode begins with a critique of the first season, including a statement from the Halbach family criticizing corporations for seeking profits from the family's loss. Those who knew the Halbach family were sickened by the documentary. The news footage also showed friends remembering, saying they want to keep her "memory as bright as her smile."[36] The only fair or balanced treatment of Teresa comes from news coverage about the documentary. This very same episode ends with new blood-splatter experiments with a mannequin taking the place of Teresa, further dehumanizing her.

The second season focuses on Kathleen Zellner taking the offender's case in the appellate jurisdiction. Zellner specializes in post-conviction appellate work and has "righted more wrongful prosecutions than any private attorney in America."[37] As the new attorney of record, she needed to go over all the evidence again, which meant a new review of the facts for the second season. This is the first time there is any kind of victimology of Teresa at all. The offender's first legal team did not give any kind of history on Teresa nor any victimology. While it is still not the fair and balanced treatment of the victim that anyone would expect from a documentary about her murder, it is at least more screen time for Teresa than the first season gave her.

Much like *The Staircase*, *Making a Murderer* forgets its victim or uses her only to further the plot of its main character, the offender. Teresa ceases to exist except in forensic reports. There are rumors of possible additional seasons for *Making a Murderer*, but it is extremely unlikely that a third or fourth season would treat Teresa any differently than the first two seasons.

Unlike Kathleen Peterson, Teresa Halbach did not get the attention of multiple true crime shows after the airing of her documentary. Perhaps it has something to do with the licensing of the case with the streaming juggernaut Netflix. Regardless, it means that Teresa has only received treatment from one source, making that treatment entirely skewed. Even though it has only been a few years since the first season, additional coverage on the Teresa Halbach case is needed if for no other reason than to make sure that Teresa's story is covered for more than a few moments here and there.

Podcasts

This is where true crime podcasts have stepped in for better treatment for the women involved in true crime. Just like Kathleen, Teresa is a focused topic of the podcast *Real Crime Profile*, being featured on the very first six episodes of the podcast. Before each episode actually gets underway, the hosts, Jim Clemente, Laura Richards, and Lisa Zambetti, make it clear that while they are going to focus on the cases of the offender and his nephew, they are "here for Teresa Halbach."[38] They state the mission of the podcast is to "help people protect themselves and their loved ones"; and to "ask [the] victimology questions that documentary doesn't ask."[39] Right away, the *RCP* hosts have offered up more sympathy for Teresa than the entire eighteen episodes of *Making a Murderer* did. That continues for the rest of *RCP*'s coverage. In episode two, they want everyone to "remember that someone has lost their life here"; and that "[i]t's not just entertainment."[40]

Jim and Laura, both with long careers in law enforcement, are appalled at the treatment of Teresa. If, like the documentarians intended, the audience sympathizes with the offenders, *RCP* points out that it is impossible to separate wanting justice for the two possibly wrongly incarcerated men and also wanting to find out what happened to Teresa. During their discussion of the offender's arrest, the teenaged offender's confession, and the potentially damning investigation by Manitowoc County, the hosts of *RCP* acknowledge that it is really important to put together the truth. In this case, Teresa had a "horrific end" and gets lost in the narrative of the Netflix documentary. As Laura Richards succinctly puts it, "This is a real person—it's really tragic to have her humanity lost—she's not just a baggie of evidence—she's a person that we really don't know the true story."[41] *RCP*'s coverage of Teresa's case and the documentary series is the best podcast coverage, but as it is the first series covered by the podcast, one wonders how differently they might represent Teresa now that they are hundreds of episodes into their podcast.

With the popularity of the *Making a Murderer* series, several podcasts have covered the series and the offender's case. While most of the episodes focus entirely on the offender and the series, a few do mention the lack of attention on Teresa. *Crime Scene* spends several episodes on the series, where they point out that Teresa is merely "an afterthought."[42] While discussing the final episodes of the series, host Jordan Fenster points out that it is impossible to separate wanting "justice for Steven and Brendan and wanting to find out what happened to Teresa."[43] If, as the narrative of the documentary suggests, the offender is actually innocent, then that means that the person responsible for her death is "still out there ... [and] it's really important to put together the truth."[44]

Conclusion

According to the end of each miniseries, justice has been served to Kathleen Peterson and Teresa Halbach. The offender in Kathleen's case signed an Alford plea, which is entered into the record as technically a guilty plea. He served more than eight years in prison before his release on appeal and eventual Alford plea. The convicted offenders in Teresa's case are still serving time in two different prisons in Wisconsin, even after several appeal attempts. While the justice system seems to have done its job for the two women, pop culture has certainly not.

The cases of Kathleen Peterson and Teresa Halbach are two in which true crime podcasts have stepped in to give the women what the documentaries failed to provide—remotely adequate coverage. The fact that these documentaries were produced in the 21st century and still need this kind of assistance is all the more damning. It makes far more sense for films or shows produced in decades past to be outdated in their approach to women, but not shows released on Netflix in 2015 and 2018 respectively. The documentaries are barely informational coverage and border on the exploitative. Perhaps that is why podcasts like *Real Crime Profile* stepped in so strongly to speak for Kathleen and Teresa. While this only proves that documentaries are incredibly fallible, even those made a few years ago, it also shows the importance of true crime podcasts. Especially with its social media campaigns like #HerNameWasKathleenPeterson, *RCP* continues to advocate for not only Kathleen as the victim of a crime, but also the victim of pop culture.

Given that the documentaries have become so iconic, one must wonder whether there will ever be any other visual iterations that could offer a better interpretation of Kathleen or Teresa—one that not only offers a full-bodied portrayal of them, but advocates for them as victims and as women.

CHAPTER 11

Social Media Crimes

In the 21st century, social media became ubiquitous in the lives of Americans, indeed everyone on Earth. We became increasingly connected with Facebook, Twitter, Instagram, Snapchat, and dozens of other platforms. When combined with the democratization of technologies like Wi-Fi and smartphones, these social media platforms are available to most Americans. Therefore, it is not surprising that social media and message boards like Reddit became a part of true crime during the 2010s. There were two crimes in particular involving women and some kind of online phenomenon that occurred in this decade: the murder of Gypsy Rose Blanchard's mother and the attempted murder of Payton Leutner.

Gypsy Rose Blanchard used Facebook and Christian online dating sites to meet the boyfriend who ended up murdering her mother, Dee Dee Blanchard, in 2015 in Springfield, Missouri. Payton Leutner, the young woman who was stabbed 19 times by two friends in Wisconsin in 2014, managed to crawl out of the forest and find help. The friends, young women who went to school with Payton, decided to kill her after reading about Slenderman, an "urban legend" that was created as a result of a Photoshop contest on the website Something Awful in 2009.

These two crimes were heavily influenced by internet culture and have been the subject of multiple pop culture iterations, even given the short time since the crimes themselves, 2014 and 2015 respectively. Continuing with the theme of this project, this chapter will examine how both of these women have been interpreted by pop culture since the crime, but now with the added influence of the internet and social media to make the 2010s a unique decade.

◇◇

Gypsy Rose Blanchard

Just the Facts

Gypsy Rose Blanchard was born on July 27, 1991, to Clauddine (aka Dee Dee) and Rod Blanchard in Louisiana. Dee Dee was 24 at the time of Gypsy's birth, and Rod, only 17, left Dee Dee shortly before Gypsy's birth, saying he "got married for the wrong reasons."[1] Gypsy was born a healthy child, but her long medical history began at the tender age of three months when Dee Dee rushed her to the hospital over concerns of sleep apnea. According to Rod Blanchard, there were several rounds of tests without any results that pointed towards a diagnosis. Nevertheless, Dee Dee told Rod that Gypsy had a chromosomal defect, and all of the health issues that suddenly began to appear stemmed from that one problem.[2]

Dee Dee's professional past as a nurse's aide assisted her in convincing a variety of doctors in several states that Gypsy suffered from a laundry list of conditions. Also helping in this ruse is the fact that doctors rely heavily on a child's mother to report on a child's health, especially if a child may not be able to speak or advocate for herself. For example, Dee Dee told doctors at the Tulane University Hospital and Clinic and the Children's Hospital that Gypsy had seizures every few months, leading to Gypsy being put on anti-seizure medications.[3] Also assisting Dee Dee in her plot was, ironically, Hurricane Katrina. After the hurricane hit Louisiana in 2005, wherever they moved after that point, Dee Dee was able to blame the hurricane for the lack of medical records and say essentially whatever she wished.

When Gypsy and Dee Dee finally moved into a Habitat for Humanity house in Springfield, Missouri, in 2008, Dee Dee told the neighbors that her daughter suffered from "chromosomal defects, muscular dystrophy, epilepsy, severe asthma, sleep apnea, [and] eye problems," among several other ailments.[4] Gypsy had her salivary glands removed because Dee Dee told doctors that she had a drooling problem. She also had a feeding tube inserted when Dee Dee told Gypsy's doctors that she was not able to stand to eat orally. Gypsy had been in a wheelchair since she was seven, and she had lost her teeth due to the amount and severity of medications she was prescribed.

Those same neighbors who pitched in whenever possible to help the Blanchards were shocked to wake up in 2015 to find two posts to Gypsy and

Dee Dee's joint Facebook account that were very out of character. On June 14, 2015, the first post simply said, "That Bitch is dead!" As those neighbors, friends, and family debated about the first post and what it meant, a second post appeared: "I fucken SLASHED THAT FAT PIG AND RAPED HER SWEET INNOCENT DAUGHTER ... HER SCREAM WAS SOOOO FUCKEN LOUD LOL."[5] One neighbor, Kim, worried about Dee Dee, called 911. The police could not enter the Blanchards' house without a warrant, so Kim's husband, David, entered the house through a window. After finding Gypsy's wheelchairs and no Gypsy, the police began the paperwork for a warrant. Once it came through at 10:45 that night, the police entered the home and found Dee Dee's body.

Gypsy, missing from the home in Springfield, Missouri, was found later in a house in Waukesha County, Wisconsin. More than a year before Dee Dee's death, Gypsy had created a secret Facebook account and an account for a Christian dating site. Straining against her mother's yoke, Gypsy was desperate for some kind of normal attention—friends, a social life, even a boyfriend. She met a man from Waukesha County, Wisconsin, named Nicholas Godejohn. During their online relationship, Gypsy opened up to Nicholas about the abuse she was suffering at the hands of her mother. Likewise, Nicholas told Gypsy about what he called his various personalities, though he had never been officially diagnosed with dissociative identity disorder. He introduced Gypsy to BDSM and they both dressed up in cosplay, taking photos and sending them to each other.[6]

Nicholas had no history of violence but did have a prior arrest in 2013 for lewd conduct when he was arrested after watching pornography and masturbating in a McDonalds for nine hours. Even though he had no history of violence, it was Nicholas who wielded the knife. The police found Gypsy and the offender in his parents' house in Wisconsin by tracing the geo-tagging Facebook posts and following them from Missouri to Wisconsin. After the pair were arrested, Gypsy petitioned for and was granted a separate trial after details of Dee Dee's abuse were entered into the court record. On July 5, 2015, Gypsy "pleaded guilty to second-degree murder" and received the minimum sentence of ten years.[7] She is eligible for parole at the end of 2023, when she will be 32 years old.[8] In February 2019 the offender was sentenced to life in prison without the possibility of parole for the murder of Dee Dee.[9]

As the details of Gypsy's medical history became public record after Dee Dee's murder, Gypsy's lawyer and true crime experts began commenting on the possibility of Munchausen Syndrome by Proxy. This syndrome, also called Factitious Disorder Imposed on Another, occurs when "people, usually caregivers (such as a parent), intentionally produce or falsify physical or psychologic [sic] symptoms or signs in a person in their care (usually a child), rather than in themselves (as in factitious disorder imposed on self)."[10] The description continues, saying that "[t]he caregiver falsifies history and may injure the child with drugs or other agents … to simulate disease. The caregiver seeks medical care for the child and appears to be deeply concerned and protective. The child typically has a history of frequent hospitalizations, usually for a variety of nonspecific symptoms, but no firm diagnosis."[11] This diagnosis, while it cannot officially be placed at the feet of Dee Dee now that she is dead, is a huge factor in Gypsy's role in Dee Dee's death.

TV/Documentaries

With the unique circumstances of Gypsy's childhood and the role social media played in the death of Dee Dee, it was not surprising how quickly the true crime community turned its attention towards the case. Within two years of the crime, a major documentary aired on HBO. It was followed by episodes of various true crime shows known for focusing on infamous cases. In 2019, four years after Dee Dee's death, an eight-part miniseries was released on the streaming service Hulu. *The Act* provides the most comprehensive fictional view of the Gypsy Rose Blanchard case. These pop culture iterations run the spectrum of shining a light on who Gypsy is to exploiting her story for ratings.

Mommy Dead and Dearest

Mommy Dead and Dearest first aired on HBO on May 16, 2017, and is considered the definitive documentary on the Gypsy Rose Blanchard case. Directed by Erin Lee Carr and with a runtime of eighty-two minutes, it focuses on the death of Dee Dee, but also on the abuse of Gypsy. The title is immediately telling, showing its focus on Gypsy's abuse. The title is a play on the title of a tell-all book written by Christina Crawford, the daughter of actor Joan Crawford. The book, called *Mommie Dearest*, "portrayed Joan Crawford as a sadistic perfectionist, an alcoholic prone to unpredictable squalls of maternal fury who would punish the mildest misdemeanors with disproportionate force."[12] In this tell-all, Christina alleged that her mother had abused her, including berating her for hanging her clothes on wire hangers, screaming "no wire hangers!" which "entered the vernacular as shorthand for neurotic maternal instability."[13] This obvious comparison with a pop culture touchstone allows all viewers, not just true crime aficionados, to make the connection with another abusive and unstable mother who abused her daughter.

Mommy Dead and Dearest has become the definitive documentary on the case by being the first and by giving the audience access to not only Gypsy herself but also other crucial players of this case who give greater understanding to Gypsy and Dee Dee. Gypsy walks on screen, wearing her prison uniform, presumably in a prison interview room that was decorated for this occasion. More than a year after her sentencing, this Gypsy looks and even sounds different than she did the last time she was on camera. Her hair is longer; she looks healthier; and, even while looking contrite, she looks happy. In this interview, a viewer can see the damage done by Dee Dee. During the documentary, footage and photos of Gypsy during her time under Dee Dee's control are shown in stark contrast to this now healthy young woman. While it can be hard to understand exactly what her mother put Gypsy through, comparing the images of her before her mother's death to this young woman sitting in the prison uniform, that damage is clear. Even her voice is lower, more measured, and clearer than it was in any footage taken while Gypsy was under Dee Dee's control.

Hearing Gypsy's story in her own words also allows Gypsy to take control of her own narrative. For her entire life, Gypsy had been under her mother's control, not even able to speak for herself to her own doctors. During this interview, Gypsy says that this is "the first time being this honest."[14] She describes her mother's death and her role in it, taking responsibility for the part that she played. She continues, saying that after her arrest, she seriously considered suicide as she began her sentence at Chillicothe Correctional Center in Missouri.

Not only does this documentary give Gypsy her voice back, but it also allows viewers to see Gypsy as a "normal" young woman. Normal here is obviously being used in relative terms, but Gypsy's life in prison is far more normal than it was before prison. The documentary shows Gypsy spending time with her father, Ron, and her stepmother, Kristy. Ron, in his interview, reports that Dee Dee refused to let him see, and later, even speak to, his daughter. However, here, Gypsy is seen lifting her shirt to show them both her port site, where her feeding tube had been.[15]

In addition to giving Gypsy a platform to speak her truth, *Mommy Dead and Dearest* also provided greater clarity on Dee Dee Blanchard, allowing even more understanding in Gypsy's case. Dee Dee's father and stepmother, with their strong Louisiana accents, describe their suspicions of Dee Dee's involvement in her mother's death in 1997, as well as her stepmother's illness that mysteriously cleared up after Dee Dee moved out. Dee Dee's nephew calls her evil and lists a history of offenses that included credit card fraud and writing bad checks. When Dee Dee's father and stepmother are asked what was done with her remains—whether the family had a funeral—her father says that no one wanted her remains and that as far as the family was concerned, they could flush her remains down the toilet.[16] While obviously not about Gypsy, this insight into Dee Dee's history and how her own family feels about her, even after her death, allows a viewer to see that what Dee Dee did to Gypsy was not a one-time offense.

The Act

Four years after the crime, the streaming service Hulu released an eight-episode mini-series called *The Act* based on the case. Starring Joey King as Gypsy and Patricia Arquette as Dee Dee, *The Act* was created by Nick Antosca and Michelle Dean and was released between March 20 and May 1, 2019. Relying heavily on historical events, a cursory viewing would give a viewer a relatively faithful account of Gypsy. Some of the mistakes or alterations may have been made simply for creative license, but others may be issues of manipulating the "character" of Gypsy.

The first small alteration comes in the second episode, titled "Teeth." As the title suggests, this episode focused on Gypsy's teeth, by way of her testing her mother's true care of her. During a moment of teenage rebellion, Gypsy takes a sip of a soda, even though that much sugar, according to Dee Dee, would kill her. After not dying, Gypsy starts waking up in the middle of the night to sneak soda, ice cream, and candy while surfing the internet. Soon, her teeth begin to rot and fall out. Seeing the damage, Dee Dee forces Gypsy to have all of her teeth removed and have false teeth implanted. The result is the same, but the journey to Gypsy's false teeth has been changed. According to her medical records, her tooth decay was due to the sheer amount and damaging effects of the medication. In this iteration, the tooth decay is placed solely at the feet of Gypsy. It is her fault for drinking two-liter bottles of soda while eating gallons of ice cream as opposed to the effect of the laundry list of medications given to her by Dee Dee. It is a small piece, but it is one of a few alterations that change the story and not in Gypsy's favor.

Another small change is in the next episode, "Two Wolverines." Gypsy and Dee Dee attend a comic con where each meets a man cosplaying as Wolverine, hence the title of the episode. Gypsy buys a phone with internet capability and gets online to track down her new friend, a man named Scott—another indictment of the role the internet and social media played in Gypsy's life. After months of talking and texting, Scott texts that he had a rough night and is in an emergency room. Gypsy calls a taxi and rushes to his side. Joey King's performance is great—portraying Gypsy's hesitation, fear, and relief at walking through the hospital. Finally feeling free from her mother, she goes home with Scott. However, Dee Dee finds her, tells Scott that Gypsy is underage, and brings her home. The scene is absolutely horrifying, but the truth is even worse than what is on the screen. That is hard to believe considering that when Dee Dee and Gypsy arrive home, Dee Dee ties Gypsy to the bed as punishment for disobeying her. According to Gypsy, after this encounter, Dee Dee told her, "If you do it again, I'll break your hands," while holding a hammer. It is unclear why this line is omitted—whether it was deemed to be over the top, even if it is true, or if it is strictly hearsay. The only person left to tell this part of the story is Gypsy, but the show left in other details that come from her testimony and interviews. So, why is this detail left out? While tying Gypsy to the bed is vile, this quote from Dee Dee would make her look even worse. Was it left out to minimize Dee Dee's villainy and thereby heighten Gypsy's guilt?

The sixth episode, "A Whole New World," includes another alteration while also shining a light on a crucial point of Gypsy's story. Now two-thirds of the way through the miniseries, viewers get a look into Dee Dee's backstory, from the moment of Gypsy's birth. Emma, Dee Dee's mother, is seen as an overbearing mother who berated Dee Dee and stepped in to raise Gypsy for the six months that Dee Dee was in prison for check fraud. A few years later, Emma is sick, with Dee Dee caring for her, but by now Dee Dee's Munchausen Syndrome by Proxy is already evident. This again gives viewers insight that Gypsy was not Dee Dee's first victim nor was this her first foray into criminal behavior. These flashbacks also provide another alteration that revictimizes Gypsy, continuing the yo-yo effect of this miniseries. After Emma's death, when Dee Dee and her cousin are going through the house to get it ready for sale, Gypsy asks to go outside and play with her older cousins on a trampoline. By this time, Gypsy is six; she has already been "diagnosed" with multiple ailments. Conditioned, Gypsy backpedals and asks Dee Dee if she can go out and watch her cousins while they jump on the trampoline.[17] Even with her mother's warning, Gypsy gets on the trampoline and a scream is heard from inside the house. Dee Dee runs outside to find her daughter lying on the ground, and this is the catalyst that puts Gypsy in a wheelchair for the first time. While the ultimate blame for putting Gypsy in the wheelchair always lies with Dee Dee, this iteration essentially places blame with Gypsy for disobeying her mother. The actual story was a bike accident when Dee Dee's father had Gypsy on a bike, or a motorcycle, depending on the person telling the story. With the actual story, there is absolutely no blame to put upon Gypsy, not even a shadow, for why and how she ended up in a wheelchair for fourteen years.

It is also in this episode that Dee Dee is killed by Gypsy's boyfriend before the couple leave Springfield. In 2015, they spent a few days in a motel before getting on a bus to the offender's home in Wisconsin. There is footage, taken by Gypsy herself with a handheld camera, showing intimate moments between Gypsy and the offender. On this footage, Gypsy is heard giggling and talking about sexual acts with him, only hours after the murder of her mother. When asked about this, Gypsy says that to get through the trauma of the night, she took pills. In this episode, as soon as Joey King's Gypsy walks into the motel room, she pulls a bottle out of her pocket and dry-swallows two pills. At various points over the next few days with him, Gypsy pulls out that bottle from her pocket and dry-swallows a few more pills. For example, Gypsy wants to get out of the motel room for even a few hours, but the offender says no, he would rather just watch TV. Faced with a new life that is starkly different from the one she imagined, with a man who is definitely not the hero she had hoped for, Gypsy continues to take her mother's sedatives until the bottle is empty. Seeing this in episode six counteracts the numerous times the handheld camera footage has been played on various newscasts, documentaries, and true crime shows. In only a few of those instances is Gypsy's story of her need to take a sedative to deal with the trauma actually aired alongside that footage. Episode six and each dry-swallow of pills shows how damaged and off-kilter Gypsy was in the days following the murder. Not only does this reinforce Gypsy's story, but also it adds balance to the footage that has played numerous times.

The final episode of *The Act*, "Free," offers a flashback to Dee Dee's murder, but from Gypsy's point of view. Elements of this scene line up with Gypsy's telling of the night, but with a few key omissions. According to Gypsy, after the offender killed Dee Dee, he came into the bathroom and forced her to clean up after him, mirroring the "master/slave" relationship that he preferred in their sex life. Additionally, she said that he wanted to have sex with Dee Dee's body, but that she volunteered to have sex with him to prevent him doing that to her mother. In the episode, when he comes into the bathroom with blood dripping off the tip of the knife, Gypsy rushes over to help him. He stands, frozen, while she begins cleaning up. There are no orders or demands from the offender. Leaving the bathroom, he pulls her towards her bedroom and they have sex, but there is no mention of him wanting to have sex with Dee Dee's body or of Gypsy trying to stop that from happening. Again, one has to wonder if this was omitted because the details were hearsay or if there was another reason. It could possibly be understandable if any or all details that came solely from Gypsy's testimony were left out of the miniseries, but that would have made for a very short series. However, leaving this out only serves to make Gypsy appear more willing or even cooperative during the murder. This picking and choosing which details were included in the episodes—a lot of facts with some omissions—make Gypsy look more cooperative or guilt-ier than her own story.

The final scene of the miniseries shows Gypsy in her cell, sitting on her cot, laying her head on the shoulder of her mother's ghost, who is sitting next to her. She is taking comfort in her mother's presence, and, more importantly, this Gypsy is seeking comfort from her abusive mother. According to several interviews, Gypsy is happy in prison, and, while she regrets her mother's murder, one questions whether she would be seeking comfort like this. Again, one wonders about the manipulation of Gypsy's image to evoke the sympathies of the audience. *The Act* offers powerful acting by the cast; Patricia Arquette won both the Emmy and the Golden Globe in 2019 for her role as Dee Dee. However, it also presents a problematic portrayal of the events surrounding Gypsy Rose Blanchard, leading any person clicking on that icon in Hulu to believe its interpretation without question.

Podcasts

Podcast hosts have been enthralled by the case since the news broke in 2015. Enticed by the rare Munchausen Syndrome by Proxy and the role the social media played in the case, podcasts began dropping within six months of the offender's sentencing in November of 2018. The majority of them cover the Gypsy Rose Blanchard case in a straightforward manner. So, if the podcasts cover Gypsy in pretty much the same way, why include them at all? Again, the problem lies with omissions. The central omission is Gypsy and the offender's sex life and how it influences iterations of Gypsy.

The most comprehensive podcast, titled *The Killer Thorn of Gypsy Rose*, is hosted by Dr. Phil McGraw, who became a household name after he started appearing on *The Oprah Winfrey Show* in 1998. A former psychologist who has a Ph.D. in clinical psychology, he is not licensed to practice and hosts his own show that premiered in 2002. The season of his podcast covers the case and psychology of Gypsy Rose Blanchard over five episodes.[18] Given his background, McGraw provides psychological insights into the case, but with his entertainment background, it is also not surprising how often hyperbole appears. In the first twenty minutes of the first episode, he uses words like "maniac" to describe the offender and describes the death of Dee Dee as like a "scene from the Hitchcock film *Psycho*."[19] However, once one looks past the entertainment factor, there are some important elements to this series.

A large portion of this series was Dr. Phil's interview with Gypsy herself. The episodes were released in 2019, but there is no indication of when the interview took place. If one assumes the interview occurred within weeks of the episodes' release, it is one of the more recent interviews with Gypsy. In this interview, Gypsy describes what her life is like in prison. Dr. Phil concludes that she "seems to be doing much better" behind bars and that she has gained roughly thirty pounds because no one is overmedicating her or starving her.[20] In addition to portraying Gypsy as physically healthier than she was when she entered prison, Dr. Phil asks her if she believes she belongs in prison—effectively testing her mental status after a few years in prison. Gypsy says that she does belong in prison but believes she does not deserve such a harsh sentence. In her thinking, she would be better in a facility that is better suited to give her the help she needs. Allowing Gypsy to speak for herself, with the added benefit of time and distance from her mother and her mother's death, literally gives her her voice back.

The Killer Thorn of Gypsy Rose, by spending hours on the case, more time than any other iteration other than *The Act*, is able to provide more context to the abuse suffered by Gypsy. Gypsy describes her first memory in episode three, saying it was an eye surgery. After going into details of her various surgeries and abuse suffered at the hands of her mother, Dr. Phil wonders how far Dee Dee would have gone. Would she have "amputated her legs?"[21] Other podcasts typically give a laundry list of the abuse, which does not convey the severity or intensity of her abuse. Dr. Phil tells his listeners of the hundred hospital visits in an eleven-year period. Having a better sense of the abuse and Gypsy's experience during her years in captivity, listeners will have a much better sense of the woman herself than they would if they listened to any other podcast.

One final point that sets Dr. Phil apart from the other coverage of the case is the thoughts on Gypsy's future. The final episode, released on May 23, 2019, ends with Dr. Phil discussing her current situation; she is still in prison and engaged to a man who had written to her after seeing a documentary about her case. Dr. Phil does not approve of this relationship, saying that she needs to build a relationship with herself first, her family second, and then she can begin thinking about entering into a new romantic relationship.[22] He continues, saying that Gypsy has the potential to be the "poster person for rehabilitation."[23] Suggesting phasing her back into society, he cites her lack of real-world life experiences, which would make it difficult for her to transition directly from prison to the outside world. While most coverage of Gypsy Rose speculates on her mental state both before and during the murder, *The Killer Thorn of Gypsy Rose* is the only one to not only consider her life after prison, but also to make rational suggestions for how she might be most successful. This allows listeners to imagine a Gypsy Rose outside her abuse and her mother's murder, and not wearing a prison uniform.

Other podcasts that discuss Gypsy Rose Blanchard cover much of the same ground. *Killer Instinct, Voices of the Victim, Martinis & Murder, True Crime All the Time, Female Killers,* and *Redhanded* all have episodes on Gypsy, with large sections of fascination on Munchausen Syndrome by Proxy. The elements of the case that are up for debate in these podcasts are Gypsy's involvement/guilt and her sex life with the offender. For example, in episode 76 of *True Crime All the Time,* the hosts heavily imply that Gypsy planned the murder from the start and that the offender was no more than a hitman. They question where Gypsy learned "how to manipulate others."[24] They continue to say that they "do feel really bad for her" but that "she did orchestrate a murder."[25] The May 8, 2019, episode of *Female Killers* also implies that Gypsy was the mastermind, saying that the offender merely "participated" in the murder of Dee Dee, rather than being the actual murderer himself.[26]

Gypsy's sexual relationship with the offender is also covered differently, depending on the podcast, changing a listener's perception of Gypsy. While Gypsy has maintained that the sex after Dee Dee's murder was rape, even though she agreed to it initially to prevent him from raping Dee Dee's corpse, this is rarely called rape in the podcasts covering the case. In *The Killer Thorn of Gypsy Rose,* Dr. Phil includes the detail that Gypsy agreed to sex to stop him from raping Dee Dee after the murder, but says that she "screamed" for him to stop and calls it a "brutal rape."[27] *Redhanded* does not talk about that specific event, but the two female hosts discuss whether the sex that occurs in the motel room after the murder was consensual or not, something that many others do not even consider. Other podcasts, like *Voices of the Victims,* do not mention anything about the rape allegations, which leaves the audience with no choice but to assume that any sex between Gypsy and the offender was consensual.

Given the short time that has passed since the case, there will surely be more podcasts, which will choose to spend an hour or so on Gypsy Rose Blanchard. The real question is, with the luxury of time, will the interpretation and portrayal of Gypsy Rose become more even-keeled and gain greater perspective? As she is released from prison and continues to age, and hopefully get the help that she needs, will Gypsy's story become more confident? With that confidence, perhaps documentarians and podcast hosts will choose to believe her account and present it in full, without judgment.

◇◇

Payton Leutner

Payton Leutner is perhaps the most obscure subject of this project. While the details surrounding her stabbing are well known, as is information about the two offenders, Payton is somewhat of a mystery. It is not surprising, given Payton was 12 at the time of her stabbing and, even now (in 2022); she is only twenty years old. Just now an adult, she needed some level of anonymity to have a remotely normal childhood.

Even with her family's dedication to her privacy, it is impossible to tell the story of the "Slenderman stabbing" without talking about the victim. This section will attempt to walk the fine line between respect for privacy and historical/pop cultural analysis.

At the crux of this story is the mythic "Slenderman." To understand the events of May 31, 2014, one must first delve into the internet phenomenon first seen on June 8, 2009. On a forum of the website Something Awful, a challenge was posed to its posters—"create paranormal images." For what was essentially a Photoshop contest, Eric Knudsen, known on the forum as Victor Surge, posted two black-and-white altered photos with a "tall out-of-focus figure" standing next to a tree.[28] After two years of the community adding to the lore, Slenderman had an "official" description on Yahoo Answers:

> The Slenderman is a supernatural creature that is described as appearing as normal human being but is described as being 8 feet tall and he has vectors of extra appendages that are described to be sharp as swords. The creature is known to stalk humans and cause many disappearances…. A man named Victor Surge found this legend and made his own version of it which he called Slender man….[29]

Purely a product of the internet, Slenderman, a "dark god in an age of digital media," was Knudsen's inspiration from the stories of H.P. Lovecraft. Rather than doing the killing himself, Slenderman "encourages others to [kill] in order to please him."[30] According to the lore, if his followers, or proxies, did just that, they would become his servants and live with him in his mansion, which was rumored to be in a forest. It was this wish that the offenders who attacked Payton Leutner sought to fulfill in May 2014.

Just the Facts

Payton was born in 2002 to Stacie and Joe Leutner. In the fourth grade, a few years before the crime took place, Payton approached Morgan

Geyser while at school, "because she was sitting alone."[31] After the initial interaction, the two became fast friends. "They hung out after school, had sleepovers, and joked like little girls do. Morgan even gave Payton a sweet nickname, Bella."[32] The friendship went well for two years, until, in the sixth grade, Morgan met Anissa Weier.

With a new person, the dynamic between Payton and Morgan changed, with Payton feeling left out. When the other two became "obsessed" with the Slenderman legend, Payton said she went along with it because Morgan "liked it and thought it was real. But I went along with it. I was supportive because I thought that's what she liked."[33]

On May 30, 2014, the girls all went to Morgan's home to celebrate her birthday with a slumber party. The night included roller-skating, pizza, and playing with dolls, but Payton told *20/20* years later that the night was different from their other sleepovers; this time Morgan did not want to stay up all night.[34] Little did Payton know that Morgan and Anissa had planned to kill her that night while she slept. According to their statements to the police, the two girls put it off until the next day, choosing instead a nearby forest. They told Payton they wanted to play a game of hide and seek, but the game quickly turned violent as Morgan "stabbed Payton repeatedly with a kitchen knife while Anissa stood watch nearby."[35]

After being left in the woods, Payton crawled into a grassy area where Greg Steinberg, a passing cyclist, found her. When he stopped, she asked him, "Can you help me, please? I've been stabbed multiple times."[36] According to a doctor who treated Payton in the ER, also interviewed by *20/20* in 2019, Payton was stabbed nineteen times, with five wounds on her arm, seven on her leg, and "the rest scattered throughout her torso."[37] One of the stab wounds to her torso "missed her actual heart by a fraction of an inch," and Payton "was in intensive care for days."[38] After this lengthy recovery, Payton resumed as much of a normal life as she could.

The offenders in this case, Morgan and Anissa, fled the scene, not to avoid the police but to try and find Slenderman. They were found by police near Interstate 94, still carrying a bag containing the knife used in the attack. Given their young ages, Morgan and Anissa were not sentenced until years later. In December 2017, Anissa was sentenced to twenty-five years in a mental health facility after she pled "guilty to being an accomplice to second-degree intentional homicide."[39] Morgan, as the person whose hands had wielded the weapon, received a sentence of "40 years in a mental hospital after pleading guilty to attempted first-degree intentional homicide" in February 2018.[40]

In the less than a decade since the commission of this crime, there have been a surprising number of pop culture iterations. In addition to a well-known documentary, there is a movie and an episode of a popular television show based on the crime. And, as always, the case has been the subject of podcast episodes.

Movies/TV

The fictionalized accounts of the case center around a Lifetime movie and an episode of *Criminal Minds*; both aired in 2018. While neither specifically used Payton's name, this case has such specific details that it is very clear both iterations are about the attempted murder of Payton Leutner.

Terror in the Woods

Terror in the Woods premiered on Lifetime on October 14, 2018. It was written by Amber Benson, directed by D.J. Viola, and stars Skylar Morgan Jones as Emily, the character based on Payton. Rather than Slenderman, the imaginary boogeyman in *Terror in the Woods* is the Suzarin, with fairly similar characteristics to the original creation. As with much of the coverage of this case, Emily/Payton is barely a character up to the point of her attempted murder. The main characters are Rachel and Kaitlin (Anissa and Morgan respectively) and their growing friendship. The audience watches a substantial amount of the film dedicated to the two offenders, with only one or two scenes with Emily. Kaitlin's mother asks her why she does not hang out with Emily so much anymore. Rachel is shown calling Emily immature. However, there is not any significant screen time for the victim of this case.

The first time that Emily/Payton is brought into the main storyline of the film is Kaitlin's birthday party. Even though she is there in the room, the main plot line of Kaitlin and Rachel plotting the murder overwhelms her presence. Once the three finally find themselves in the woods, the difference between them is clear. Emily is wearing a pink fairy dress over her outfit. The other two are dressed in dark and muted colors—Rachel is wearing plastic armor over her dark clothes.

The stabbing of Emily is surprisingly more graphic and brutal than one would expect from a Lifetime movie. While Emily has stopped to smell the flowers, the two others debate who should be the one to stab her. Kaitlin tells Rachel that Rachel should do it because she "knows where all the good spots are."[41] Rachel says Kaitlin has to stab Emily—to "go bananas."[42] Kaitlin hesitates, asking for Rachel's permission first. Once she has it, she stabs Emily over and over.

While Kaitlin and Rachel go off to find the Suzarin, Emily is left to die in the forest. A fisherman in a boat finds Emily on the side of the river and presumably calls 911 to get Emily to the hospital. This Good Samaritan aside, this scene removes the agency of Payton Leutner, who fought so hard for her life that she crawled to a path to be found by a cyclist. Given the lack of attention paid to Payton by the news media or the HBO documentary, any audience stumbling upon *Terror in the Woods* could easily have no idea of Payton's heroism and sheer will to survive.

In the last moments of the film, Emily is finally given a small moment of autonomy as she is seen post-recovery, roller-blading. However, it is a very small moment. The clip of Emily is so short that if one is distracted, it would be quite easy to miss that she had lived after the attack. Rachel and Kaitlin, on the other hand, are shown post-conviction, with much more detail than given to Emily. Clearly in prison and wearing a prison uniform, Rachel is gardening. Kaitlin is in a mental facility while her mother is speaking to a group about making sure that her daughter gets the help that she needs and making sure they get her medications right. Just like the rest of the film, the bulk of the attention is paid to the offenders, their families, their lives, and their reasons for nearly killing Emily. Emily, and by extension Payton, is two-dimensional and simply a plot point for Rachel and Kaitlin.

Criminal Minds

Season 14 episode 5 of *Criminal Minds*, titled "The Tall Man," first aired on CBS on Halloween, October 31, 2018. While clearly paying homage to the case, the show has made some significant changes to the original facts. The most glaring of these changes is the aging up of the main players involved in the case. Clearly older than 12, the three main characters, identified as Ally, Chelsea, and Bethany, are in high school. There is even a line from the characters at the beginning of the episode, when they are walking through the woods, where they say, "What are we, 12?" By aging the characters out of middle school and into high school, some of the horror associated with the crime disappears. A large part of the media attention paid to the crime against Payton had to do with the fact that all three girls involved were 12 years old. By making them at least four or even five years older, an audience can feel more "comfortable" with the terrible crimes in the episode.

Another glaring deviation from the original case in this episode is the offender. As is stated above, in actuality the two offenders were the other two girls who went into the woods with Payton. In the *Criminal Minds* episode, the offender is a male sex offender who had manipulated one of the three girls into harming the other two. This humanizing of the

Slenderman, transforming him from an urban legend into an evil human, gives all of the young women an innocence, even Bethany, who held the knife in her hand.

Even without saying her name, many people who are familiar with the case were able to connect the character of Chelsea with Payton. The connection allows for a "happy ending" of the case without exploiting Payton or intruding into her life as a 17-year-old high school student. In the final scenes of the episode, Chelsea (Payton) is shown in her hospital bed, smiling with her friend, Ally. She is recovering and, unlike Payton, able to maintain her friendship with her longtime friend, who presumably would help her heal and rebuild after her trauma.

Documentaries

Beware the Slenderman

Beware the Slenderman is arguably the most famous telling of the stabbing of Payton Leutner in 2014. Directed by Irene Brodsky, it premiered at the South by Southwest festival in March of 2016 and broadcast on HBO on January 23, 2017. For most viewers, this documentary was their introduction to the case and the primary source of information on the major players, including Payton. The most damning exclusion in this documentary is that of the Leutner family—especially the lack of information about Payton herself. The only discussion of Payton outside of the commission of the crime and the trial is a short clip of her doing the Ice Bucket Challenge. While it is entirely understandable why the Leutners did not wish to participate in a documentary, especially one that was filmed less than two years after Payton was nearly killed in those woods, that does not explain why the documentary chose to spend no more than a few moments on Payton the person and not the victim. Yes, showing her participating in the Ice Bucket Challenge, a viral social media challenge where participants recorded themselves being doused with ice water to raise money for ALS research, shows Payton's caring nature. But that short moment is drowned out by the sheer weight of coverage given to the two offenders.

The only other mentions of Payton in the 117 minutes of *Beware the Slenderman* occur during the investigation of the crime and in the trial. In addition to this almost exclusive depiction as a victim, Payton is often referred to as "Bella," a nickname that was given to her by Morgan, one of the offenders. Whether intending to or not, the documentary strips Payton of much of her identity.

20/20

Five years after the crime, Payton broke her silence with an interview on *20/20* that aired on October 24, 2019. By then 17, Payton sat down with David Muir to tell her side of the story. When asked to describe herself before the incident, Payton said she was "fun" and "hopeful."[43] She tells Muir that she made friends with Morgan because it looked like Morgan "didn't have any friends" and she did not want anyone to be lonely.[44] The friendship turned sour when Morgan became friends with Anissa, who Payton says was "always cruel" to her.[45] Hearing the origins of this crime from Payton herself is haunting and empowering. This was the final piece viewed for this chapter, so the researcher had already consumed hours of content about the Slenderman stabbing—most of it without any real portrayal of Payton. Seeing a healthy Payton, who consented to the interview, tell the story in her own words finally offers some balance to the tale.

Additionally, the *20/20* special had interviews with Payton's parents, the man who found her in the woods, and the ER doctor who treated her. These provided further insight into Payton's ordeal in November of 2014. The man who found Payton takes *20/20* to the spot where he found her, saying, "Somehow she'd managed to pull herself out of the woods."[46] This is especially good after the treatment of Payton in *Terror in the Woods* where the character based on her was simply found on the side of a river rather than "pulling herself out of the woods."

This interview was heavily covered in the press as it was the first time Payton spoke out publicly. Headlines appeared like "'Slender Man' Stabbing Victim Speaks Publicly for First Time,"[47] "'Slenderman' Stabbing Victim Payton Leutner on the Friends Who Tried to Kill Her,"[48] and "'Slender Man' Attack Victim Says She Sleeps with Broken Scissors 'Just in Case.'"[49] After five years of pop culture revictimization, this interview allowed the Leutner family to retake some control.

Podcasts

Of the nine podcasts listened to for this chapter, the majority of them depend heavily on the *Beware of Slenderman* documentary and, therefore, spend far more time talking about the offenders than about Payton. Additionally, the podcast hosts are intrigued by the Slenderman mythos, further skewing the focus away from Payton.

While there was some critique of the documentary, it is overshadowed by the coverage of the two offenders and the excitement of Slenderman.

In episode 31 of *True Crime Guys*, they spend nineteen minutes discussing Slenderman before getting to the case and transitioning to covering the HBO documentary. *Dark Stuff* covered the case in their episode "Violent Crimes Day and A Slenderman Stabbing," which dropped on February 18, 2018. Suann, the female host, points out that "the victim wasn't mentioned as much as I would have liked her to be mentioned."[50] *Crime Grinds*, in its second episode, titled "Slenderman Stabbing," from October 17, 2018, draws attention to the lack of information on Payton. This leaves listeners believing that *Crime Grinds* would have included more background on Payton if that information were more readily available. While there was not, at the time of their recording, background on Payton, the show does give as much coverage as possible on what happened to her after the stabbing. They say that she made a full recovery but that she has twenty-five scars and slept with scissors under her pillow every night, after making sure that all the doors and windows were locked. This inclusion of the struggles that Payton and her family went through in the months and years following the attack ensures that the audience remembers this as well.

The worst offender in this treatment of Payton among the podcasts surveyed for this chapter is *White Wine True Crime!*. For much of the episode, the hosts cover the documentary, and as such, focus completely on the offenders. However, in the conversation about the crime, they label Anissa the Alpha and Morgan the Beta of the friendship. This is not unusual and they are not the only ones to make this Alpha/Beta comparison—*Unpopular Culture*, hosted by a licensed psychotherapist with a history in forensics, also makes it. Where *WWTC* makes a strategic error that horrifically revictimizes Payton is in the label they choose for her—"the meat." It is unconscionable to call a 12-year-old girl who was stabbed nineteen times by two people that she considered to be her best friends "the meat." They have reduced this young girl to even less than a victim, to a literal piece of meat that was tenderized by an Alpha and a Beta. Not only this, but their assumption is that any friendship of three always includes an Alpha, a Beta, and "the meat," which implies that not only do they consider Payton "the meat" but they believe that it was her destiny to always be "the meat."

Only time will tell if distance will be enough to provide more cohesive and balanced coverage of Payton Leutner. Far more information is now available after Payton herself sat down for an interview in 2019, but that does little to counteract the dearth of information in pop culture, which ignored Payton, or worse, revictimized her again and again.

Conclusion

By 2022, Gypsy Rose Blanchard was still serving her sentence while Payton Leutner entered college during the COVID-19 pandemic. At the dawn of a new decade, the social media that was so integral to the crimes in question are still vital, especially to young people like Gypsy and Payton. In addition to the enticing inclusion of social media, these crimes were committed during a perfect storm. A 24-hour news cycle, combined with channels now entirely dedicated to true crime and the cresting wave of true crime interest, has created this perfect storm that thrust Gypsy and Payton into an unwanted spotlight.

The stories of Gypsy and Payton prove that, even with only five years, pop culture will still take the opportunity to create exploitative iterations. As with many of the women chosen for this project, the coverage of Gypsy and Payton is more exploitative than informational or advocational for either of them. In most of the coverage of Payton, content creators are far more interested in the internet myth of Slenderman than the young woman who was brutally stabbed and left to die in the woods. In telling Gypsy's story, many mention the abuse she suffered at the hands of her mother, but only a few take that abuse into account when they discuss how much influence it may have had on her actions to kill her mother.

It is now being repeated for the eleventh time in this analysis that, perhaps with more time, both Gypsy and Payton will someday be treated with respect. They, like all victims, deserve advocacy and attention rather than being relegated to a minor player in their own story.

Conclusion

As this was written, the world was locked down due to the Novel Coronavirus, also known as COVID-19. Communities on local, state, and national levels were put into quarantine. Historians delved into the historical record of the last pandemic, which took place in 1918 when influenza killed millions worldwide. This again proves how 1920–2020 bookends the 20th century better than 1900–2000. As the 1920s began, the United States was recovering from a global pandemic; in 2020 it was entering into a new one. The true crime community, unsurprisingly, turned inward, relying on one another to support and fill the hours as the days melted together into a year like no other. Some podcasts increased their content output while others struggled to find their way when the hosts were not able to record in the same studio. Several weeks into the quarantine, George Floyd was murdered by Minneapolis police officers on May 25, and a series of protests began across the globe on race relations and discrimination. This confluence of events—the COVID-19 quarantine and the riots of summer 2020—has caused additional introspection into true crime.

Even as early as April 2020, the United States felt the impact of the COVID lockdown on true crime. States, particularly on the East Coast, began to issue shelter-in-place orders, requiring most Americans to stay inside their homes unless they were essential workers or they had to get necessary goods. For many, this meant hours, even more than "normal," staring at screens. Fans of true crime turned to old favorites. *Dateline* viewership went up 9 percent while a *48 Hours* episode on Lizzie Borden had ratings 35 percent higher than the same night in 2019.[1] Rebecca Reisner states in a *Daily Beast* article that traffic on her site, *Forensic Files Now*, has increased 10–20 percent since the beginning of the pandemic.[2] Reisner says that, given the serious times, it "just seems appropriate to watch this stuff when things are grim."[3]

Systemic racism was brought to attention with the deaths of George Floyd, who was choked as he told the officers that he could not breathe, and Breonna Taylor, an emergency room technician in Louisville, Kentucky, who was shot in her own apartment as she was sleeping, by officers who were executing a no-knock warrant and entered her apartment looking for someone she used to date. Even in the midst of a global pandemic, with the United States having the highest case numbers in the world, people gathered in dozens of cities to protest what they referred to as the systemic racism in the country's police departments. In the wake of the murder of George Floyd, the American Civil Liberties Union (ACLU) released a report detailing the level of police violence against Black, Indigenous, and people of color. Published in July 2020, the report says that "police in America kill people at least three times the rate of their law enforcement counterparts in Canada, a wealthy country with the next highest rate of killing, and at least 16 times the rates of Germany and England."[4] Acknowledging that police violence is now "among the leading causes of death" for young men of color, there is a lack of research on women killed by police that "mirror[s] the lack of media attention often given to women and non-binary people of color."[5] It is clear from what statistics exists that "although women are less likely than men to be killed by police overall, Black women and Native American/Indigenous women are more likely to be killed by police than white women."[6]

While 2020 was a year like no other in the memory of most people alive, a world of face masks, global death tolls, and race riots would be very familiar to the women in the first two chapters. Sabella arrived in the United States in 1916, with just enough time to settle in before the 1918 pandemic began. As she sat in prison awaiting her trial, a predominately Black town in Florida called Rosewood was wiped out by whites from a neighboring town. One must wonder how many sundown towns—towns that African Americans were warned to leave by sundown or they would not survive—Bonnie and Clyde drove through as they crisscrossed the Midwest. Several of the women experienced huge traumas before the reason for their inclusion in this book: multiple wars, economic recessions and depressions, racial and political upheavals—all in addition to what they had to deal with in their own lives. Having experienced a global pandemic, the resulting economic decline, and racial unrest boiling over in dozens of cities while also trying to telecommute and maintain relationships has given unique insight into all of these women.

The ultimate goal for historians of both true crime and those of the more traditional vein, is to tell people's stories. For some women, like Sabella and Marilyn, their stories have seldom been told and rarely with any real justice. For other women, like Sharon and Nicole, histories of their lives run the spectrum from barely acknowledged to manipulated to the point where they are unrecognizable. The question remains—where are the histories of these women that show them the same respect that their offenders are often awarded? And, as many people get their information about history from popular culture, where are the pop culture iterations of these and other women that offer even an informational look at them and stop exploiting them?

In the wake of the #MeToo movement, the true depth of the destructive patriarchal Hollywood system was revealed. Dozens of women came forward with accusations against a powerful Hollywood producer who refused roles if they did not perform sexual favors.[7] In a study conducted in 2017 at USC Annenberg's School for Communication and Journalism, young women are more likely to be shown on media platforms in "sexy attire," "with some nudity," and to be thin.[8] A five-year study, also by USC Annenberg, looking at 2007–2012, indicates that the categories of wearing sexy attire and some nudity actually increased during that time. Female characters in the ever-popular action films are now written as take-charge, kickass women, but, as actor Jessica Chastain points out, "[T]hey have to be in some cat suit."[9] A 2018 report by Plan International found that "female leaders were four times more likely to be shown naked on screen than similar male roles."[10] With this kind of insidious sexualization of women across the entire industry, both on and off screen, there is little hope of widespread change. A patriarchal system, now more than a century old, combined with audiences who still pay for the salacious and sexual, means a massive cultural shift is needed before women receive treatment equal to men.

Unsurprisingly, and as expected, the majority of advocacy for these and other women comes from podcasts and independent content creators. The world of podcasting offers many freedoms, which allows content creators to treat women and female victims very differently than more traditional Hollywood films and television. Outside of the rigid Hollywood system, podcast hosts are able to choose what they cover and how they cover it. As shown in the previous chapters, the majority of women covered in this project have received the best coverage from podcasts, most of those episodes hosted by women. Statistics on the diversity of podcasting have not been collected, but more importantly, may be too difficult to easily collect. As mentioned in an online article written by David Hooper for *Big Podcast Bulletin*, a podcast is more than the hosts, but the hosts are often the only ones who are mentioned on any social media.[11]

In the aftermath of the deaths of George Floyd, Breonna Taylor, and far too many others, many podcasts have made concerted efforts to include more episodes on Black, Indigenous, and people of color—those who have been left out of the narrative for decades. One of the systemic changes that will hopefully come from this season of protest will be a greater inclusion in media, not only podcasts, so the stories of victims of all backgrounds are told.

Chapter Notes

Introduction

1. Rachel Monroe, *Savage Appetites: True Stories of Women, Crime, and Obsession* (New York: Scribner, 2020), 1.

2. Jean Murley, *The Rise of True Crime: 20th Century Murder and American Popular Culture* (Westport, CT: Praeger, 2008), 15.

3. Murley, 80.

4. Matt Zoller Seitz, *TV (The Book): Two Experts Pick the Greatest American Shows of All Time* (New York: Grand Central, 2016), 372.

5. Scaachi Koul, "Being 'Polite' Often Gets Women Killed," *Buzzfeed News*, February 15, 2017, accessed May 10, 2019, https://www.buzzfeednews.com/article/scaachikoul/whats-your-favorite-murder.

6. Scaachi Koul, "Being 'Polite' Often Gets Women Killed," *Buzzfeed News*, February 15, 2017, accessed May 10, 2019, https://www.buzzfeednews.com/article/scaachikoul/whats-your-favorite-murder.

7. Amanda Vicary and R. Chris Fraley, "Captured by True Crime: Why Are Women Drawn to Tales of Rape, Murder, and Serial Killers," *Social Psychological and Personality Science* (2010), 83.

8. Vicary and Fraley, "Captured by True Crime," 83.

9. Megan Abbott, "Why Do We—Women in Particular—Love True Crime Books?" *Los Angeles Times*, June 14, 2018.

10. Molly Fitzpatrick, "How Two Hilarious Women Turned a Comedy-Murder Podcast Into a Phenomenon," *Rolling Stone*, May 30, 2017, https://www.rollingstone.com/culture/culture-features/how-two-hilarious-women-turned-a-comedy-murder-podcast-into-a-phenomenon-113785/.

11. Further proving the comradery of the true crime podcast community, *MFM* fans know the hosts simply by the names of Karen and Georgia. Therefore, this project refers to them as such.

12. Molly Fitzpatrick, "How Two Hilarious Women Turned a Comedy-Murder Podcast Into a Phenomenon," *Rolling Stone*, May 30, 2017, https://www.rollingstone.com/culture/culture-features/how-two-hilarious-women-turned-a-comedy-murder-podcast-into-a-phenomenon-11378.

13. Connecticut Law Tribune Editorial Board, "Crimes Against Blacks, Women Still Underreported in Media," *Law.com*, February 21, 2020, https://www.law.com/ctlawtribune/2020/02/21/crimes-against-blacks-women-still-underreported-in-media/?slreturn=20200704193937.

14. Anne-Marie O'Connor, "Not Only Natalee Is Missing," *Los Angeles Times*, August 5, 2005, https://www.latimes.com/archives/la-xpm-2005-aug-05-et-aruba5-story.html.

15. Anne-Marie O'Connor, "Not Only Natalee Is Missing," *Los Angeles Times*, August 5, 2005, https://www.latimes.com/archives/la-xpm-2005-aug-05-et-aruba5-story.html.

16. Anne-Marie O'Connor, "Not Only Natalee Is Missing," *Los Angeles Times*, August 5, 2005, https://www.latimes.com/archives/la-xpm-2005-aug-05-et-aruba5-story.html.

17. Anne-Marie O'Connor, "Not Only Natalee Is Missing," *Los Angeles Times*, August 5, 2005, https://www.latimes.com/archives/la-xpm-2005-aug-05-et-aruba5-story.html.

Chapter 1

1. Kori Rumore and Marianna Mather, *He Had It Coming: Four Murderous Women and the Reporter Who Immortalized Their Stories* (Chicago: Midway Press, 2019), 111.

2. Sabella's first husband shares his name with a fairly famous mobster. The Francesco Nitti that has a Wikipedia page and can be researched easily online is not the husband of Sabella.

3. Emilie Le Beau Lucchesi, *Ugly Prey: An Innocent Woman and the Death Sentence That Scandalized Jazz Age Chicago* (Chicago: Chicago Review Press, 2017), 34.

4. Rumore and Mather, *He Had It Coming*, 111.

5. Runmore and Mather, *He Had It Coming*, 116.

6. Runmore and Mather, *He Had It Coming*, 119.

7. Runmore and Mather, *He Had It Coming*, 124.

8. Erik Rivenes, "1923 Chicago's Accused Murderess Sabella Nitti with Emilie La Beau Lucchesi," *Most Notorious*, October 25, 2018, accessed May 13, 2020, https://radiopublic.com/most-notorious-a-true-crime-histo-GyZRpW/s1!fa5e8.

9. Lucchesi, *Ugly Prey*, 288.

10. Lucchesi, *Ugly Prey*, 288.

11. Runmore and Mather, *He Had It Coming*, 144.

12. Runmore and Mather, *He Had It Coming*, 144.

13. For more research on the shifting and changing racial definitions, please read *The History of White People* by Nell Painter.

14. "Oct. 12 Is Set as Date to Hand Woman Slayer," *Chicago Tribune*, July 15, 1923, 5.

15. "'My Children Die with Me' Is Mrs. Nitti's Cry," *Chicago Tribune*, July 31, 1923, 7.

16. "'My Children Die with Me' Is Mrs. Nitti's Cry," *Chicago Tribune*, July 31, 1923, 7.

17. Genevieve Forbes, "Mrs. Nitti and Consort Given Noose Penalty," *Chicago Tribune*, July 10, 1923, 1.

18. Genevieve Forbes, "Mrs. Nitti and Consort Given Noose Penalty," *Chicago Tribune*, July 10, 1923, 1.

19. Genevieve Forbes, "Mrs. Nitti and Consort Given Noose Penalty," *Chicago Tribune*, July 10, 1923, 1.

20. Genevieve Forbes, "Mrs. Nitti and Consort Given Noose Penalty," *Chicago Tribune*, July 10, 1923, 1.

21. Genevieve Forbes, "Mrs. Nitti and Consort Given Noose Penalty," *Chicago Tribune*, July 10, 1923, 1.

22. Genevieve Forbes, "Mrs. Nitti and Consort Given Noose Penalty," *Chicago Tribune*, July 10, 1923, 1.

23. "State Launches Trial of Belva of Law Killing," *Chicago Tribune*, June 5, 1924, 12.

24. Maurine Watkins, "Select Jury to Pronounce Fate of Beulah Annan," *Chicago Tribune*, May 23, 1924, 6.

25. Genevieve Forbes, "Dialect Jargon Makes 'Em Dizzy Aa Nitti Trial," *Chicago Tribune*, July 7, 1923, 2.

26. Genevieve Forbes, "Mrs. Nitti's Tragedy Melts Hearts of Women in Jail," *Chicago Tribune*, July 12, 1923, 3.

27. Genevieve Forbes, "Mrs. Nitti's Tragedy Melts Hearts of Women in Jail," *Chicago Tribune*, July 12, 1923, 3.

28. Genevieve Forbes, "Mrs. Nitti's Tragedy Melts Hearts of Women in Jail," *Chicago Tribune*, July 12, 1923, 3.

29. Runmore and Mather, *He Had It Coming*, 3.

30. Douglas Perry, *The Girls of Murder City: Fame, Lust, and the Beautiful Killers Who Inspired Chicago* (New York: Penguin, 2010), 57.

31. Perry, *The Girls of Murder City*, 116.

32. Emilie Le Beau Lucchesi, *Ugly Prey: An Innocent Woman and the Death Sentence That Scandalized Jazz Age Chicago* (Chicago: Chicago Review Press, 2017), 4.

33. Lucchesi, *Ugly Prey*, 4–5.

34. Lucchesi, *Ugly Prey*, 5.

35. Lucchesi, *Ugly Prey*, 5.

36. Lucchesi, *Ugly Prey*, 4.

37. Lucchesi, *Ugly Prey*, 107.

38. Lucchesi, *Ugly Prey*, 107.

39. Lucchesi, *Ugly Prey*, 107.

40. Jon Seidel, *Second City Sinners: True Crime from Historic Chicago's Deadly Streets* (Guilford, CT: Lyons Press, 2019), 120.

41. *Chicago*, directed by Cecil B. DeMille (1927; Culver City, CA: Amazon.com Services LLC), Streaming, https://www.amazon.com/Chicago-Phyllis-Haver/dp/

B078X312QS/ref=sr_1_2?dchild=1&keyw
ords=chicago+1927&qid=1596561573&s
r=8-2.

42. Runmore and Mather, *He Had It Coming*, 177–179.

43. This is the only time I will mention this term and I apologize for its use here now. It is only included because of its rampant use in the film because of the connotations the word usage has towards Sabella.

44. Lucchesi, *Ugly Prey*, 288.

45. Rivenes, *Most Notorious*, October 25, 2018.

46. Rivenes, *Most Notorious*, October 25, 2018.

47. Rebekah Buchanan, host, "Ugly Prey: An Innocent Woman and the Death Sentence That Scandalized Jazz Age Chicago," *Books on Law* (podcast), May 2, 2018, accessed June 1, 2020, https://newbooksnetwork.com/emilie-lucchesi-ugly-prey-an-innocent-woman-and-the-death-sentence-that-scandalized-jazz-age-chicago-chicago-review-2017/.

Chapter 2

1. Jeff Guinn, *Go Down Together: The True, Untold Story of Bonnie and Clyde* (New York: Simon & Schuster, 2010), 45.

2. Guinn, *Go Down Together*, 48.

3. Guinn, *Go Down Together*, 49.

4. Guinn, *Go Down Together*, 51.

5. Guinn, *Go Down Together*, 82.

6. Guinn, *Go Down Together*, 88.

7. "Barrow's Auto Found in Kansas," *El Paso Times*, April 9, 1934.

8. "Hunt Dillinger in Oklahoma," *El Paso Times*, April 9, 1934.

9. "Cigar-Smoking Woman Seized at Clebune," *El Paso Times*, April 9, 1934.

10. "Clyde Barrow Linked with New Crimes," *The Brownsville Herald* (Brownsville, TX), November 26, 1933.

11. "Clyde Barrow and Girl 'Put On Spot' in Deal with Felon, Report Says," *El Paso Times*, May 24, 1934.

12. Guinn, *Go Down Together*, 137.

13. "Clyde Barrow and Girl 'Put On Spot' in Deal with Felon, Report Says," *El Paso Times*, May 24, 1934.

14. Jan I. Fortune, *The True Story of Bonnie and Clyde: As Told by Bonnie's Mother and Clyde's Sister, Mrs. Emma*

Parker and Mrs. Nell Barrow Cowan (New York: Signet, 1968).

15. Fortune, *The True Story of Bonnie and Clyde*, 43–44.

16. Fortune, *The True Story of Bonnie and Clyde*, 57.

17. Fortune, *The True Story of Bonnie and Clyde*, 57.

18. Fortune, *The True Story of Bonnie and Clyde*, 57.

19. *The Bonnie Parker Story*, directed by William Witney (1958; Los Angeles, CA), found on YouTube at https://www.youtube.com/watch?v=WlnhFqW2ivg.

20. Which is very confusing if you haven't yet figured out that his name is Guy.

21. *The Bonnie Parker Story*.

22. Guinn, *Go Down Together*, 362.

23. Guinn, *Go Down Together*, 362.

24. Guinn, *Go Down Together*, 363.

25. *Bonnie and Clyde*, directed by Arthur Penn (1967; Burbank, CA: Amazon.com Services LLC), Streaming, https://www.amazon.com/Bonnie-Clyde-Warren-Beatty/dp/B0097JUIQG/ref=sr_1_1?crid=SVT0YKZJ9O46&dchild=1&keywords=bonnie+and+clyde+1967&qid=1596561660&sprefix=bonnie+and+clyde+19%2Caps%2C165&sr=8-1.

26. *Bonnie and Clyde*.

27. *Bonnie and Clyde*.

28. Guinn, *Go Down Together*, 364.

29. *Bonnie & Clyde*, episode 1, "Part One," directed by Bruce Beresford, written by John Rice and Joe Batteer, featuring Emile Hirsch and Holliday Granger, aired on December 8, 2013, Storyline Entertainment, 2020, Amazon.com Streaming. https://www.amazon.com/Bonnie-Clyde/dp/B00I2TMNSI/ref=sr_1_1?dchild=1&keywords=bonnie+and+clyde+2013&qid=1596561687&sr=8-1.

30. Up to this point, the only time the two had interacted was at Bonnie's wedding to Roy. Clyde, having crashed the wedding, had simply seen her and nothing more. Yet, he shows up now to take her out.

31. *Bonnie & Clyde*, episode 1, "Part One."

32. *Bonnie & Clyde*, episode 1, "Part One."

33. *Bonnie & Clyde*, episode 1, "Part One."

34. *Bonnie & Clyde*, episode 1, "Part One."

35. Ben Kissel, Marcus Parks,

and Henry Zebrowski, hosts, "Episode 371: Bonnie and Clyde Part III—Filthy, Smelly, and Surly," *The Last Podcast on the Left* (podcast), November 8, 2017, accessed December 7, 2019, https://www.lastpodcastontheleft.com/episodes/2019/6/28/episode-371-bonnie-and-clyde-part-iii-filthy-smelly-and-surly.

36. *The Highwaymen*, directed by John Lee Hancock (2019; Santa Monica, CA: Netflix), Streaming, https://www.netflix.com/search?q=the%20highwaymen.

37. *The Highwaymen*.

38. None of the pop culture fictionalizations shows the true nature of Bonnie's injuries. She was horribly injured and, by the end of her life, needed be carried from place to place as her leg had begun to heal in an unnatural position.

39. *The Highwaymen*.

40. *Highlander*, Season 5, Episode 6, "Money No Object," directed by Rafel Zielinski, written by James Thorpe, featuring Adrian Paul, Stan Kirsch, and Elizabeth Gracen, aired on November 4, 1996, Rysher Entertainment, 2020, Amazon Streaming, https://www.amazon.com/gp/video/detail/B07HFL339C/ref=atv_dp_season_select_s5.

41. *Highlander*, "Money No Object," 1996.

42. Vanessa Richardson and Sami Nye, hosts, "'Bonnie & Clyde'—Bonnie Parker," *Female Criminals* (podcast), April 2, 2018, accessed December 10, 2019, https://www.parcast.com/criminals.

43. *Last Podcast on the Left*, Episode 371.

44. *Last Podcast on the Left*, Episode 371.

Chapter 3

1. Morgan Korzik, "The Life of Elizabeth Short," *The Black Dalia: The 1947 Murder of Elizabeth Short*, December 2, 2016, Accessed May 13, 2019, http://blackdahlia.web.unc.edu/the-life-of-elizabeth-short/

2. Korzik, "The Life of Elizabeth Short."

3. Korzik, "The Life of Elizabeth Short."

4. Camp Cooke is now Vandenberg Air Force Base.

5. Korzik, "The Life of Elizabeth Short."

6. Piu Eatwell, *Black Dahlia, Red Rose: The Crime, Corruption, and Cover-Up of America's Greatest Unsolved Murder* (New York: Liveright, 2018), Page 5.

7. In the words of *My Favorite Murder*—It is never a mannequin.

8. Eatwell, *Black Dahlia, Red Rose*, 6.

9. Eatwell, *Black Dahlia, Red Rose*, 34.

10. The name Black Dahlia is said to have been a nickname given to Elizabeth by people at a soda fountain she would frequent. It is also said that the name was, at least in part, based upon the 1946 movie *The Blue Dahlia* starring Veronica Lake and Alan Ladd.

11. "M.P. Admits Slaying of Black Dahlia," *Washington Post*, February 9, 1947.

12. "M.P. Admits Slaying of Black Dahlia," *Washington Post*, February 9, 1947.

13. "Police Seek Mad Pervert in Girl's Death," *Washington Post*, January 18, 1947.

14. "Medford Girl Murder Victim: Mutilated Body Found in Los Angeles Vacant Lot," *Boston Daily Globe*, January 17, 1947.

15. "Police Seeking Former Marine in L.A. Slaying," *The Hartford Sentinel* (Hartford, CT), January 18, 1947.

16. "Police Seek Mad Pervert in Girl's Death," *Washington Post*, January 18, 1947.

17. "Black Dahlia's Love Life Traced in Search for Her Fiendish Murderer," *Los Angeles Times*, January 18, 1947.

18. "Black Dahlia's Love Life Traced in Search for Her Fiendish Murderer," *Los Angeles Times*, January 18, 1947.

19. "Black Dahlia's Love Life Traced in Search for Her Fiendish Murderer," *Los Angeles Times*, January 18, 1947.

20. Steve Hodel, *The Black Dahlia Avenger: A Genius for Murder: The True Story* (New York: Arcade, 2019), 18.

21. Hodel, *The Black Dahlia Avenger*, 337.

22. Hodel, *The Black Dahlia Avenger*, 337.

23. Hodel, *The Black Dahlia Avenger*, 337.

24. Hodel, *The Black Dahlia Avenger*, 337.

25. Hodel, *The Black Dahlia Avenger*, 338.

26. Hodel, *The Black Dahlia Avenger*, 338.

27. Hodel, *The Black Dahlia Avenger*, 338.

28. Hodel, *The Black Dahlia Avenger*, 338.

29. According to an obituary, Hansen was "haunted by the death" until his death in 1983, fifteen years after he retired from the LAPD.

30. Eatwell, *Black Dahlia, Red Rose*, 196.

31. *Who Is the Black Dahlia?*, directed by Joseph Pevney (1975; Los Angeles, California), YouTube, https://www.youtube.com/watch?v=Y921yIpz4KI.

32. *Who Is the Black Dahlia?*.

33. *Who Is the Black Dahlia?*.

34. *Who Is the Black Dahlia?*.

35. *Who Is the Black Dahlia?*.

36. This character, Doctor Wallace Coppin, seems to be based on Robert "Red" Manley. In the film, Coppin is shown giving her the ride from Santa Barbara to LA that Manley gave to her from San Diego to Los Angeles. As the police investigation in the film focuses so wholly on a medical professional, Manley was changed to a doctor to add to his viability as a suspect.

37. The screenplay was co-written by Gregory and Joan Didion.

38. *True Confessions*, directed by Ulu Grosbard (1981; Los Angeles, California: Amazon.com Services LLC), Streaming, https://www.amazon.com/True-Confessions-Robert-Niro/dp/B01D81RE4M/ref=sr_1_2?dchild=1&keywords=true+confessions&qid=1596562131&s=instant-video&sr=1-2.

39. The word, beginning with a c, is highly offensive to many and will not be included here.

40. *True Confessions*.

41. *The Black Dahlia*, directed by Brian De Palma (2006; Culver City, California: Amazon.com Services, LLC), Streaming, https://www.amazon.com/Black-Dahlia-Josh-Hartnett/dp/B000M86HPC/ref=sr_1_1?dchild=1&keywords=black+dahlia+2006&qid=1596562156&s=instant-video&sr=1-1.

42. *The Black Dahlia*.

43. *The Black Dahlia*.

44. *Hunter*, Season 4, Episode 13, "The Black Dahlia," directed by Michael Preece, written by Robert Hamner, featuring Fred Dryer, Stefanie Kramer, and Charles Hallahan, aired on January 9, 1988, Stephen J. Cannell Productions, 2020, Amazon Streaming, https://www.amazon.com/gp/video/detail/B07NQ2MDWT/ref=atv_dp_season_select_s4.

45. *Hunter*, "The Black Dahlia."

46. *American Horror Story*, Season 1, Episode 9, "Spooky Little Girl," directed by John Scott, written by Jennifer Salt, featuring Connie Britton, Dylan McDermott, and Jessica Lange, aired on November 30, 2011, Ryan Murphy Productions, 2019, Netflix, https://www.netflix.com/watch/70260298?trackId=13752289&tctx=0%2C8%2C2b3dd968-fb33-4910-9d4c-e68c77e984c9-89225307%2C9d41289a9a2b2003ef1fc950d974d6bd490fd678%3A260cfda58771787b7eb8afee8ff489e19ac2a7e7%2C%2C.

47. *American Horror Story*, "Spooky Little Girl."

48. *American Horror Story*, "Spooky Little Girl."

49. *American Horror Story*, "Spooky Little Girl."

50. *American Horror Story*, "Spooky Little Girl."

51. *American Horror Story*, "Spooky Little Girl."

52. *American Horror Story*, "Spooky Little Girl."

53. *James Ellroy's L.A.: City of Demons*, Season 1, Episode 1, "Dead Women Own Me," directed by Brian Coughlin, featuring James Ellroy, aired on January 19, 2011, Digital Ranch Productions, 2020, Amazon Streaming, https://www.amazon.com/Dead-Women-Own-Me/dp/B078WCWNMQ/ref=sr_1_1?crid=1717DBWUI68CV&dchild=1&keywords=james+ellroy%27s+la+city+of+demons&qid=1596562346&s=instant-video&sprefix=james+ellroy%27s%2Cinstant-video%2C147&sr=1-1.

54. He again refers to her as Betty but historians agree that she was Betty to her family and friends. As Ellroy was born in 1948, more than a year after Elizabeth's death, there is no way he could have met her. There is no evidence that his family knew the Short family, so this use of Betty is a familiarization that he has not earned. This is why, out of respect to Elizabeth Short, she is referred to in this project exclusively as Elizabeth.

55. *James Ellroy's L.A.: City of Demons*, "Dead Women Own Me."

56. *James Ellroy's L.A.: City of Demons*, "Dead Women Own Me."

57. Daniel Fienberg, "'I Am The Night': TV Review," *Hollywood Reporter*, January 15, 2019, accessed June 15, 2020, https://www.hollywoodreporter.com/review/i-am-night-review-1175463.

58. *I Am the Night*, Episode 3, "Dark Flower," directed by Victoria Mahoney, written by Sam Sheridan, featuring Chris Pine, India Eisley, and Jefferson Mays, aired on February 2, 2019, Jenkins + Pine, 2020, Hulu Streaming, https://www.hulu.com/series/i-am-the-night-e89d16c0-99e3-4431-a7a1-c3d4076477b0.

59. "The Black Dahlia—Elizabeth Short," *True Crimecast* (podcast), July 24, 2018, accessed June 12, 2020, https://www.stitcher.com/podcast/true-crimecast/e/55462897?autoplay=true.

60. *True Crimecast*, "The Black Dahlia."

61. "Black Dahlia, the Unsolved Murder of Elizabeth Short." *Thinking Out Loud* (podcast), July 1, 2019, accessed June 10, 2020, https://podtail.com/en/podcast/thinking-out-loud-3/.

62. Diana and Gina, hosts, "20. Elizabeth Short—Part One," *Talk More About That* (podcast), April 2, 2018, accessed May 28, 2020, http://tmatpodcast.blubrry.net/20-elizabeth-short-part-one/.

63. *Talk More About That*, "20. Elizabeth Short—Part One."

64. *Talk More About That*, "20. Elizabeth Short—Part One."

65. *Talk More About That*, "20. Elizabeth Short—Part One."

66. Mark Shostrom, a special effects makeup artist, has done extensive research and interviews on Elizabeth Short. His interview over two episodes of *True Crime Garage* dramatically changed the tone and outline of these episodes. For example, Mark and Nic spend 42 minutes talking about Elizabeth's life before getting to her murder. In their own coverage of "The Black Dahlia Case," the hosts immediately begin with the discovery of Elizabeth's body. More of Mark Shostrom's research can be found here: http://www.theblackdahliainhollywood.com/.

67. *Talk More About That*, "20. Elizabeth Short—Part One."

68. Richard O. Jones, host, "The Black Dahlia," *True Crime Historian* (podcast), November 17, 2017, accessed June 2, 2020, https://www.truecrimehistorian.com/.

69. *Talk More About That*, "20. Elizabeth Short—Part One."

70. Ash and Alaina, hosts, "Episode 38: The Black Dahlia—Part 1," *Morbid* (podcast), January 22, 2019, accessed June 3, 2020, http://morbidpodcast.blubrry.net/tag/black-dahlia/.

71. Karen Kilgariff and Georgia Hardstark, hosts, "7 Murders in Heaven," *My Favorite Murder* (podcast), March 11, 2016, accessed May 10, 2019, https://www.stitcher.com/podcast/exactly-right/my-favorite-murder/e/45613056?autoplay=true.

72. Nic and The Captain, hosts, "Black Dahlia, Part 2," *True Crime Garage* (podcast), August 1, 2016, accessed June 4, 2020, https://truecrimegarage.com/blogs/true-crime-garage/posts/black-dahlia-part-1-2-episodes-44-45.

73. *Talk More About This*, "Episode 20: Black Dahlia."

74. Diana and Gina, hosts, "21: Elizabeth Short—Part Two," *Talk More About That* (podcast), April 9, 2018, accessed June 10, 2020, https://www.stitcher.com/podcast/talk-more-about-that/e/54021265.

75. Obviously, attempting to find her killer is a way of advocating for Elizabeth. However, in many of those situations, the content creators seem more interested in solving the mystery than finding justice for Elizabeth.

Chapter 4

1. James Neff, *The Wrong Man: The Verdict on the Dr. Sam Sheppard Murder Case* (New York: Random House, 2002), 42.

2. Sam Sheppard will not be referred to as an offender or alleged offender as he was found not guilty and recent forensic evidence has indicated his innocence.

3. Donald Greyfield, "Marilyn Reese Sheppard," *Find a Grave*, https://www.findagrave.com/memorial/6876/marilyn-sheppard.

4. Neff, *The Wrong Man*, 4.

5. Neff, *The Wrong Man*, 47.

6. Relman Morin, "The Sheppard Murder: Police Still Contend Doctor Killed Wife; Defense Certain It Was Someone Else," *Akron Beacon Journal* (Akron, OH), August 29, 1954.

7. Relman Morin, "The Sheppard

Murder: Police Still Contend Doctor Killed Wife; Defense Certain It Was Someone Else," *Akron Beacon Journal* (Akron, OH), August 29, 1954.

8. Relman Morin, "The Sheppard Murder: Police Still Contend Doctor Killed Wife; Defense Certain It Was Someone Else," *Akron Beacon Journal* (Akron, OH), August 29, 1954.

9. Relman Morin, "The Sheppard Murder: Police Still Contend Doctor Killed Wife; Defense Certain It Was Someone Else," *Akron Beacon Journal* (Akron, OH), August 29, 1954.

10. Relman Morin, "The Sheppard Murder: Police Still Contend Doctor Killed Wife; Defense Certain It Was Someone Else," *Akron Beacon Journal* (Akron, OH), August 29, 1954.

11. Relman Morin, "The Sheppard Murder: Police Still Contend Doctor Killed Wife; Defense Certain It Was Someone Else," *Akron Beacon Journal* (Akron, OH), August 29, 1954.

12. Relman Morin, "The Sheppard Murder: Police Still Contend Doctor Killed Wife; Defense Certain It Was Someone Else," *Akron Beacon Journal* (Akron, OH), August 29, 1954.

13. Sheppard wrestled under the name "Killer Sam Sheppard" in more than 40 matches before his death.

14. Neff, *The Wrong Man*, 289.

15. Fox Butterfield, "DNA Test Absolves Sam Sheppard of Murder, Lawyer Says," *New York Times*, March 5, 1998.

16. "Prosecutors Exhume Body of Marilyn Sheppard, Fetus," *Chicago Tribune*, October 5, 1999, https://www.chicagotribune.com/news/ct-xpm-1999-10-05-9910060224-story.html.

17. "Fantasy Is State's View: On New Blood Theory of Dr. Sam Side—Court Rules Wednesday," *Cincinnati Enquirer*, April 30, 1955.

18. "Intensive Search Fails to Locate Blunt Weapon, Indicated in Ohio Slaying," *Cincinnati Enquirer*, July 6, 1954.

19. "Six Magnets to Search Lake: Bay Village Police Want Weapon Used in Murder of Doctor's Wife," *Cincinnati Enquirer*, July 7, 1954.

20. "Village Seeks Help in Solving Murder of Doctor's Spouse," *Cincinnati Enquirer*, July 20, 1954.

21. Chip is not a junior. As stated earlier, his middle name is Reese, which was Marilyn's maiden name.

22. Morin, *Akron Beacon Journal*, August 29, 1954.

23. "Doctor Wakened by Scream of Wife Being Murdered," *Lancaster Eagle-Gazette* (Lancaster, OH), July 5, 1954.

24. Cynthia Cooper and Sam Reese Sheppard, *Mockery of Justice: The True Story of the Sheppard Murder Case* (Lebanon, NH: Northeastern University Press, 1995), 5.

25. Cooper and Sheppard, *Mockery of Justice*, 4.

26. Copper and Sheppard, *Mockery of Justice*, 13.

27. Cooper and Sheppard, *Mockery of Justice*, 13.

28. Cooper and Sheppard, *Mockery of Justice*, 15.

29. Cooper and Sheppard, *Mockery of Justice*, 15.

30. Throughout the book, Sam H. Sheppard is referred to only as Dr. Sam, humanizing him even further.

31. Cooper and Sheppard, *Mockery of Justice*, 57.

32. Cooper and Sheppard, *Mockery of Justice*, 57.

33. Cooper and Sheppard, *Mockery of Justice*, 58.

34. Cooper and Sheppard, *Mockery of Justice*, 199.

35. Keith Phipps, "James Neff: The Wrong Man: The Final Verdict on the Dr. Sam Sheppard Murder," *The AV Club*, March 29, 2002, accessed February 12, 2020, https://aux.avclub.com/james-neff-the-wrong-man-the-final-verdict-on-the-dr-1798193037.

36. Neff, *The Wrong Man*, 5.

37. Neff, *The Wrong Man*, 43.

38. Neff, *The Wrong Man*, 43.

39. Neff, *The Wrong Man*, 389.

40. Neff, *The Wrong Man*, 43.

41. Neff, *The Wrong Man*, 47.

42. Neff, *The Wrong Man*, 49.

43. Deanna, "Postpartum Depression in the 1950s, My Grandmother's Story (of A Short History of Postpartum Depression, from 1950s-Now)," *Maple Leaf Mommy*, accessed February 15, 2020, https://mapleleafmommy.com/mom-life/postpartum-depression-in-1950s-my/.

44. Deanna, "Postpartum Depression

in the 1950s, My Grandmother's Story (of A Short History of Postpartum Depression, from 1950s-Now)," *Maple Leaf Mommy*, accessed February 15, 2020, https://mapleleafmommy.com/mom-life/postpartum-depression-in-1950s-my/.

45. Neff, *The Wrong Man*, 50.

46. Neff, *The Wrong Man*, 50.

47. Here, I break from the pattern of previous and subsequent chapters. Instead of separating the television and film iterations here, I have kept all incarnations of *The Fugitive* in the same section to help the reader see the clear similarities and differences between the 1963, 1993, and 2000 versions.

48. "The Fugitive (1963)," *IMDB.com*, accessed February 15, 2020, https://www.imdb.com/title/tt0056757/.

49. "The Girl from Little Egypt—The Fugitive (1963)," *IMDB.com*, accessed February 15, 2020, https://www.imdb.com/title/tt0584014/?ref_=ttep_ep14.

50. Karen Kilgariff and Georgia Hardstark, "Let's Hear Your Podcast!" *My Favorite Murder* (podcast), February 9, 2017, accessed February 22, 2020, https://www.stitcher.com/podcast/exactly-right/my-favorite-murder/e/49081289?autoplay=true.

51. Carter Roy and Wenndy Mackenzie, "Episode 101: Dead on the Fourth of July: Marilyn Reese Sheppard," *Unsolved Murders* (podcast), June 25, 2018, accessed February 21, 2020, https://www.stitcher.com/podcast/parcast/unsolved-murders-true-crime-stories/e/55050920?autoplay=true.

Chapter 5

1. Given the number of offenders in this case, it is impossible to not name them as part of the system to honor the victims as in other chapters. To avoid confusion, all perpetrators will be named, but named as few times as possible as to not add to the idolization of the offenders.

2. Vincent Bugliosi, *Helter Skelter: The True Story of the Manson Murder* (New York: W.W. Norton, 2001), 52.

3. Bugliosi, *Helter Skelter*, 52.

4. Bugliosi, *Helter Skelter*, 55.

5. Bugliosi, *Helter Skelter*, 55.

6. Bugliosi, *Helter Skelter*, 56.

7. "Actress Sharon Tate Found Murdered," *San Mateo Times and Daily News Leader* (San Mateo, California), August 9, 1969.

8. "Actress, Bay Heiress, 3 Others: Hollywood 'Ritual Slayings,'" *San Francisco Examiner*, August 10, 1969.

9. "Actress, Bay Heiress, 3 Others."

10. "9 Hippie Mystics Held in Bizarre Tate Murders," *Oakland Tribune*, December 2, 1969.

11. Alisa Statman and Brie Tate, *Restless Souls: The Sharon Tate's Account of Stardom, the Manson Murders, and a Crusade for Justice* (New York: HarperCollins, 2012), xiii.

12. Also released in 2004 was the film *The Manson Family*, an account of the murders from the Family's point of view. While released in 2004, it was originally produced in 1997.

13. Mark Kermode, "Wolves at the Door," BBC5 Radio Live, March 17, 2017, YouTube, 01:43, https://www.youtube.com/watch?v=IuqSarxR9KM.

14. "Wolves at the Door," *Rotten Tomatoes*," accessed August 10, 2019, https://rottentomatoes.com/m/wolves_at_the_door.

15. A fact that gave the author hope as the cast was filled with potential up and comers; a sign that occasionally leads to a surprise hit.

16. "The Haunting of Sharon Tate," *Rotten Tomatoes*, accessed August 18, 2020, https://www.rottentomatoes.com/m/the_haunting_of_sharon_tate.

17. In this film, it appears that Steven Parent is the new caretaker and that he lived in a trailer. In reality, Steven was visiting the caretaker, William Garretson, to sell Garretson a radio. Also, Garretson lived in a guest house, not a trailer. Garretson survived the murders and was briefly considered a suspect before being cleared.

18. "Clark Collis, Sharon Tate's Sister Wept at Margot Robbie's *Once Upon a Time in Hollywood* Portrayal," Entertainment Weekly, July 26, 2019, https://ew.com/movies/2019/07/26/once-upon-a-time-hollywood-sharon-tate-sister-debra/#:~:text=Debra%20Tate%2C%20the%20sister%20of,which%20Tarantino's%20movie%20is%20set.

19. Aisha Harris, "Sharon Tate Is a Woman in a Tarantino Movie. It's Complicated," *New York Times*, August 7, 2019,

https://www.nytimes.com/2019/08/07/movies/sharon-tate-tarantino-women.html.

20. Aisha Harris, "Sharon Tate Is a Woman in a Tarantino Movie. It's Complicated," *New York Times*, August 7, 2019, https://www.nytimes.com/2019/08/07/movies/sharon-tate-tarantino-women.html.

Chapter 6

1. The Hell's Angels were hired as security and alleged paid in beer.

2. From all contemporary news coverage of Patricia, it is clear to the researcher that Patricia prefers Patricia to Patty, so this chapter will refer to her as Patricia unless the sources or the pop culture iterations refer to Patricia as Patty.

3. Howard Kohn and David Weird, "The Inside Story," *Rolling Stone*, October 23, 1975, 41.

4. Kohn and Weir, "The Inside Story."

5. Kohn and Weir, "The Inside Story."

6. Kohn and Weir, "The Inside Story."

7. The "hole" refers to solitary confinement in the infamous San Quentin prison.

8. Kohn and Weir, "The Inside Story," 46.

9. Kohn and Weir, "The Inside Story," 45.

10. Kohn and Weir, "The Inside Story," 46.

11. Howard Kohn and David Weir, "The Inside Story: Part Two," *Rolling Stone*, November 20, 1975, accessed February 26, 2020, https://www.rollingstone.com/culture/culture-news/tanias-world-the-inside-story-of-the-patty-hearst-kidnapping-part-two-people-in-need-109403/.

12. Kohn and Weir, "The Inside Story: Part Two."

13. Kohn and Weir, "The Inside Story: Part Two."

14. Louis Jolyn West, "Patricia Hearst's Torment Is a Disgrace," *Los Angeles Times*, December 22, 1978.

15. Louis Jolyn West, "Patricia Hearst's Torment Is a Disgrace," *Los Angeles Times*, December 22, 1978.

16. Dr. Singer worked for the United States Army and Dr. West worked for the United States Air Force. Members of the U.S. military were victims of coercive persuasion during the Korean Conflict, 1950–1953. When those men returned to the United States, they were studied by doctors like Singer and West. Twenty years later, those studies would be put to use during the Hearst trial.

17. Louis Jolyn West, "Patricia Hearst's Torment Is a Disgrace," *Los Angeles Times*, December 22, 1978.

18. Louis Jolyn West, "Patricia Hearst's Torment Is a Disgrace," *Los Angeles Times*, December 22, 1978.

19. Louis Jolyn West, "Patricia Hearst's Torment Is a Disgrace," *Los Angeles Times*, December 22, 1978.

20. Louis Jolyn West, "Patricia Hearst's Torment Is a Disgrace," *Los Angeles Times*, December 22, 1978.

21. Louis Jolyn West, "Patricia Hearst's Torment Is a Disgrace," *Los Angeles Times*, December 22, 1978.

22. Gerald Higgins, "The History of Confidentiality in Medicine," *Can Fam Physician*, April 1989; 35, 921–926.

23. "Confidentiality, Patient/Physician," *American Academy of Family Physicians*, accessed March 1, 2020, https://www.aafp.org/about/policies/all/patient-confidentiality.html.

24. Louis Jolyn West, "Patricia Hearst's Torment Is a Disgrace," *Los Angeles Times*, December 22, 1978.

25. William Graebner, *Patty's Got a Gun: Patricia Hearst in 1970s America* (Chicago: University of Chicago Press, 2008), 7.

26. Graebner, *Patty's Got a Gun*, 8.

27. Graebner, *Patty's Got a Gun*, 8.

28. Graebner, *Patty's Got a Gun*, 119.

29. *Patty Hearst*, directed by Paul Schrader (1988; Culver City, California: MGM, DVD, 2011).

30. *Patty Hearst*.

31. It was assumed to be consensual because Patricia had held onto a memento from Wolf and still had it with her when she was arrested.

32. *Patty Hearst*.

33. *Patty Hearst*.

34. While the six SLA members died during this confrontation, they died due to a fire that tore through the house.

35. "The Arrest of Patty Hearst," *FBI.gov*, February 4, 2009, accessed Feb-

ruary 28, 2020, https://www.fbi.gov/audio-repository/news-podcasts-inside-the-arrest-of-patty-hearst.mp3/view.

36. *Patty Hearst.*

37. *Patty Hearst.*

38. *Patty Hearst.*

39. CNN stands for Cable News Network—one of the most famous news networks in the world. It has recently begun to branch into the true crime and historical documentary arena.

40. *The Radical Story of Patty Hearst,* Episode 1, "Part One: The Kidnapping," directed by Pat Kondelis, featuring Jeffrey Toobin and Bill Harris, aired on February 11, 2018, CNN, 2020, Amazon Streaming, https://www.amazon.com/Radical-Story-Patty-Hearst-Season/dp/B079K2SGPC.

41. *The Radical Story of Patty Hearst,* Episode 1, 2018.

42. Please see that coverage later in the chapter.

43. *The Radical Story of Patty Hearst,* Episode 2, "Part Two: The Captive," directed by Pat Kondelis, featuring Jeffrey Toobin and Bill Harris, aired on February 11, 2018, CNN, 2020, Amazon Streaming, https://www.amazon.com/Radical-Story-Patty-Hearst-Season/dp/B079K2SGPC.

44. *The Radical Story of Patty Hearst,* Episode 2, 2018.

45. *The Radical Story of Patty Hearst,* Episode 3, "Part Three: The Robbery," directed by Pat Kondelis, featuring Jeffrey Toobin and Bill Harris, aired on February 18, 2018, CNN, 2020, Amazon Streaming, https://www.amazon.com/Radical-Story-Patty-Hearst-Season/dp/B079K2SGPC.

46. The fourth episode, aptly named "The Lost Year," concentrates on the year between the Hibernia Bank robbery and the time that Patricia and the Harrises spent in Pennsylvania.

47. *The Radical Story of Patty Hearst,* Episode 5, "Part Five: The Conversion," directed by Pat Kondelis, featuring Jeffrey Toobin and Bill Harris, aired on February 25, 2018, CNN, 2020, Amazon Streaming, https://www.amazon.com/Radical-Story-Patty-Hearst-Season/dp/B079K2SGPC.

48. *The Radical Story of Patty Hearst,* Episode 5.

49. *The Radical Story of Patty Hearst,* Episode 5.

50. *The Radical Story of Patty Hearst,* Episode 6, "Part 6: The Verdict," directed by Pat Kondelis, featuring Jeffrey Toobin and Bill Harris, aired on February 25, 2018, CNN, 2020, Amazon Streaming, https://www.amazon.com/Radical-Story-Patty-Hearst-Season/dp/B079K2SGPC.

51. *The Radical Story of Patty Hearst,* Episode 6, 2018.

52. Jeffrey Toobin and Brian Stelter, hosts, "The Kidnapping," *Patty Has a Gun* (podcast), January 26, 2018, accessed February 17, 2020, https://www.cnn.com/interactive/2018/02/us/patty-hearst-podcast/.

53. Jeffrey Toobin and Brian Stelter, hosts, "The Kidnapping," *Patty Has a Gun* (podcast), January 26, 2018, accessed February 17, 2020, https://www.cnn.com/interactive/2018/02/us/patty-hearst-podcast/.

54. Jeffrey Toobin and Brian Stelter, hosts, "Inside the SLA," *Patty Has a Gun* (podcast), February 2, 2018, accessed February 17, 2020, https://www.cnn.com/interactive/2018/02/us/patty-hearst-podcast/.773702?autoplay=true.

55. Irma Blanco and Carter Roy, hosts, "Patty Hearst: Part 1: The Kidnapping," *Hostage* (podcast), October 17, 2018, accessed March 2, 2020, https://www.stitcher.com/podcast/parcast/hostage/e/56773702?autoplay=true.

56. Patty Hearst: Part 2: Girl on the Run," *Hostage* (podcast), October 24, 2018, accessed March 2, 2020, https://open.spotify.com/episode/0pTB7DrRQCuEbkktIljMwe.x.

57. Irma Blanco and Carter Roy, hosts, "Patty Hearst: Part 3: Captive of the SLA," *Hostage* (podcast), October 31, 2018, accessed March 2, 2020, https://open.spotify.com/episode/6S1zA7t4eEikMGwjDfymUx.

58. 628?autoplay=true" https://www.stitcher.com/podcast/hollywood-crime-scene/e/67280628?autoplay=true.

59. Desi Jedeikin and Rachel Fisher, hosts, "Episode 129—Patty Hearst," *Hollywood Crime Scene* (podcast), February 11, 2020, accessed March 4, 2020, https://www.stitcher.com/podcast/hollywood-crime-scene/e/67280628?autoplay=true.

60. Caitlin Cutt and Kari Martin, "WWTC055:#WCW Rachael O'Brien, Patty Hearst, and Broken Limbs," *White Wine True Crime* (podcast), October 19, 2016, accessed March 3, 2020, https://www.stitcher.com/podcast/white-wine-true-crime/e/wwtc055-wcw-rachael-obrien-patty-hearst-and-broken-limbs-47970483.

61. Cutt and Martin, "O'Brien."

62. Cutt and Martin, "O'Brien."

63. Cutt and Martin, "O'Brien."

Chapter 7

1. Les Steed, "Speaking Out: Who Is Elizabeth Kendall and Where Is Ted Bundy's Former Girlfriend Now?" *The US Sun*, January 30, 2020, accessed April 12, 2020, https://www.the-sun.com/news/333527/who-is-elizabeth-kendall-and-where-is-ted-bundys-former-girlfriend-now/.

2. Elizabeth Kendall, *The Phantom Prince: My Life with Ted Bundy, Updated and Expanded Edition* (New York: Abrams Press, 2020), 4.

3. Kendall, *The Phantom Prince*, 4.

4. Kendall, *The Phantom Prince*, 4.

5. Kendall, *The Phantom Prince*, 5.

6. Kendall, *The Phantom Prince*, 7.

7. Kendall, *The Phantom Prince*, 8.

8. Con Psarras, "Life with Killer Ted Bundy, the Phantom Prince," *Salt Lake Tribune*, October 25, 1981.

9. Con Psarras, "Life with Killer Ted Bundy, the Phantom Prince," *Salt Lake Tribune*, October 25, 1981.

10. George Thurston, "Authors Try to Make Sense of Bundy," *Tallahassee Democrat*, January 22, 1989.

11. Salim Jiwa, "Trail of Death: Bundy Killed," *The Providence* (British Columbia, Canada), February 2, 1989.

12. Salim Jiwa, "Trail of Death: Bundy Killed," *The Providence* (British Columbia, Canada), February 2, 1989.

13. Salim Jiwa, "Trail of Death: Bundy Killed," *The Providence* (British Columbia, Canada), February 2, 1989.

14. Les Steed, "Speaking Out: Who is Elizabeth Kendall and Where Is Ted Bundy's Former Girlfriend Now?" *The U.S. Sun*, January 30, 2020, accessed April 12, 2020, https://www.the-sun.com/news/333527/who-is-elizabeth-kendall-and-where-is-ted-bundys-former-girlfriend-now/.

15. Lindsay Geller, "Who Is Ted Bundy's Ex-Girlfriend, Elizabeth 'Liz' Kendall, from 'Falling for a Killer'?" *Women's Health*, January 31, 2020. https://www.womenshealthmag.com/life/a27031703/ted-bundy-girlfriend-liz-kendall/.

16. Heather Finn, "Who Is Ted Bundy's Ex-Girlfriend Liz Kendall? Here's What You Need to Know," *Good Housekeeping*, January 31, 2020, https://www.goodhousekeeping.com/life/a30719690/ted-bundy-girlfriend-liz-kendall/.

17. As the title of the article includes her real name, the title and the URL will not be included here.

18. Kendall, *The Phantom Prince*, ix.

19. Kendall, *The Phantom Prince*, ix.

20. Kendall, *The Phantom Prince*, ix.

21. Kendall, *The Phantom Prince*, x.

22. Kendall, *The Phantom Prince*, x.

23. Kendall, *The Phantom Prince*, xi.

24. Kendall, *The Phantom Prince*, 185.

25. Kendall, *The Phantom Prince*, 186.

26. Kendall, *The Phantom Prince*, 186–187.

27. It is worth noting that the screenwriter of this movie was a woman. It is interesting that a female screenwriter was able to write Bundy so well, while writing Liz so poorly. One wonders if this could possibly be explained because of the source material—Larsen's book?

28. Polly Nelson, *Defending the Devil: My Story as Ted Bundy's Last Lawyer* (Brattleboro, VT: Echo Point Books and Media, 2019), 66.

29. *The Deliberate Stranger*, directed by Marvin J. Chomsky (1986, Los Angeles, CA: Warner Bros. Home Video, 2010), DVD.

30. *The Deliberate Stranger*.

31. *The Deliberate Stranger*.

32. *The Deliberate Stranger*.

33. *The Deliberate Stranger*.

34. *The Deliberate Stranger*.

35. *The Deliberate Stranger*.

36. On the film's Wikipedia page, they also use Liz's real name rather than her pseudonym.

37. *Ted Bundy*, directed by Matthew Bright (2002, Century City, California: Amazon.com Services LLC), Streaming, https://www.amazon.com/Ted-Bundy-Michael-Reilly-Burke/dp/B07JN41Y3S/ref=sr_1_2?dchild=1&keywords=bundy&qid=1596564109&s=instant-video&sr=1-2.

38. *Ted Bundy.*

39. *Ted Bundy.*

40. *Ted Bundy.*

41. *Ted Bundy.*

42. *Extremely Wicked, Shockingly Evil and Vile*, directed by Joe Berlinger (2019, Los Angeles, California: Netflix), Streaming, https://www.netflix.com/watch/81028 570?trackId=13752289&tctx=0%2C0%2C 7e50eba91c4679bac2c40bff7163d5c3b61b 71a7%3A7e66a918a626127888a69a5b5a32 87d30e452e49%2C7e50eba91c4679bac2c4 0bff7163d5c3b61b71a7%3A7e66a918a6261 27888a69a5b5a3287d30e452e49%2C%2C.

43. *Extremely Wicked, Shockingly Evil and Vile.*

44. *Extremely Wicked, Shockingly Evil and Vile.*

45. *Ted Bundy: Mind of a Monster* (2019, Los Angeles, California: Amazon.com Services, LLC), Streaming, https://www. amazon.com/Ted-Bundy-Mind-Monster/ dp/B07WQGRPRZ/ref=sr_1_3?dchild=1 &keywords=mind+of+a+monster&qid=15 96564182&s=instant-video&sr=1-3.

46. *Ted Bundy: Mind of a Monster.*

47. *Ted Bundy: Mind of a Monster.*

48. As this was being written in the summer of 2020.

49. *Conversations with a Killer: The Ted Bundy Tapes*, episode 1, "Handsome Devil," directed by Joe Berlinger, written by Joe Berlinger, featuring Stephen Michaud, Hugh Aynesworth, and Kathleen McChesney, aired January 24, 2019, https://www.netflix.com/watch/80226550 ?trackId=13752289&tctx=0%2C0%2Cb99 747a7719d416b06dee9bc320d7c7809918d 35%3A760752c1813c7f54eb57217773de84 9314874d21%2Cb99747a7719d416b06dee 9bc320d7c7809918d35%3A760752c1813c7 f54eb57217773de849314874d21%2C%2C.

50. *Conversations with a Killer: The Ted Bundy Tapes*, "Handsome Devil," 2019.

51. Kendall, *The Phantom Prince*, x.

52. Kendall, *The Phantom Prince*, x.

53. Kendall, *The Phantom Prince*, x.

54. *Ted Bundy: Falling for a Killer*, episode 1, "Boy Meets Girl," directed by Trish Wood, written by Richard O'Regan and Carolyn Saunders, featuring Elizabeth Kendall and Molly Kendall, aired January 31, 2020, https://www.amazon.com/Boy-Meets-Girl/dp/B08BYYX1HM/ref=sr_1_1 ?dchild=1&keywords=falling+for+a+kille r&qid=1596500074&sr=8-1.

55. *Ted Bundy: Falling for a Killer*, "Boy Meets Girl."

56. *Ted Bundy: Falling for a Killer*, "Boy Meets Girl."

57. *Ted Bundy: Falling for a Killer*, episode 2, "Falling," directed by Trish Wood, written by Richard O'Regan and Carolyn Saunders, featuring Elizabeth Kendall and Molly Kendall, aired January 31, 2020, https://www.amazon.com/Boy-Meets-Girl/dp/B08BYYX1HM/ref=sr_1_1?dchil d=1&keywords=falling+for+a+killer&qid =1596500074&sr=8-1.

58. After two women disappeared in one day from Lake Sammamish State Park, witnesses worked with a police sketch artist to create a sketch of a man they identified as "Ted."

59. *Ted Bundy: Falling for a Killer*, episode 3, "Gone Girls," directed by Trish Wood, written by Richard O'Regan and Carolyn Saunders, featuring Elizabeth Kendall and Molly Kendall, aired January 31, 2020, https://www.amazon.com/Boy-Meets-Girl/dp/B08BYYX1HM/ref=sr_1_1 ?dchild=1&keywords=falling+for+a+kille r&qid=1596500074&sr=8-1.

60. *Ted Bundy: Falling for a Killer*, "Gone Girls."

61. *Ted Bundy: Falling for a Killer*, "Gone Girls."

62. *Ted Bundy: Falling for a Killer*, "Gone Girls."

63. *Ted Bundy: Falling for a Killer*, "Gone Girls."

64. *Ted Bundy: Falling for a Killer*, "Gone Girls."

65. This study would be remiss in not mentioning that Kathleen McChesney joined the FBI in 1978 and eventually became the third highest ranking officer in the Bureau as the Executive Assistant Director of the FBI.

66. *Ted Bundy: Falling for a Killer*, "Gone Girls."

67. *Ted Bundy: Falling for a Killer*, "Gone Girls."

68. *Ted Bundy: Falling for a Killer*, "Gone Girls."

69. *Ted Bundy: Falling for a Killer*, "Gone Girls."

70. *Ted Bundy: Falling for a Killer*, episode 5, "Collateral Damage," directed by Trish Wood, written by Richard O'Regan and Carolyn Saunders, featuring Elizabeth Kendall and Molly Kendall, aired January

31, 2020, https://www.amazon.com/Boy-Meets-Girl/dp/B08BYYX1HM/ref=sr_1_1?dchild=1&keywords=falling+for+a+killer&qid=1596500074&sr=8-1.

71. *Ted Bundy: Falling for a Killer*, "Collateral Damage."

72. *Ted Bundy: Falling for a Killer*, "Collateral Damage."

73. By popularity, the author means general knowledge and awareness of the crimes of Bundy.

74. Jill and Dick, hosts, "Surviving Ted Bundy," *True Crime Brewery* (podcast), released June 5, 2017, accessed May 12, 2020, https://www.stitcher.com/podcast/tiegrabber-podcasts/true-crime-brewery/e/surviving-ted-bundy-50394290.

75. Alaina and Ash, hosts, "Ted Bundy Part 1," *Morbid* (podcast), released May 29, 2018, accessed May 12, 2020, https://www.morbidpodcast.com/listen/2019/1/5/episode-5-ted-bundy-part-1.

76. *Morbid*, "Ted Bundy Part 1."

77. *Morbid*, "Ted Bundy Part 1."

78. *Morbid*, "Ted Bundy Part 1."

79. Lucy and Lily, hosts, "Minisode A: Extremely Wicked, Shockingly Evil and Vile," *Two Girls, One Murder!* (podcast), released June 12, 2019, accessed May 10, 2020, https://twogirlsonemurder.podbean.com/e/minisode-a-extremely-wicked-shockingly-evil-and-vile/.

80. *Two Girls, One Murder!*, "Minisode A: Extremely Wicked, Shockingly Evil and Vile."

81. Rebecca Lavoie and Kevin Flynn, hosts, "Extremely Wicked, Shockingly Evil, and Vile," *You Can't Make This Up* (podcast), released May 8, 2019, accessed May 11, 2020, https://www.stitcher.com/podcastnetflix/e/60552790?autoplay=true.

82. Hayley Langan and Kaitlin Mahar, hosts, "63: Extremely Wicked, Shockingly Evil, and Vile (Review)," *Crime Culture* (podcast), released May 8, 2019, accessed May 9, 2020, https://www.stitcher.com/podcast/crime-culture/e/60576511.

83. *Crime Culture*, "63: Extremely Wicked, Shockingly Evil and Vile (Review)."

Chapter 8

1. Carol Pogash, "The Cheerleader Murder," *Ladies Home Journal*, November 1985, found on Click Americana, https://clickamericana.com/topics/crime/the-real-death-of-a-cheerleader-1985.

2. Pogash, "The Cheerleader Murder."

3. Pogash, "The Cheerleader Murder."

4. Pogash, "The Cheerleader Murder."

5. Pogash, "The Cheerleader Murder."

6. Pogash, "The Cheerleader Murder."

7. Pogash, "The Cheerleader Murder."

8. This is the equivalent of $1217 in 2020.

9. Pogash, "The Cheerleader Murder."

10. The only account of what happened on this night is from the offender, which must be taken with a grain of salt.

11. Pogash, "The Cheerleader Murder."

12. Pogash, "The Cheerleader Murder."

13. Pogash, "The Cheerleader Murder."

14. Nancy appears in *The 1980s: The Deadliest Decade*, using her real name. Given this, the research has assumed that she no longer wishes for anonymity and will use her real name.

15. Pogash, "The Cheerleader Murder."

16. Pogash, "The Cheerleader Murder."

17. "Witness Surfaces in Teen Murder," *The Californian* (Salinas, California), June 25, 1984.

18. Andrew Ross and Jon Bashor, "Last Hours of Orinda Teen's Life," *San Francisco Examiner*, June 23, 1984.

19. Andrew Ross and Jon Bashor, "Last Hours of Orinda Teen's Life," *San Francisco Examiner*, June 23, 1984.

20. Jon Bashor, "Friends Attend Funeral for Slain Orinda Girl," *San Francisco Examiner*, June 28, 1984, 28

21. While the film was initially released on NBC under the name *A Friend to Die For*, it was subsequently sold to Lifetime, where it was renamed *Death of a Cheerleader*. As it is generally known now as *Death of a Cheerleader*, that is how it will be referred to in this project.

22. *Death of a Cheerleader*, directed by William A. Graham (1994; Los Angeles, California: Amazon.com Services LLC), Streaming, https://www.amazon.com/Death-Cheerleader-Kellie-Martin/dp/B077SH8YJQ/ref=sr_1_1?dchild=1&keywords=death+of+a+cheerleader&qid=1596547621&sr=8-1.

23. As there are no reliable sources from before her death, the research can only rely upon the quotes about Kirsten and her character made by her friends and

family in news accounts after her death. While those sources may be colored by grief, the accounts are far afield from the behavior seen in this movie.

24. This is equal to roughly $182 in 2020.

25. *Death of a Cheerleader.*

26. *Death of a Cheerleader.*

27. *Death of a Cheerleader.*

28. *Death of a Cheerleader.*

29. *Death of a Cheerleader.*

30. *1980s: The Deadliest Decade*, season 1, episode 3, "The Cheerleader Murder," directed by Andrea De Brito, featuring Patrick Gallagher, aired on November 28, 2016, Investigation Discovery, https://www.amazon.com/The-Yuppie-Murder/dp/B01MYMJMP3/ref=sr_1_1?crid=17U9CLA3JMZ68&dchild=1&keywords=1980s+deadliest+decade&qid=1596548223&sprefix=1980s+dead%2Caps%2C154&sr=8-1.

31. *1980s: The Deadliest Decade*, "The Cheerleader Murder."

32. *1980s: The Deadliest Decade*, "The Cheerleader Murder."

33. *Death of a Cheerleader*, directed by Paul Shapiro (2019; Los Angeles, California: Amazon.com Services LLC), Streaming, https://www.amazon.com/DEATH-CHEERLEADER-Inc-Reunion-Pictures/dp/B07N965B5H/ref=sr_1_2?dchild=1&keywords=death+of+a+cheerleader&qid=1596548587&sr=8-2.

34. Jen and Cam, hosts, "#34: Dying to Fit In: Kirsten Costas," *Our True Crime Podcast* (podcast), released April 10, 2019, accessed June 3, 2020, https://www.ourtruecrimepodcast.com/2019/04/34-dying-to-fit-in-kirsten-costas.html.

35. Esther Ludlow, host, "Episode 58 with Friends Like These Kirsten Costas," *Once Upon a Crime* (podcast), aired on September 4, 2017, accessed June 5, 2020, https://www.truecrimepodcast.com/episode-058-with-friends-like-these-kirsten-costas/.

36. Alysa Lucas, host, "Kirsten Costas," *Fatal*i*teas* (podcast), released August 14, 2019, accessed May 31, 2020, https://fataliteas.libsyn.com/kirsten-costas.

37. Patrick Serrano, host, "Death of a Cheerleader (2019 Lifetime)," *Lifetime Uncorked* (podcast), released on February 14, 2019, accessed on June 3, 2020, https://lifetimeuncorked.com/2019/02/05/death-of-a-cheerleader-2019-lifetime/.

38. *Lifetime Uncorked*, "Death of a Cheerleader (2019 Lifetime)," 2019.

Chapter 9

1. Sheila Weller, *Raging Heart: The Intimate Story of the Tragic Marriage of O.J. and Nicole Brown Simpson* (Los Angeles: Graymalkin Media, 2016), 123.

2. Weller, *Raging Heart: The Intimate Story of the Tragic Marriage of O.J. and Nicole Brown Simpson*, 260.

3. Weller, *Raging Heart: The Intimate Story of the Tragic Marriage of O.J. and Nicole Brown Simpson*, 275.

4. Weller, *Raging Heart: The Intimate Story of the Tragic Marriage of O.J. and Nicole Brown Simpson*, 281.

5. The Bronco was driven by O.J.'s friend Al Cowlings and at notoriously low speeds, shutting down several Los Angeles highways.

6. How many "Trials of the Century" have there been now?

7. Sue Manning, "Police Question O.J. Simpson in Wife's Death; Hall of Famer Denies Involvement," *Napa Valley Register* (Napa Valley, California), June 14, 1994.

8. "Simpson's Ex-Wife and Man Killed," *North County Times* (Oceanside, CA), June 14, 1994.

9. Jim Newman and Eric Malnic, "Police Sources Link Evidence to Simpson," *Los Angeles Times*, June 15, 1994.

10. Jeffrey Toobin, *The Run of His Life: The People v. O.J. Simpson* (New York: Random House, 2015), 15.

11. Toobin, *The Run of His Life: The People v. O.J. Simpson*, 14.

12. Toobin, *The Run of His Life: The People v. O.J. Simpson*, 244–245.

13. Toobin, *The Run of His Life: The People v. O.J. Simpson*, 245.

14. Fred Goldman and Kim Goldman, *If I Did It: Confessions of a Killer* (New York: Beaufort Books, 2007), xxiii.

15. Goldman and Goldman, *If I Did It: Confessions of a Killer*, xxiii.

16. Goldman and Goldman, *If I Did It: Confessions of a Killer*, 84.

17. Goldman and Goldman, *If I Did It: Confessions of a Killer*, 96.

18. Goldman and Goldman, *If I Did It: Confessions of a Killer*, 91.

19. Goldman and Goldman, *If I Did It: Confessions of a Killer,* 71 and 86.

20. *The O.J. Simpson Story,* Directed by Jerrold Freedman (as Alan Smithee) (1995; Los Angeles: YouTube), Streaming, https://www.youtube.com/watch?v=k97yjE0V3yI.

21. *The O.J. Simpson Story.*

22. This is the same actor who plays Elizabeth Short in American Horror Story, covered in chapter three.

23. *The Murder of Nicole Brown Simpson,* directed by Daniel Farrands (2020; Los Angeles: Amazon.com Services LLC), Streaming, https://www.amazon.com/Murder-Nicole-Brown-Simpson/dp/B0833K57DP/ref=sr_1_1?dchild=1&keywords=the+murder+of+nicole+brown+simpson&qid=1596554955&sr=8-1.

24. This alter-ego of Charlie is discussed further in *O.J.: The Lost Confession.*

25. There is another killer known as the Casanova Killer. The other is Paul John Knowles who was killed in custody in Georgia in 1974.

26. Katie Rife, "The Director of the Haunting of Sharon Tate Sets His Ghoulish Sights on the Murder of Nicole Brown Simpson," *AV Club,* January 10, 2020, https://film.avclub.com/the-director-of-the-haunting-of-sharon-tate-sets-his-gh-1840935191.

27. "Kelly Dowdle," *Internet Movie Database,* accessed February 10, 2020, https://www.imdb.com/name/nm1942596/?ref_=ttfc_fc_cl_t77.

28. Gil Garcetti was the Los Angeles Attorney General at the time of the trial.

29. *The People vs. O.J. Simpson: American Crime Story,* season 1, episode 1, "From the Ashes of Tragedy," directed by Ryan Murphy, written by Scott Alexander and Larry Karaszewski, featuring Cuba Gooding, Jr., and Sarah Paulson, aired on February 2, 2016, https://www.netflix.com/watch/80127673?trackId=200257859.

30. *The People vs. O.J. Simpson: American Crime Story,* season 1, episode 4, "100% Not Guilty," directed by Anthony Hemingway, written by Scott Alexander, Larry Karaszewski, Maya Forbes, and Wallace Wolodarsky, featuring Cuba Gooding Jr, and Sarah Paulson, aired on February 23, 2016, https://www.netflix.com/watch/80127676?trackId=200257859.

31. *The People vs. O.J. Simpson: American Crime Story,* "100% Not Guilty."

32. *The People vs. O.J. Simpson: American Crime Story,* season 1, episode 10, "The Verdict," directed by Ryan Murphy, written by Scott Alexander and Larry Karaszewski, featuring Cuba Gooding Jr, and Sarah Paulson, aired on April 5, 2016, https://www.netflix.com/watch/80127682?trackId=200257859.

33. *The People vs. O.J. Simpson: American Crime Story,* "The Verdict."

34. Laura Bradley, "*O.J. Simpson: The Lost Confession*: Was FOX's *American Idol* Counter Genius or Gross?" *Vanity Fair,* March 12, 2018, https://www.vanityfair.com/hollywood/2018/03/oj-simpson-the-lost-confession-reviews-exploitative-ratings.

35. *O.J. Simpson: The Lost Confession?,* featuring Soledad O'Brien, Eve Shakti Chin, and Jim Clemente, aired on March 11, 2018, YouTube, https://www.youtube.com/watch?v=CfM-7TERCMw.

36. Kristen Baldwin, "With O.J. Interview, FOX Falls Off the Human Decency Wagon: EW Review," *Entertainment Weekly,* March 12, 2018, https://ew.com/tv/2018/03/12/oj-simpson-lost-confession-review/.

37. Kristen Baldwin, "With O.J. Interview, FOX Falls Off the Human Decency Wagon: EW Review," *Entertainment Weekly,* March 12, 2018, https://ew.com/tv/2018/03/12/oj-simpson-lost-confession-review/.

38. Laura Bradley, "*O.J. Simpson: The Lost Confession*: Was FOX's *American Idol* Counter Genius or Gross?" *Vanity Fair,* March 12, 2018, https://www.vanityfair.com/hollywood/2018/03/oj-simpson-the-lost-confession-reviews-exploitative-ratings.

39. Laura Bradley, "*O.J. Simpson: The Lost Confession*: Was FOX's *American Idol* Counter Genius or Gross?" *Vanity Fair,* March 12, 2018, https://www.vanityfair.com/hollywood/2018/03/oj-simpson-the-lost-confession-reviews-exploitative-ratings.

40. *True Crime with Aphrodite Jones,* season 1, episode 2, "O.J. Simpson," written and directed by Tom Jennings, featuring Nicole Brown Simpson, Maria Clark, and F. Lee Bailey, aired March 18, 2010, https://www.amazon.com/Scott-Peterson/

dp/B00APE0NOO/ref=sr_1_1?dchild=1&
keywords=true+crime+with+aphrodite+j
ones&qid=1596559024&sr=8-1.

41. Please see Chapter 10 for coverage
of these episodes.

42. Jim Clemente, Laura Richards,
and Lisa Zambetti, hosts, "Episode 7: The
People vs. O.J.: The Crime Scene and the
Scheme Team," *Real Crime Profile* (podcast), released on March 16, 2016, accessed
December 12, 2019, https://www.stitcher.
com/podcast/wondery/real-crime-profile/
e/43495357?autoplay=true.

43. *Real Crime Profile*, "Episode 7: The
People vs. O.J.: The Crime Scene and the
Scheme Team."

44. *Real Crime Profile*, "Episode 7: The
People vs. O.J.: The Crime Scene and the
Scheme Team."

45. Jim Clemente, Laura Richards, and
Lisa Zambetti, hosts, "Episode 8: People
vs. O.J.: Nicole's 911 Call," *Real Crime Profile* (podcast), released on March 23, 2016,
accessed December 12, 2019, https://www.
stitcher.com/podcast/real-crime-profile/
e/episode-8-the-people-vs-oj-simpson-
nicoles-911-call-43495356.

46. Jim Clemente, Laura Richards, and
Lisa Zambetti, hosts, "Episode 9: The People vs. O.J.: BONUS EPISODE: Analyzing
Two Letters by Nicole," *Real Crime Profile* (podcast), released March 27, 2016,
accessed December 12, 2019, https://www.
stitcher.com/podcast/real-crime-profile/
e/episode-9-the-people-vs-o-j-simpson-
bonus-episode-analyzing-43495355.

47. Jim Clemente, Laura Richards, and
Lisa Zambetti, hosts, "Episode 15: The
People vs. O.J.: The Verdict," *Real Crime
Profile* (podcast), released May 4, 2016,
accessed December 12, 2019, https://www.
stitcher.com/podcast/real-crime-profile/e/-
episode-15-the-people-vs-oj-simpson-the-
verdict-44338872.

48. Sarah Marshall and Michael
Hobbes, hosts, "The O.J. Simpson Trial:
Nicole Brown Simpson Part 1," *You're
Wrong About...* (podcast), released October 3, 2019, accessed July 7, 2020, https://
www.stitcher.com/podcast/michael-
hobbes/youre-wrong-about/e/64342603.

49. Sarah Marshall and Michael
Hobbes, hosts, "The O.J. Simpson Trial:
Nicole Brown Simpson Part 2," *You're
Wrong About...* (podcast), released Octo-
ber 17, 2019, accessed July 7, 2020, https://

www.stitcher.com/podcast/michael-
hobbes/youre-wrong-about/e/64661334.

50. Meg and Joe, hosts, "The Trial of
O.J. Simpson," *Two Ghouls One Grave*
(podcast), released September 1, 2019,
accessed December 22, 2019, https://www.
stitcher.com/podcast/two-ghouls-one-
grave/e/63611727.

51. Nic and The Captain, hosts, "O.J.
Simpson///Part 2///25," *True Crime Garage*
(podcast), released April 19, 2016, accessed December 19, 2020, https://www.
stitcher.com/podcast/true-crime-
garage/e/44171939.

52. DJ Schwartz, "O.J. Simpson,"
Conspiracy Asylum (podcast), released
May 31, 2019, accessed December 15,
2020, https://www.podchaser.com/
podcasts/conspiracy-asylum-745919/
episodes/oj-simpson-40138618.

53. *Conspiracy Asylum*, "O.J. Simpson."

54. There is also a wonderful podcast
called *Confronting O.J. Simpson with Kim
Goldman* where Ron Goldman's sister Kim
honors her brother and discusses her experience in the trial and the years since in
depth.

Chapter 10

1. Angela Heywood Bible, "Wife of
1999 Mayoral Candidate Found Dead,"
The News and Observer (Raleigh, North
Carolina), December 10, 2001.

2. Angela Heywood Bible, "Wife of
1999 Mayoral Candidate Found Dead,"
The News and Observer (Raleigh, North
Carolina), December 10, 2001.

3. Angela Heywood Bible, "Wife of
1999 Mayoral Candidate Found Dead,"
The News and Observer (Raleigh, North
Carolina), December 10, 2001.

4. J. Andrew Curliss and Vicki
Cheng, "Death of Wife of Ex-Candidate
Under Scrutiny," *The News and Observer*
(Raleigh, North Carolina), December 11,
2001.

5. Aisling Swift, "Friends Remember Arts
Patron," *The News and Observer* (Raleigh,
North Carolina), December 14, 2001.

6. Ruth Sheehan, "It Wasn't Just About
Mike Peterson," *The News and Observer*
(Raleigh, North Carolina), October 11,
2003.

7. Ruth Sheehan, "It Wasn't Just About

Mike Peterson," *The News and Observer* (Raleigh, North Carolina), October 11, 2003.

8. Ruth Sheehan, "It Wasn't Just About Mike Peterson," *The News and Observer* (Raleigh, North Carolina), October 11, 2003.

9. "Diane Fanning," Accessed July 15, 2020, https://dianefanning.com/.

10. Diane Fanning, *Written in Blood* (New York: St. Martin's Press, 2005), 173.

11. Fanning, *Written in Blood*, 198.

12. Fanning, *Written in Blood*, 201.

13. Fanning, *Written in Blood*, 201.

14. Kathleen died at the base of the back staircase, not the staircase seen in their wedding photos.

15. Brooke Cain, "Another 'Staircase' twist: Michael Peterson had a romance with documentary's editor," *The News-Observer* (Raleigh, North Carolina), June 13, 2018.

16. *True Crime with Aphrodite Jones*, season 1, episode 3, "The Staircase Killer: Michael Peterson," directed by Tom Jennings, written by Tom Jennings and John McLaughlin, featuring Aphrodite Jones and Freda Black, aired on March 25, 2010, Amazon Streaming, https://www.amazon.com/Scott-Peterson/dp/B00APE0NOO/ref=sr_1_1?dchild=1&keywords=true+crime+with+aphrodite+jones&qid=1596565983&sr=8-1.

17. *True Crime with Aphrodite Jones*, "The Staircase Killer: Michael Peterson."

18. Jim Clemente, Laura Richards, Lisa Zambetti, "Episode 143: The Autopsy from 'The Staircase,'" *Real Crime Profile* (podcast), released September 12, 2018, accessed December 9, 2019, https://www.stitcher.com/podcast/real-crime-profile/e/56219253?autoplay=true.

19. Jim Clemente, Laura Richards, Lisa Zambetti, "Episode 140: Her Name was Kathleen Peterson," *Real Crime Profile* (podcast), released August 22, 2018, accessed December 9, 2019, https://www.stitcher.com/podcast/wondery/real-crime-profile/e/55893950?autoplay=true

20. Jim Clemente, Laura Richards, Lisa Zambetti, "Episode 151: Controlling the Edit and the Narrative of the Staircase," *Real Crime Profile* (podcast), released November 5, 2018, accessed December 9, 2019, https://www.stitcher.com/podcast/wondery/real-crime-profile/e/57064451?autoplay=true.

21. *Real Crime Profile*, "Episode 151."

22. *Real Crime Profile*, "Episode 151."

23. Jess Commons, "Who Was Teresa Halbach, The Real Victim of Making a Murderer?" *Grazia*, March 27, 2016, https://graziadaily.co.uk/life/tv-and-film/teresa-halbach-real-victim-making-murderer/.

24. Jess Commons, "Who Was Teresa Halbach, the Real Victim of Making a Murderer?" *Grazia*, March 27, 2016, https://graziadaily.co.uk/life/tv-and-film/teresa-halbach-real-victim-making-murderer/.

25. Jess Commons, "Who Was Teresa Halbach, the Real Victim of Making a Murderer?" *Grazia*, March 27, 2016, https://graziadaily.co.uk/life/tv-and-film/teresa-halbach-real-victim-making-murderer/.

26. Ken Kratz and Peter Wilkinson, *The Case Against Steven Avery and What "Making a Murderer" Gets Wrong* (Dallas: BenBella Books, 2017), 19.

27. Kratz and Wilkinson, *The Case Against Steven Avery*, 19.

28. Kratz and Wilkinson, *The Case Against Steven Avery*, 20.

29. Kratz and Wilkinson, *The Case Against Steven Avery*, 21.

30. Kratz and Wilkinson, *The Case Against Steven Avery*, 21.

31. Kratz and Wilkinson, *The Case Against Steven Avery*, 160.

32. Kratz and Wilkinson, *The Case Against Steven Avery*, 160–161.

33. *Making a Murderer*, season 1, episode 2, "Turning the Tables," written and directed by Moira Demos and Laura Ricciardi, featuring Dolores Avery and Steven Avery, aired December 18, 2015, Netflix Streaming, https://www.netflix.com/watch/80000772?trackId=13752289&tctx=0%2C1%2Ca8b00922-504a-446e-b0a0-0ffc822f949b-84164254%2Cdf36033ebc1c48022b83e5169928f9f3c0938a12%3Ab80a0d553155873a172bce10f58bf8696f076fc3%2C%2C.

34. *Making a Murderer*, "Turning the Tables."

35. *Making a Murderer*, season 1, episode 9, "Lack of Humility," written and directed by Moira Demos and Laura Ricciardi, featuring Dolores Avery and Steven

Avery, aired on December 18, 2015, Netflix Streaming, https://www.netflix.com/watch/80075830?trackId=200257859.

36. *Making a Murderer*, season 2, episode 1, "Number 18," written and directed by Moira Demos and Laura Ricciardi, featuring Dolores Avery and Steven Avery, aired October 19, 2018, https://www.netflix.com/watch/80115431?trackId=13752289&tctx=0%2C0%2Ca8b00922-504a-446e-b0a0-0ffc822f949b-84164254%2Cdf36033ebc1c48022b83e5169928f9f3c0938a12%3Ab80a0d553155873a172bce10f58bf8696f076fc3%2C%2C.

37. "Truth Wins: The Law Offices of Kathleen Zellner," accessed June 10, 2020, http://www.kathleenzellner.com/.

38. Jim Clemente, Laura Richards, Lisa Zambetti, "Episode 1—Making a Murderer: The Arrest of Steven Avery," *Real Crime Profile* (podcast), released January 1, 2016, accessed August 29, 2019, https://www.stitcher.com/podcast/real-crime-profile/e/episode-1-making-a-murderer-the-arrest-of-steven-avery-43495363.

39. *Real Crime Profile*, "Episode 1—Making a Murderer: The Arrest of Steven Avery."

40. Jim Clemente, Laura Richards, Lisa Zambetti, "Episode 2—The Investigation and the Detectives," *Real Crime Profile* (podcast), released January 30, 2016, accessed August 29, 2019, https://www.stitcher.com/podcast/real-crime-profile/e/episode-2-making-a-murderer-the-investigation-and-detectives-43495362.

41. Jim Clemente, Laura Richards, Lisa Zambetti, "Episode 6—Making a Murderer: Microscopic Look at Colborn and Sturm Phone Calls," *Real Crime Profile* (podcast), released March 9, 2016, accessed August 29, 2019, https://www.stitcher.com/podcast/real-crime-profile/e/episode-6-making-a-murderer-microscopic-look-at-colborn-and-43495358.

42. "Making A Murderer Season 1—Teresa Halbach, Steven Avery, and Brendan Dassey," *Crime Screen* (podcast), released October 26, 2018, accessed August 19, 2019. (This podcast has stopped production and cannot be found except in podcatcher apps).

43. "Making a Murderer Season 1 Episode 5, 6, and 7—Teresa Halbach, Steven Avery, and Brendan Dassey," *Crime Screen* (podcast), released November 7, 2018, accessed August 19, 2019. (This podcast has stopped production and cannot be found except in podcatcher apps).

44. *Crime Screen*, "Making a Murderer Season 1 Episode 5, 6, and 7."

Chapter 11

1. Michelle Dean, "Dee Dee Wanted Her Daughter to Be Sick, Gypsy Wanted Her Mom Murdered," *Buzzfeed*, August 18, 2016, https://www.buzzfeednews.com/article/michelledean/dee-dee-wanted-her-daughter-to-be-sick-gypsy-wanted-her-mom.

2. Michelle Dean, "Dee Dee Wanted Her Daughter to Be Sick, Gypsy Wanted Her Mom Murdered," *Buzzfeed*, August 18, 2016, https://www.buzzfeednews.com/article/michelledean/dee-dee-wanted-her-daughter-to-be-sick-gypsy-wanted-her-mom.

3. Michelle Dean, "Dee Dee Wanted Her Daughter to Be Sick, Gypsy Wanted Her Mom Murdered," *Buzzfeed*, August 18, 2016, https://www.buzzfeednews.com/article/michelledean/dee-dee-wanted-her-daughter-to-be-sick-gypsy-wanted-her-mom.

4. Michelle Dean, "Dee Dee Wanted Her Daughter to Be Sick, Gypsy Wanted Her Mom Murdered," *Buzzfeed*, August 18, 2016, https://www.buzzfeednews.com/article/michelledean/dee-dee-wanted-her-daughter-to-be-sick-gypsy-wanted-her-mom.

5. Michelle Dean, "Dee Dee Wanted Her Daughter to Be Sick, Gypsy Wanted Her Mom Murdered," *Buzzfeed*, August 18, 2016, https://www.buzzfeednews.com/article/michelledean/dee-dee-wanted-her-daughter-to-be-sick-gypsy-wanted-her-mom.

6. Michelle Dean, "Dee Dee Wanted Her Daughter to Be Sick, Gypsy Wanted Her Mom Murdered," *Buzzfeed*, August 18, 2016, https://www.buzzfeednews.com/article/michelledean/dee-dee-wanted-her-daughter-to-be-sick-gypsy-wanted-her-mom.

7. Michelle Dean, "Dee Dee Wanted Her Daughter to Be Sick, Gypsy Wanted Her Mom Murdered," *Buzzfeed*, August 18, 2016, https://www.buzzfeednews.com/

article/michelledean/dee-dee-wanted-her-daughter-to-be-sick-gypsy-wanted-her-mom.

8. *Ibid.*

9. Harrison Keegan, "The offender Godejohn Sentenced to Life in Prison for Murder of Dee Dee Blanchard," *Springfield News Leader*, February 22, 2019, https://www.news-leader.com/story/news/crime/2019/02/22/theoffender-godejohn-sentenced-life-prison-blanchard-murder/2949249002/.

10. Merck Manual Professional Version, "Factitious Disorder Imposed on Another." https://www.merckmanuals.com/en-ca/professional/psychiatric-disorders/somatic-symptom-and-related-disorders/factitious-disorder-imposed-on-another.

11. *Ibid.*

12. Elizabeth Day, "I'll Never Forgive Mommie: Joan Crawford's Daughter Gives First Interview in 10 Years," *The Guardian*, May 24, 2008, https://www.theguardian.com/film/2008/may/25/biography.film.

13. Elizabeth Day, "I'll Never Forgive Mommie: Joan Crawford's Daughter Gives First Interview in 10 Years," *The Guardian*, May 24, 2008, https://www.theguardian.com/film/2008/may/25/biography.film.

14. *Mommy Dead and Dearest*, directed by Erin Lee Carr, featuring Gypsy Rose Blanchard, Jim Arnott, David Blanchard, aired March 11, 2017, Amazon Streaming, https://www.amazon.com/Mommy-Dead-Dearest-Erin-Carr/dp/B0779CKQ7Z/ref=sr_1_1?dchild=1&keywords=mommy+dead+and+dearest&qid=1596570609&sr=8-1.

15. *Mommy Dead and Dearest.*

16. *Mommy Dead and Dearest.*

17. *The Act*, episode 6, "A Whole New World," directed by Laure de Clermont-Tonnerre, written by Heather Marion, featuring Joey King, Patricia Arquette, and Calum Worthy, aired April 17, 2019, Hulu Streaming, https://www.hulu.com/series/the-act-8cc910fe-b59e-46a5-9966-16c4e0ed208d.

18. Other seasons cover Chris Watts, Aaron Hernandez, and Lori Vallow. The tenth season of the podcast was released in spring 2020.

19. Phil McGraw, host, "S1E1: The Killer Thorn of Gypsy Rose," *Analysis of Murder by Dr. Phil* (podcast), released April 25, 2019, accessed March 2, 2020, https://www.drphilpodcasts.com/killer-thorn-of-gypsy-rose.

20. Phil McGraw, host, "S1E2: The Killer Thorn of Gypsy Rose," *Analysis of Murder by Dr. Phil* (podcast), released May 8, 2019, accessed March 2, 2020, https://www.drphilpodcasts.com/killer-thorn-of-gypsy-rose.

21. *Analysis of Murder by Dr. Phil*, "S1E2: The Killer Thorn of Gypsy Rose."

22. As of May 2020, Gypsy Rose has ended that relationship and is currently single.

23. Phil McGraw, host, "S1E5: The Killer Thorn of Gypsy Rose," *Analysis of Murder by Dr. Phil* (podcast), released May 23, 2019, accessed March 2, 2020, https://www.drphilpodcasts.com/killer-thorn-of-gypsy-rose.

24. Mike Ferguson and Mike Gibson, hosts, "Gypsy Rose Blanchard," *True Crime All the Time* (podcast), released April 29, 2019, accessed March 4, 2020, https://www.stitcher.com/podcast/true-crime-all-the-time/e/54286126.

25. *True Crime All the Time*, "Gypsy Rose Blanchard."

26. Shevonne, host, "9. Munchausen de Proxy: Gypsy Rose Blanchard," *Female Killers* (podcast), released May 9, 2019, accessed March 10, 2020, https://femalekillers.com/episode/9-munchausen-de-proxy-gypsy-rose-blanchard/.

27. *Analysis of Murder by Dr. Phil*, "S1E5: The Killer Thorn of Gypsy Rose."

28. John Biggs, "The Story of Slenderman, The Internet's Own Monster," *Tech Crunch*, June 30, 2014, https://techcrunch.com/2014/06/30/the-story-of-slenderman-the-internets-own-monster/.

29. John Biggs, "The Story of Slenderman, The Internet's Own Monster," *Tech Crunch*, June 30, 2014, https://techcrunch.com/2014/06/30/the-story-of-slenderman-the-internets-own-monster/.

30. John Biggs, "The Story of Slenderman, The Internet's Own Monster," *Tech Crunch*, June 30, 2014, https://techcrunch.com/2014/06/30/the-story-of-slenderman-the-internets-own-monster/.

31. DeAnna Janes, "The Complete Timeline and True Story Behind the Slender Man Stabbing," *O: The Oprah Magazine*, October 25, 2019, https://www.oprahmag.com/entertainment/tv-movies/

a29591703/slender-man-stabbing-true-story/.

32. DeAnna Janes, "The Complete Timeline and True Story Behind the Slender Man Stabbing," *O: The Oprah Magazine*, October 25, 2019, https://www.oprahmag.com/entertainment/tv-movies/a29591703/slender-man-stabbing-true-story/.

33. DeAnna Janes, "The Complete Timeline and True Story Behind the Slender Man Stabbing," *O: The Oprah Magazine*, October 25, 2019, https://www.oprahmag.com/entertainment/tv-movies/a29591703/slender-man-stabbing-true-story/.

34. DeAnna Janes, "The Complete Timeline and True Story Behind the Slender Man Stabbing," *O: The Oprah Magazine*, October 25, 2019, https://www.oprahmag.com/entertainment/tv-movies/a29591703/slender-man-stabbing-true-story/.

35. DeAnna Janes, "The Complete Timeline and True Story Behind the Slender Man Stabbing," *O: The Oprah Magazine*, October 25, 2019, https://www.oprahmag.com/entertainment/tv-movies/a29591703/slender-man-stabbing-true-story/.

36. DeAnna Janes, "The Complete Timeline and True Story Behind the Slender Man Stabbing," *O: The Oprah Magazine*, October 25, 2019, https://www.oprahmag.com/entertainment/tv-movies/a29591703/slender-man-stabbing-true-story/.

37. DeAnna Janes, "The Complete Timeline and True Story Behind the Slender Man Stabbing," *O: The Oprah Magazine*, October 25, 2019, https://www.oprahmag.com/entertainment/tv-movies/a29591703/slender-man-stabbing-true-story/.

38. DeAnna Janes, "The Complete Timeline and True Story Behind the Slender Man Stabbing," *O: The Oprah Magazine*, October 25, 2019, https://www.oprahmag.com/entertainment/tv-movies/a29591703/slender-man-stabbing-true-story/.

39. DeAnna Janes, "The Complete Timeline and True Story Behind the Slender Man Stabbing," *O: The Oprah Magazine*, October 25, 2019, https://www.oprahmag.com/entertainment/tv-movies/

40. DeAnna Janes, "The Complete Timeline and True Story Behind the Slender Man Stabbing," *O: The Oprah Magazine*, October 25, 2019, https://www.oprahmag.com/entertainment/tv-movies/a29591703/slender-man-stabbing-true-story/.

41. *Terror in the Woods*, directed by D.J. Viola (2018; Atlanta, Georgia, Amazon.com Services LLC), Streaming, https://www.amazon.com/Terror-Woods-Inc-ThinkFactory-Media/dp/B07JVPMJH5/ref=sr_1_2?dchild=1&keywords=terror+in+the+woods&qid=1596577644&sr=8-2.

42. *Terror in the Woods*.

43. *20/20*, season 43, episode 5, "The Wicked," featuring David Muir and Payton Leutner, aired on October 25, 2019, Hulu Streaming, https://www.hulu.com/watch/6e9f4cad-db66-43d9-8800-d5cce7102e52.

44. *20/20*, "The Wicked."

45. *20/20*, "The Wicked."

46. *20/20*, "The Wicked."

47. Kelley Robinson, "'Slender Man' Stabbing Victim Speaks Publicly for First Time: 'Without the Whole Situation, I Wouldn't Be Who I Am,'" *ABC News*, October 24, 2019, https://abcnews.go.com/U.S./slender-man-stabbing-victim-speaks-publicly-time-situation/story?id=66268385.

48. Yaron Steinbuch, "'Slender Man' Stabbing Victim Payton Leutner on the Friends Who Tried to Killer Her," *New York Post*, October 24, 2019, https://nypost.com/2019/10/24/slender-man-stabbing-victim-payton-leutner-on-the-friends-who-tried-to-kill-her/.

49. "'Slender Man' Attack Victim Says She Sleeps with Broken Scissors 'Just in Case,'" *CBS News*, October 25, 2019, https://www.cbsnews.com/news/slender-man-attack-victim-payton-leutner-i-sleep-with-broken-scissors-just-in-case/.

50. Christian and Suann, hosts, "Episode 10: Violent Crimes Day and a Slenderman Stabbing," *Dark Stuff* (podcast), released February 18, 2018, accessed February 27, 2020, https://podtail.com/fr/podcast/dark-stuff-with-christian-suann/010-violent-crimes-day-a-slenderman-stabbing/.

Conclusion

1. Alaina Demopoulos, "Why True Crime TV Has Become So Popular During the Coronavirus Pandemic," *Daily Beast*, April 10, 2020, https://www.thedailybeast.com/as-coronavirus-rages-true-crime-tv-shows-provide-a-strange-and-popular-comfort.

2. Demopoulous, "Why True Crime TV Has Become So Popular During the Coronavirus Pandemic."

3. Demopoulous, "Why True Crime TV Has Become So Popular During the Coronavirus Pandemic."

4. "The Other Epidemic: Fatal Police Shootings in the Time of COVID-19," ACLU https://www.aclu.org/sites/default/files/field_document/aclu_the_other_epidemic_fatal_police_shootings_2020.pdf, 2.

5. "The Other Epidemic: Fatal Police Shootings in the Time of COVID-19," 2.

6. "The Other Epidemic: Fatal Police Shootings in the Time of COVID-19," 3.

7. As with the other offenders, this offenders name will not be mentioned here as to not give him any additional notoriety.

8. Dr. Stacy L. Smith, Dr. Katherine Pieper, and Marc Choueiti, "The Future Is Female? Examining the Prevalence and Portrayal of Girls and Teens in Popular Movies," 2017, http://assets.uscannenberg.org/docs/the-future-is-female.pdf.

9. Yohana Deta, "Jessica Chastain Is So Over Hollywood Sexualizing Female Characters in Action Movies," *Mashable*, September 30, 2015, https://mashable.com/2015/09/30/jessica-chastain-characters/.

10. Sonia Elks, "Women Are Four Times More Likely to Be Shown Undressed in Films Than Men," *World Economic Forum*, October 11, 2019, https://www.weforum.org/agenda/2019/10/harmful-female-gender-stereotypes-film-industry/.

11. David Hooper, "Is Podcasting More Diverse Than We Thought?" https://bulletin.bigpodcast.com/podcasting-diversity.

Works Cited

Introduction

Abbott, Megan. "Why Do We—Women in Particular—Love True Crime Books?" *Los Angeles Times* (Los Angeles, CA), June 14, 2018.

Connecticut Law Tribune Editorial Board. "Crimes Against Blacks, Women Still Underreported in Media." Law.com, February 21, 2020. https://www.law.com/ctlawtribune/2020/02/21/crimes-against-blacks-women-still-underreported-in-media/?slreturn=20200704193937.

Fitzpatrick, Molly. "How Two Hilarious Women Turned a Comedy-Murder Podcast Into a Phenomenon." *Rolling Stone*, May 30, 2017. https://www.rollingstone.com/culture/culture-features/how-two-hilarious-women-turned-a-comedy-murder-podcast-into-a-phenomenon-113785/.

Koul, Scaachi. "Being 'Polite' Often Gets Women Killed." *Buzzfeed News*, February 15, 2017. Accessed May 10, 2019. https://www.buzzfeednews.com/article/scaachikoul/whats-your-favorite-murder.

O'Connor, Anne-Marie. "Not Only Natalee Is Missing." *Los Angeles Times*, August 5, 2005. https://www.latimes.com/archives/la-xpm-2005-aug-05-et-aruba5-story.html.

Vicary, Amanda, and R. Chris Fraley. "Captured by True Crime: Why Are Women Drawn to Tales of Rape, Murder, and Serial Killers?" *Social Psychological and Personality Science*, 2010.

Zoller Seitz, Matt. *TV (The Book): Two Experts Pick the Greatest American Shows of All Time*, New York: Grand Central Publishing, 2016.

Chapter 1: Sabella Nitti

Buchanan, Rebekah, host. "Ugly Prey: An Innocent Woman and the Death Sentence that Scandalized Jazz Age Chicago." *Books on Law* (podcast), May 2, 2018. Accessed June 1, 2020. https://newbooksnetwork.com/emilie-lucchesi-ugly-prey-an-innocent-woman-and-the-death-sentence-that-scandalized-jazz-age-chicago-chicago-review-2017/.

DeMille, Cecil, dir. *Chicago*. 1927; Culver City, CA: Amazon.com Services LLC, Streaming. https://www.amazon.com/Chicago-Phyllis-Haver/dp/B078X312QS/ref=sr_1_2?dchild=1&keywords=chicago+1927&qid=1596561573&sr=8-2.

Forbes, Genevieve. "Dialect Jargon Makes 'Em Dizzy At Nitti Trial." *Chicago Tribune* (Chicago, IL), July 7, 1923.

Forbes, Genevieve. "Mrs. Nitti and Consort Given Noose Penalty." *Chicago Tribune* (Chicago, IL), July 10, 1923.

Forbes, Genevieve. "Mrs. Nitti's Tragedy Melts Hearts of Women in Jail." *Chicago Tribune* (Chicago, IL), July 12, 1923.

Lucchesi, Emilie Le Beau. *Ugly Prey: An Innocent Woman and the Death Sentence that Scandalized Jazz Age Chicago*. Chicago: Chicago Review Press, 2017.

"'My Children Die with Me' Is Mrs. Nitti's Cry." *Chicago Tribune* (Chicago, IL), July 31, 1923.

"Oct. 12 Is Set as Date to Hang Woman Slayer." *Chicago Tribune* (Chicago, IL), July 15, 1923.

Perry, Douglas. *The Girls of Murder City: Fame, Lust, and the Beautiful Killers Who Inspired Chicago*. New York: Penguin Books, 2010.

Rivenes, Erik. "1923 Chicago's Accused Murderess Sabella Nitti with Emilie La Beau Lucchesi." *Most Notorious*, October 25, 2018. Accessed May 13, 2020. https://radiopublic. com/most-notorious-a-true-crime-histo-GyZRpW/s1!fa5e8.

Rumore, Kori, and Marianna Mather. *He Had It Coming: Four Murderous Women and the Reporter Who Immortalized Their Stories*. Chicago: Midway Press, 2019.

Seidel, Jon. *Second City Sinners: True Crime from Historic Chicago's Deadly Streets*. Guilford, CT: Lyons Press, 2019.

"State Launches Trial of Belva of Law Killing." *Chicago Tribune* (Chicago, IL), June 5, 1924.

Watkins, Maurine. "Select Jury to Pronounce Fate of Beulah Annan." *Chicago Tribune* (Chicago, IL), May 23, 1924.

Chapter 2: Bonnie Parker

"Barrow's Auto Found in Kansas." *El Paso Times* (El Paso, TX), April 9, 1934.

"Cigar-Smoking Woman Seized at Clebune." *El Paso Times* (El Paso, TX), April 9, 1934.

"Clyde Barrow Linked With New Crimes." *Brownsville Herald* (Brownsville, TX), November 26, 1933.

"Clyde Barrow and Girl 'Put On Spot' in Deal with Felon, Report Says." *El Paso Times* (El Paso, TX), May 24, 1934.

Fortune, Jan I. *The True Story of Bonnie and Clyde: As Told by Bonnie's Mother and Clyde's Sister, Mrs. Emma Parker and Mrs. Nell Barrow Cowan*. New York: Signet Publishing, 1968.

Guinn, Jeff. *Go Down Together: The True, Untold Story of Bonnie and Clyde*. New York: Simon & Schuster, 2010.

Hancock, John Lee, dir. *The Highwaymen*. 2019; Santa Monica, CA: Netflix. Streaming. https://www.netflix.com/search?q=the%20highwaymen.

"Hunt Dillinger in Oklahoma." *El Paso Times* (El Paso, TX), April 9, 1934.

Kissell, Ben, Marcus Parks, and Henry Zebrowski, hosts. "Episode 371: Bonnie and Clyde Part III—Filthy, Smelly, and Surly." *The Last Podcast on the Left* (podcast), November 8, 2017. Accessed December 7, 2019. https://www.lastpodcastontheleft.com/episodes/2019/6/28/episode-371-bonnie-and-clyde-part-iii-filthy-smelly-and-surly.

Penn, Arthur, dir. *Bonnie and Clyde*. 1967; Burbank, CA: Amazon.com Services LLC, Streaming. https://www.amazon.com/Bonnie-Clyde-Warren-Beatty/dp/B0097JUIQG/ref=sr_1_1?crid=SVT0YKZJ9O46&dchild=1&keywords=bonnie+and+clyde+1967&qid=1596561660&sprefix=bonnie+and+clyde+19%2Caps%2C165&sr=8-1.

Rice, John, and Joe Batteer, writers. *Bonnie & Clyde*, Episode 1, "Part One." Directed by Bruce Beresford, featuring Emile Hirsch and Holliday Granger. Aired on December 8, 2013, Storyline Entertainment, 2020. Amazon.com Streaming. https://www.amazon. com/Bonnie-Clyde/dp/B00I2TMNSI/ref=sr_1_1?dchild=1&keywords=bonnie+and+clyde+2013&qid=1596561687&sr=8-1.

Richardson, Vanessa, and Sami Nye, hosts. "'Bonnie & Clyde'—Bonnie Parker." *Female Criminals* (podcast), April 2, 2018. Accessed December 10, 2019. https://www.parcast. com/criminals.

Thorpe, James, writer. *Highlander*, Season 5, Episode 6, "Money No Object." Directed by Rafel Zielinski, featuring Adrian Paul, Stan Kirsch, and Elizabeth Gracen. Aired on November 4, 1996, Rysher Entertainment, 2020. Amazon Streaming. https://www. amazon.com/gp/video/detail/B07HFL339C/ref=atv_dp_season_select_s5.

Witney, William, dir. *The Bonnie Parker Story*. 1958; Los Angeles, CA: YouTube. https:// www.youtube.com/watch?v=WlnhFqW2ivg.

Chapter 3: Elizabeth Short

Ash and Alaina, hosts. "Episode 38: The Black Dahlia—Part 1." *Morbid* (podcast), January 22, 2019. Accessed June 3, 2020. http://morbidpodcast.blubrry.net/tag/black-dahlia/.

"The Black Dahlia—Elizabeth Short." *True Crimecast* (podcast), July 24, 2018. Accessed June 12, 2020. https://www.stitcher.com/podcast/true-crimecast/e/55462897?autoplay=true.

"Black Dahlia, the Unsolved Murder of Elizabeth Short." *Thinking Out Loud* (podcast), July 1, 2019. Accessed June 10, 2020. https://podtail.com/en/podcast/thinking-out-loud-3/.

"Black Dahlia's Love Life Traced in Search for Her Fiendish Murderer." *Los Angeles Times*, January 18, 1947.

De Palma, Brian, dir. *The Black Dahlia*. 2006; Culver City, CA: Amazon.com Services, LLC. Streaming. https://www.amazon.com/Black-Dahlia-Josh-Hartnett/dp/B000M86HPC/ref=sr_1_1?dchild=1&keywords=black+dahlia+2006&qid=1596562156&s=instant-video&sr=1-1.

Diana and Gina, hosts. "20: Elizabeth Short—Part One," *Talk More About That* (podcast), April 2, 2018. Accessed May 28, 2020. http://tmatpodcast.blubrry.net/20-elizabeth-short-part-one/.

Diana and Gina, hosts. "21: Elizabeth Short—Part Two." *Talk More About That* (podcast), April 9, 2018. Accessed June 10, 2020. https://www.stitcher.com/podcast/talk-more-about-that/e/54021265.

Eatwell, Piu. *Black Dahlia, Red Rose: The Crime, Corruption, and Cover-up of America's Greatest Unsolved Murder*. New York: Liveright Publishing Corp., 2018.

Fienberg, Daniel. "'I Am the Night': TV Review," *Hollywood Reporter*, January 15, 2019. Accessed June 15, 2020. https://www.hollywoodreporter.com/review/i-am-night-review-1175463.

Grosbard, Ulu, dir. *True Confessions*. 1981; Los Angeles, CA: Amazon.com Services LLC. Streaming. https://www.amazon.com/True-Confessions-Robert-Niro/dp/B01D81RE4M/ref=sr_1_2?dchild=1&keywords=true+confessions&qid=1596562131&s=instant-video&sr=1-2.

Hamner, Robert, writer. *Hunter*, Season 4, Episode 13, "The Black Dahlia," directed by Michael Preece, featuring Fred Dryer, Stephanie Kramer, and Charles Hallahan. Aired on January 9, 1988, Stephen J. Cannell Productions, 2020. Amazon Streaming. https://www.amazon.com/gp/video/detail/B07NQ2MDWT/ref=atv_dp_season_select_s4.

Hodel, Steve. *The Black Dahlia Avenger: A Genius for Murder: The True Story*. New York: Arcade Publishing, 2019.

James Ellroy's L.A.: City of Demons, Season 1, Episode 1, "Dead Women Own Me." Directed by Brian Coughlin, featuring James Ellroy. Aired on January 19, 2011, Digital Ranch Productions, 2020, Amazon Streaming. https://www.amazon.com/Dead-Women-Own-Me/dp/B078WCWNMQ/ref=sr_1_1?crid=1717DBWUI68CV&dchild=1&keywords=james+ellroy%27s+la+city+of+demons&qid=1596562346&s=instant-video&sprefix=james+ellroy%27s%2Cinstant-video%2C147&sr=1-1.

Jones, Richard O., host. "The Black Dahlia." *True Crime Historian* (podcast), November 17, 2017. Accessed June 2, 2020. https://www.truecrimehistorian.com/.

Kilgaiff, Karen, and Georgia Hardstark, hosts. "7 Murders in Heaven." *My Favorite Murder* (podcast), March 11, 2016. Accessed May 10, 2019. https://www.stitcher.com/podcast/exactly-right/my-favorite-murder/e/45613056?autoplay=true.

Korzik, Morgan. "The Life of Elizabeth Short." *The Black Dahlia: The 1947 Murder of Elizabeth Short*. December 2, 2016. Accessed May 13, 2019. http://blackdahlia.web.unc.edu/the-life-of-elizabeth-short/.

"Medford Girl Murder Victim: Mutilated Body Found in Los Angeles Vacant Lot." *Boston Daily Globe*, January 17, 1947.

"M.P. Admits Slaying of Black Dahlia." *Washington Post*, February 9, 1947.

Nic and The Captain, hosts. "Black Dahlia, Part 2." *True Crime Garage* (podcast), August 1, 2016. Accessed June 4, 2020. https://truecrimegarage.com/blogs/true-crime-garage/posts/black-dahlia-part-1-2-episodes-44-45.

Pevney, Joseph, dir. *Who Is the Black Dahlia?* 1975; Los Angeles, CA. YouTube. https://www.youtube.com/watch?v=Y921yIpz4KI.

"Police Seeking Former Marine in L.A. Slaying." *Hartford Sentinel* (Hartford, CT), January 18, 1947.

"Police Seek Mad Pervert in Girl's Death." *Washington Post*, January 18, 1947.

Salt, Jennifer, writer. *American Horror Story*, Season 1, Episode 9, "Spooky Little Girl." Directed by John Scott, featuring Connie Britton, Dylan McDermott, and Jessica Lange. Aired on November 30, 2011, Ryan Murphy Productions, 2019, Netflix. https://www. netflix.com/watch/70260298?trackId=13752289&tctx=0%2C8%2C2b3dd968-fb33-4910-9d4c-e68c77e984c9-89225307%2C9d41289a9a2b2003ef1fc950d974d6bd490fd678%3A2 60cfda58771787b7eb8afee8ff489e19ac2a7e7%2C%2C.

Sheridan, Sam, writer. *I Am the Night*, Episode 3, "Dark Flower." Directed by Victoria Mahoney, featuring Chris Pine, India Eisley, and Jefferson Mays. Aired on February 2, 2019, Jenkins + Pine, 2020. Hulu Streaming. https://www.hulu.com/series/i-am-the-night-e89d16c0-99e3-4431-a7a1-c3d4076477b0.

Chapter 4: Marilyn Sheppard

Butterfield, Fox. "DNA Test Absolves Sam Sheppard of Murder, Lawyer Says." *New York Times*, March 5, 1998.

Cooper, Cynthia, and Sam Reese Sheppard. *Mockery of Justice: The True Story of the Sheppard Murder Case*. Lebanon, NH: Northeastern University Press, 1995.

Deanna. "Postpartum Depression in the 1950s, My Grandmother's Story (of A Short History of Postpartum Depression, from 1950s–Now)." *Maple Leaf Mommy*. Accessed February 15, 2020. https://mapleleafmommy.com/mom-life/postpartum-depression-in-1950s-my/.

"Doctor Wakened by Scream of Wife Being Murdered." *Lancaster Eagle-Gazette* (Lancaster, OH), July 5, 1954.

"The Girl From Little Egypt—The Fugitive." 1963; IMDb.com. Accessed February 15, 2020. https://www.imdb.com/title/tt0584014/?ref_=ttep_ep14.

Greyfield, Donald. "Marilyn Reese Sheppard." *Find a Grave*. https://www.findagrave.com/memorial/6876/maryn-sheppard.

"Fantasy Is State's View: On New Blood Theory of Dr. Sam Side—Court Rules Wednesday." *Cincinnati Enquirer*, April 30, 1955.

"The Fugitive." 1963; IMDb.com. Accessed February 15, 2020. https://www.imdb.com/title/tt0056757/.

"Intensive Search Fails to Locate Blunt Weapon, Indicated in Ohio Slaying." *Cincinnati Enquirer*, July 6, 1954.

Kilgariff, Karen, and Georgia Hardstark. "Let's Hear Your Podcast!" *My Favorite Murder* (podcast), February 9, 2017. Accessed February 22, 2020. https://www.stitcher.com/podcast/exactly-right/my-favorite-murder/e/49081289?autoplay=true.

Morin, Relman. "The Sheppard Murder: Police Still Contend Doctor Killed Wife; Defense Certain it Was Someone Else." *Akron Beacon Journal* (Akron, OH), August 29, 1954.

Neff, James. *The Wrong Man: The Verdict on the Dr. Sam Sheppard Murder Case*. New York: Random House, 2002.

Phipps, Keith. "James Neff: The Wrong Man: The Final Verdict on the Dr. Sam Sheppard Murder." *The AV Club*. March 29, 2002. Accessed February 12, 2020. https://aux.avclub.com/james-neff-the-wrong-man-the-final-verdict-on-the-dr-1798193037.

"Prosecutors Exhume Body of Marilyn Sheppard, Fetus." *Chicago Tribune* (Chicago, IL), October 5, 1999. https://www.chicagotribune.com/news/ct-xpm-1999-10-05-9910060224-story.html.

Roy, Carter, and Wenndy Mackenzie. "Episode 101: Dead on the Fourth of July: Marilyn Reese Sheppard." *Unsolved Murders* (podcast), June 25, 2018. Accessed February 21, 2020. https://www.stitcher.com/podcast/parcast/unsolved-murders-true-crime-stories/e/55050920?autoplay=true.

"Six Magnets to Search Lake: Bay Village Police Want Weapon Used in Murder of Doctor's Wife." *Cincinnati Enquirer*, July 7, 1954.

"Village Seeks Help in Solving Murder of Doctor's Spouse." *Cincinnati Enquirer*, July 20, 1954.

Chapter 5: Sharon Tate

"9 Hippie Mystics Held in Bizarre Tate Murders." *Oakland Tribune* (Oakland, CA), December 2, 1969.

"Actress, Bay Heiress, 3 Others: Hollywood 'Ritual Slayings.'" *San Francisco Examiner* (San Francisco, CA), August 10, 1969.

"Actress Sharon Tate Found Murdered." *San Mateo Times and Daily News Leader* (San Mateo, CA), August 9, 1969.

Bugliosi, Vincent. *Helter Skelter: The True Story of the Manson Murder.* New York: W.W. Norton Company, 2001.

Collis, Clark. "Sharon Tate's Sister Wept at Margot Robbie's *Once Upon a Time in Hollywood* Portrayal." *Entertainment Weekly*, July 26, 2019. https://ew.com/movies/2019/07/26/once-upon-a-time-hollywood-sharon-tate-sister-debra/#:~:text=Debra%20Tate%2C%20the%20sister%20of,which%20Tarantino's%20movie%20is%20set.

Harris, Aisha. "Sharon Tate Is a Woman in a Tarantino Movie. It's Complicated." *New York Times*, August 7, 2019. https://www.nytimes.com/2019/08/07/movies/sharon-tate-tarantino-women.html.

"The Haunting of Sharon Tate." Rotten Tomatoes. ND, Accessed August 18, 2020. https://www.rottentomatoes.com/m/the_haunting_of_sharon_tate.

Kermode, Mark. "Wolves at the Door." BBC5 Radio Live. March 17, 2017, YouTube, 01:43. https://www.youtube.com/watch?v=IuqSarxR9KM.

Stateman, Alisa, and Brie Tate. *Restless Souls: The Sharon Tate's Account of Stardom, the Manson Murders, and a Crusade for Justice.* New York: HarperCollins, 2012.

"Wolves at the Door." Rotten Tomatoes. ND, Accessed August 10, 2019. https://rottentomatoes.com/m/wolves_at_the_door.

Chapter 6: Patricia Hearst

"The Arrest of Patty Hearst." FBI.gov. February 4, 2009. Accessed February 28, 2020. https://www.fbi.gov/audio-repository/news-podcasts-inside-the-arrest-of-patty-hearst.mp3/view.

Blanco, Irma, and Carter Roy, hosts. "Patty Hearst: Part 1: The Kidnapping." *Hostage* (podcast). October 17, 2018. Accessed March 2, 2020. https://www.stitcher.com/podcast/parcast/hostage/e/56773702?autoplay=true.

Blanco, Irma, and Carter Roy, hosts. "Patty Hearst: Part 2: Girl on the Run." *Hostage* (podcast). October 24, 2018. Accessed March 2, 2020. https://open.spotify.com/episode/0pTB7DrRQCuEbkktIljMwe.

Blanco, Irma, and Carter Roy, hosts. "Patty Hearst: Part 3: Captive of the SLA." *Hostage* (podcast). October 31, 2018. Accessed March 2, 2020. https://open.spotify.com/episode/6S1zA7t4eEikMGwjDfymUx.

"Confidentiality, Patient/Physician." *American Academy of Family Physicians.* Accessed March 1, 2020. https://www.aafp.org/about/policies/all/patient-confidentiality.html.

Cutt, Caitlin, and Kari Martin. "WWTC055:#WCW Rachael O'Brien, Patty Hearst, and Broken Limbs." *White Wine True Crime!* (podcast), October 19, 2016. Accessed March 3, 2020. https://www.stitcher.com/podcast/white-wine-true-crime/e/wwtc055-wcw-rachael-obrien-patty-hearst-and-broken-limbs-47970483.

Graebner, William. *Patty's Got a Gun: Patricia Hearst in 1970s America.* Chicago: University of Chicago Press, 2008.

Higgins, Gerald. "The History of Confidentiality in Medicine." *Can Fam Physician.* April 1989; 35, 921–926.

Jedeikin, Desi, and Rachel Fisher, hosts. "Episode 129—Patty Hearst." *Hollywood Crime Scene* (podcast), February 11, 2020. Accessed March 4, 2020. https://www.stitcher.com/podcast/hollywood-crime-scene/e/67280628?autoplay=true.

Kohn, Howard, and David Weir. "The Inside Story." *Rolling Stone.* Vol 196, October 23, 1975.

Kohn, Howard, and David Weir. "The Inside Story: Part Two." *Rolling Stone*. Vol 200, November 20, 1975. Accessed February 26, 2020. https://www.rollingstone.com/culture/culture-news/tanias-world-the-inside-story-of-the-patty-hearst-kidnapping-part-two-people-in-need-109403/.

The Radical Story of Patty Hearst. Episode 1, "Part One: The Kidnapping." Directed by Pat Kondelis, featuring Jeffrey Toobin and Bill Harris. Aired on February 11, 2018, CNN, 2020, Amazon Streaming. https://www.amazon.com/Radical-Story-Patty-Hearst-Season/dp/B079K2SGPC.

The Radical Story of Patty Hearst. Episode 2, "Part Two: The Captive." Directed by Pat Kondelis, featuring Jeffrey Toobin and Bill Harris. Aired on February 11, 2018, CNN, 2020, Amazon Streaming. https://www.amazon.com/Radical-Story-Patty-Hearst-Season/dp/B079K2SGPC.

The Radical Story of Patty Hearst. Episode 3, "Part Three: The Robbery." Directed by Pat Kondelis, featuring Jeffrey Toobin and Bill Harris. Aired on February 18, 2018, CNN, 2020, Amazon Streaming. https://www.amazon.com/Radical-Story-Patty-Hearst-Season/dp/B079K2SGPC.

The Radical Story of Patty Hearst. Episode 5, "Part Five: The Conversion." Directed by Pat Kondelis, featuring Jeffrey Toobin and Bill Harris. Aired on February 25, 2018, CNN, 2020, Amazon Streaming. https://www.amazon.com/Radical-Story-Patty-Hearst-Season/dp/B079K2SGPC.

The Radical Story of Patty Hearst. Episode 6, "Part 6: The Verdict." Directed by Pat Kondelis, featuring Jeffrey Toobin and Bill Harris. Aired on February 25, 2018, CNN, 2020, Amazon Streaming. https://www.amazon.com/Radical-Story-Patty-Hearst-Season/dp/B079K2SGPC.

Schrader, Paul, dir. *Patty Hearst*. 1988; Culver City, CA: MGM, DVD, 2011.

Toobin, Jeffrey, and Brian Stelter, hosts. "Inside the SLA." *Patty Has a Gun* (podcast), February 2, 2018. Accessed February 17, 2020. https://www.cnn.com/interactive/2018/02/us/patty-hearst-podcast/.

Toobin, Jeffrey, and Brian Stelter, hosts. "The Kidnapping." *Patty Has a Gun* (podcast), January 26, 2018. Accessed February 17, 2020. https://www.cnn.com/interactive/2018/02/us/patty-hearst-podcast/.

West, Louis Jolyn. "Patricia Hearst's Torment Is a Disgrace." *Los Angeles Times*, December 22, 1978.

Chapter 7: Elizabeth Kendall

Alaina and Ash, hosts. "Ted Bundy Part 1." *Morbid* (podcast). Released May 29, 2018. Accessed May 12, 2020. https://www.morbidpodcast.com/listen/2019/1/5/episode-5-ted-bundy-part-1.

Berlinger, Joe, writer. *Conversations With a Killer: The Ted Bundy Tapes*. Episode 1, "Handsome Devil." Directed by Joe Berlinger, featuring Stephen Michaud, Hugh Aynesworth, and Kathleen McChesney. Aired January 24, 2019. https://www.netflix.com/watch/80226550?trackId=13752289&tctx=0%2C0%2Cb99747a7719d416b06dee9bc320d7c7809918d35%3A760752c1813c7f54eb57217773de849314874d21%2Cb99747a7719d416b06dee9bc320d7c7809918d35%3A760752c1813c7f54eb57217773de849314874d21%2C%2C.

Berlinger, Joe, dir. *Extremely Wicked, Shockingly Evil, and Vile*. 2019, Los Angeles, CA: Netflix. Streaming. https://www.netflix.com/watch/81028570?trackId=13752289&tctx=0%2C0%2C7e50eba91c4679bac2c40bff7163d5c3b61b71a7%3A7e66a918a626127888a69a5b5a3287d30e452e49%2C7e50eba91c4679bac2c40bff7163d5c3b61b71a7%3A7e66a918a626127888a69a5b5a3287d30e452e49%2C%2C.

Bright, Matthew, dir. *Ted Bundy*. 2002, Century City, CA: Amazon.com Services LLC. Streaming. https://www.amazon.com/Ted-Bundy-Michael-Rely-Burke/dp/B07N41Y3S/ref=sr_1_2?dchd=1&keywords=bundy&qid=1596564109&s=instant-video&sr=1-2.

Chomsky, Marvin J., dir. *The Deliberate Stranger*. 1986; Los Angeles, CA: Warner Bros. Home Video, 2010, DVD.

Finn, Heather. "Who Is Ted Bundy's Ex-Girlfriend Liz Kendall? Here's What You Need to Know." *Good Housekeeping*, January 31, 2020. https://www.goodhousekeeping.com/life/a30719690/ted-bundy-girlfriend-liz-kendall/.

Geller, Lindsay. "Who Is Ted Bundy's Ex-Girlfriend, Elizabeth 'Liz' Kendall, From 'Falling For a Killer'?" *Women's Health*, January 31, 2020. https://www.womenshealthmag.com/life/a27031703/ted-bundy-girlfriend-liz-kendall/.

Jill and Dick, hosts. "Surviving Ted Bundy." *True Crime Brewery* (podcast). Released June 5, 2017. Accessed May 12, 2020. https://www.stitcher.com/podcast/tiegrabber-podcasts/true-crime-brewery/e/surviving-ted-bundy-50394290.

Jiwa, Salim. "Trail of Death: Bundy Killed." *The Providence* (British Columbia, Canada), February 2, 1989.

Kendall, Elizabeth. *The Phantom Prince: My Life with Ted Bundy, Updated and Expanded Edition*. New York: Abrams Press, 2020.

Langan, Hayley, and Kaitlin Mahar, hosts. "63: Extremely Wicked, Shockingly Evil, and Vile (Review)." *Crime Culture* (podcast). Released May 8, 2019. Accessed May 9, 2020. https://www.stitcher.com/podcast/crime-culture/e/60576511.

Lavoie, Rebecca, and Kevin Flynn, hosts. "Extremely Wicked, Shockingly Evil, and Vile." *You Can't Make This Up* (podcast). Released May 8, 2019. Accessed May 11, 2020. https://www.stitcher.com/podcast/netflix/e/60552790?autoplay=true.

Lucy and Lily, hosts. "Minisode A: Extremely Wicked, Shockingly Evil, and Vile." *Two Girls, One Murder!* (podcast). Released June 12, 2019. Accessed May 10, 2020. https://twogirlsonemurder.podbean.com/e/minisode-a-extremely-wicked-shockingly-evil-and-vile/.

Nelson, Polly. *Defending the Devil: My Story as Ted Bundy's Last Lawyer*. Brattleboro, VT: Echo Point Books and Media, 2019.

O'Regan, Richard, and Carolyn Saunders, writers. *Ted Bundy: Falling for a Killer*. Episode 1, "Boy Meets Girl," directed by Trish Wood, featuring Elizabeth Kendall and Molly Kendall. Aired January 31, 2020. https://www.amazon.com/Boy-Meets-Girl/dp/B08BYYX1HM/ref=sr_1_1?dchild=1&keywords=falling+for+a+killer&qid=1596500074&sr=8-1.

O'Regan, Richard, and Carolyn Saunders, writers. *Ted Bundy: Falling for a Killer*. Episode 2, "Falling." Directed by Trish Wood, featuring Elizabeth Kendall and Molly Kendall. Aired January 31, 2020. https://www.amazon.com/Boy-Meets-Girl/dp/B08BYYX1HM/ref=sr_1_1?dchild=1&keywords=falling+for+a+killer&qid=1596500074&sr=8-1.

O'Regan, Richard, and Carolyn Saunders, writers. *Ted Bundy: Falling for a Killer*. Episode 3, "Gone Girls." Directed by Trish Wood, featuring Elizabeth Kendall and Molly Kendall. Aired January 31, 2020. https://www.amazon.com/Boy-Meets-Girl/dp/B08BYYX1HM/ref=sr_1_1?dchild=1&keywords=falling+for+a+killer&qid=1596500074&sr=8-1.

O'Regan, Richard, and Carolyn Saunders, writers. *Ted Bundy: Falling for a Killer*. Episode 5, "Collateral Damage." Directed by Trish Wood, featuring Elizabeth Kendall and Molly Kendall. Aired January 31, 2020. https://www.amazon.com/Boy-Meets-Girl/dp/B08BYYX1HM/ref=sr_1_1?dchild=1&keywords=falling+for+a+killer&qid=1596500074&sr=8-1.

Psarras, Con. "Life With Killer Ted Bundy, the Phantom Prince." *Salt Lake Tribune*, October 25, 1981.

Steed, Les. "Speaking Out: Who is Elizabeth Kendall and Where Is Ted Bundy's Former Girlfriend Now?" *The U.S. Sun*, January 30, 2020. Accessed April 12, 2020. https://www.the-sun.com/news/333527/who-is-elizabeth-kendall-and-where-is-ted-bundys-former-girlfriend-now/.

Ted Bundy: Mind of a Monster. 2019; Los Angeles, CA: Amazon.com Services, LLC. Streaming. https://www.amazon.com/Ted-Bundy-Mind-Monster/dp/B07WQGRPRZ/ref=sr_1_3?dchd=1&keywords=mind+of+a+monster&qid=1596564182&s=instant-video&sr=1-3.

Thurston, George. "Authors Try to Make Sense of Bundy." *Tallahassee Democrat* (Tallahassee, FL), January 22, 1989.

Chapter 8: Kirsten Costas

1980s: The Deadliest Decade. Season 1, Episode 3, "The Cheerleader Murder." Directed by Andrea De Brito, featuring Patrick Gallagher. Aired on November 28, 2016, Investigation Discovery. https://www.amazon.com/The-Yuppie-Murder/dp/B01MYMJMP3/ref=s r_1_1?crid=17U9CLA3JMZ68&dchild=1&keywords=1980s+deadliest+decade&qid=1596 548223&sprefix=1980s+dead%2Caps%2C154&sr=8-1.

Bashor, Jon. "Friends Attend Funeral for Slain Orinda Girl." *San Francisco Examiner*, June 28, 1984.

Graham, William, dir. *Death of a Cheerleader*. 1994; Los Angeles, CA: Amazon.com Services LLC. Streaming. https://www.amazon.com/Death-Cheerleader-Kellie-Martin/dp/ B077SH8YJQ/ref=sr_1_1?dchild=1&keywords=death+of+a+cheerleader&qid=15965476 21&sr=8-1.

Jen and Cam, hosts. "#34: Dying to Fit In: Kirsten Costas." *Our True Crime Podcast* (podcast). Released April 10, 2019. Accessed June 3, 2020. https://www.ourtruecrimepodcast. com/2019/04/34-dying-to-fit-in-kirsten-costas.html.

Lucas, Alysa, host. "Kirsten Costas." *Fatal*i*teas* (podcast). Released August 14, 2019. Accessed May 31, 2020. https://fataliteas.libsyn.com/kirsten-costas.

Ludlow, Esther, host. "Episode 58: With Friends Like These: Kirsten Costas." *Once Upon a Crime* (podcast). Aired on September 4, 2017. Accessed June 5, 2020. https://www. truecrimepodcast.com/episode-058-with-friends-like-these-kirsten-costas/.

Pogash, Carol. "The Cheerleader Murder." *Ladies Home Journal*, November 1985. Click Americana. https://clickamericana.com/topics/crime/the-real-death-of-a-cheerleader-1985.

Ross, Andrew, and Jon Bashor. "Last Hours of Orinda Teen's Life." *San Francisco Examiner*, June 23, 1984.

Serrano, Patrick, host. "Death of a Cheerleader (2019 Lifetime)." *Lifetime Uncorked* (podcast). Released on February 14, 2019. Accessed on June 3, 2020. https://lifetimeuncorked. com/2019/02/05/death-of-a-cheerleader-2019-lifetime/.

Shapiro, Paul, dir. *Death of a Cheerleader*. 2019; Los Angeles, CA: Amazon.com Services LLC. Streaming. https://www.amazon.com/DEATH-CHEERLEADER-Inc-Reunion-Pictures/dp/B07N965B5H/ref=sr_1_2?dchild=1&keywords=death+of+a+cheerleader& qid=1596548587&sr=8-2.

"Witness Surfaces in Teen Murder." *The Californian* (Salinas, CA), June 25, 1984.

Chapter 9: Nicole Brown

Alexander, Scott, and Larry Karaszewski, writers. *The People v. O.J. Simpson: American Crime Story*, Season 1, Episode 1, "From the Ashes of Tragedy." Directed by Ryan Murphy, featuring Cuba Gooding, Jr., and Sarah Paulson. Aired on February 2, 2016. https:// www.netflix.com/watch/80127673?trackId=200257859

Alexander, Scott, Larry Karaszewski, Maya Forbes, and Wallace Wolodarsky, writers. *The People v. O.J. Simpson: American Crime Story*, Season 1, Episode 4, "100% Not Guilty." Directed by Anthony Hemingway, featuring Cuba Gooding, Jr., and Sarah Paulson. Aired on February 23, 2016. https://www.netflix.com/watch/80127676?trac kId=200257859.

Alexander, Scott, and Larry Karaszewski, writers. *The People v. O.J. Simpson: American Crime Story*, Season 1, Episode 10, "The Verdict." Directed by Ryan Murphy, featuring Cuba Gooding, Jr., and Sarah Paulson. Aired on April 5, 2016. https://www.netflix.com/ watch/80127682?trackId=200257859.

Baldwin, Kristen. "With O.J. Interview, FOX Falls Off the Human Decency Wagon: EW Review." *Entertainment Weekly*, March 12, 2018. https://ew.com/ tv/2018/03/12/oj-simpson-lost-confession-review/.

Bradley, Laura. "*O.J. Simpson: The Lost Confession*: Was FOX's *American Idol* Counter Genius or Gross?" *Vanity Fair*, March 12, 2018. https://www.vanityfair.

com/hollywood/2018/03/oj-simpson-the-lost-confession-reviews-exploitative-ratings.

Clemente, Jim, Laura Richards, and Lisa Zambetti, hosts. "Episode 7: The People vs. O.J.: The Crime Scene and the Scheme Team." *Real Crime Profile* (podcast). Released on March 16, 2016. Accessed December 12, 2019. https://www.stitcher.com/podcast/wondery/real-crime-profe/e/43495357?autoplay=true.

Clemente, Jim, Laura Richards, and Lisa Zambetti, hosts. "Episode 8: People vs. O.J.: Nicole's 911 Call." *Real Crime Profile* (podcast). Released on March 23, 2016. Accessed December 12, 2019. https://www.stitcher.com/podcast/real-crime-profile/e/episode-8-the-people-vs-oj-simpson-nicoles-911-call-43495356.

Clemente, Jim, Laura Richards, and Lisa Zambetti, hosts. "Episode 9: The People vs. O.J.: BONUS EPISODE: Analyzing Two Letters by Nicole." *Real Crime Profile* (podcast). Released on March 27, 2016. Accessed December 12, 2019. https://www.stitcher.com/podcast/real-crime-profile/e/episode-9-the-people-vs-o-j-simpson-bonus-episode-analyzing-43495355.

Clemente, Jim, Laura Richards, and Lisa Zambetti, hosts. "Episode 15: The People vs. O.J.: The Verdict." *Real Crime Profile* (podcast). Released on May 4, 2016. Accessed December 12, 2019. https://www.stitcher.com/podcast/real-crime-profile/e/episode-15-the-people-vs-oj-simpson-the-verdict-44338872.

Farrands, Daniel, dir. *The Murder of Nicole Brown Simpson*. 2020; Los Angeles: Amazon.com Services LLC. Streaming. https://www.amazon.com/Murder-Nicole-Brown-Simpson/dp/B0833K57DP/ref=sr_1_1?dchild=1&keywords=the+murder+of+nicole+brown+simpson&qid=1596554955&sr=8-1.

Freedman, Jerrold (as Alan Smithee), dir. *The OJ Simpson Story*. 1995; Los Angeles: YouTube. Streaming. https://www.youtube.com/watch?v=k97yjE0V3yI.

Goodman, Fred, and Kim Goldman. *If I Did It: Confessions of a Killer*. New York: Beaufort Books, 2007.

Jennings, Tom, writer. *True Crime with Aphrodite Jones*. Season 1, Episode 2, "O.J. Simpson." Directed by Tom Jennings, featuring Nicole Brown Simpson, Maria Clark, and F. Lee Bailey. Aired March 18, 2010. https://www.amazon.com/Scott-Peterson/dp/B00APE0NOO/ref=sr_1_1?dchild=1&keywords=true+crime+with+aphrodite+jones&qid=1596559024&sr=8-1.

"Kelly Dowdle." *Internet Movie Database*. Accessed February 10, 2020. https://www.imdb.com/name/nm1942596/?ref_=ttfc_fc_cl_t77.

Manning, Sue. "Police Question O.J. Simpson in Wife's Death; Hall of Famer Denies Involvement." *Napa Valley Register* (Napa Valley, CA), June 14, 1994.

Marshall, Sarah, and Michael Hobbes, hosts. "The OJ Simpson Trial: Nicole Brown Simpson Part 1." *You're Wrong About...* (podcast). Released October 3, 2019. Accessed July 7, 2020. https://www.stitcher.com/podcast/michael-hobbes/youre-wrong-about/e/64342603.

Marshall, Sarah, and Michael Hobbes, hosts. "The OJ Simpson Trial: Nicole Brown Simpson Part 2." *You're Wrong About...* (podcast). Released October 17, 2019. Accessed July 7, 2020. https://www.stitcher.com/podcast/michael-hobbes/youre-wrong-about/e/64661334.

Meg and Joe, hosts. "The Trial of OJ Simpson." *Two Ghouls One Grave* (podcast). Released September 1, 2019. Accessed December 22, 2019. https://www.stitcher.com/podcast/two-ghouls-one-grave/e/63611727.

Newman, Jim, and Eric Malnic. "Police Sources Link Evidence to Simpson." *Los Angeles Times*, June 15, 1994.

Nic and the Captain, hosts. "OJ Simpson///Part 2///25." *True Crime Garage* (podcast). Released on April 19, 2016. Accessed December 19, 2020. https://www.stitcher.com/podcast/true-crime-garage/e/44171939.

O.J. Simpson: The Lost Confession? Featuring Soledad O'Brien, Eve Shakti Chin, and Jim Clemente. Aired on March 11, 2018. YouTube. https://www.youtube.com/watch?v=CfM-7TERCMw.

Rife, Katie. "The director of The Haunting of Sharon Tate sets his ghoulish sights on The Murder of Nicole Brown Simpson." *AV Club*. January 10, 2020. https://film.avclub.com/the-director-of-the-haunting-of-sharon-tate-sets-his-gh-1840935191.

Schwartz, DJ. "OJ Simpson." *Conspiracy Asylum* (podcast). Released on May 31, 2019. Accessed December 15, 2020. https://www.podchaser.com/podcasts/conspiracy-asylum-745919/episodes/oj-simpson-40138618.

"Simpson's Ex-Wife and Man Killed," *North County Times* (Oceanside, CA), June 14, 1994.

Toobin, Jeffrey. *The Run of His Life: The People v. O.J. Simpson*. New York: Random House Publishing, 2015.

Weller, Sheila. *Raging Heart: The Intimate Story of the Tragic Marriage of O.J. and Nicole Brown Simpson*. Los Angeles: Graymalkin Media, 2016.

Chapter 10: Kathleen & Teresa

Bible, Angela Heywood. "Wife of 1999 Mayoral Candidate Found Dead." *The News and Observer* (Raleigh, NC), December 10, 2001.

Cain, Brooke. "Another 'Staircase' twist: Michael Peterson had a romance with documentary's editor." *The News and Observer* (Raleigh, NC), June 13, 2018.

Clemente, Jim, Laura Richards, and Lisa Zambetti, hosts. "Episode 1—Making a Murderer: The Arrest of Steven Avery." *Real Crime Profile* (podcast). Released January 1, 2016. Accessed August 29, 2019. https://www.stitcher.com/podcast/real-crime-profile/e/-episode-1-making-a-murderer-the-arrest-of-steven-avery-43495363.

Clemente, Jim, Laura Richards, and Lisa Zambetti, hosts. "Episode 2—The Investigation and the Detectives." *Real Crime Profile* (podcast). Released January 30, 2016. Accessed August 29, 2019. https://www.stitcher.com/podcast/real-crime-profile/e/episode-2-making-a-murderer-the-investigation-and-detectives-43495362.

Clemente, Jim, Laura Richards, and Lisa Zambetti, hosts. "Episode 6—Making a Murderer: Microscopic Look at Colborn and Sturm Phone Calls." *Real Crime Profile* (podcast). Released March 9, 2016. Accessed August 29, 2019. https://www.stitcher.com/podcast/real-crime-profile/e/episode-6-making-a-murderer-microscopic-look-at-colborn-and-43495358.

Clemente, Jim, Laura Richards, and Lisa Zambetti, hosts. "Episode 140—Her Name was Kathleen Peterson." *Real Crime Profile* (podcast). Released August 22, 2018. Accessed December 9, 2019. https://www.stitcher.com/podcast/wondery/real-crime-profe/e/55893950?autoplay=true.

Clemente, Jim, Laura Richards, and Lisa Zambetti, hosts. "Episode 143—The Autopsy from "The Staircase." *Real Crime Profile* (podcast). Released September 12, 2018. Accessed December 9, 2019. https://www.stitcher.com/podcast/wondery/real-crime-profe/e/56219253?autoplay=true.

Clemente, Jim, Laura Richards, and Lisa Zambetti hosts. "Episode 151—Controlling the Edit and the Narrative of the Staircase." *Real Crime Profile* (podcast). Released November 5, 2018. Accessed December 9, 2019. https://www.stitcher.com/podcast/wondery/real-crime-profe/e/57064451?autoplay=true.

Commons, Jess. "Who Was Teresa Halbach, The Real Victim of Making a Murderer?" *Grazia*. March 27, 2016. https://graziadaily.co.uk/life/tv-and-film/teresa-halbach-real-victim-making-murderer/.

Curliss, J. Andrew, and Vicki Cheng. "Death of Wife of Ex-Candidate Under Scrutiny." *The News and Observer* (Raleigh, NC), December 11, 2001.

Demos, Moira, and Laura Ricciardi, writers. *Making a Murderer*, Season 1, Episode 2, "Turning the Tables." Directed by Moira Demos and Laura Ricciardi, featuring Dolores Avery and Steven Avery. Aired on December 18, 2015, Netflix Streaming. https://www.netflix.com/watch/80000772?trackId=13752289&tctx=0%2C1%2Ca8b00922-504a-446e-b0a0-0ffc822f949b-84164254%2Cdf36033ebc1c48022b83e5169928f9f3c0938a12%3Ab80a0d553155873a172bce10f58bf8696f076fc3%2C%2C.

Demos, Moira, and Laura Ricciardi, writers. *Making a Murderer*, Season 1, Episode 9, "Lack of Humility." Directed by Moira Demos and Laura Ricciardi, featuring Dolores Avery and Steven Avery. Aired on December 18, 2015, Netflix Streaming. https://www.netflix.com/watch/80075830?trackId=200257859.

Demos, Moira, and Laura Ricciardi, writers. *Making a Murderer*, Season 2, Episode 1, "Number 18." Directed by Moira Demos and Laura Ricciardi, featuring Dolores Avery and Steven Avery. Aired on October 19, 2018. https://www.netflix.com/watch/80115 431?trackId=13752289&tctx=0%2C0%2Ca8b00922-504a-446e-b0a0-0ffc822f949b-84164254%2Cdf36033ebc1c48022b83e5169928f9f3c0938a12%3Ab80a0d553155873a172b ce10f58bf8696f076fc3%2C%2C.

"Diane Fanning." Accessed July 15, 2020. https://dianefanning.com/.

Fanning, Diane. *Written in Blood*. New York: St. Martin's Press, 2005.

Jennings, Tom, and John McLaughlin, writers. *True Crime with Aphrodite Jones*, Season 1, Episode 3, "The Staircase Killer: Michael Peterson." Directed by Tom Jennings, featuring Aphrodite Jones and Freda Black. Aired on March 25, 2010, Amazon Streaming. https://www.amazon.com/Scott-Peterson/dp/B00APE0NOO/ref=sr_1_1?dchild=1&keywords=true+crime+with+aphrodite+jones&qid=1596565983&sr=8-1.

Kratz, Ken, and Peter Wilkinson. *The Case Against Steven Avery and What "Making a Murderer" Gets Wrong*. Dallas, TX: BenBella Books, 2017.

"Making a Murderer Season 1—Teresa Halbach, Steven Avery, and Brendan Dassey," *Crime Screen* (podcast). Released October 26, 2018. Accessed August 19, 2019. (This podcast has stopped production and cannot be found except in podcatcher apps).

"Making a Murderer Season 1 Episodes 5, 6, and 7—Teresa Halbach, Steven Avery, and Brendan Dassey," *Crime Screen* (podcast). Released November 7, 2018. Accessed August 19, 2019. (This podcast has stopped production and cannot be found except in podcatcher apps).

Sheehan, Ruth. "It Wasn't Just About Mike Peterson." *The News and Observer* (Raleigh, NC), October 11, 2003.

Swift, Aisling. "Friends Remember Arts Patron." *The News and Observer* (Raleigh, NC), December 14, 2001.

"Truth Wins: The Law Offices of Kathleen Zellner." Accessed June 10, 2020. http://www.kathleentzellner.com/.

Chapter 11: Gypsy and Payton

20/20, Season 43, Episode 5, "The Wicked." Featuring David Muir and Payton Leutner. Aired October 25, 2019, Hulu Streaming. https://www.hulu.com/watch/6e9f4cad-db66-43d9-8800-d5cce7102e52.

Biggs, John. "The Story of Slenderman, The Internet's Own Monster." *Tech Crunch*, June 30, 2014. https://techcrunch.com/2014/06/30/the-story-of-slenderman-the-internets-own-monster/.

Carr, Erin Lee, dir. *Mommy Dead and Dearest*. Featuring Gypsy Rose Blanchard, Jim Arnott, and David Blanchard. Aired March 11, 2017. Amazon Streaming. https://www.amazon.com/Mommy-Dead-Dearest-Erin-Carr/dp/B0779CKQ7Z/ref=sr_1_1?dchild=1&keywords=mommy+dead+and+dearest&qid=1596570609&sr=8-1.

Christian and Suann, hosts. "Episode 10: Violent Crimes Day and A Slenderman Stabbing." *Dark Stuff* (podcast). Released February 18, 2018. Accessed February 27, 2020. https://podta.com/fr/podcast/dark-stuff-with-christian-suann/010-violent-crimes-day-a-slenderman-stabbing/.

Day, Elizabeth. "I'll Never Forgive Mommie: Joan Crawford's Daughter Gives First Interview in 10 Years." *The Guardian*, May 24, 2008. https://www.theguardian.com/fm/2008/may/25/biography.fm.

Dean, Michelle. "Dee Dee Wanted Her Daughter To Be Sick, Gypsy Wanted Her Mom Murdered." *Buzzfeed*, August 18, 2016. https://www.buzzfeednews.com/article/michelledean/dee-dee-wanted-her-daughter-to-be-sick-gypsy-wanted-her-mom.

Ferguson, Mike, and Mike Gibson, hosts. "Gypsy Rose Blanchard." *True Crime All The Time* (podcast). Released Apr 29, 2019. Accessed March 4, 2020. https://www.stitcher.com/podcast/true-crime-all-the-time/e/54286126.

Janes, DeAnna. "The Complete Timeline and True Story Behind the Slender Man

Stabbing." *O: The Oprah Magazine*, October 25, 2019. https://www.oprahmag.com/entertainment/tv-movies/a29591703/slender-man-stabbing-true-story/.

Keegan, Harrison. "The offender Godejohn Sentenced to Life in Prison For Murder of Dee Dee Blanchard." Springfield News Leader, February 22, 2019. https://www.news-leader.com/story/news/crime/2019/02/22/theoffender-godejohn-sentenced-life-prison-blanchard-murder/2949249002/.

Marion, Heather, writer, *The Act*, Episode 6, "A Whole New World." Directed by Laure de Clermont-Tonnerre, featuring Joey King, Patricia Arquette, and Calum Worthy. Aired Apr 17, 2019. Hulu Streaming. https://www.hulu.com/series/the-act-8cc910fe-b59e-46a5-9966-16c4e0ed208d.

McGraw, Phil, host. "S1E1: The Killer Thorn of Gypsy Rose." *Analysis of Murder by Dr. Phil* (podcast). Released Apr 25, 2019. Accessed March 2, 2020. https://www.drphilpodcasts.com/killer-thorn-of-gypsy-rose.

McGraw, Phil, host. "S1E2: The Killer Thorn of Gypsy Rose." *Analysis of Murder by Dr. Phil* (podcast). Released May 8, 2019. Accessed March 2, 2020. https://www.drphilpodcasts.com/killer-thorn-of-gypsy-rose.

McGraw, Phil, host. "S1E5: The Killer Thorn of Gypsy Rose." *Analysis of Murder by Dr. Phil* (podcast). Released May 23, 2019. Accessed March 2, 2020. https://www.drphilpodcasts.com/killer-thorn-of-gypsy-rose.

Merck Manual Professional Version. "Factitious Disorder Imposed on Another." https://www.merckmanuals.com/en-ca/professional/psychiatric-disorders/somatic-symptom-and-related-disorders/factitious-disorder-imposed-on-another.

Robinson, Kelley. "'Slender Man' Stabbing Victim Speaks Publicly for First Time: 'Without the Whole Situation, I Wouldn't Be Who I Am'" *ABC News*, October 24, 2019. https://abcnews.go.com/US/slender-man-stabbing-victim-speaks-publicly-time-situation/story?id=66268385.

Shevonne, host. "9. Munchausen de Proxy: Gypsy Rose Blanchard." *Female Killers* (podcast). Released May 9, 2019. Accessed March 10, 2020. https://femalekillers.com/episode/9-munchausen-de-proxy-gypsy-rose-blanchard/.

"'Slender Man' Attack Victim Says She Sleeps with Broken Scissors 'Just in Case.'" *CBS News*, October 25, 2019. https://www.cbsnews.com/news/slender-man-attack-victim-payton-leutner-i-sleep-with-broken-scissors-just-in-case/.

Steinbuch, Yaron. "'Slender Man' Stabbing Victim Payton Leutner on the Friends Who Tried to Kler Her." *New York Post*, October 24, 2019, https://nypost.com/2019/10/24/slender-man-stabbing-victim-payton-leutner-on-the-friends-who-tried-to-kl-her/.

20/20, Season 43, Episode 5, "The Wicked." Featuring David Muir and Payton Leutner. Aired October 25, 2019, Hulu Streaming. https://www.hulu.com/watch/6e9f4cad-db66-43d9-8800-d5cce7102e52.

Viola, D.J., dir. *Terror in the Woods*. 2018; Atlanta, GA, Amazon.com Services LLC. Streaming. https://www.amazon.com/Terror-Woods-Inc-ThinkFactory-Media/dp/B07JVPMJH5/ref=sr_1_2?dchild=1&keywords=terror+in+the+woods&qid=1596577644&sr=8-2.

Conclusion

Demopoulos, Alaina. "Why True Crime TV Has Become So Popular During the Coronavirus Pandemic." *Daily Beast*, April 10, 2020. https://www.thedailybeast.com/as-coronavirus-rages-true-crime-tv-shows-provide-a-strange-and-popular-comfort.

Deta, Yohana. "Jessica Chastain Is So Over Hollywood Sexualizing Female Characters in Action Movies." *Mashable*, September 30, 2015. https://mashable.com/2015/09/30/jessica-chastain-characters/.

Elks, Sonia. "Women Are Four Times More Likely to Be Shown Undressed in Films Than Men." World Economic Forum, October 11, 2019. https://www.weforum.org/agenda/2019/10/harmful-female-gender-stereotypes-film-industry/.

Hooper, David. "Is Podcasting More Diverse Than We Thought?" https://bulletin.bigpodcast.com/podcasting-diversity.

Smith, Stacy L., Katherine Pieper, and Marc Choueiti. "The Future Is Female? Examining the Prevalence and Portrayal of Girls and Teens in Popular Movies." 2017. http://assets. uscannenberg.org/docs/the-future-is-female.pdf.

"The Other Epidemic: Fatal Police Shootings in the Time of COVID-19." ACLU. https:// www.aclu.org/sites/default/files/field_document/aclu_the_other_epidemic_fatal_ police_shootings_2020.pdf.

Index